Lecture Notes in Computer

Edited by G. Goos, J. Hartmanis and J

T0237762

Springer

Berlin
Heidelberg
New York
Barcelona
Hong Kong
London
Milan
Paris
Singapore
Tokyo

Dirk Craeynest   Alfred Strohmeier (Eds.)

Reliable
Software Technologies –

Ada-Europe 2001

6th Ada-Europe International Conference
on Reliable Software Technologies
Leuven, Belgium, May 14-18, 2001
Proceedings

 Springer

Series Editors

Gerhard Goos, Karlsruhe University, Germany
Juris Hartmanis, Cornell University, NY, USA
Jan van Leeuwen, Utrecht University, The Netherlands

Volume Editors

Dirk Craeynest
Offis & K.U. Leuven
Offis nv/sa - Aubay Group
Weiveldlaan 41/32, 1930 Zaventem, Belgium
E-mail: dirk.craeynest@offis.be

Alfred Strohmeier
Swiss Federal Institute of Technology Lausanne (EPFL)
EPFL-DI-LGL, 1015 Lausanne EPFL, Switzerland
E-mail: alfred.strohmeier@epfl.ch

Cataloging-in-Publication Data applied for

Die Deutsche Bibliothek - CIP-Einheitsaufnahme

Reliable software technologies : Ada Europe ... ; ... Ada Europe
international conference ... ; proceedings. - 5. 2000 (Juni 2000)-. -
Berlin ; Heidelberg ; New York ; Barcelona ; Hong Kong ; London ;
Milan ; Paris ; Singapore ; Tokyo : Springer, 2000
    Erscheint unregelmäßig. - Früher begrenztes Werk in verschiedenen
    Ausg. - Bibliographische Deskription nach 6. 2001
    (Lecture notes in computer science ; ...)
6. Ada Europe 2001 : Leuven, Belgium, May 14 - 18, 2001. - (2001)
    (Lecture notes in computer science ; Vol. 2043)
    ISBN 3-540-42123-8

CR Subject Classification (1998): D.2, D.1.2-5, D.3, C.2.4, C.3, K.6

ISSN 0302-9743
ISBN 3-540-42123-8 Springer-Verlag Berlin Heidelberg New York

Springer-Verlag Berlin Heidelberg New York
a member of BertelsmannSpringer Science+Business Media GmbH

http://www.springer.de

© Springer-Verlag Berlin Heidelberg 2001
Printed in Germany

Typesetting: Camera-ready by author, data conversion by PTP Berlin, Stefan Sossna
Printed on acid-free paper   SPIN 10782549   06/3142   5 4 3 2 1 0

Foreword

The Sixth International Conference on Reliable Software Technologies, Ada-Europe 2001, took place in Leuven, Belgium, May 14-18, 2001. It was sponsored by Ada-Europe, the European federation of national Ada societies, in cooperation with ACM SIGAda, and it was organized by members of the K.U. Leuven and Ada-Belgium. This was the 21st consecutive year of Ada-Europe conferences and the sixth year of the conference focusing on the area of reliable software technologies.

The use of software components in embedded systems is almost ubiquitous: planes fly by wire, train signalling systems are now computer based, mobile phones are digital devices, and biological, chemical, and manufacturing plants are controlled by software, to name only a few examples. Also other, non-embedded, mission-critical systems depend more and more upon software. For these products and processes, reliability is a key success factor, and often a safety-critical hard requirement.

It is well known and has often been experienced that quality cannot be added to software as a mere afterthought. This also holds for reliability. Moreover, the reliability of a system is not due to and cannot be built upon a single technology. A wide range of approaches is needed, the most difficult issue being their purposeful integration. Goals of reliability must be precisely defined and included in the requirements, the development process must be controlled to achieve these goals, and sound development methods must be used to fulfill these non-functional requirements.

All artifacts produced must be verified. Useful verification techniques are numerous and complementary: reviewing design documents, proving properties of a program, including its correctness, reasoning about a program, performing static analysis, but also dynamic testing based on program execution, to mention just a few.

Development of software requires tools, and some are more helpful than others for tracking down or avoiding errors. Some techniques are well established, such as strong type checking of the source code by the language compiler. Here, the Ada programming language excels, for it was designed with reliability as a goal. Other techniques are less common and considered as more advanced, such as automatic test generation based on formal specifications.

Clearly, the domain is vast and not all issues related to reliable software technologies can be covered in a single conference, but we are proud to say that these proceedings span a wide range of them and constitute a rich collection of contributions.

Invited Speakers

The conference presented five distinguished speakers, who delivered state-of-the-art information on topics of great importance, for now and for the future of software engineering in general, and reliable software in particular:

- Building Formal Requirements Models for Reliable Software
  Axel van Lamsweerde, Université Catholique de Louvain, Belgique
- Using Ada in Interactive Digital Television Systems
  Pascal Héraud, CANAL+ Technologies, France

- Testing from Formal Specifications, a Generic Approach
  Marie-Claude Gaudel, Université de Paris-Sud, France
- Logic versus Magic in Critical Systems
  Peter Amey, Praxis Critical Systems, UK
- Can Java Meet its Real-Time Deadlines?
  Brian Dobbing, Aonix Europe Ltd, UK, and co-author Ben Brosgol, ACT, USA

We would like to express our sincere gratitude to these distinguished speakers, well known to the community, for sharing their insights with the conference participants and for having written up their contributions for the proceedings.

Submitted Papers

A large number of papers were submitted. The program committee worked hard to review them, and the selection process proved to be difficult, since many papers had received excellent reviews. Finally, the program committee selected 27 papers for inclusion in the proceedings, and 2 contributions for presentation only. The final result was a truly international program with authors from Australia, Belgium, China, France, Germany, Israel, Portugal, Russia, Spain, Sweden, Switzerland, the United Kingdom, and the USA, covering a broad range of software technologies: Formal Methods, Testing, High-Integrity Systems, Program Analysis, Distributed Systems, Real-Time Systems, Language and Patterns, Dependable Systems, APIs and Components, Real-Time Kernels, Standard Formats: UML & XML, System Evolution, and Software Process.

Tutorials

The conference also included an exciting selection of tutorials, featuring international experts who presented introductory and advanced material in the domain of the conference:

- Non-Standard Techniques in Ada
  Art Duncan, RPI, USA
- Practical Experiences of Safety-Critical Ada Technologies
  Peter Amey and Rod Chapman, Praxis Critical Systems, UK
- Early Reliability Measurement and Improvement
  Jeff Tian, SMU, USA
- An Introduction to XML
  Gregory Neven, Maarten Coene, and Roel Adriaensens, K.U. Leuven, Belgium
- From Full Concurrency to Safe Concurrency
  John Harbaugh, Boeing, USA
- Building Distributed Systems with Ada
  Samuel Tardieu, Laurent Pautet, and Thomas Quinot, ENST, France
- Implementing Design Patterns in Ada: Sequential Programming Idioms
  Matthew Heaney, USA
- Architecture Centred Development and Evolution of Reliable Real-Time Systems
  Bruce Lewis and Ed Colbert, USA

Workshop on Exception Handling

At the initiative of Alexander Romanovsky, Alfred Strohmeier, and Andy Wellings, a full-day workshop was held on "Exception Handling for a 21st Century Programming Language". As the complexity of modern software systems grows, so does the need to deal reliably and efficiently with an increasing number of abnormal situations. The most general mechanism for this is exception handling, which is becoming a standard feature in modern languages. Ada has been the first mainstream programming language integrating exceptions in the procedural paradigm, and Java has fused exceptions with object-orientation. However, integration of exceptions and concurrency are still the subject of research, and the performance of "object-oriented exceptions" for hard real-time systems should be investigated.

The aims of the workshop were therefore:

- to share experience on how to build modern systems that have to deal with abnormal situations;
- to discuss how solutions to those needs can be developed employing standard Ada features including the current exception handling paradigm;
- to propose new exception handling mechanisms/paradigms that can be included in future revisions of the Ada language and also fit high integrity language profiles for safety critical systems.

Participation to the workshop was by invitation upon acceptance of a submission, e.g. a brief position paper, an experience report, or a full research paper. The papers were made available to the participants before the workshop. The workshop included talks based on the submitted papers and intensive shepherded discussion sessions. Selected submissions will be published in Ada Letters.

Acknowledgements

Many people contributed to the success of the conference. The program committee, made up of international experts in the area of reliable software technologies, spent long hours carefully reviewing all the papers and tutorial proposals submitted to the conference. A subcommittee comprising Luc Bernard, Johann Blieberger, Dirk Craeynest, Erhard Ploedereder, Juan Antonio de la Puente, and Alfred Strohmeier met in Leuven to make the final paper selection. Some program committee members were assigned to shepherd some of the papers. We are grateful to all those who contributed to the technical program of the conference. Special thanks to Alexander Romanovsky, whose dedication was key to the success of the workshop. We are also grateful to Raul Silaghi who did most of the clerical work for the preparation of this volume.

We would also like to thank the members of the organizing committee, and especially the people of the K.U. Leuven, for the work spent in the local organization. Karel De Vlaminck and Yolande Berbers were in charge of the overall coordination and took care of all the clerical details for the successful running of the conference. Luc Bernard supervised the preparation of the attractive tutorial program. Yvan Barbaix worked long hours contacting companies and people to prepare the conference exhibition. Dirk Walravens created and maintained the conference Web site, and supported the paper submission and review process. Special thanks to Andrew Hately for publicizing the conference by post and e-mail, and for preparing the brochure with the conference program. A great help in organizing the submission process and the paper reviews was the START Conference Manager, provided graciously by Rich Gerber.

Last but not least, we would like to express our appreciation to the authors of the papers submitted to the conference, and to all the participants who helped in achieving the goal of the conference, providing a forum for researchers and practitioners for the exchange of information and ideas about reliable software technologies. We hope they all enjoyed the technical program as well as the social events of the 6th International Conference on Reliable Software Technologies.

May 2001   Alfred Strohmeier
                                                           Dirk Craeynest

Organizing Committee

Conference Chair
Karel De Vlaminck, K.U. Leuven, Belgium

Program Co-chairs
Dirk Craeynest, Offis nv/sa & K.U. Leuven, Belgium
Alfred Strohmeier, Swiss Fed. Inst. of Technology Lausanne (EPFL), Switzerland

Tutorial Chair
Luc Bernard, Offis nv/sa, Belgium

Exhibition Chair
Yvan Barbaix, K.U. Leuven, Belgium

Publicity Chair
Andrew Hately, Eurocontrol - CFMU, Belgium

Finance Co-chairs
Karel De Vlaminck, K.U. Leuven, Belgium
Marc Gobin, Royal Military Academy, Belgium

Local Organization Chair
Yolande Berbers, K.U. Leuven, Belgium

Organizing Board
Karel De Vlaminck, Dirk Craeynest, Yolande Berbers

Ada-Europe Conference Liaison
Alfred Strohmeier, Swiss Fed. Inst. of Technology Lausanne (EPFL), Switzerland

Advisory Board

Brad Balfour, Objective Interface, USA
Ben Brosgol, Ada Core Technologies, USA
Roderick Chapman, Praxis, UK
Robert Dewar, ACT, USA
Franco Gasperoni, ACT Europe, France
Ian Gilchrist, IPL Information Processing, UK
Mike Kamrad, Top Layer Networks, USA
Hubert B. Keller, Forschungszentrum Karlsruhe, Germany
Rudolf Landwehr, CCI, Germany
John Robinson, John Robinson & Associates, UK
Jean-Pierre Rosen, Adalog, France
Bill Taylor, Rational Software, UK
Theodor Tempelmeier, Rosenheim University of Applied Sciences, Germany
Joyce Tokar, DDC-I, USA
Andy Wellings, University of York, UK

Program Committee

Ángel Álvarez, Technical University of Madrid, Spain
Lars Asplund, Uppsala University, Sweden
Ted Baker, Florida State University, USA
Yvan Barbaix, K.U. Leuven, Belgium
Stéphane Barbey, Paranor AG, Switzerland
John Barnes, UK
Yolande Berbers, K.U. Leuven, Belgium
Luc Bernard, Offis nv/sa, Belgium
Guillem Bernat, University of York, UK
Johann Blieberger, Technical University of Vienna, Austria
Jim Briggs, University of Portsmouth, UK
Bernd Burgstaller, Technical University of Vienna, Austria
Alan Burns, University of York, UK
Agusti Canals, CS-SI, France
Ulf Cederling, Växsjö University, Sweden
Dirk Craeynest, Offis nv/sa & K.U. Leuven, Belgium
Alfons Crespo, Universidad Politécnica de Valencia, Spain
Juan A. de la Puente, Universidad Politécnica de Madrid, Spain
Peter Dencker, Aonix GmbH, Germany
Raymond Devillers, Université Libre de Bruxelles, Belgium
Michael Feldman, George Washington University, USA
Jesús M. González-Barahona, Universidad Rey Juan Carlos, Spain
Michael González Harbour, Universidad de Cantabria, Spain
Gerhard Goos, University of Karlsruhe, Germany
Thomas Gruber, Austrian Research Centers, Austria
Helge Hagenauer, University of Salzburg, Austria
Günter Hommel, Technische Universität Berlin, Germany
Yvon Kermarrec, ENST Bretagne, France
Jörg Kienzle, Swiss Fed. Inst. of Technology Lausanne (EPFL), Switzerland
Fabrice Kordon, Université P.& M. Curie, France
Björn Källberg, SaabTech, Sweden
Albert Llamosí, Universitat de les Illes Balears, Spain
Kristina Lundqvist, Uppsala University, Sweden
Franco Mazzanti, Ist. di Elaborazione della Informazione, Italy
John W. McCormick, University of Northern Iowa, USA
Hugo Moen, Navia Aviation AS, Norway
Pierre Morere, Aonix, France
Paolo Panaroni, Intecs Sistemi, Italy
Laurent Pautet, ENST Paris University, France
Erhard Plödereder, University of Stuttgart, Germany
Ceri Reid, Coda Technologies, UK
Jean-Marie Rigaud, Université Paul Sabatier, France
Sergey Rybin, Moscow State University, Russia & ACT Europe, France

Table of Contents

Real-Time Systems

Language and Patterns

Dependable Systems

APIs and Components

Real-Time Kernels

Standard Formats: UML & XML

System Evolution

Building Formal Requirements Models
for Reliable Software

Axel van Lamsweerde

Université catholique de Louvain, Département d'Ingénierie Informatique
B-1348 Louvain-la-Neuve (Belgium)
avl@info.ucl.ac.be

Abstract. Requirements engineering (RE) is concerned with the elicitation of the goals to be achieved by the system envisioned, the operationalization of such goals into specifications of services and constraints, and the assignment of responsibilities for the resulting requirements to agents such as humans, devices, and software. Getting high-quality requirements is difficult and critical. Recent surveys have confirmed the growing recognition of RE as an area of primary concern in software engineering research and practice.

The paper first briefly introduces RE by discussing its main motivations, objectives, activities, and challenges. The role of rich models as a common interface to all RE processes is emphasized. We review various techniques available to date for system modeling, from semi-formal to formal, and discuss their relative strengths and weaknesses when applied during the RE stage of the software lifecycle.

The paper then discusses some recent efforts to overcome such problems through RE-specific techniques for goal-oriented elaboration of requirements, multiparadigm specification, the integration of non-functional requirements, the anticipation of abnormal agent behaviors, and the management of conflicting requirements.

1 Introduction

The requirements problem is among the oldest in software engineering. An early empirical study over a variety of software projects revealed that inadequate, inconsistent, incomplete, or ambiguous requirements are numerous and have a critical impact on the quality of the resulting software [Bel76]. Late correction of requirements errors was observed to be incredibly expensive [Boe81]. A consensus has been growing that engineering high-quality requirements is difficult; as Brooks noted in his landmark paper on the essence and accidents of software engineering, "the hardest single part of building a software system is deciding precisely what to build" [Bro87].

In spite of such early recognition, the requirements problem is still with us – more than ever. A recent survey over 8000 projects in 350 US companies showed that only 16% of them were considered to be successful; 33% of them failed while 51% were in the space between, providing only partial functionalties, with major cost overruns and late deliveries. [Sta95]; when asked about the main reasons for this, 50% of the project managers mentioned poor requirements as the major source of

A. Strohmeier and D. Craeynest (Eds.): Ada-Europe 2001, LNCS 2043, pp. 1-20, 2001.

failure. An independent survey of 3800 European organizations in 17 countries confirmed this; when asked where their main software problems are, more than half of the managers mentioned requirements specification and requirements management in first position [ESI96]. The problem gets even more serious in areas where reliability is a key concern. Many accidents in the safety-critical systems literature have been attributed to poor requirements engineering [Lev95].

Software requirements should thus be engineered with great care and precision. *Methods* should therefore be used to elicit them in a systematic way, organize them in a coherent structure, and check them against desired qualities such as completeness, consistency, and adequacy with respect to the real needs.

In spite of much recent interest in RE, the current state of the art in RE methods is still fairly limited [Lam2Ka]. There are many reasons for this, notably,

- the broad scope and inherent complexity of the RE process,
- some frequent misunderstanding of what the basic notions are really about (such as "requirements", "consistency", or "completeness"),
- the lack of abstraction of most software modeling techniques when used for engineering requirements,
- the lack of support for reasoning about the software-to-be and its environment taken together,
- the natural propensity to invent new notations and a posteriori checking techniques rather than constructive approaches,
- the conflicting concerns of formality (for analyzability) and simplicity (for usability).

This paper elaborates on some of the issues raised in this list. Section 2 introduces the scope and concerns of RE; we discuss the role of "rich" models as a common interface to the multiple activities involved in the RE process. Section 3 briefly reviews the main software modeling techniques available to date, from semi-formal to formal; we argue that these techniques while appropriate for the later stages of software design are not the ones needed in the context of engineering requirements. The second part of the paper then outlines an approach aimed at supporting the elaboration, structuring, and analysis of requirements models [Dar93, Lam98a, Lam2Kc]. The approach combines a goal-oriented method for deriving requirements and responsibility assignments from system objectives (Section 4), a systematic technique for generating exceptional behaviors to be handled in order to produce more complete and realistic requirements (Section 5), and a systematic technique for detecting and resolving conflicts among requirements as they usually arise from multiple viewpoints among the stakeholders involved (Section 6).

2   What Is RE Really about?

The RE process addresses three kinds of intertwined issues.

- **WHY** issues: The goals for a new system need to be identified, analyzed, and refined. Such goals are usually obtained by analyzing problems with the current situation, identifying new opportunities, exploring scenarios of interaction, and so on. Beside functional goals (e.g., satisfaction of requests, information of the state of affairs) there are many non-functional ones (e.g., safety, security, performance, evolvability, etc.). The identification and refinement of such goals usually makes heavy use of domain-specific knowledge.

- *WHAT* issues: The requirements operationalizing the various goals identified need to be defined precisely and related to each other; in parallel, the assumptions made in the operationalization process need to be made explicit and documented. Beside functional requirements about services to be provided there is a wide spectrum of non-functional requirements about quality of service.

- *WHO* issues: The requirements need to be assigned as contractual obligations among the various agents forming the composite system-to-be. These include the software to be developed, human agents, sensors/actuators, existing software, etc. The boundary between the software-to-be and its environment results from this distribution of responsibilities; different agent assignments define different system proposals.

Requirements engineering is thus by no means limited to WHAT issues as often suggested in the literature on software specifications.

In view of some confusions being frequently made, it is also worth clarifying what requirements are really about.

A first important distinction must be made between *requirements* and *domain properties* [Jac95, Par95]. Physical laws, organizational policies, regulations, or definitions of objects or operations in the environment are not requirements. For example, the precondition that the doors must be closed for an operation OpenDoors to be applied in a train control system is a domain property, not a requirement; on another hand, a precondition requiring that the train be at some station is a requirement on that same operation in order to achieve the goal of safe transportation.

A second important distinction must be made between requirements and software specifications. *Requirements* are formulated in terms of objects in the real world, in a vocabulary accessible to stakeholders [Jac95]; they capture required relations between objects in the environment that are monitored and controlled by the software, respectively [Par95]. *Software specifications* are formulated in terms of objects manipulated by the software, in a vocabulary accessible to programmers; they capture required relations between input and output software objects. *Accuracy goals* are non-functional goals at the boundary between the software and the environment that require the state of input/output software objects to accurately reflect the state of the corresponding monitored/controlled objects they represent [Myl92, Dar93]. In our train example, there should be an accuracy goal stating that the (physical) doors are open iff the corresponding Doors.State software variable has the value 'open'.

A third distinction has to be made between requirements and assumptions. Although they are both optative properties, *requirements* are to be enforced by the software whereas *assumptions* can be enforced by agents in the environment only [Lam98a]. For example, the software can enforce that trains be at station when doors get open, but cannot enforce that passengers get in.

If R denotes the set of requirements, As the set of assumptions, D the set of domain properties, S the set of software specifications, Ac the set of accuracy goals, and G the set of goals under consideration, the following satisfaction relations must hold:

$$S, Ac, D \models R \quad \text{with} S, Ac, D \not\models \text{false}$$

$$R, As, D \models G \quad \text{with} R, As, D \not\models \text{false}$$

The reasons why RE is such a complex step of the software lifecycle should now appear in this overall setting.

- The scope of RE is fairly broad. It addresses two systems –the system as it is and the system as it will be. It includes the software to be developed but also for the environment in which the software will operate. The latter may embody complex organizational policies or physical phenomena that need to be taken into account. The scope also covers a whole range of concerns and descriptions, from very high-level objectives to low-level constraints and from the initially vague to the eventually precise, sometimes formal.

- The RE process is composed of multiple intertwined subprocesses such as domain analysis, stakeholder analysis, elicitation of goals and scenarios, exploration of alternatives, risk analysis, negotiation, documentation of choices, specification, validation and verification, and change management.

- Usually there are many different parties involved which do not necessarily share the same objectives and background –clients, domain experts, managers, analysts, developers, etc.

- The large number and diversity of raised concerns inevitably leads to conflicts that need to be detected and resolved appropriately. In our train control example, the goal of safe transportation requires trains not to be too close to each other which conflicts with the goal of serving more passengers. In an electronic payment system, anonymity and accountability are conflicting goals, security through passwords conflicts with usability, and so on. Requirements engineers live in a world where conflicts are the rule, not the exception; conflict management is a driving force of the RE process.

- There are many other types of errors and deficiencies a requirements specification can contain beside conflicts and inconsistencies; some of them may be critical, such as incompleteness, inadequacies, or ambiguities; others, such as noises, overspecifications, forward references, or wishful thinking, are generally less severe but hamper understandability and generate new problems [Mey85]. Errors in requirements specifications are known to be numerous, persistent, expensive, and dangerous [Boe81, Lev95].

Rich *models* appear to be the best interfaces to the various RE subprocesses mentioned above. They provide a structured way of capturing the output of domain analysis and goal/requirement elicitation; they offer good support for exploring alternatives and negotiating choices; they provide structure to complex specifications and individual units for their compositional analysis; they may guide further elicitation, specification, and analysis. Models also provide the basis for documentation and evolution.

3 Candidate Techniques for Requirements Modeling and Specification

If modeling turns out to be a core activity in the RE process, the basic questions to be addressed are:

- what aspects to model in the *WHY-WHAT-WHO* range,
- how to model such aspects,
- how to define the model precisely,
- how to reason about the model.

The answer to the first question determines the *ontology* of conceptual units in terms of which models will be built - e.g., data, operations, events, goals, agents, and so forth. The answer to the second question determines the *structuring relationships* in terms of which such units will be composed and linked together - e.g., input/output, trigger, generalization, refinement, responsibility assignment, and so forth. The answer to the third question determines the informal, semi-formal, or formal *specification technique* used to define the properties of model components precisely. The answer to the fourth question determines the kind of *reasoning technique* available for the purpose of elicitation, specification, and analysis.

As will be seen below, the main candidate approaches for requirements modeling and specification are limited to *WHAT* aspects only. We review them briefly before arguing about their limitation for RE tasks.

3.1 Semi-formal Approaches

The principle here is to *formally declare* conceptual units and their links; the properties of such units and links are generally *asserted informally*. We just list some of the main standard techniques.

Entity-Relationship Diagrams. The conceptual units denote autonomous classes of objects of interest with distinct identities and shared features; the conceptual links denote subordinate classes of objects of interest. Both can be characterized by attributes with specific value ranges. Diagrams can be hierarchically structured through specialization mechanisms. Figure 1 depicts a fragment for our train control example.

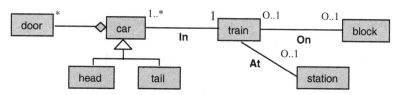

Fig. 1. Entities and relationships

State Transition Diagrams. The conceptual units denote object states of interest whereas the conceptual links denote guarded transitions triggered by events. Diagrams can be hierarchically structured through various parallel composition mechanisms. Figure 2 depicts a fragment for our train control example.

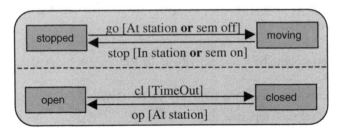

Fig. 2. States and transitions

Dataflow Diagrams. The conceptual units denote operations of interest whereas the conceptual links denote input/output data flows. Diagrams can be hierarchically structured through functional decomposition mechanisms Figure 3 depicts a fragment for our train control example.

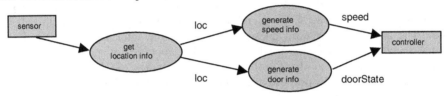

Fig. 3. Operations and data flows

The strengths of semi-formal approaches are fairly obvious:

- graphical notations are easier to use and communicate;
- different kinds of diagrams may provide complementary views of the same system; such views can be related to each other through inter-view consistency rules [Nus94].

These strengths together with notational standardization are probably the main reasons for the current popularity of UML [Rum99].

On the down side, these approaches have strong limitations:

- in general they can only cope with functional aspects;
- since they only capture declaration-level features of a system, they generally support highly limited forms of specification and analysis;
- the box-and-arrow semantics of their graphical notations is most often fairly fuzzy; the same model may often be interpreted in different ways by different people.

3.2   Formal Approaches

The principle here is to model a system in terms of structured collections of declarations and assertions, *both* specified in a formal language, which provides a precise syntax, semantics, and proof theory. The standard approaches here differ according to the specification paradigm they rely on (see [Lam2Kb] for more details and references).

History-Based Specification. A system is characterized by its maximal set of admissible behaviors over time. The properties of interest are specified by temporal logic assertions about system objects; such assertions involve operators referring to past, current and future states. The assertions are interpreted over time structures which can be discrete, dense or continuous. Most often it is necessary to specify properties over time bounds; real-time temporal logics are therefore necessary. In our train control example, we could specify a progress requirement about trains moving from one station to the other, such as

$$\forall tr: Train,\ st: Station$$
$$At\ (tr,\ st) \Rightarrow \Diamond_{\leq T}\ At\ (tr,\ next(st))$$

Our requirement of doors staying closed between stations would be specified by

$$\forall tr: Train,\ st: Station$$
$$\bullet\ At\ (tr,\ st) \land \neg At\ (tr,\ st) \Rightarrow$$
$$tr.Doors = \text{``closed''}\ \mathcal{U}\ At\ (tr,\ next(st))$$

In the assertion above, $\Diamond_{\leq T}$ means "some time in the future before deadline T" [Koy92] whereas the $\bullet$ and $\mathcal{U}$ temporal operators mean "in the previous state" and "always in the future until", respectively [Man92].

Built-in historical references allow the specifier to avoid introducing extra variables for encoding the past or the future in behavioral requirements; this paradigm seems thus particularly appropriate for the early stages of requirements specification.

State-Based Specification. Instead of characterizing the admissible system histories, one may characterize the admissible system states at some arbitrary snapshot. The properties of interest are specified by invariants constraining the system objects at any snapshot, and by pre- and post-assertions constraining the application of system operations at any snapshot. In our train control example, we could specify the operation to control door openings by a Z schema [Pot96] such as

OpenDoors _____
Δ TrainSystem
st?: Station
_____
Doors = "closed " $\land$ At (tr, st?)
Doors' = "open"

The state-based paradigm is more operational than the previous one; it seems more appropriate for the later stages of requirements specification where specific software services have been elicited from more abstract requirements.

Transition-Based Specification. Instead of characterizing admissible system histories or system states, one may characterize the required transitions from state class to state class. The properties of interest are specified by a set of transition functions; the transition function for a system object gives, for each input state and triggering event, the corresponding output state. The occurrence of a triggering event is a sufficient condition for the corresponding transition to take place (unlike a precondition, it captures an obligation); necessary preconditions may also be specified to guard the transition. In our train control example, we could specify the required dynamics of doors by a SCR table [Par95, Heit96] such as

Old Mode	Event	New Mode
open	@T TimeOut	closed
closed	@T AtStation	open

Functional Specification. The principle here is to specify a system as a structured set of mathematical functions. Two approaches may be distinguished.

Algebraic specification. The functions are grouped by object types that appear in their domain or codomain, thereby defining abstract data types. The properties of interest are then specified as conditional equations that capture the effect of composing functions. In the context of our train control example, we might introduce a signature such as

WhichTrain: Blocks →Trains
EnterBlock: Trains × Blocks → Blocks

together with a law of composition such as

WhichTrain (EnterBlock (tr, bl)) = tr

Higher-Order Functions. The functions are grouped into logical theories. Such theories contain type definitions, variable declarations, and axioms defining the various functions in the theory. Functions may have other functions as arguments which significantly increases the power of the language. In the context of our train control example, we might introduce a PVS [Owr95] function specification such as

TRACKING: TYPE = [Blocks →Trains]
trk: **VAR** TRACKING
AddTrain: [TRACKING, Blocks, Trains → TRACKING]
*AddTrain (trk, bl, tr) = trk   **WITH** [(bl) := tr]*

Operational Specification. Much closer to the programming level, a system may be characterized as a collection of concurrent processes that can be executed by some more or less abstract machine. Operational techniques such as Petri nets or process algebras rely on this general paradigm.

Formal approaches have numerous strengths:

- they offer precise rules of interpretation of statements;
- they support much more sophisticated forms of analysis, e.g., animation, algorithmic verification such as model checking, or deductive verification;
- they allow other useful products to be generated automatically, e.g., counterexamples, failure scenarios, test cases, proof obligations, refinements, code fragments, and so on.

On the down side, these approaches are not really accessible to practitioners. Formal specifications are hard to write, read, and communicate. Writing the input required by analysis tools is generally difficult, error-prone and thus requires high expertise; coping with their output is generally hard as well.

3.3 Common Inadequacies to RE Needs

Popular semi-formal and formal approaches both have common limitations with respect to the nature and scope of RE discussed in Section 2.

- *Restricted scope.* The approaches outined above address WHAT issues only; they do not cover WHY and WHO issues. RE methods need richer ontologies than those based on programming abstractions (viz. data, operation or state). To address WHY and WHO issues, RE ontologies must offer higher-level abstractions such as goals, goal refinements, agents, responsibility assignments, and so forth.

- *Alternative choices out of the picture.* The above approaches do not allow alternatives to be represented, related to each other, and compared for selection. RE methods must provide support for reasoning about alternative goal refinements, alternative conflict resolutions, alternative responsibility assignments, and so forth.

- *Non-functional aspects out of the picture.* The above approaches generally do not consider non-functional concerns. The latter form an important part of any requirements specification and play a prominent role in alternative selection, conflict management, and architecture derivation. RE methods must provide support for representing and reasoning about them.

- *Poor separation of concerns.* The above techniques in general make no distinction between domain properties, requirements, assumptions, and software specifications. In the above Z schema, for example, the domain property Doors = "closed " and the requirement At (tr, st?) have the same status. As discussed in Section 2, such distinctions are important in RE.

- *Monolithic frameworks.* With the techniques above there is no way to be formal at some critical places and semi-formal at others, or to combine multiple specification paradigms. In order to be usable, flexible, and customizable to specific types of concerns, RE methods should ideally be "multi-button", that is, support multiparadigm specification and integrate multiple forms of reasoning – from qualitative to formal, and from lightweight to heavyweight when needed.

- *Poor guidance.* Most techniques essentially provide sets of notations and tools for a posteriori analysis. Therefore they tend to induce an approach of elaborating models and specifications by iterative debugging. In view of the inherent complexity of the RE process, one should ideally favor a more constructive approach in which the quality of the requirements model and specification obtained is guaranteed by the method followed.

4 Shifting to Goal-Oriented RE

This section reviews some attempts to address those inadequacies, with special emphasis on a goal-oriented approach we have developed for that purpose.

Broadly speaking, a *goal* corresponds to an objective the system should achieve through cooperation of agents in the software-to-be and in the environment. It may refer to a functional or a non-functional concern.

Goals play a prominent role in the RE process [Dar93, Lam98a]. They drive the elaboration of requirements to support them. They provide a completeness criterion for the requirements specification; the specification is complete if all stated goals are met by the specification [Yue87]. Goals are generally more stable than the requirements to achieve them. They provide a rationale for requirements; a requirement exists because of some underlying goal which provides a base for it. In short, requirements "implement" goals much the same way as programs implement design specifications.

Goal-oriented approaches to RE are therefore receiving growing attention. Two complementary frameworks have been proposed for integrating goals and goal refinement in requirements models: a formal framework and a qualitative one.

In the *formal* framework [Dar93], goals can be specified semi-formally or formally. Goal refinements are captured through AND/OR graphs. AND-refinement links relate a goal to a set of subgoals (called refinement); this means that satisfying all subgoals in the refinement is a sufficient condition for satisfying the goal. OR-refinement links relate a goal to an alternative set of refinements; this means that satisfying one of the refinements is a sufficient condition for satisfying the goal. AND/OR operationalization links are also introduced to relate goals to requirements on operations/ objects; AND/OR responsibility links are introduced to relate primitive goals to individual agents. Goals are formalized in a real-time temporal logic whereas operations/objects are formalized by invariants and pre/post-conditions. Formal schemes are available for reasoning about goal refinement [Dar96], operationalization [Dar93, Let01], conflict [Lam98a], obstruction [Lam2Kc], assignment to agents [Let01], inference from scenarios [Lam98b], and acquisition by analogy [Mas97].

In the *qualitative* framework [Myl92], weaker link types are introduced to relate "soft" goals [Myl92]. The idea is that such goals cannot be said to be satisfied in a clear-cut sense. Instead of goal satisfaction, goal satisficing is introduced to express that lower-level goals or requirements are expected to achieve the goal within acceptable limits, rather than absolutely. A subgoal is then said to contribute partially to the goal, regardless of other subgoals; it may contribute positively or negatively. If a goal is AND-decomposed into subgoals and all subgoals are satisficed, then the goal is satisficeable; but if a subgoal is denied then the goal is deniable. If a goal contributes negatively to another goal and the former is satisficed, then the latter is deniable. In the AND/OR goal graph, goals are specified by names, parameters, and degrees of satisficing/denial by child goals. This framework is particularly well-suited for high-level goals that cannot be formalized . It can be used for evaluating alternative goal refinements. A qualitative labeling procedure may determine the degree to which a goal is satisfied/denied by lower-level requirements, by propagating such information along positive/negative support links in the goal graph.

The formal framework gave rise to the KAOS method for eliciting, specifying, and analyzing goals, requirements, scenarios, and responsibility assignments. Our aim here is to briefly suggest how the method works using a few excerpts from the requirements elaboration for a non-trivial, safety-critical system: the Bay Area Rapid Transit system [BART99, Let2K, Lam2Ka].

Figure 4 summarizes the steps of the method by showing the corresponding sub-models obtained. The goal refinement graph is elaborated by eliciting goals from available sources and asking *why* and *how* questions (goal elaboration step); objects, relationships and attributes are derived from the goal specifications (object modeling step); agents are identified, alternative responsibility assignments are explored, and agent interfaces are derived (responsibility assignment step); operations and their domain pre- and postconditions are identified from the goal specifications, and strengthened pre-/postconditions and trigger conditions are derived so as to ensure the corresponding goals (operationalization step). These steps are not strictly sequential as progress in one step may prompt parallel progress in the next one or backtracking to a previous one.

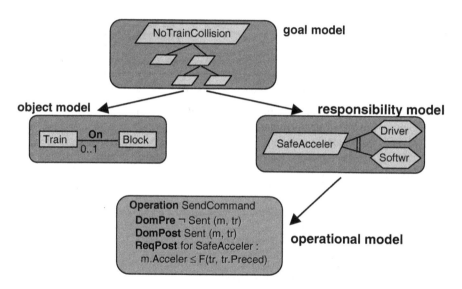

Fig. 4. Goal-oriented RE with KAOS

Goal Identification from the Initial Document. A first set of goals is identified from a first reading of the available source [BART99] by searching for intentional keywords such as "objective", "purpose", "intent", "concern", "in order to", etc. A number of soft goals are thereby identified, e.g., "ServeMorePassengers", "NewTracksAdded", "Minimize[DevelopmentCosts]", "Minimize[DistanceBetweenTrains]", "SafeTransportation", etc. These goals are qualitatively related to each other through support links: Contributes (+), ContributesStrongly (++), Conflicts (-), ConflictsStrongly (- -). These weights are used to select among alternatives. Where possible, keywords from the semi-formal layer of the KAOS language are used to indicate the goal category. The *Maintain* and *Avoid* keywords specify "always" goals having the temporal pattern $\Box(P \rightarrow Q)$ and $\Box (P \rightarrow \neg Q)$, respectively. The *Achieve* keyword specifies "eventually" goals having the pattern $P \Rightarrow \Diamond Q$. The "$\rightarrow$" connective denotes logical implication; $\Box(P \rightarrow Q)$ is denoted by $P \Rightarrow Q$ for short.

Figure 5 shows the result of this first elicitation. Clouds denote soft-goals, parallelograms denote formalizable goals, arrows denote goal-subgoal links, and a double line linking arrows denotes an OR-refinement into alternative subgoals.

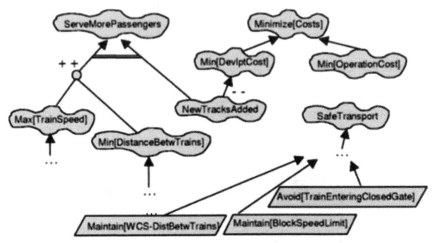

Fig. 5. Preliminary goal graph for the BART system

Formalizing Goals and Deriving the Object Model. The object modeling step can start as soon as goals can be formulated precisely enough. The principle here is to identify objects, relationships and attributes from goal specifications. Consider, for example, the goal Maintain[BlockSpeedLimit] at the bottom of Figure 5. It may be specified as follows:

Goal Maintain[BlockSpeedLimit]
   InformalDef *A train should stay below the maximum speed the track segment can handle.*
   FormalDef   ∀ tr: Train, bl: Block:
             On(tr, bl) ⇒ tr.Speed ≤ bl.SpeedLimit

From the predicate, objects, and attributes appearing in this goal formalization we derive the following portion of the object model:

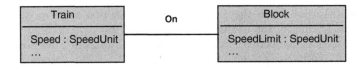

Similarly, the other goal at the bottom of Figure 5 is specified as follows:

Goal Maintain[WCS-DistBetweenTrains]
   InformalDef *A train should never get so close to a train in front so that if the train in front stops suddenly (e.g., derailment) the next train would hit it.*
   FormalDef ∀ tr1, tr2: Train :
             Following (tr1, tr2) ⇒ tr1.Loc - tr2.Loc > tr1.WCS-Dist

(The InformalDef statements in those goal definitions are taken literally from the initial document; WCS-Dist denotes the physical worst-case stopping distance based on the physical speed of the train.) This new goal specification allows the above portion of the object model to be enriched with Loc and WCS-Dist attributes for the Train object together with a reflexive Following relationship on it. *Goals thus provide a precise driving criterion for identifying elements of the object model.*

Eliciting More Abstract Goals by WHY Questions. It is often the case that higher-level goals underpinning goals easily identified from initial sources are kept implicit in such sources. They may, however, be useful for finding out other important subgoals of the higher-level goal that were missing for the higher-level goal to be achieved.

Higher-level goals are identified by asking WHY questions about the goals available. For example, asking a WHY question about the goal

Maintain[WCS-DistBetweenTrains]

yields the parent goal

Avoid[TrainCollision]

On another hand, asking a WHY question about the goal

Avoid[TrainEnteringClosedGate]

yields the parent goal

Avoid[TrainOnSwitchInWrongPosition].

The formalizations of this parent goal and of the initial subgoal Avoid[TrainEnteringClosedGate] match the root and one of the two child nodes of a formal refinement pattern from our pattern library [Dar96, Let2K]. This pattern, pre-proved once for all to produce a correct and complete goal refinement using a temporal logic verifier, reveals by reinstantiation that the companion subgoal was missing from the initial document, that is, the goal

Maintain[GateClosedWhenSwitchInWrongPosition].

Missing goals can thus be discovered formally by a combination of WHY questions and refinement patterns.

Eliciting More Concrete Goals by HOW Questions. Goals need to be refined until subgoals are reached that can be assigned to individual agents in the software-to-be and in the environment. Terminal goals become requirements in the former case and assumptions in the latter.

More concrete subgoals are elicited by asking HOW questions. For example, a HOW question about the goal

Maintain[WCS-DistBetweenTrains]

Yields the following three companion subgoals:

Maintain [SafeSpeed/AccelerationCommanded],
Maintain [SafeTrainResponseToCommand],
Maintain [NoSuddenStopOfPrecedingTrain].

The formalization of these subgoals may be used to formally prove that together they entail the father goal Maintain[WCS-DistBetweenTrains] formalized above [Let2K]. These subgoals have to be refined in turn until assignable subgoals are reached. A complete refinement tree may be found in [Lam2Ka].

Exploring Alternative Responsibility Assignments. The responsibility assignment step relies on precise formulations of goals from the goal elaboration step. Assignments of individual agents to terminal goals in the refinement graph are captured by AND/OR responsibility links. For example, the initial BART document suggests assigning the *Accuracy* goal

> Maintain[AccurateSpeed/PositionEstimates]

to the TrackingSystem agent, the goal

> Maintain[SafeTrainResponseToCommand]

to the OnBoardTrainController agent, and the goal

> Maintain[SafeCmdMsg]

to the Speed/AccelerationControlSystem agent.

Alternative goal refinements and agent assignments could be explored. For example, the parent goal

> Maintain[WCS-DistBetweenTrains]

may alternatively be refined by the following three *Maintain* subgoals:

> PreceedingTrainSpeed/PositionKnownTo**Following**Train,
>
> SafeAccelerationBasedOn**PreceedingTrain**Speed/Position,
>
> NoSuddenStopOfPreceedingTrain

The second subgoal could now be assigned to the **OnBoard**TrainController agent. This alternative responsibility assignment would produce a fully distributed system. Qualitative reasoning techniques in the style of [Myl99] might then be applied to the soft goals identified in Figure 5 to help selecting the most preferable responsibility assignment.

Deriving Agent Interfaces. Once terminal subgoals have been assigned to individual software or environmental agents, the interfaces of each agent in terms of monitored and controlled variables can be derived systematically from the goal specifications. The formal technique is described in [Let01]; we just suggest the idea here on a simple example. Consider the goal Maintain[SafeCmdMsg] that has been assigned to the Speed/AccelerationControlSystem agent. We give its general form here for sake of simplicity:

> **Goal** Maintain[SafeCmdMsg]
> **FormalDef** $\forall$ cm: *CommandMessage*, tr1, tr2: *Train*
> Sent (cm, tr1) $\wedge$ Following (tr1, tr2) $\wedge$ Refers (cm, tr2.Info)
> $\Rightarrow$ cm.Accel $\leq$ F (tr1, tr2) $\wedge$ cm.Speed > G (tr1)

To fulfil its responsibility for this goal the Speed/AccelerationControlSystem agent must be able to *evaluate* the goal antecedent and *establish* the goal consequent. The agent's monitored variable is therefore *Train.Info* whereas its controlled variables are *CommandMessage.Accel* and *CommandMessage.Speed*. The latter will in turn become monitored variables of the OnBoardTrainController agent, by similar analysis.

Identifying Operations. The final operationalization step starts by identifying the operations relevant to goals and defining their domain pre- and postconditions. Goals refer to specific state transitions; for each such transition an operation causing it is identified; its domain pre- and postcondition captures the state transition. For the goal Maintain[SafeCmdMsg] formalized above we get, for example,

Operation SendCommandMessage
   Input Train {**arg** tr}
   Output ComandMessage {**res** cm}
   DomPre ¬ Sent (cm, tr)
   DomPost Sent (cm, tr)

This definition minimally captures what any sending of a command to a train is about in the domain considered; it does not ensure any of the goals it should contribute to.

Operationalizing Goals. The next operationalization sub-step is to strengthen such domain conditions so that the various goals linked to the operation are ensured. For goals assigned to software agents, this step produces *requirements* on the operations for the corresponding goals to be achieved. Derivation rules for an operationalization calculus are available [Dar93, Let01]. In our example, they yield the following requirements that strengthen the domain pre- and postconditions:

Operation SendCommandMessage
   Input ...; **Output** ...
   DomPre ... ; **DomPost** ...
   ReqPost for SafeCmdMsg:
      Following (tr, t2)
         → cm.Accel ≤ F (tr, tr2) ∧ cm.Speed > G (tr)
   ReqTrig for CmdMsgSentInTime:
      ■$_{\leq 0.5\ sec}$ ¬ ∃ cm': CommandMessage:
         Sent (cm', tr)

(The trigger condition captures an obligation to trigger the operation as soon as the condition gets true, and provided the domain precondition is true. In the example above the condition says that no command has been sent in every past state up to one half-second [BART99].)

Using a mix of semi-formal and formal techniques for goal-oriented requirements elaboration, we have reached the level at which most formal specification techniques would start.

5 Analyzing Obstacles to Requirements Satisfaction

First-sketch specifications of goals, requirements and assumptions are often too ideal; they are likely to be violated from time to time in the running system due to unexpected behavior of agents. The lack of anticipation of exceptional behaviors may result in unrealistic, unachievable and/or incomplete requirements. We capture such exceptional behaviors by formal assertions called *obstacles* to goal satisfaction.

An obstacle O is said to obstruct a goal G iff

$$\{O, \text{Dom}\} \models \neg G \qquad \textit{obstruction}$$
$$\text{Dom} \not\models \neg O \qquad\ \textit{domain consistency}$$

Obstacles need to be identified and resolved at RE time in order to produce robustness requirements and hence more reliable software. We have developed a set of formal and heuristic techniques for:

- the abductive generation of obstacles from goal specifications and domain properties,
- the systematic generation of various types of obstacle resolution, e.g., goal substitution, agent substitution, goal weakening, goal restoration, obstacle mitigation, or obstacle prevention.

The interested reader may refer to [Lam2Kc] for details. We just illustrate a few results from obstacle analysis for some of the terminal goals in the goal refinement graph of the BART system.

The following obstacles were generated to obstruct the subgoal Achieve[CommandMsgIssuedInTime]:

> CommandMsgNotIssued,
> CommandMsgIssuedLate,
> CommandMsgSentToWrongTrain

For the companion subgoal Achieve[CommandMsgDeliveredInTime] we similarly generated obstacles such as:

> CommandMsgDeliveredLate,
> CommandMsgCorrupted

The last companion subgoal Maintain[SafeCmdMsg] may be obstructed by the condition

> UnsafeAcceleration,

and so on. The obstacle generation process for a single goal results in a goal-anchored fault-tree, that is, a refinement tree whose root is the goal negation. Compared with standard fault-tree analysis [Lev95], obstacle analysis is goal-oriented, formal, and produces obstacle trees that are provably complete with respect to what is known about the domain [Lam2Kc].

Alternative obstacle resolutions may then be generated to produce new or alternative requirements. For example, the obstacle CommandMsgSentLate above could be resolved by an alternative design in which accelerations are calculated by the on-board train controller instead; this would correspond to a *goal substitution* strategy. The obstacle UnsafeAcceleration above could be resolved by assigning the responsibility for the subgoal SafeAccelerationCommanded of the goal Maintain[SafeCmdMsg] to the VitalStationComputer agent instead [BART99]; this would correspond to an *agent substitution* strategy. An *obstacle mitigation* strategy could be applied to resolve the obstacle OutOfDateTrainInfo obstructing the accuracy goal Maintain[AccurateSpeed/PositionEstimates], by introducing a new subgoal of the goal Avoid[TrainCollisions], namely, the goal Avoid[CollisionWhenOutOfDateTrainInfo]. This new goal has to be refined in turn, e.g., by subgoals requiring full braking when the message origination time tag has expired.

6 Handling Conflicting Requirements

As mentioned before, requirements engineers live in a world where conflicts are the rule, not the exception [Eas94]. Conflicts generally arise from multiple viewpoints and concerns. They must be detected and eventually resolved even though they may be temporarily useful for eliciting further information [Hun98]. In [Lam98] we have studied various forms of conflict and, in particular, a weak form called *divergence* which occurs frequently in practice.

The goals G_1, ..., G_n are said to be divergent iff there exists a non-trivial *boundary condition B* such that :

$$\{ B, \forall i\ G_i, Dom\} \models \textbf{false} \qquad \textit{inconsistency}$$
$$\{ B, \forall_{j\neq i}\ G_j, Dom\} \not\models \textbf{false} \qquad \textit{minimality}$$

("Non-trivial" means that B is different from the bottom **false** and the complement $\neg\ \forall i\ G_i$). Note that the traditional case of conflict, in the sense of logical inconsistency, amounts to a particular case of divergence.

Divergences need to be identified and resolved at RE time in order to eventually produce consistent requirements and hence more reliable software. We have also developed a set of formal and heuristic techniques for:

- the abductive generation of boundary conditions from goal specifications and domain properties,

- the systematic generation of various types of divergence resolution.

The interested reader may refer to [Lam98] for details. The initial BART document suggests an interesting example of divergence [BART99, p.13]. Roughly speaking, the train commanded speed may not be too high, because otherwise it forces the distance between trains to be too high, in order to achieve the DistanceIncreasedWithCommandedSpeed subgoal of the SafeTransportation goal; on the other hand, the commanded speed may not be too low, in order to achieve the LimitedAccelerAbove7mphOfPhysicalSpeed subgoal of the SmoothMove goal. There seems to be a flavor of divergence here. We therefore look at the formalization of the suspect goals:

> **Goal** Maintain [CmdedSpeedCloseToPhysicalSpeed]
> > **FormalDef** $\forall$ tr: Train
> > > tr.CmAccel$\geq$ 0 $\Rightarrow$ tr.CmSpeed $\leq$ tr.Speed + f (dist-to-obstacle)

and

> **Goal** Maintain [CmdedSpeedAbove7mphOfPhysicalSpeed]
> > **FormalDef** $\forall$ tr: Train
> > > tr.CmAccel$\geq$ 0 $\Rightarrow$ tr.CmSpeed > tr.Speed + 7

These two goals are formally detected to be divergent using the regression technique described in [Lam98]. The generated boundary condition for making them logically inconsistent is

> $\Diamond\ \exists$ tr: Train
> > tr.CmAccel$\geq$ 0 $\wedge$ f (dist-to-obstacle) $\leq$ 7

The resolution operators from [Lam98] may be used to generate alternative resolutions; in this case one should keep the safety goal as it is and *weaken* the other conflicting goal to remove the divergence:

Goal Maintain [CmdedSpeedAbove7mphOfPhysicalSpeed]
   FormalDef $\forall$ tr: Train
                    tr.CmAccel $\geq$ 0 $\Rightarrow$ tr.CmSpeed > tr.Speed + 7 $\vee$ **f (dist-to-obstacle)** $\leq$ 7

7 Conclusion

Standard modeling and specification techniques were reviewed in this paper to argue that most of them are inappropriate to the scope, concerns, processes, and actors involved in requirements engineering. Although they provide useful paradigms for RE methodologies, these techniques provide too low-level ontologies, do not support the representation and exploration of alternatives, mix up different kinds of assertions, are too monolithic, and provide little guidance in the requirements elaboration process.

We used a real, complex safety-critical system as a running example to show the benefits of a constructive, multiparadigm, and goal-oriented approach to requirements modeling, specification and analysis. The key points illustrated are the following:

*   object models and operational requirements can be derived constructively from goal specifications;
*   goals provide the rationale for the requirements that operationalize them, and a correctness criterion for requirements completeness;
*   the goal refinement structure provides a rich way of structuring the entire requirements document;
*   alternative system proposals are explored by alternative goal refinements and assignments;
*   a multiparadigm, multibutton framework allows one to combine different levels of expression and reasoning: semi-formal for modeling and navigation, qualitative for selection among alternatives, and formal, when needed, for more accurate reasoning;
*   goal formalization allows RE-specific types of analysis to be carried out, such as
    - checking the correctness and completeness of a goal refinement,
    - completing an incomplete refinement,
    - generating obstacles to requirements satisfaction, and resolutions to yield new requirements for more robust systems,
    - generating boundary conditions for conflict among requirements together with alternative resolutions.

Goals, especially non-functional ones, may also play a leading role in the process of deriving a software architecture from requirements, and of defining architectural views [Lam98a]. Goal-based reasoning is thus central to RE but also to architectural design. From our experience in using KAOS in a wide variety of industrial projects at our tech transfer institute, we have observed that domain experts, managers, and decision makers are in fact much more interested by goal structures than, e.g., UML models. Getting such early involvement and feedback turns out to be crucial to the development of reliable software, as the empirical studies mentioned at the beginning of this paper suggest.

References

[BART99] Bay Area Rapid Transit District, Advance Automated Train Control System, Case Study Description. Sandia National Labs, http://www.hcecs.sandia.gov/bart.htm.

[Bel76] T.E. Bell and T.A. Thayer, "Software Requirements: Are They Really a Problem?", *Proc. ICSE-2: 2nd Intrnational Conference on Software Enginering,* San Francisco, 1976, 61-68.

[Boe81] B.W. Boehm, Software Engineering Economics. Prentice-Hall, 1981.

[Bro87] F.P. Brooks "No Silver Bullet: Essence and Accidents of Software Engineering". *IEEE Computer*, Vol. 20 No. 4, April 1987, pp. 10-19.

[Dar93] A. Dardenne, A. van Lamsweerde and S. Fickas, "Goal-Directed Requirements Acquisition", *Science of Computer Programming*, Vol. 20, 1993, 3-50.

[Dar96] R. Darimont and A. van Lamsweerde, "Formal Refinement Patterns for Goal-Driven Requirements Elaboration", *Proc. FSE'4 - Fourth ACM SIGSOFT Symposium on the Foundations of Software Engineering*, San Francisco, October 1996, 179-190.

[Eas94] S. Easterbrook, "Resolving Requirements Conflicts with Computer-Supported Negotiation". In *Requirements Engineering: Social and Technical Issues*, M. Jirotka and J. Goguen (Eds.), Academic Press, 1994, 41-65.

[ESI96] European Software Institute, "European User Survey Analysis", Report USV_EUR 2.1, ESPITI Project, January 1996.

[Heit96] C. Heitmeyer, R. Jeffords and B. Labaw, "Automated Consistency Checking of Requirements Specificatons", *ACM Transactions on Software Engineering and Methodology* Vol. 5 No. 3, July 1996, 231-261.

[Hun98] A. Hunter and B. Nuseibeh, "Managing Inconsistent Specifications: Reasoning, Analysis and Action", *ACM Transactions on Software Engineering and Methodology*, Vol. 7 No. 4. October 1998, 335-367.

[Jac95] M. Jackson, Software Requirements & Specifications - A Lexicon of Practice, Principles and Pejudices. ACM Press, Addison-Wesley, 1995.

[Koy92] R. Koymans, Specifying message passing and time-critical systems with temporal logic, LNCS 651, Springer-Verlag, 1992.

[Lam98a] A. van Lamsweerde, R. Darimont and E. Letier, "Managing Conflicts in Goal-Driven Requirements Engineering", *IEEE Trans. on Sofware. Engineering*, Special Issue on Inconsistency Management in Software Development, November 1998.

[Lam98b] A. van Lamsweerde and L. Willemet, "Inferring Declarative Requirements Specifications from Operational Scenarios", *IEEE Trans. on Sofware. Engineering*, Special Issue on Scenario Management, December 1998, 1089-1114.

[Lam2Ka] A. van Lamsweerde, "Requirements Engineering in the Year 00: A Research Perspective", Keynote paper, *Proc. ICSE'2000 - 22nd Intl. Conference on Software Engineering,* IEEE Press, June 2000.

[Lam2Kb] A. van Lamsweerde, "Formal Specification: a Roadmap". In *The Future of Software Engineering*, A. Finkelstein (ed.), ACM Press, 2000.

[Lam2Kc] A. van Lamsweerde and E. Letier, "Handling Obstacles in Goal-Oriented Requirements Engineering", *IEEE Transactions on Software Engineering*, Special Issue on Exception Handling, October 2000.

[Let2K] þE. Letier and A. van Lamsweerde, "KAOS in Action: the BART System". IFIP WG2.9 meeting, Flims, http:// www.cis.gsu.edu/~wrobinso/ifip2_9/Flims00.

[Let01] E. Letier, Reasoning About Agents in Goal-Oriented Requirements Engineering. PhD Thesis, University of Louvain, 2001.

[Lev95] N. Leveson, *Safeware - System Safety and Computers*. Addison-Wesley, 1995.

[Man92] Z. Manna and A. Pnueli, *The Temporal Logic of Reactive and Concurrent Systems,* Springer-Verlag, 1992.

[Mas97] P. Massonet and A. van Lamsweerde, "Analogical Reuse of Requirements Frameworks", Proc. RE-97 - *3rd Int. Symp. on Requirements Engineering,* Annapolis, 1997, 26-37.

[Mey85] B. Meyer, "On Formalism in Specifications", IEEE Software, Vol. 2 No. 1, January 1985, 6-26.

[Myl92] Mylopoulos, J., Chung, L., Nixon, B., "Representing and Using Nonfunctional Requirements: A Process-Oriented Approach", *IEEE Trans. on Sofware. Engineering,* Vol. 18 No. 6, June 1992, pp. 483-497.

[Myl99] J. Mylopoulos, L. Chung and E. Yu, "From Object-Oriented to Goal-Oriented Requirements Analysis", Communications of the ACM, Vol. 42 No. 1, January 1999, 31-37.

[Nus94] B. Nuseibeh, J. Kramer and A. Finkelstein, "A Framework for Expressing the Relationships Between Multiple Views in Requirements Specifications", *IEEE Transactions on Software Engineering,* Vol. 20 No. 10, October 1994, 760-773.

[Owr95] S. Owre, J. Rushby, and N. Shankar, "Formal Verification for Fault-Tolerant Architectures: Prolegomena to the Design of PVS", *IEEE Transactions on Software Engineering* Vol. 21 No. 2, Feb. 95, 107-125.

[Par95] D.L. Parnas and J. Madey, "Functional Documents for Computer Systems", *Science of Computer Programming,* Vol. 25, 1995, 41-61.

[Pot96] B. Potter, J. Sinclair and D. Till, *An Introduction to Formal Specification and Z.* Second edition, Prentice Hall, 1996.

[Rum99] J. Rumbaugh, I. Jacobson and G Booch, The Unified Modeling Language Reference Manual. Addison-Wesley, Object Technology Series, 1999.

[Sta95] The Standish Group, "Software Chaos", http:// www.standishgroup.com/chaos.html.

[Yue87] K. Yue, "What Does It Mean to Say that a Specification is Complete?", *Proc. IWSSD-4, Fourth International Workshop on Software Specification and Design,* IEEE, 1987.

Using Ada in Interactive Digital Television Systems

Pascal Héraud and Thierry Lelégard

Canal+ Technologies
34, Place Raoul Dautry
75516 Paris Cedex 15
France
pascal.heraud@canal-plus.fr
thierry.lelegard@canal-plus.fr

Abstract. Since 1996, the Digital Television (DTV) market has been exponentially growing. Based on widely accepted MPEG and DVB standards, the digital television offers a higher image quality as well as an unlimited number of interactive services.

Canal+ Technologies provides a complete end-to-end solution for Digital Television operators, from the central broadcast centers to the set-top boxes at home. The DTV broadcast center systems have availability, reliability and load constraints which require a robust implementation. For this reason, the server-side components of the Canal+ Technologies software have been developed in Ada.

This paper explains the architecture of a Digital Television system and how Ada is used inside this system. It also describes how this system is currently re-engineered from a proprietary Ada 83 / OpenVMS implementation using the DEC Ada compiler to an Ada 95 multi-platform implementation using the GNAT compiler.

1 What Is Digital Television ?

The first part of this paper gives some background information about digital television since most readers may not be familiar with this technology. The second part is more Ada specific.

1.1 Analog vs. Digital Television

Analog television is the technology which is still currently used in most television networks. The analog signal of each TV channel is modulated and broadcast on one allocated frequency.

Also successfully used for years, this technology has a number of drawbacks. First, using one frequency (one carrier) for only one TV channel is a poor usage of the bandwidth. Then, the analog encoding of the audio and video is very sensitive to noisy

A. Strohmeier and D. Craeynest (Eds.): Ada-Europe 2001, LNCS 2043, pp. 21-34, 2001.

signals, which often leads to a poor image quality (especially with the NTSC standard). Finally, since the signal is a direct encoding of the audio and video, there is no support for data services. At best, a basic Teletext service can be embedded in the signal, between lines of the image.

The digital television technology was introduced to answer these issues. First, the audio and video are separately sampled to obtain a digital encoding. Then, these data are compressed using the MPEG standard (currently MPEG-2 in most operational digital television systems). The MPEG encoding defines *packets*. Each packet belongs to a virtual flow, identified by a *Packet Identifier* or PID. Such a virtual flow contains, for instance, the video or audio stream of a TV channel (we use the term *service* for a TV channel).

One frequency (or carrier) is a modulated flow of MPEG packets. We call this flow a *transport stream* or TS. In this transport stream, you will find packets belonging to different PID's. This means that one frequency contains several multiplexed services. In other words, several TV channels can be transported on one frequency. Moreover, since the packets contains digital data, they may contain any kind of data: video and audio but also executable code for interactive applications, data for these applications, etc.

We will not elaborate further on the structure of the MPEG transport streams and the MPEG encoding since some good literature is available on the subject. You simply need the remember the following basics:

- The audio and video signals are digitally encoded, compressed and segmented into packets.
- Since these data are compressed, there is room for multiple TV channels on the same transport stream.
- The various packets on a transport stream may contain any kind of data, not only audio and video.

As a consequence, some (but not all) of the advantages of digital television over analog television are:

- Better bandwidth usage (several services per frequency).
- Better image quality (noisy signals have less influence on digital encoding).
- Virtually unlimited support for data services.

The number of services that can be multiplexed on one transport stream depends on several factors such as the transport medium (terrestrial, satellite or cable) and the requested image quality (the more compressed a video stream is, the poorer image quality you get). Here are some typical figures:

- The bandwidth of a transport stream varies from 24 MB/s (terrestrial) to 38 MB/s (satellite), occasionally up to 50 MB/s on some satellites.
- The bandwidth usage of one service varies from 3 MB/s (slowly moving pictures) to 6 MB/s (typically sports channels).

- There are typically 6 to 10 different services which are multiplexed on one transport stream.
- A TV operator typically operates from 3 to 20 different transport streams.

1.2 Canal+ Technologies

Canal+ Technologies is part of the Canal+ Group, the largest Pay-TV operator in Europe. The group has over 14,000,000 subscribers in 10 countries, including France, Spain, Italy, Belgium, the Netherlands, Poland, Northern Europe, etc.

The group is both a content provider (with several premium channels) and a television broadcast company through various media (terrestrial, satellite and cable). Although a majority of subscribers still receive analog TV, the proportion of customers using digital TV is increasing every year.

As an entertainment company, the group is also a major actor in the film industry. In France, most movie productions are partially financed by Canal+. Additionally, the group includes "Studio Canal", a film-maker company, and recently acquired Universal Studios in Hollywood.

Canal+ Technologies is a subsidiary of the Canal+ Group which provides end-to-end solutions for digital television operators. A digital television system can be seen through several views:
- By function:
  - Conditional access (*MediaGuard* product line).
  - Interactive television services (*MediaHighway* product line).
- By location:
  - Broadcast center (also called *Head-End*)
  - Set-top box at each subscriber's (also called *IRD* for Integrated Receiver-Decoder, or simply *decoder*).

Canal+ Technologies provides all the software in the head-end and the set-top boxes, as well as the integration services. The hardware part is supplied through a number of partners for computer and network, MPEG encoding and multiplexing, set-top boxes. However, the Canal+ Technologies software is hardware and vendor independent. As an example, the set-top box software currently runs on hardware from 26 different vendors.

Canal+ Technologies is based in Paris (France) with 600 people (including 450 in R&D). The company also have an American branch in Cupertino (California) with 50 people. Its technologies are currently used by 20 TV operators (both inside and outside the Canal+ Group) in 13 countries (Europe, UK, USA, Japan, China, India, Malaysia, etc.) The Canal+ Technologies software currently powers more than 8,000,000 set-top boxes in the world.

1.3 Digital Television Systems

After introducing the basics of digital television and the company Canal+ Technologies, this section of the paper briefly describes the overall structure of an end-to-end digital television system. We will cover the requirements of the various parts of the systems and you will instantly see where Ada is a good candidate as implementation language. The second part of the paper will focus on the way Ada is used in the Canal+ Technologies systems.

First, have a look at the global structure of a digital television system. The following diagram describes its various parts and their interactions.

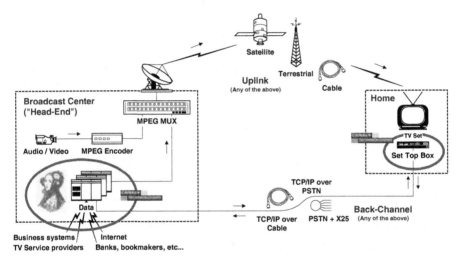

Fig. 1. Digital television system overview

As you may see, there are two major geographical locations in the system:
- The left side of the diagram represents the Head-End. There is usually one such center for a TV operator. However, due to operational constraints, an operator may have several of them. The audio/video component of each service (only one is represented on the diagram) is encoded in MPEG format and injected into a multiplexer (also called MUX). The data are generated by computer equipment and are formatted into MPEG packets which are injected in the same multiplexer. Each MUX generates one transport stream which is modulated and broadcast over any type of medium (terrestrial, satellite or cable).
- The signal is received on the right side at each subscriber's home by the set-top box. The set-top box demodulates the signal, demultiplexes the MPEG stream, descrambles the audio and video (if the subscriber is entitled to) and generates a normal TV signal which is transmitted to the TV set. The set-top box also receives the executable code of the interactive applications and their data. These applications are executed in the set-top box and displayed on the TV set.

You may also notice the "back-channel" at the bottom of the diagram. Each set-top box may optionally connect back to the head-end (the broadcast stream on top is unidirectional). This connection can be established over a telephone line (and then forwarded over X25 or TCP/IP) or directly through the TV cable. The choice of the medium depends on the type of television network and the telecommunication infrastructure of the country.

As mentioned in the previous section, there are two main kinds of data services in the system: the *conditional access system* and the *interactive services*.

Conditional access system: MediaGuard Canal+ Technologies product line. This is the basis of the Pay-TV system which guarantees the revenues of the TV operator. The paying services (TV channels) are scrambled at the head-end according various access criteria. Each subscriber pays for a number of selected services, either on a subscription basis (a given service can be viewed at any time) or on a pay-per-view (PPV) basis. In the later case, the subscriber pays for one specific event (a movie, a football match, etc.) and is authorized to view this event only.

The purpose of the conditional access system is the management of subscribers, the generation and broadcasting of the access rights to each of them, the management of the PPV events. On the set-top box side, the conditional access system is responsible for the descrambling of the audio/video and is implemented in a removable smart-card.

Interactive services: MediaHighway Canal+ Technologies product line. The digital set-top box is a complete computer environment which may execute any kind of application. The actual implementation of the set-top box hardware is not specified as long as it follows a number of interface specifications. On top of this hardware, Canal+ Technologies provides a virtual machine which supports Java, HTML as well as older languages. The interactive applications are now usually written in Java. The generated byte-code is broadcast in the transport stream and can be executed by any set-top box from any supported vendor.

There are two kinds of interactivity:

- Weak interactivity: All possible data for an application are broadcast in the MPEG stream. They are received by everyone and the application browses through them. Typical applications include electronic television program guide, weather forecast, jobs advertisements, etc.
- Strong interactivity: The application connects back to the head-end through the back-channel and starts a personal dialog. Typical applications include PPV event ordering, telebanking, e-commerce, e-mail, Internet access, horse race betting, networked games between subscribers. In some countries, the set-top boxes include a credit card reader for secure payment. Depending on the applications, the head-end acts either as a complete back-office server or as a transaction router and is connected to the relevant organizations or companies such as banks, merchants or bookmakers.

Related standards: Digital television is an evolving technology and so are the related standards. However, some strongly established standards are used across almost all digital television systems. The main ones are listed below and are all implemented in the Canal+ Technologies systems.

- MPEG (Motion Picture Expert Group): This international standard defines the audio and video encoding as well as the structure of the transport stream. This transport stream may contain "private tables", the format of which are defined by other standards, such as the following ones.
- DVB (Digital Video Broadcasting): This European standard defines various structural information such as a scrambling method and the *Service Information* (SI), which is the way the television programs are described.
- Application-level standards: Some emerging standards attempt to define a common format for the interactive applications and data. MHEG-5 defines a specific format of interpreted applications. DVB-HTML defines a subset of HTML with TV-oriented extensions. DVB-MHP defines a standard profile and API's for Java applications.

As you may guess, a digital television head-end is a critical environment. 24 hours a day, 365 days a years, many subscribers (sometimes millions of them) are watching TV. They need to receive the correct access right information, the correct applications and data. They also may want to spend some money for a PPV event, a commerce transaction, etc. Well, building such critical systems is not unusual to Ada developers. This is the reason why most Canal+ Technologies software running in a head-end is written in Ada, hence the famous face of lady Ada you may see in the diagram...

2 Ada in Digital Television

Ada 83 was used to implement head-end systems, now Ada 95 is. Ada has the answers to some of our questions but market and technical constraints raises new questions.

2.1 Head-End Systems

A head-end center is the nervous system of an operator. It should satisfy important technical and market constraints.

2.1.1 System Requirements

The main requirement for head-end systems is reliability. Television is a non-stop business. Application servers must be able to answer requests anytime of the day, any day of the year. Failure of a pay-par-view server, a home shopping or a home betting application may result in an important loss of revenue.

Another requirement is the capacity to develop a project in less than a year. Once operators has the idea of a new service, they should deploy it as soon as possible.

Head-end servers and applications must interface with a wide range of external systems (Subscriber management system of the operator, MPEG encoders, ciphering units, multiplexers, bank servers for payment identification, …). These equipment can be accessed through specific API or protocols.

2.1.2 Application Characteristics

Applications running in an head-end systems are mostly soft real-time ones. Data processing cycle is always greater than 10 milliseconds and are more often greater than 1 second. However, applications load is non-constant, very high peak of activity over a short time follows a low average activity over long period of time. This is specially true for pay-per-view servers.

Most applications are based on the following scheme: receiving data from some equipment or application, processing it, sending the processed data to some equipment or application. Such a scheme reflects an highly parallel activity. Furthermore, a cluster may support up to 50 different applications.

Finally we are making commercial products. Our applications are managed like a classical product, they must be highly customizable since not two system configurations are the same. The type and volume of activity depends on the customer needs (type and number of interactive services, number of customers). They should be easily configurable to answer pricing constraints.

2.2 Canal+ Systems Initial Implementation

Products available in the early 90's leaded the choice of platform and tools used to develop head-end systems.

2.2.1 System Environment

Cluster of systems was (and still is) the best technique to satisfy the reliability requirement. In 1993 when the first head-end systems were designed OpenVMS clusters were the only choice. They were offering an unique set of clustering features (cluster file system, locking management across cluster, quick restart time of failover) doubled with a highly operating system.

Moreover, applications relying heavily on database stored data had their performance requirements answered with the DEC Rdb database.

2.2.2 Ada 83 Language

Ada 83 language satisfies head-end applications requirements.

Ada tasking allows an easier development of highly parallel applications which implies a shorter cycle development cycle. Ada rigorous definition and strong typing policy makes applications debug period shorter.

Reliability is better achieved with strong typing and through Ada run-time checks. Unlike embedded systems we are delivering our application to the customer still with run-time checks. When a bug is detected on a customer site, it helps up to analyze it. Of course our applications are fully optimized to satisfy both cost and performance constraints.

Dec Ada compiler on VMS is a highly reliable compiler (few bugs) generating excellent code and including a full set of operating system interface libraries.

2.3 Usage of Ada

Almost all head-end applications and servers are coded using Ada. It represents currently around 1.2 million lines of Ada code (1.9 million with comments).

2.3.1 Where Ada Is Used

Applications coded in Ada are of the following kinds:

- Broadcasting: These applications provide a continuous flow of data for distribution. They are characterized by a constant level of activity with a short cycle of processing.
- Telecommunication servers: These applications manage incoming calls from set-top boxes. They are characterized by an erratic level of activity (high peaks over short period of time then low activity most of the time).
- Data processing: This kind of application is used for conditional access and generation of data for set-top box applications. They are highly parallel applications with a constant level of activity.
- Database and transactional processing: These applications mostly rely on the performance of the database system to support concurrent accesses. They are also characterized by a non-constant level of activity.

2.3.2 Programming Rules

Having different kinds of applications, there is not a common set of programming rules for all of them. However all applications are making an unrestricted use of tasking and generic units.

Dynamic memory allocation is restricted as much as possible for telecommunications servers in order to be able to deal with high peak of activity. No restrictions apply for other kinds of applications.

Broadcasting applications are the only ones setting specific priorities. Emitting tasks are set with higher priorities.

Exceptions were used at the beginning for error management but it is not well adapted for an application under the monitoring of an operator. The quality of reporting is not good enough. We are now using a "bottom up" status management to report information from the origin of the problem up to its consequences as the highest level. Having a better reporting operators can act more efficiently to either fix it or describe it to our hotline.

2.3.3 Where Ada Is Not Used

Ada is not used to code the following kinds of applications:

- GUI: These applications are used by the operators to monitor the whole system. They are running on Windows NT.
- Internet applications: These applications interacts with too many existing non-Ada applications and APIs.
- Set-top box software: These applications are embedded ones which fall within the Ada domain but people working on set-top box software are not Ada developers. Moreover, its easier to get third parties companies to develop applications using our middleware when API are written with a language having a large market acceptance. Since our newest generation of set-top box comes with a Java Virtual Machine, Ada to Java compiler could be used to develop applications but market acceptance here is the main drag.

2.4 Current Issues and New Directions

New customers desiderata and evolution of our programming tools push us to question the OpenVMS cluster/Ada 83 initial choice.

2.4.1 System Environment

Current applications are running only on OpenVMS. Applications are using a lot of low level system dependent features (socket programming, inter-processes communications, locking across cluster, X25 communications, file management, time management, process management, memory mapping features). Moreover early time to market constraints have generated low level dependencies in almost all layers of the existing code.

Due to market constraints, we need to port these applications on different operating systems. Wanting to keep application code completely portable we had to write a system layer with a common interface tailored to our needs providing access to low level system dependent features and perform a cleanup to remove low level dependencies.

2.4.2 Programming Language

Programming language is also an another issue because Compaq will no longer support the Dec Ada compiler at the end of 2001. Moreover, our market is growing exponentially so we constantly need to hire new developers with Ada experience which is not an easy task. Digital TV technologies are evolving a lot so the life expectancy of a given application is quite short and the pace of renewal is quick. Therefore new applications can be coded using an another programming language.

Other programming language evaluated were Java, C++ and Ada95. Java is getting a wide market acceptance but it is an interpreted language which implies a major hit in performance which would increase the cost of our solutions (more expensive hardware). C++ is widely available with a lot of programming tools but it is a very unsafe language. Ada 95 is a safe language but with a small market acceptance and few development tools available.

Having a big repository of existing Ada code and the reliability requirement make us choose Ada 95 rather than an another language.

2.4.3 Applications Architecture

All applications are being modified to use the multiple O/S support library. At the same time they are completely or partly reengineered. UML is used to specify and design new applications, oriented object programming is applied whenever possible. Finally we are now using CORBA for distribution. Most of our applications follow the layered architecture presented in the next figure.

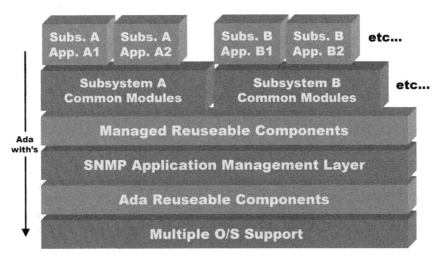

Fig. 2. Application modular composition.

2.5 Ada 95 Experience Report

We started using Ada 95 as a programming language for our applications in the middle of 1999. Here is our experience of transiting to Ada 95 from Ada 83 and our first Ada 95 impressions.

2.5.1 Ada 95 Benefits

The most useful Ada 95 features used by our applications are:

- Controlled types,
- Tagged types,
- Child units,
- Protected objects.

Even tough our applications used a lot of dynamic memory allocation, our applications running without interruption must not have any memory leak so controlling the memory allocation and deallocation is therefore a big improvement.

Object oriented programming is now greatly improved with the usage of tagged types. Our new applications try to get the most out of type extension and dispatching.

Packages of a same subsystem are now part of a unique hierarchical name space. Private package definition allow us to tightly control which packages can be "withed" by the upper layer units hiding completely implementation packages. It avoids having high level packages "withing" low level ones even if it was not allowed in the documentation it is now enforced by the language in an efficient way.

Highly parallel applications face problems related to concurrent access of shared data. Access to this data was done through a task, we can now do it using a protected type.

Others useful features are:
- Interfaces packages (Annex B),
- Elaboration control,
- Modular types,
- Readable "out" parameters, use type clause.

Annex B packages Interface are heavily used for the implementation of the multiple O/S support library to interface with system libraries.

Our applications usually rely on the code executed during the elaboration of lower level services. In Ada 83 we ran a small script to insert elaborate pragmas matching each with clause. We now use the *pragma elaborate_all* to guarantee the elaboration of all the packages of the closure.

2.5.2 Ada 95 Pitfalls and Suggestions for Ada 0Y

Others Ada 95 specific features look promising but with flaws that kept us from using them for our applications. Those features are streams and distributed systems.

Ada 95 Streams

The Ada 95 language defines the concept of streams (see sections 13.13 and A.12 of the "Ada 95 Language Reference Manual"). However, this view of the streams has some characteristics which prevents them from being used into an heterogeneous environment.
- The Ada 95 definition of streams does not guarantee the interoperability between different platforms. The base type of the stream, the type *Stream_Element*, is unfortunately "implementation-defined". There is no guarantee that all compilers use 8-bits bytes on all platforms for the type *Stream_Element*. Even on strange platforms such as old 36-bits machines, interoperability means exchanging 8-bits bytes. But the language does not guarantee this.
- The Ada 95 streams implicitly assume that each type is represented the same way on each protocol. A protocol P1 may require little endian byte order when another

protocol P2 may need big endian. However, for each type, there can be only one Write attribute.

- The Ada 95 streams do not offer a sufficiently strict control on the transmitted data. When a structure is sent over an Ada 95 stream, the Write procedure of each element is invoked. But, if the programmer forgot to declare one Write attribute, a default one is provided by the language and the programmer loses control on the representation.

For all these reasons, we have developed our own implementation of streams. They are similar, in principles, to the Ada 95 streams but they guarantee full control on data representation, full interoperability between heterogeneous platforms and structured data flow.

Distributed Systems (Annex E)

The Ada 95 language defines facilities for supporting the implementation of distributed systems. However, it is not applicable for our applications working within an heterogeneous environment.

- The Ada 95 definition of the Annex E does not guarantee the interoperability between two implementations of this annex. The reference manual does not define a data presentation layer as it is done for CORBA with the General Inter-ORB Protocol (GIOP) or the Internet Inter-ORB Protocol (IIOP). Two annex implementations from two different vendors are not guaranteed to communicate together and even two annex implementations on different platforms from the same vendor are not guaranteed to work together (endianness of exchanged data).
- The annex is designed for distribution of Ada only applications. This does not match our needs of openness with external systems or equipment.
- Only the GNAT compiler provides an implementation of the Annex E.

Suggestions for Ada 0Y

Ada 95 defines high level means for interoperability between applications running in an heterogeneous environment but the representation of exchanged data could not be completely defined. Therefore it is practically unusable. Ada 0Y could propose an interface or a mean (a low level entry point) to completely defined the representation of data.

We would like also to have a "with private" clause definition. Packages listed in this clause shall be used only within the private part of the package. It would fit with the private package definition and allow the definition of types in a private part using types defined in a private package. For example:

```
package P is
end P;

private package P.Priv_Child is
   type Priv_Type is ...
end P.Priv_Child;
```

```
with private P.Priv_Child; -- new clause
package P.Public_Child is
   type T is private;
private
   type T is record
      Comp : P.Priv_Child.Priv_Type;
   end record;
end P.Public_Child;
```

The combination of object oriented programming and hierarchical library makes private parts bigger and bigger increasing the number of packages "withed" by the specification. Limiting the usage of a with clause to the private part only would help to clarify the real exported interface.

2.5.3 GNAT Compiler

Our primary platforms are OpenVMS and Sun Solaris because they provide clustering features. Our secondary platforms are Linux and Windows NT. The GNAT compiler is the only one existing for all our platforms. It is the only one Ada 95 compiler for OpenVMS.

The support provided by ACT is fast and efficient for bug fixes. We are usually receiving a wavefront less than a week after reporting a problem.

Generated code performance on OpenVMS platform is not on par when compared with Dec Ada compiler generated code but ACT is going to improve it.

The lack of library tools is a major hurdle to manage modular applications. Modules composing an application evolve and several versions of the same module exist. An application of a specific version is the composition of specific version of those modules. We associate a library for each version of each module. A parent relationship is established between these libraries to respect dependencies between modules as presented in fig 2. Our integration team is in charge of maintaining a coherent set of libraries and providing "official" libraries to derive from. With Dec Ada library environment, a developer who needs to work on a specific version of an application just has to choose the right starting (or high level) library and automatically inherits of the right parent libraries. Such an approach is almost impossible with GNAT. The developer must specify the whole and exact list of source and object file directories with the ADA_OBJECTS_PATH and ADA_INCLUDE_PATH environment variables. A single error is the list may result in a configuration inconsistency. In our quite complex set of modules, this is not the role of a developer working on a specific application to determine which module version to use and their relationship.

Therefore we have developed a GNAT Wrapper utility. Our purpose was not to develop a sophisticated environment. The GNAT Wrapper defined a simple concept of library. A library is a directory where compilation products are stored, it defines a list of search directories where related sources are located, it may have one or more parent libraries. Those additional data are stored in a text file located in the directory. A GNAT command must be preceded by the command "gw" (such as gw gnatmake foo). The GNAT wrapper defines on the fly the appropriate environment variables

ADA_OBJECTS_PATH and ADA_INCLUDE_PATH by browsing the entire library path (the library itself and its parents recursively) and execute the command passed as a parameter. This command is not interpreted, it is just executed. The GNAT Wrapper also generate when needed a GNAT configuration file (gnat.adc) which is the concatenation of all the GNAT configuration files in the library path. This was very useful for us because the file naming convention of GNAT for child units (foo.bar gives foo-bar.ads) conflicts with the file naming convention of our configuration management system. We are using the pragma *Source_File_Name* located in GNAT configuration files to enforce our child units naming convention (foo.bar gives foo__bar.ads).

Then when a developer needs to work a specific version of an application, he just has to create a library with its parent being the official entry point and it inherits of the whole library path prepared by our integration team.

This utility is coded with Ada 95 (8000 lines of code) and built upon our multiple operating system layer.

2.6 Ada's Future in Digital Television

The television is a very competitive market where price and time constraints are strong. Ada remains an expensive language compared to other programming language environment (compiler and tools), the cost is counter balanced by the benefits of the language in term of reliability but also time of development meaning money. But it is getting harder to justify this choice.

Moreover, there are very few Ada vendors because of the small Ada market acceptance and we are increasingly worried about their continuity.

Small market acceptance also limits the number and quality of software engineering tools available for the Ada language.

Training our seasoned Ada 83 programmers to Ada 95 was not difficult even tough Ada 95 is perceived as a very complex language. But hiring Ada developers is quite difficult and training non Ada developers is even more difficult because of a cultural shift with other programmers.

Ada is the most adapted and our favorite language to develop digital television applications but we cannot afford to be the "last of the Adaists".

Testing from Formal Specifications, a Generic Approach

Marie-Claude Gaudel

L.R.I, Université de Paris-Sud et CNRS, Bât. 490, F-91405 Orsay-cedex, France
mcg@lri.fr

Abstract. Deriving test cases from specifications is now recognised as a major application of formal methods to software development. Several methods have been proposed for various formalisms: behavioural descriptions such as transition systems, model-based specifications, algebraic specifications, etc. This article presents a general framework for test data selection from formal specifications. A notion of "exhaustive test set" is derived from the semantics of the formal notation and from the definition of a correct implementation. Then a finite test set is selected via some "selection hypotheses", This approach has been illustrated by its application to algebraic specifications, object-oriented Petri nets (CO-OPN2), LUSTRE, and full LOTOS.

1 Introduction

Selecting test cases for software systems is a complex and difficult task, due to the variety of faults that a piece of software can exhibit. Among several complementary approaches, specification-based software testing was recognised as unavoidable since the very first studies and experiments. In their pioneering paper [1], Goodenough and Gerhart pointed out that test cases based on code coverage were not sufficient. They recommended complementing it with test cases derived from informal specifications expressed by "condition tables". Numerous authors have advocated for the same ideas under the terms of functional testing [2] or black-box testing.

The first paper where testing was based on some formal description of the system under test, was by Chow [3] on testing software modelled by finite state machines. It has been very influential on all the subsequent works on testing based on formal specifications.

The emergence of formal specifications in the 1990s gave rise to several works on testing based on formal specifications. Several methods have been proposed for various formalisms: algebraic specifications by Gannon, McMullin and Hamlet [4], and then by Bernot, Gaudel and Marre [5]; model-based specifications (VDM, Z) by Dick and Faivre [6]; finite state machines and specification languages based on them such as basic LOTOS by Brinksma [7] and Pitt and Freestone [8], etc. This field of research has been especially active in the area of communication protocols as it can be seen in

A. Strohmeier and D. Craeynest (Eds.): Ada-Europe 2001, LNCS 2043, pp. 35–48, 2001.
© Springer-Verlag Berlin Heidelberg 2001

the series of proceedings of the Workshops on Protocol Specification, Testing and Verification.

This article presents a unified framework for test data selection from formal specifications. A notion of "exhaustive test set" is derived from the semantics of the formal notation and from the definition of a correct implementation. Then, assuming some "testability hypothesis" on the implementation under test, a finite test set is selected via some "selection hypotheses".

A word of warning before going further: it is definitely not the claim of this paper that specification based testing is the unique solution to the verification of software. It is clear that diverse software fault detection techniques need to be combined [9], [10]. The aim of this paper is to show that formal specifications are quite fundamental to a rigorous and systematic approach to software testing, and to propose a general framework for black-box testing based on formal specifications, applicable to arbitrary formalisms.

The paper is organised as follows. Section 2 is an informal introduction to the general principles of the approach. Section 3 briefly reports their application to the case of algebraic specifications. Section 4 summarises the case of full LOTOS as presented in [11] and gives some conclusions on the detection power of the method based on the experiment presented in [12].

2   Informal Introduction to the General Principles

Given a specification *SP* and a proposed implementation *P*, any verification activity (proving or testing) must be based on a *relation of satisfaction* (sometimes called conformance relation) that we note *P sat SP*. This relation is usually defined on a semantic domain common to implementations and specifications. Namely, there is some domain D such that $sat \subseteq D \times D$. For instance, in the case of algebraic specifications the semantic domain is some class of sorted algebra; in the case of model based or behavioural specifications it is some variants of finite state automata or finite state machines.

In this section, we present how to design test methods for specification formalisms.

2.1   Test Experiments, Exhaustivity, and Testability

The satisfaction relation *P sat SP* is generally a large conjunction of elementary properties (for instance it may begin by "for all paths in the specification..."). These elementary properties are the basis for the definition of what is a *test experiment*, a test data, and the *verdict* of a test experiment, i.e. the decision whether a implementation *P* passes a test *t*. The satisfaction relation as a whole is used for the definition of an *exhaustive test set, Exhaust(SP)*. It is generally unrealistic, but it aims at providing a reference, as close as possible to correctness, for the definition of testing strategies and the selection of finite test sets.

However, an implementation's passing all the tests in the exhaustive test set does not necessarily mean that it satisfies the specification. This is true for a class of reasonable implementations. But a totally erratic system or a diabolic one may pass the exhaustive test set and then fail. More formally, the implementation under test must fulfil some basic requirements coming from the semantic domain D considered for the specifications and the implementations. For instance, in the case of finite automata, the implementation must behave like an automaton, without memory of its history. The new state after a transition t must depend on the previous state and t only. Such properties of the implementation must be assumed as soon as a satisfaction relation is used as a basis for testing. We call them the *minimal hypothesis*, or the *testability hypothesis*. We note it $Hmin_D(P)$ or *Hmin* when there is no ambiguity.

Hmin, *Exhaust*, and *sat* must satisfy:

$$Hmin(P) \wedge P \text{ passes } Exhaust(SP) \Leftrightarrow P \text{ sat } SP . \tag{1}$$

There are some cases where several choices are possible for the pair $< H\ min, Exhaust >$ [13]. Intuitively, when restricting the class of testable implementations, it is possible to weaken *Exhaust(SP)*.

Note that the verification of $H\ min_D$ may be ensured by various techniques, such as static analysis, proof, or other kind of testing.

2.2 Selection Hypotheses, Uniformity, Regularity

A black-box testing strategy can be formalised as the selection of a finite subset of *Exhaust(SP)*. Let us consider as an example the classical partition testing strategy (more exactly, it should be called sub-domain testing strategy). It consists in defining a collection of (possibly non-disjoint) subsets which covers the exhaustive test set. Then an element of each subset is selected and submitted to the implementation under test.

The choice of such a strategy corresponds to stronger hypotheses than *Hmin* on the implementation under test. We call such hypotheses *selection hypotheses*. In this case, it is a *uniformity hypothesis*. The implementation under test is assumed to uniformly behave on the test subsets UTS_i:

$$UTS_1 \cup \ldots \cup UTS_p = Exhaust(SP), \text{ and } \forall i = 1, \ldots, p$$

$$\forall t \in UTS_i, P \text{ passes } t \Rightarrow P \text{ passes } UTS_i. \tag{2}$$

This notion is similar to the reliability property of partition criteria introduced by Goodenough and Gerhart in [1].

Various selection hypotheses can be formulated and combined depending on some knowledge of the program, some coverage criteria of the specification and ultimately cost considerations. A *regularity hypothesis* uses a size function on the tests and has the form "if the subset of *Exhaust(SP)* made up of all the tests of size less than or equal to a given limit is passed, then *Exhaust(SP)* also is". Other hypotheses have been proposed. For example, Phalippou presented some independence and fairness hypotheses in [14] for the test of communication protocols against Input-Output State Machines specifications. All these hypotheses are important from a theoretical point of view because they formalise common test practices and express the gap between the success of a test strategy and correctness. They are also important in practice because exposing them makes clear the assumptions made on the implementation. It gives some indication of complementary verifications [9].

2.3 Validity and Unbias

A pair *(H, T)* of a set of hypotheses and one of tests is considered *valid* if *H* implies that if *T* is passed then *Exhaust(SP)* is as well. It is considered *unbiased* if *H* implies that if *Exhaust(SP)* is passed then *T* is as well. Assuming *H*, validity guarantees that all incorrect implementations are rejected, and being unbiased guarantees that no correct implementation is rejected.

From (1), *(Hmin(P), Exhaust(SP))* is both valid and unbiased. Another extreme example that is both valid and unbiased is *(Hmin(P) ∧ P passes Exhaust(SP), Ø)*, which indicates that if the implementation is assumed to be correct then no tests are needed! Interesting pairs are those that are valid and unbiased, with reasonable hypotheses stronger enough to reduce the set of tests to a tractable size.

2.4 The Oracle Problem

The interpretation of the results of a test is often very difficult. This difficulty is known as the *oracle problem*: deciding whether the result of a test execution is acceptable or not requires a procedure (manual, automated, or both) which relies upon knowledge of the expected results. The problem is difficult as soon as the program yields the results in a way which may depends on some representation choices and makes the comparison with the specified results difficult. This is an important issue in the case of black-box testing, since the test is based on a specification which is (normally) more abstract than the program. Thus program results may appear in a form which is not obviously equivalent to the specified results. This contradicts a common belief that the existence of a formal specification is sufficient to directly decide whether a test is a success. Solutions to this problem depend on the specification formalism, and to a less extent, on the implementation context. This point is discussed in Section 3 for algebraic specifications, and in Section 4 for LOTOS processes.

3 Instantiation to Algebraic Specifications

Algebraic specifications make it possible to describe abstract data types in an axiomatic way [15]. A piece of a toy specification is given below. The syntax is the one of the data type part of LOTOS [16]. We assume the existence of a basic specification

"Text " with the usual notations and properties of character strings. The example describes an unbounded priority queue of textual messages.

```
type PriorityQueue is Text, NaturalNumber, Boolean
   sorts   Queue, Message
   opns    emptyq:    -> Queue
           add:       Message, Queue -> Queue
           get:       Queue -> Message
           remove:    Queue -> Queue
           isEmpty:   Queue -> Boolean
           (_._):     Nat, Text -> Message
           priority:  Message -> Nat
           text:      Message -> Text
   eqns
     forall s: Text, n:Nat, q:Queue, m:Message
     ofsort Message
        get(emptyq)) = (0.<>) ;        {<> is the empty text}
        get(add(m, emptyq)) = m ;
        isEmpty(q) = false,            {, is for ʌ }
           priority(get(q)) ge priority(m) =>
              get(add(m,q)) = get(q) ;
        isEmptyq(q) = false,
           priority(get(q)) lt priority(m) =>
                 get(add(m,q)) = m ;
        ...
endtype
```

3.1 Test Experiments, Exhaustivity, and Testability

Such a specification has two parts: a signature $\Sigma = (S, OP)$ where S is a finite set of *sorts* and OP is a finite set of *operation names* over the sorts in S, and Ax, a finite set of *axioms*. These axioms are equations or positive conditional equations built on Σ-terms using a family of S-sorted variables $X = \{X_s / s \in S\}$.

If SP is a specification (Σ, Ax) and P is an implementation under test against SP, we assume that P provides some way to execute the operations of SP[1]. Let t be a Σ-term without variable and t_p its computation by P.

Given an equation $\tau = \tau'$, a test for this equation is any ground instantiation $t = t'$ of it. A test experiment of P against $t = t'$ consists of evaluating t_p and t'_p and comparing the result values. In the example, a possible test inspired by the second equation is

```
get(add((0.'HELLO_WORLD'), emptyq)) = (0.'HELLO_WORLD')
```

---

[1] It means that there is a mapping from the operations of SP into some "procedures" in P. Here, "procedure" may be understood in a broad sense, i. e. as a way of using P to execute these operations.

The corresponding test experiment consists in two computations and a comparison, namely
- computing the construction in P of the message (0,'HELLO_WORLD') and of an empty queue, calling the add_p function on them, then the get_p function;
- computing again the message (or reusing it);
- comparing the two results.

In the case of positive conditional equations, the equations in premise are evaluated as well. When they all return the same values for both sides, the results of both sides of the equation in conclusion must be equal.

A program performing these experiments is called a *tester* and can be easily derived from the axioms.

As a first approximation, let us say that the exhaustive test set for a specification SP is the set of all the possible well-typed ground instantiations of all the axioms.

$$Exhaust(SP) = \{P\sigma => E\sigma \mid \forall P => E \in Ax, \ \forall \sigma = \{\sigma_s : X_s -> (T_\Sigma)_s \mid s \in S\} \} \qquad (3)$$

This notion is directly derived from the definition of the satisfaction of a set of axioms by a Σ-algebra [15][2]. It turns out that this exhaustive test set can be reduced, since it contains useless tests, namely the tests corresponding to those instantiations of conditional equations where the premise $P\sigma$ is not valid [5].

However, considering all the well-typed ground instantiations is not the same thing as considering all the well-sorted assignments to the values of the set implementing a sort. It may be the case that some values are not expressible by ground terms of the specification. In other words, the test set is exhaustive with respect to the specification, but may be not with respect to the values used by the program. It is why some testability hypothesis on the implementation under test is necessary: the success of the exhaustive test set ensures the satisfaction of the specification by the implementation only if this implementation behaves as a "finitely generated Σ-algebra". Practically, it means the following testability hypothesis:
- The realisations of the operations of Σ are deterministic; the results do not depend on some hidden, non specified, internal state;
- The implementation has been developed following reasonable programming techniques; any computed value of a data type must always be a result of the specified operations of this data type.

Note that these properties are easily ensured by good programming languages. For instance, the Ada language provides some safe linguistic support for the second one.

3.2 Selection Hypotheses in the Case of Algebraic Specifications

As said in Section 2, the choice of the selection hypotheses may depend on many factors. However, the text of the specification provides very useful guidelines. For algebraic specifications these guidelines rely on coverage of the axioms and composi-

---

[2] A Σ-algebra A satisfies an equation L = R if for all well-sorted assignment $\alpha = \{\alpha_s : X_s -> A_s \mid s \in S\}$, there is $\overline{\alpha}(L) = \overline{\alpha}(R)$, where $\overline{\alpha}$ is the unique extension of α to Σ-terms.

tion of the cases appearing in premise of the axioms defining the operations via a technique called *unfolding* [5].

In the given subset of the example, the coverage of the axioms requires four tests. These tests correspond to three uniformity hypotheses: one for the messages contained in the queues of size one; and two for the queues of size greater than one. More precisely there is one test only for the case where the last input has priority less or equal than all the messages present in the queue and one for the case it has greater priority. It is possible to weaken the second hypothesis by using the specification of ge to split the uniformity sub-domain into one where the priority of the last input is equal to the maximum priority in the queue and one where it is strictly less. These possibilities, and several other ones, has been automated in the LOFT tool developed by Bruno Marre [17], [18].

3.3   The Oracle Problem in the Case of Algebraic Specifications

In this case, the oracle problem reduces to the problem of deciding the equality of two results computed by the implementation. For some sorts it is possible to use the equality test provided by the programming language. Such sorts are called *observable*. They generally correspond to built-in types (Boolean, Integer...). The situation is different for those sorts corresponding to specific aspects of the system to be developed, which may be implemented by tricky data structures. Even if an equality function is available for these sorts, it is a part of the implementation under test. Thus, it may be faulty.

In theory, it is possible to use the *observable contexts* provided by the specification to translate the equality of a non-observable sort s into a set of observable equalities [5], [19]. Given a signature Σ, a Σ-context over some non-observable sort s is a Σ-term with a distinguished variable z_s of sort s. An observable context over s is a Σ-context of observable sort. If two non-observable ground Σ-terms t and t' are equal, there is $C[z_s \leftarrow t] = C[z_s \leftarrow t']$ for all observable contexts C. Conversely, if two t and t' are not distinguishable by any C, it means that at the level of the specification they are observationally equivalent. Their implementations may differ, but they correspond to the same abstract notion.

A major problem here is that the number of observable contexts is generally infinite. A possibility is to select a finite subset of them, but, as shown in [5], validity may not be preserved unless risky *oracle hypotheses* are assumed. In [20] Doong and Frankl experimented two approaches: an approximate abstract equality based on selected observable contexts, and an eqn_p implementation of equality for every class, which is tested together with the other operations of the class, introducing some risk of bias and invalidity. There are pragmatic advantages and disadvantages in both cases.

Recently, Machado has suggested interesting compromises in [21] and Chen et al. in [9]. Machado complements the approximate abstract equality with a hidden part, while Chen and his colleagues give a heuristic white-box technique to select a relevant finite subset of observable contexts.

3.4 Some Applications

A first experiment, performed at LRI by Pierre Dauchy and Bruno Marre, was on the on-board part of the driving system of an automatic subway. An algebraic specification was written. Then two modules of the specification were used for experiments with LOFT. The experiment is reported in details in [22].

A second experiment is reported in [23] and was performed within collaboration between LRI and the LAAS laboratory in Toulouse. The experiment was performed on a rather small piece of software written in C, which was extracted from a nuclear safety shutdown system. For some previous work, 1345 mutants of this procedure had been built by the LAAS team using classical fault injection methods. Five different test sets of 282 tests were selected using the LOFT system, with the same selection hypotheses: we were interested in studying both the quality and the stability of the method with respect to the arbitrary choices in the uniformity sub-domains. The rate of rejected mutants turned out to be rather stable, from 0.9651 to 0.9784, and good for a black-box strategy. The results were better than the ones of the all-paths structural strategy, which is supposed to be the most powerful structural testing strategy.

An experiment of "intensive" testing of a family of Ada components have been led by Didier Buchs and Stéphane Barbey in the Software Engineering Laboratory at EPFL [24]. First an algebraic specification of the component was reengineered: the signature was derived from the package specifications of the family, and the axioms were written manually. Then the LOFT system was used with a standard choice of hypotheses.

LOFT has been also used for the validation of a transit node specification [25] and for the test of the data types of an implementation of the Two-Phase-Commit protocol [12].

4   Instantiation to LOTOS

Specifications in LOTOS [16] describe processes that communicate by sending synchronous messages through shared, untyped gates. Processes take as parameters both data values and the gates that are to be used to communicate with other processes. Data values are described with an algebraic specification language (the one used in the example above). The processes have *guarded commands* and *recursion* as control structures, as well as mechanisms for *synchronisation* and *parallelism* (with interleaving semantics).

The specification below describes a process parameterised by a queue. It is a recursive process which begins by a choice (noted [ ]). At any moment, the process is ready to accept a message. In this case, it will start again with the new message added in the queue. Moreover, if the queue is not empty, the process has the choice to send its oldest message among the ones with the greatest priority. Then it will start again with this message removed from the queue.

As it can be seen below, when [isEmpty(Q)= false], both actions in-Gate?M:Message and outGate!get(Q) are executable by Transmitter[inGate,outGate](Q), depending on its environment.

```
behaviour
  Transmitter[inGate, outGate](emptyq)
where
process Transmitter[inGate, outGate](Q:Queue):noexit :=
  inGate?M:Message ;
        Transmitter[inGate, outGate] (add(M,Q))
[ ]
  [isEmpty(Q)= false] -> outGate!get(Q) ;
        Transmitter[inGate, outGate] (remove(Q))
endproc
```

The semantics of such a LOTOS specification is an infinite transition system where the transitions are labelled by pairs *<gate, value>* meaning that there is a communication of the value via the gate. In the above example the transitions are labelled by *<inGate, some message>* and *<outGate, some message>*; the states can be characterised by the value of the queue.

In a parallel composition with total synchronisation, for instance $P//Q$, a communication can occur if both P and Q are ready to execute synchronisable actions. For example, it is possible to synchronise the following couples of actions:

- *g!exp* and *g?x:s* : if the result r of *exp* is of sort s, then the communication *<g, r>* occurs in both processes. The value r is assigned to the variable x.
- *g!exp1* and *g!exp2* : if *exp1* and *exp2* have the same result r, then the communication *<g, r>* occurs in both processes

An important remark is that a process can block (deadlock) in case of incompatibility of gate or value. For instance, there is no executable action for the following process:

```
Transmitter[inGate, outGate](emptyq) || out-
Gate?M:Message ; …
```

Since the queue is empty, *Transmitter* only accepts to receive a message via *inGate*; it refuses any action *outGate?M:Message*.

Another important remark, in the context of testing, is that *g?x:s* can be considered as abbreviation of an unbounded choice between communications of some value of sort s, i. e.: $[ ]_{exp:s}g!exp$.

There is a special action known as *stop*, which leads to a state where there is no executable action. There is also an internal action i which does not need to synchronise. For instance, in $P//i ; Q$, the action i can be executed whatever are the executable actions of P and leads to the state[3] $P//Q$. The action i is said to be *non observable*.

Thus, in the sequel observable actions are either *stop* or some *g!exp*.

---

[3] There is an identification of the initial state of a process with the expression of this process.

A sequence of observable actions σ is executable by a process P if the successive actions of σ can be successfully executed possibly with interspersed internal actions. Such sequences correspond to observable behaviours of the process. The set of these sequences is called the traces of the process and will be noted *traces(P)*.

4.1 Test Experiments, Exhaustivity

Observing the execution of their parallel composition with a tester is the usual way of testing reactive processes. Given a test experiment $P//T$, where P is the implementation under test, and T is the tester process, the observations that can be made are the occurrence or the non occurrence of sequences of observable actions. More precisely, some sequences can be executed, and among them, some lead to a deadlock of the test experiment. These observations are the basis for the conformance relation most often used for LOTOS specifications.

Definition. An implementation P conforms to a specification SP if and only if: for all traces σ of SP which can be executed by P and can lead to a state where all the actions of a set A of observable actions are refused, then, the same sequence σ when executed by SP may lead to a state where all the actions of A are refused.

In other words, when the implementation follows some trace of the specification, when there is a deadlock, it must be a specified one.

Paraphrasing the above definition, the exhaustive test set is given by the following set of processes:

$$Exhaust(SP) = \{ \ \sigma \ ; [\ ]_{a_i \in A} \ a_i \ ; stop \ | \ \sigma \in traces(SP), \ A \subseteq L \ \} \qquad (4)$$

where L is the set of all action $g!v$ where g is any gate of SP and v is any value of a sort s used by SP. This test set contains all the traces of SP followed by (a choice in) all the subsets of L

4.2 Oracle and Testability

The verdict of a test experiment $P//T$, where $T = \sigma \ ; [\ ]_{a_i \in A} \ a_i \ ; stop$ is defined by:
- If σ is not executed by P, then success.
- If σ is executed by P, and some action in A is accepted, then success.
- If σ is executed by P, and no action in A is accepted, then
  - If SP may block after σ, then success
  - Otherwise failure.

The first of the three main cases corresponds to a deadlock before the end of σ. Thus, σ is not executable by P. In the second case there is no deadlock after σ. In both cases the premise in the conformance definition is false, thus there is conformance. The third case corresponds to the observation of a deadlock after σ. This deadlock must be possible in the specification.

As pointed out in [11], it is possible to simplify *Exhaust(SP)*. If all the actions in *A* may be refused after σ in *SP* then, from the definition of the verdict, the test experiment $P // T$ is a success for any implementation *P*, and thus it is useless. After this simplification, *Exhaust(SP)* coincides with the "must tests" defined by Hennessy and De Nicola [26]. It is also possible to factorise some tests, since some of them are prefixes of the others. Moreover, many subsets *A* of actions are redundant as shown in [27] by Tretmans.

Now, let us consider the minimal hypothesis required for ensuring property (1). It must include the fact that *P* and *SP* have the same set of observable actions, in order to avoid meaningless deadlocks. Moreover, atomicity of these actions must be ensured by the implementation. However, more is needed to ensure that the tests of Exhaust(SP) are all successful if and only if P conforms to SP, since in LOTOS a trace σ can lead to several states. In practice, the only way to cope with non-determinism, when testing with a black-box strategy, is to repeat each experiment "a sufficient number of times". This corresponds to an assumption that the non-determinism of the implementation is such that after a number *k* of executions of the same experiment, all the possible choices in the implementation are covered. For instance, if *c* is known as the maximum number of choices at any step in *P*, then $k(\sigma)$ must be chosen greater or equal to $/\sigma/ \times c$. Its precise value depends on the way the non-determinism is known to be balanced in the implementation.

Hmin(P) is the conjunction of the three properties above. We now require $k(\sigma)$ successful test experiments for each test to pass the test set *Exhaust(SP)*.

4.3 Selection Hypotheses in the Case of LOTOS Specifications

Regularity hypotheses have been implicitly used for a long time to deal with processes with infinite behaviours. When a specification SP describes a non-terminating process, for instance because of a recursive definition, *traces(SP)* contains infinite traces, and thus *Exhaust(SP)* contains arbitrary long testers. It means non-terminating test experiments, which are not practically acceptable. A natural selection strategy is to limit the length of the testers. The "length" may be defined as the number of observable actions or as the number of recursive calls performed. A regularity hypothesis based on the number of recursive calls seems more natural and can be supported by an analysis of the dependencies between the arguments along successive calls.

Uniformity hypotheses can be stated in a way to ensure that the control structure of the specified process is covered. Namely, for each variable occurring in the specification, being a parameter or a communication variable, some relevant values are chosen in such a way that every syntactical path of the process is exercised.

In our example, an example of a test set of Transmitter [inGate, outGate] (emptyq) could be

```
{inGate!(1,'HELLO') ; outGate!(1,'WORLD') ; stop, in-
Gate!(1,'SALUT') ; inGate!(3,'LE_MONDE') ; stop }
```

Here, there is a uniformity hypothesis on the messages, and a regularity hypothesis that two recursive calls are enough. This test set is obviously weaker than what would be proposed by an experienced tester. The point is that the control structure of the process does not reflect the complexity of the used data type. Weakening the regularity hypothesis, i. e. increasing the length of the tests, does not significantly improve the solution.

As explained in [11], it is possible to consider both the data type part and the behaviour part in the selection process by unfolding the operations occurring in the process definition.

Unfolding once the get operation of the example introduces three sub-cases to be tested, corresponding to the three axioms in the PriorityQueue data type. Then, the above regularity hypothesis appears to be too strong: the two last axioms require at least two additions in the queue, and then a use of get. A possible test set, with regularity three, is

```
{ inGate!(1,'HELLO');outGate!(1,'HELLO');stop, in-
Gate!(2,'HEL');inGate!(1,'LO');outGate!(2,'LO');stop,
in-
Gate!(1,'WO');inGate!(2,'RLD');outGate!(2,'RLD');stop,
… }
```

4.4 Some Application

This approach has been used by Perry James for testing an implementation of the Two-Phase-Commit Protocol [28] developed from a LOTOS specification into Concert/C [29]. The results of this experiment are reported in [12].

The tests for the data types were obtained first with the LOFT system. Then a set of testers was derived manually from the process part of the specification. The submission of these tests, was preceded by a test campaign of the implementation of the atomic actions of the specification by the Concert/C library, i. e. the communication infrastructure (the set of gates connecting the processes), which was developed step by step. Coming back to the testability hypothesis, this phase of development and testing was a way of ensuring the fact that the actions in the implementation were the same as in the specification, and that they were atomic.

No errors were found in the data types implementations, but an undocumented error of the Concert/C preprocessor was detected when testing them. Some errors were discovered in the implementation of the main process. They were related to memory management, and to the treatment of the time-outs. There are always questions on the interest of testing pieces of software, which have been formally specified and almost directly derived from the specification. But this experiment shows that problems may arise: The first error-prone aspect, memory management, was not expressed in the LOTOS specification. The second one was specified in a tricky way due to the absence of explicit time in the classical LOTOS, which was used. Such unspecified aspects are unavoidable when developing efficient implementation.

5 Conclusion

The approach presented here provides a systematic way of using formal specifications for deriving test cases, independently of the used formalism. Moreover, the fact that the testability and selection hypotheses are made explicit is a serious advantage: It helps at choosing sound strategies. It gives some guidelines on the kind of development constraints or verification activities, which must complement the submission of the derived test cases.

This approach has been applied to other formalisms: CO-OPN2 by Cécile Peraire and Didier Buchs at EPFL [30], and Lustre by Bruno Marre [31], in collaboration with the French Commissariat à l'Énergie Atomique.

References

1. Goodenough, J. B., Gerhart, S.: Toward a Theory of Test Data Selection. IEEE Transactions on Software Engineering, vol. SE-1, n° 2, (1975) 156-173.
2. Howden, W.: Errors, Design Properties, and Functional Program Tests. in Chandraskaran, B., Radicchi, S. (eds.), Computer Program Testing, North-Holland (1981).
3. Chow, T. S.: Testing Software Design Modeled by Finite-State Machines. IEEE Transactions on Software Engineering, vol. SE-4, n° 3, (1978) 178-187.
4. Gannon, J., McMullin, P., Hamlet, R.: Data Abstraction Implementation, Specification and Testing. ACM Transactions on Programming Languages and Systems, vol. 3, n°3, (1981) 211-223.
5. Bernot, G., Gaudel, M.-C., Marre B.: Software Testing based on Formal Specifications: a theory and a tool. Software Engineering Journal, vol. 6, n° 6, (1991) 387-405.
6. Dick, J., Faivre, A.: Automating the Generation and Sequencing of test cases from model-based specifications. FME'93, LNCS n°670, Springer-Verlag (1993) 268-284.
7. Brinksma, E., A Theory for the Derivation of Tests, 8th International Conference on Protocol Specification, Testing and Verification, Atlantic City, North-Holland (1988).
8. Pitt, D.H., Freestone, D.: The Derivation of Conformance Tests from LOTOS specifications, IEEE Transactions on Software Engineering, vol. 16, n°12, (1990) 1337-1343.
9. Chen, H. Y., Tse, T. H., Chan, F. T., Chen, T. Y.: In Black and White: an Integrated Approach to Class-level Testing of Object-Oriented Programs. ACM transactions on Software Engineering and Methodology, vol. 7, n° 3, (1998) 250-295.
10. Littlewood, B., Popov, P. T., Strigini, L., Shryane, N.: Modeling the Effects of Combining Diverse Software Fault Detection Techniques. IEEE Transactions on Software Engineering, vol. 26, n° 12, (2000) 1157-1167.
11. Gaudel, M.-C., James, P. R.: Testing Algebraic Data Types and Processes: a unifying theory. Formal Aspects of Computing, 10(5-6), (1999) 436-451.
12. James, P. R., Endler M., Gaudel M.-C.: Development of an Atomic Broadcast Protocol using LOTOS. Software Practice and Experience, 29(8), (1999) 699-719.
13. Bernot, G., Gaudel, M.-C, Marre, B.: A Formal Approach to Software Testing. 2nd International Conference on Algebraic Methodology and Software Technology, AMAST, Iowa City, 1991, Workshops in Computing Series, Springer-Verlag, (1992).
14. Phalippou, M.: Relations d'Implantation et Hypothèses de Test sur des Automates à Entrées et Sorties. Thèse de l'université de Bordeaux 1, (1994).

15. Kreowski, H.-J. ed.: Foundations of Algebraic Specifications. Springer-Verlag, (1999).
16. ISO: LOTOS, a Formal Description Technique based on the Temporal Ordering of Observational Behaviours. Technical report 8807, International Standards Organisation (1989).
17. Marre, B.: Toward Automatic Test Data Selection using Algebraic Specifications and Logic Programming. International Conference on Logic Programming, MIT Press (1991) 202-219.
18. Marre, B.: LOFT, a Tool for Assisting Selection of Test Data Sets from Algebraic Specifications. LNCS n°915, Springer-Verlag (1995) 799-800.
19. Le Gall, P., Arnould, A.: Formal Specifications and Test: Correctness and Oracle. LNCS n°1130, Springer-Verlag (1996) 342-358.
20. Doong, R.-K., Frankl, P. G.: The ASTOOT Approach to Testing Object-Oriented Programs. ACM Transactions on Software Engineering and Methodology, 3(2), (1994) 101-130.
21. Machado, P. D. L: On Oracles for Interpreting Test Results against Algebraic Specifications. LNCS n° 1548, Springer-Verlag (1998) 502-518.
22. Dauchy, P., Gaudel, M.-C, Marre, B.: Using Algebraic Specifications in Software Testing : a Case Study on the Software of an Automatic Subway. Journal of Systems and Software, 21(3), (1993) 229-244.
23. Marre, B., Thévenod-Fosse, P., Waeselink, H., Le Gall, P., Crouzet, Y.: An Experimental Evaluation of Formal Testing and Statistical Testing, SAFECOMP'92, Zurich, Oct. 1992.
24. Barbey, S., Buchs, D.: Testing Ada abstract data types using formal specifications, in Ada in Europe, 1st Int. Eurospace-Ada-Europe Symposium. LNCS n°887, Springer-Verlag, (1994) 76-89.
25. Arnold, A., Gaudel, M.-C., Marre, B.: An Experiment on the Validation of a Specification by Heterogeneous Formal Means: the Transit Node. 5th IFIP Working Conference on Dependable Computing for Critical Applications, (1995) 24-34.
26. Hennessy, M.: An Algebraic Theory of Processes. MIT Press (1988).
27. Tretmans, J.: A Formal Approach to Conformance Testing. 6th Int. Workshop on Protocol Test Systems, IFIP Transactions C-19, North-Holland, (1994) 257-276.
28. Birman, K. P.: Building Secure and Reliable Network Applications. Manning Publications (1997)
29. Auerbach, J. S. et al.: High-level Language Support for Programming Distributed Systems. IEEE Int. Conf. on Computer Languages, IEEE, (1992) 320-330.
30. Péraire, C., Barbey, S., Buchs, D.: Test Selection for Object-Oriented Software Based on Formal Specifications. IFIP Working Conference on Programming Concepts and Methods, Shelter Island, USA, Chapman & Hall, (1998) 385-403.
31. Marre, B., Arnould, A.: Test Sequences Generation from LUSTRE Descriptions: GATEL. IEEE Automated Software Engineering Conference, IEEE, (2000) 229-237.

Logic versus Magic in Critical Systems

Peter Amey

Praxis Critical Systems, 20 Manvers St., Bath, BA1 1PX, UK
`pna@praxis-cs.co.uk`

Abstract. A prevailing trend in software engineering is the use of tools which apparently simplify the problem to be solved. Often, however, this results in complexity being concealed or "magicked away". For the most critical of systems, where a credible case for safety and integrity must be made prior to there being any service experience, we cannot tolerate concealed complexity and must be able to reason logically about the behaviour of the system. The paper draws on real-life project experience to identify some historical and current magics and their effect on high-integrity software development; this is contrasted with the cost and quality benefits that can be made from taking a more logical and disciplined approach.

1 Introduction

We live in an irrational and magical world. While more and more aspects of our daily lives are governed by technology—itself the product of 2 millennia of rational thought and science—society is increasingly seduced by the comforting delusions of the "new age". The lack of rational thought and numeracy in today's society is striking. A rail crash, front page news because of its very rarity, will cause thousands to abandon the trains and drive instead. More will die as a result; however, this goes unnoticed because, perversely, road accidents are so common they don't make the news. Opinion formers in the media wear their ignorance of science and mathematics with pride but would regard themselves as profoundly uncivilized if they didn't have a working knowledge of Shakespeare.

Paradoxically, some of this "anti-science" may stem directly from the very successes of science and its impact on our daily lives. Most of the devices we use daily, and rely on, are now too complex for anyone but a specialist to understand. This is in marked contrast to the situation only a few years ago. I am just old enough to be of the generation where an informed amateur could expect to be able to understand the workings of all the complex machines with which they came in contact: the telephone, gramophone, vacuum cleaner and car for example. Furthermore, the reasonably physically adept would expect to be able to repair most of them as well. When such a level of understanding becomes infeasible—for example, the cellular telephone—perhaps we give up and accept the device as being "magic". As Arthur C. Clarke observed in 1962: *"Any sufficiently advanced technology is indistinguishable from magic"*.

A. Strohmeier and D. Craeynest (Eds.): Ada-Europe 2001, LNCS 2043, pp. 49-67, 2001.
© Springer-Verlag Berlin Heidelberg 2001

At first sight, we might think the world of software engineering to be poles apart from the rather sad[1] image portrayed above. After all it is a modern discipline and one which is increasingly prevalent in our lives; especially the fashionable modern bits of our lives such as the communications and entertainment industries. It is also a relentlessly binary and Boolean world where the consequences of everything we do are unavoidable, predictable and exact. Yet even here we find the language of magic. Every software product (even tiny utilities like Winzip) comes with a full set of "wizards"; search the web for a simple Windows macro tool and you find "Macro Magic"; want to re-organize your disk drive? then "Partition Magic" is the answer; Unix has its "daemons" and senior hackers are "gurus".

This is more than just a problem of style, it shapes an environment in which we expect our problems to be magically made easier for us, an environment where rational thought and hard work is supplanted by magic wands and silver bullets.

In this paper I will illustrate some of the historical and current magics of the software engineering industry; highlight the inadequacies of these approaches (especially in the context of high-integrity systems); and show how we need to re-discover logic to make real progress in future. Comparisons with the history of aeronautical engineering are used to illustrate some of the points made.

2   An Historical Magic-Order out of Chaos

An early example of the desire to have our problems magically removed arose after publication of Dijkstra's seminal article: "Go To Statement Considered Harmful" [1]. Ultimately this led to "structured programming", which was one of the earliest attempts to solve the software crisis. It also alerted the software world to the millions of lines of "spaghetti Fortran" that existed. The magicians were quick to provide an answer in the form of code restructuring tools. Into these could be poured unstructured code and out would come structured code (a kind of software entropy reduction that is probably contrary to the second law of thermodynamics). It is worth examining one of the means by which this illusion can be achieved. I will use as an example a small program (or, more accurately, subprogram) written to implement the following specification: *"Add up the first N (positive) values of the array of integers supplied"*

Before introducing the example itself it is worth noting that even this simple English specification is ambiguous. Does it mean "traverse the array until N positive values have been found and sum them" or "traverse N elements of the array and sum any positive ones (ignoring any negative ones)"? Only more (potentially ambiguous) English or a little bit of formal mathematics can make the meaning clear. For the example I am taking the latter meaning.

---

[1] It is interesting to note how even this simple word has been subtly redefined. To me it is "sad" that so many people have so little interest in, or understanding of, how their world works. To a much younger generation it is the exact opposite: showing such an interest or understanding would be a prime qualification for being thought "sad"!

Some Fortran-like Ada code which implements the specification might be:

```
function Sum (A : Atype; Count : Aindex)
    return Integer
is
    Accumulator, Value : Integer;
    Index              : Aindex;

begin
    Accumulator := 0;
    Index := 1;
    <<Label1>> Value := A(Index);
              if Value <= 0 then
                  goto Label2;
              end if;
              Accumulator := Accumulator + Value;

    <<Label2>> if Index = Count then
                  goto Label3;
              end if;
              Index := Index + 1;
              goto Label1;

    <<Label3>> return Accumulator;
end Sum;
```

This example is not very badly structured. It has no jumps into loops and only one upward go to. Still what we want is proper structured code so into the magic tool it goes which gives us:

```
function Sum (A      : Atype;
              Count : Aindex) return Integer
is
    IC                   : Counter;
    Accumulator, Value : Integer;
    Index               : Aindex;
begin
    IC := 1;
    Accumulator := 0;
    Index := 1;
    while IC < 6 loop
        case IC is
            when 1 => Value := A(Index);
                      IC := 2;
            when 2 => if Value <= 0 then
                          IC := 4;
                      else
                          IC := 3;
                      end if;
```

```
        when 3 => Accumulator := Accumulator + Value;
                  IC := 4;
        when 4 => if Index = Count then
                      IC := 6;
                  else
                      IC := 5;
                  end if;
        when 5 => Index := Index + 1;
                  IC := 1;
        when 6 => null;
     end case;
  end loop;
  return Accumulator;
end Sum;
```

We now have a case statement inside a while loop. Both of these constructs are pillars of structured programming orthodoxy. The code is now unquestionably "structured" but the interesting question is whether it is actually any better than it was before. Well how has this miracle been achieved? Closer examination of the restructured code shows that we have introduced an extra variable, IC. The convoluted semantics of code which makes excessive use of the go to statement arises from all the meaning being locked up in the behaviour of the processor's instruction counter and the contents of the instructions in the memory map. The variable IC is simply the instruction counter in disguise. All the semantics of the program are now locked up in the behaviour of IC and the instructions in the case statement. We have achieved the illusion of structure but nothing has really changed. Illusions are, of course, a principal tool of magicians. The risks, incidentally, were recognized by Dijkstra himself in the same paper: "*The exercise to translate an arbitrary flow diagram more or less mechanically into a jump-less one, however, is not to be recommended. Then the resulting flow diagram cannot be expected to be more transparent than the original one.*"

Why do we allow ourselves to be fooled? Because it is easier than solving the real problem. Perhaps the contract says we must deliver structured code and the alternative is understanding sufficient graph theory to do the job properly.

The lesson of this historical example is that it is extremely hard to retrofit quality and that it is impossible to retrofit quality *automatically*. If we want a well-engineered product then we must build it well to start with. This should not be a surprise: it is a lesson written throughout the history of engineering in all its disciplines.

More contemporary magics will be revealed later on.

3   The Software Process

3.1   Development as a Process of Refinement

Whatever lifecycle we choose to use, the software development process is one of *refinement*. We start with a *need*, move through *requirements* to a *specification*, a *design*, *source code* and finally *object code*. Each of these stages is accompanied by a move from the abstract to the concrete. It may also, but does not have to be, a move from the vague to the precise (although often confused, vagueness and abstraction are not the same thing).

Needs are inevitably abstract and are usually vague as well. We might want a flight control system, a secure internet trading system or a better mousetrap; these are all aspirations rather than artefacts and do not directly lead us to a sound implementation. To a certain extent *requirements* must also be abstract for if they become too prescriptive they risk becoming specifications; however, there is no reason why they should be vague.

Specifications are interesting. Potentially they give us our first opportunity to make a really rigorous but abstract description of required system properties. Formal specifications have a good track record for allowing early reasoning and hence early error detection (see Section 8.2 for an example). There remain reservations about the scalability of such Formal Methods and about the availability of tools and training so typical specifications today are insufficiently precise to allow any kind of rigorous reasoning about projected system behaviour.

Design is a much overlooked phase of development. The more extreme advocates of Object Oriented Programming deny that there is a design phase at all. In their concept, identification of the objects modelling the real world and their accurate implementation is sufficient to ensure that a correct system will emerge. More realistically design should be seen as a key stage in the refinement of abstract requirements and specifications to concrete code. We face real design choices here: our abstract *ordered queue* can become a *linked list*, an *array* which we regularly quick sort or even a *set of temporary files* which we merge sort together. There is no right answer and the solution is not implied by the required abstract property "ordered". For high-integrity systems a further layer of complexity may be introduced at this stage. The relatively simple concept: "is the trigger pulled?" at the specification level may require considerable extra design to achieve the necessary level of integrity. It might become the rather more complex: "does the code show the trigger is pulled via two separate calculation methods using real and complementary arithmetic and with a checksum on each answer showing that each calculation has followed the expected processing path?". It is this area that is most likely to cause communications difficulties between software engineers and their system counterparts who cannot understand why their relatively simple control laws are proving so hard to code.

Source code, like specifications, provides another rather interesting case. It is substantially more concrete than even a formal specification since it purports to represent instructions that will be used directly by the compiler to implement our design, fulfil our specification, embody our requirements and thus meet our needs. It even looks precise and mathematical. Therein lies the trap: the apparent precision of our source code masks considerable uncertainty. Dig a little deeper beneath the mathematical veneer of $X := X + 1$; and we find a rather less pure world of machine representations, overflows, aliasing and function side effects. There is clear evidence that attention paid to source code in the form of reviews and walkthroughs is of considerable value; however, this is despite its lack of precision and falls short of being a precise, logical reasoning process. Like dynamic testing, we may hope to detect some shortcomings by such inspections but we cannot ensure, let alone prove, their absence unless the source language is completely unambiguous and precise.

Finally we have *object code*, something which is unequivocally concrete. There is no uncertainty about its behaviour; this is determined solely by the ones and zeros of the machine code and the mask and micro-code of the processor. Unfortunately, we cannot *reason* about it, we can only *observe* its behaviour.

3.2   Some Consequences

So overall, our typical development process never results in an artefact which is susceptible to rigorous reasoning. The first really exact representation we have is object code and that arrives late in the project life and is amenable only to observation not reasoning.

For the reasons outlined above much of the software industry seems to have abandoned attempts to reason logically about software during each stage of its development. Instead we have become extremely focussed on observing the behaviour of the finished product during dynamic testing. This mindset has become so prevalent that there is a strong current trend towards effectively eliminating all lifecycle stages between requirements and object code by the use of code generators. We are encouraged to express requirements graphically and generate the code directly from the diagrams. Since all our verification activity will consist of testing the finished code the opacity of this process does not matter. Apparently we will also save time because we will get to test faster (even though our inputs to the code generator are semantically vague). The same mindset leads to another current nostrum: that the choice of programming language is not important to the quality of the finished product.

Even widely used standards such as DO-178B [2] have gone down this route with a major emphasis on one particular form of dynamic testing and little available credit for any other contributors to quality.

The obsession with getting to test quickly is, I believe, inappropriate. If we accept the software development process as being one of decreasing abstraction then as the artefacts we deal with become more concrete, contradictions and complications overlooked in earlier stages become more apparent. We are all familiar with trying to come up with a design and finding, in the course of that process, a contradiction in the specification. Even more common is to find out during coding that some overlooked deficiency of the design makes further progress impossible. It is this process that leads to late error detection and a tendency to compromise designs by "patching" when problems are found.

It is widely agreed that correction of errors is increasingly expensive the later in the development process that they are found. A development process that largely abandons attempts to reason about the earlier stages is predestined to find most errors in the later, more expensive stages. Late error detection also adds risk, especially of cost and time overruns.

These problems are, I believe, significant in most cases. They are particularly important for the development of safety-critical and other high-integrity software because of the unique properties required of such systems.

4   High-Integrity Software

High-integrity software is software where reliability is the pre-eminent requirement. Certainly it is more important than cost, efficiency, time to market and functionality. All are important; however, for systems which must work reliably, correct behaviour is the most important property of all and achieving it will dominate the development process. Historically the most common form of high-integrity software has been safety-critical software. Where loss of life, perhaps widespread, can result from software failure, the need for high integrity is self evident; however, there is an increasing trend towards the development of systems which must be regarded as high-integrity for other reasons. The economic consequences of software failure are growing all the time. At the lower end of the scale we have the costs (direct and indirect in terms of loss of consumer confidence) of product recalls of consumer products such as cars. At the upper end we have financial systems where the potential losses are incalculably high. For example the Mondex Purse [3] will provide electronic cash with (intentionally) no audit trail, so a failure of software or failure of encryption could lead to unquantifiable financial loss or the creation of arbitrary amounts of undetectable "forged" money.

Producing such systems is challenging enough but in fact the problem is rather harder than it seems at first sight. The problem is not just to produce a reliable system but to produce a system for which a credible case can be made that it *will* be reliable in advance of its deployment and *prior to any service experience* being available. The scale of this challenge cannot be over exaggerated. For avionics systems we routinely talk of failure rates as low as 10^{-9} per flying hour. Either we are being extremely disingenuous or else we really believe we can produce systems—systems reliant on software for their correct behaviour—that will not malfunction for 114000 years after deployment! That we should believe this at all is open to question; to believe we can do so by a process of informal development followed by a period of observation of the system's behaviour during dynamic testing borders on the absurd. The Bayesian mathematics involved is unequivocal [4, 5, 6]: we cannot provide the necessary assurance by testing alone. We may be able to produce systems which turn out to be reliable enough but we cannot produce a convincing case that they *will* be reliable enough by these means alone.

So it is clear that the development of ultra high-integrity software is a qualitatively different process, with different demands and requirements, to the development of systems with lower integrity requirements. We cannot expect to use the same processes for all systems and we certainly cannot expect to achieve high reliability just by being more careful, doing a few more walkthroughs or a bit (or even a lot) more testing. Only a process optimized for the development of high-integrity software can hope to achieve it.

5   The Need to Reason

One of the characteristics of high-integrity systems is the very large percentage of the overall effort that goes into the verification processes. For critical avionics systems it is reasonable to assume that over half of the overall development budget will be used for integration testing and for verification. Sources I respect put the figure as high as

80% [7]. This heavy weighting of effort towards the back end of the development lifecycle interacts in a malign manner with the increasing cost of error correction the later errors are found.   The result is that we spend most of our time in the most expensive part of the development; an economic vicious circle that is largely responsible for the perceived high cost of high-integrity software.

Only by finding ways of bringing error detection forward can we unlock this vicious circle and produce high-integrity software at a lower cost.   To bring error detection forward we must start reasoning about the characteristics of the software earlier in the development process.

5.1   Barriers to Reasoning

We can only reason logically about things which have reasonably precise meanings and which don't conceal essential information from us.   Unfortunately the entire typical development process described earlier seems to be purpose-designed to prevent such reasoning.   We write informal specifications, often too close to being designs to be truly specifications at all.   We use notations such as UML whose semantic vagueness seems almost to be a positive virtue.   Finally, we code in languages with the most obscure and imprecise semantics.   So we find ourselves relying on observation of actual behaviour rather than prediction of desired behaviour.

The UML diagram seems attractive precisely because it ignores the very concrete details that will emerge later as the development process takes us relentlessly towards the absolute concrete of object code.   Ignoring that detail, not by true abstraction but by vagueness, makes the diagrams easier to understand and allows them to be used as a means of communication between different stakeholders in the project.   Although this sounds beneficial it is only useful if the communication that takes place is useful. If the communication succeeds because the vague semantics of the diagram allows each participant to see what they want to see rather than because they have achieved a common understanding, then no real progress has been made and the contradictions and difficulties remain concealed to emerge at some more costly stage in the future. Until this time arrives, the illusion is maintained and everyone is pleased: apparent progress is being made; the specification has been discussed and agreed by everyone; and we have tools that will let us generate code from it.   The reality behind the illusion is that we have a specification which is only agreed by everyone because it contains insufficient information to allow effective debate or dissent.   Furthermore, the semantic vagueness of the specification prevents fully effective code generation since we cannot go from a vague description to concrete code automatically; this would be to create order out of chaos in an even cleverer way than the spaghetti restructuring example outlined earlier.   What is likely to happen in practice is that the code generator will take some pragmatic view of what a diagram means and generate code accordingly.   In many cases that view will be what was needed (but still with attendant difficulty that we must show it to be so), but in others some subtle mismatch between what was intended and what is generated may arise which will lurk awaiting detection at a later, more expensive, point in the development process.

Note that the semantic vagueness of these diagrams is very different from the, superficially similar, situation with computer-aided design tools in other engineering disciplines.   The structural engineer using such a design tool will have a picture of the object he is designing on his screen.   That picture may show stress levels in different colours to make them easy to understand; however, behind the scenes there is some rigorous mathematics, probably finite element analysis, going on. The coloured picture is providing an abstract view of a rigorous mathematical model. Similarly, an aerodynamicist using a computational fluid mechanics tool may look at a picture of flow fields but this too is underpinned by some heavyweight mathematics providing numerical solutions to families of partial differential equations.

In stark contrast, the user of a contemporary CASE tool is not looking at an abstract view of a precise mathematical model but at a vague illustration not underpinned by anything other than the informal design decisions of the tool vendors.

When we finally arrive at some code, whether automatically generated or not, there remains the problems of showing it to be correct to the exacting standards required for high-integrity software. Here there are further barriers to reasoning. All widely-used programming languages contain ambiguities and insecurities [8]. Ambiguities arise where the language definition permits certain implementation freedoms for the compiler writer. Typical examples are expression and parameter list evaluation orders and the method of passing subprogram parameters. Insecurities arise where language rules or coding standards cannot effectively be checked. So, for example, function side effects lead to ambiguities if evaluation order is undefined but a prohibition of function side effects simply leads to a language insecurity if there is no effective way of detecting their presence. Even Ada is not immune from these difficulties despite its attempts to wriggle out of the problem through introduction of the idea of "erroneous" programs: these are programs where ambiguity allows construction of a program of uncertain meaning, insecurity means the compiler cannot warn you about it but it is still your fault because such a program is defined to be erroneous! As a tiny example of a language ambiguity consider the completely legal Ada subprogram:

```
procedure Init (X, Y : out Integer)
is
begin
    X := 1;
    Y := 2;
end Init;
```

What, however, is the meaning of the statement: Init(A, A); ? What value does A take? The answer depends on the order of parameter association chosen by the compiler vendor and I have found different behaviours in commercial, validated compilers. The subprogram is legal but the call to it is erroneous.

These difficulties are likely to prove an irritant and waste time during the final stages of development. A larger barrier to reasoning about source code is the wilful hiding not just of detail—which is essential for abstraction—but of information vital to the reasoning process. A significant example is the location of persistent data items or program "state". The presence of state in a piece of software greatly adds to the complexity of understanding it, reasoning about it and even testing it. It is the presence of state that makes software behave in a non-functional manner so that, for example, the outputs obtained depend not only on the inputs provided but on the history of all previous inputs. More significantly still, it is the location of state which generates and governs the flow of information through a program. Values of state variables have to be calculated and set using information from other parts of the system and current values of state have to be conveyed from their location to the places which need those values; these are information flows. Information flows lead to couplings between components. A desired characteristic of good software designs is that they result in loose coupling of highly cohesive components; indeed this is a prime claim made for object orientation. So it is clear that the location of state has a major impact on information flow and component coupling and so should be a prime design driver. Yet OOP typically regards object state as an implementation detail and UML does not have a notation to express it. For more observations on the connection between state location, information flow and coupling see [9].

Making things disappear is another popular magical illusion. So here is the trick in a software context.

5.2   Objects and Vanishing "State"

Consider a simple subprogram to exchange its parameters.

```
procedure Swap (X, Y : in out T)
is
    Temp : T;
begin
    Temp := X;
    X := Y;
    Y := Temp;
end Swap;
```

We need a temporary variable to perform the swap operation. Where should it be located? Clearly the correct place is where it has been declared here; as a local variable of the subprogram. This is the right place because it is close to the point of use and cannot cause malign information flows because it ceases to exist as soon as the swap operation is completed. The alternative, making the temporary variable a global variable is unattractive for all the opposite reasons. It creates an unnecessary flow of information outside the swap operation, reducing its cohesion, and we have to take care that the value left in the variable does not cause a flow of information, and undesired coupling, to somewhere inappropriate. That I think is clear cut, but what happens when we introduce a nicely parameterized store object?

```
package Store
is
    procedure Put (X : in T);

    function Get return T;

end Store;
```

This provides all the encapsulation expected of object orientation and nicely hides the information about what might or might not be stored in the object itself. We can now use this object in our swap operation.

```
procedure Swap (X, Y : in out T) is
begin
    Store.Put (X);
    X := Y;
    Y := Store.Get;
end Swap;
```

The illusion is now complete, the state has vanished completely. We don't have a global variable or even a local variable any more, it has gone.

Of course like all such conjuring tricks this is just an illusion. The state has not disappeared; it is just hidden. By hiding it we make it impossible to reason about. So where is it. Well it might be inside the Store package or, it might be in the heap somewhere and simply be pointed at by the store object. Either way it is outside the Swap operation and is therefore global to it. Just as in the case of the unnecessary global variable, performing a swap operation causes unnecessary information to flow outside the operation and sets an unnecessary piece of state. The apparently atomic swap operation can now become coupled to other parts of the system. This may not matter unless that information gets used in some way. Unfortunately, another claimed benefit of object orientation—re-use—makes this highly possible. Suppose another operation called Consumer makes use of the store object to retrieve a value left there by Donor. The objects are composed thus (with the arrows showing the direction of data flows):

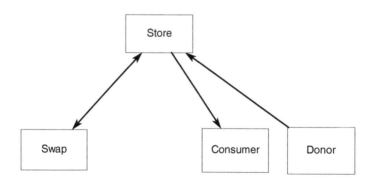

We can happily unit test Store, Swap, Consumer and Donor. More worryingly we may be able to integration test the Donor-Store-Consumer sub-system and the Swap-Store sub-system successfully; however, the overall behaviour of the system depends on whether a swap operation ever occurs between Donor setting the store value and Consumer reading it. If this sequence does occur then the expected value does not arrive at Consumer; instead, the junk value left by Swap is received instead—there is an unexpected coupling and information flow between Swap and Consumer. The presence of this potential coupling cannot be predicted by reasoning about the specifications of the objects involved. There is nothing about the specification of Store that alerts us to the potential danger. The way in which we can hide detail (to aid abstraction) but retain the ability to reason, is by having adequate abstract descriptions of the specifications of the objects we use. See for example [10].

It is the discovery of this kind of unexpected interaction during system integration that makes a major contribution to what is often called the "integration bottleneck". Finding out why the individually thoroughly-tested objects do not always behave correctly in composition is a difficult and time-consuming task that occurs, unavoidably, late in the development with the attendant risk to schedule and budget.

So contemporary approaches to object oriented programming are potentially the biggest magic of them all. We deliberately hide all state and, worse, distribute it arbitrarily in small packets amongst the objects making up the system. We typically ignore all hierarchy between objects in the sense that some should be regarded as components of others and be encapsulated by them. We even hide the control flow through polymorphism.

Why do we do this? Because solving our problem looks so much easier without all that tiresome detail—just as designing an aeroplane would be much easier if it wasn't for all those annoying compressible flows and that inconvenient metal fatigue.

We might very well end up with a system that happens to work by following this approach. What is certain is that we will not end up with a system for which it will be possible to construct a credible logical argument, *prior to deployment*, that the system *will* be suitable for its purpose; this, you will recall, is the especial challenge posed by high-integrity and safety-critical software. As Professor Hoare observed:

> *"There are two ways of constructing a software design. One way is to make it so simple that there are obviously no deficiencies. And the other way is to make it so complicated that there are no obvious deficiencies."* [11]

The current state of the object oriented programming world provides an extremely powerful way of designing systems with no obvious deficiencies. Unfortunately, when operating in the rarefied atmosphere of ultra high-integrity systems it is the non-obvious deficiencies that are potentially fatal.

5.3   Other Magics

There are of course many other contemporary magics.

There is *metric magic* where we make no attempt to understand the behaviour of our system but we "measure" it instead. So we still don't know whether it works but we know it must better than it was before because it now measures 10.6 on some arbitrary scale where it was 4.2 before!

Then there is *process improvement magic* where we give up any attempt at understanding the system we are building and concentrate instead on improving the efficiency of the building process itself. This is like optimizing the production line rather than the product.

All of these magics have a role but as slave rather than master: control flow analysis may reveal better ways of structuring code; object orientation may provide better insights into the systems we are trying to model; metrics may indicate problem areas; and quality systems and process improvements may increase our ability repeatably to produce correct systems (but only if we already knew how to do it once) or, more usefully, learn from both the successes and failures of others.

6   Social Issues

Many of these difficulties are compounded by non-technical and social issues. Common problem areas include:

Fashion. Choosing technologies because they are popular rather than because they are appropriate.

Low Expectations. So prevalent is buggy software that it has come to be regarded as the norm. Saying "it was only a software glitch" has almost become a socially acceptable way of excusing failure. In this environment it is hard to persuade people to make the investment necessary to do a better job.

Poor Contracting. Many conventional contract models seem ill-suited to the development of software. Time-hire terms give the developer little incentive to do a more efficient job. Fixed-price terms set the producer and customer in opposition with even mutually beneficial changes hard to negotiate. Complex software can probably only be developed effectively under terms providing partnerships and risk sharing.

Difficulty of Maintaining Standards. In a market containing more than its share of magicians and charlatans it is sometimes hard to maintain high standards of engineering integrity. If the right engineering answer is "no" then this does not mean that there will be no one willing to say "yes" (and perhaps charge you less!).

Gurus and Tactical Knowledge. Too many decisions are made at a tactical rather than strategic level. This trend is encouraged by the equating of engineering skill with experience of a particular tool or programming language. If the company software guru is an experienced C (or X or Y or Z) hacker then it is likely that he will recommend what he already knows for any job that comes along; this is the best way of preserving his guru status. Much recruitment of software engineers suffers from this kind of confusion. Agencies frequently send out lists of available engineers listing their skills as Visual Basic, C++ etc. These are not skills, they are programming languages. Listing them provides no indication about whether the engineer in question can be trusted to build a safe, software-intensive system. As an aeronautical engineer I am amused by the idea of applying for a job at Boeing or Airbus quoting my "skills" as: screwdriver, metric open-ended spanners and medium-sized hammers!

7   Can We Do Better?

We are increasingly reliant on software for our safety and for the functioning of society; the systems we seek to build are becoming increasingly complex; and testing alone cannot provide the necessary levels of assurance. It is therefore clear that we *must* seek to do better. Even if we believe we can continue to build high-integrity systems by current (or worse: by decreasingly suitable) means, the economic argument for doing a better and more rigorous job is inescapable. High-integrity software is seen to be very expensive—typically 5 times the cost of "normal" code of the same size and complexity. Much of this cost comes from the extensive testing required and the vicious circle of the high cost and risk of late error detection. We can only unlock this vicious circle by an engineering approach of "correctness by construction".

7.1   Aerodynamics: A Lesson from History

Many other engineering disciplines have been plagued by magics of their own. Generally they have become fully established engineering disciplines when they have put magic behind them and espoused science, mathematics and logic.

For many years aeronautical engineering had the kind of split between theoreticians and practitioners that is prevalent in computer science and software engineering today. Before the Wright brothers flew at Kittyhawk on December 17th 1903 the theoretical study of aerodynamics was already very old. Aristotle, Leonardo da Vinci and Newton had all made significant observations or theoretical contributions to the science. The relationship between gas pressure and velocity was established by Bernoulli in 1738. The governing equations of frictionless low-speed incompressible flow were fully established by Euler in 1752 and then, with friction, by Navier and Stokes in 1840. However, the gulf between these researchers and the mad fools trying to make man fly was enormous. Certainly the theoreticians did not see manned flight as their goals and history clearly shows the practical aviators to be largely ignorant of the theory.

The first successful aviators, Lilienthal in Germany and the Wright brothers in the USA, leaned heavily on empirical evidence. With whirling test arms and primitive wind tunnels they developed an intuitive understanding of which aerofoil shapes were effective in practice. The rapid development in aviation that took place between the Wrights' first manned, powered flight and the end of the First World War built on this largely pragmatic approach. Designers copied each other, established a "best practice" and built largely similar aircraft. There was even an element of fashion with early monoplanes being replaced by bi- and tri-planes until the final re-emergence of the monoplane in the 1930s.

One particular aspect of this empirical approach to design is interesting: the merits of thin versus thick aerofoil sections. All early aircraft used very thin wings; this was partly intuitive because it seemed obvious that thick wings would produce more drag. The intuition was backed up by the inadequate experimental capability of the period because the effect of scale on wind tunnel results was not well understood (despite the effect being known and published in 1883 by Osborne Reynolds whose name is now used for the dimensionless number that characterizes the effect). At the low Reynolds numbers possible in early wind tunnels, thin wings were indeed superior to thick ones; a result which does not hold at the flight speeds of real aircraft of the period.

Just as this explosion of practical aviation success was taking place, advances in theoretical aerodynamics suggested that perhaps thin wings weren't so obviously correct after all.   The work of Ludwig Prandtl on lifting line theory, itself built on foundations laid by Frederick Lanchester, pointed to the superiority of the thick aerofoil sections.   Of all the gifted aeronautical engineers of the period only Dutchman Anthony Fokker took notice and incorporated a radically thicker wing section firstly into his Fokker Triplane and later, more significantly, into the DVII biplane. The result was an aircraft which radically outperformed the opposition and, produced in sufficient numbers, might have changed the course of the war. Significantly the terms of the 1918 armistice specified only one German aircraft type to be handed over to the allies: the Fokker DVII.

From that time onwards the aeronautical engineering industry has been characterized by the way that practical experience and theoretical, mathematical study have been made to work together. The magic of early aviation has been replaced by the logic of the current industry.

7.2   Correctness by Construction

So magic is not enough. It is attractive because it appears to make our lives simpler and offers us an easy way to achieve our goals. Unfortunately it is an illusion; the real enemy is complexity and the complexity remains even if it has been concealed by magic. Of course, mindful of Professor Hoare, we should start by trying to minimise it rather than concealing it.   To use another aeronautical engineering quote (usually attributed to Bill Stout, designer of the Ford Tri-Motor), the secret of good design is to: "*simplicate, and add lightness*". The only way of dealing with the unavoidable complexity that remains is by reasoning about it.

An engineering, correctness by construction approach emphasizes the need to reason about the system and the software in it at all stages of development.   The semantic gaps between each stage in the development process are kept small so that we can show that each stage preserves the required properties from the one before. We are not aiming to meet any particular development standard but to produce a system which can be shown to be acceptable by logical reasoning; such a system can be certified to any reasonable standard. We may still have to do extensive testing, indeed standards may demand it, but we enter that test process with a system we expect to be correct, to demonstrate its correctness rather than to seek an expected crop of bugs. Structural engineers often proof-load structures but they are doing so not "to find out if it is strong enough" but to demonstrate that their stress calculations and design have been done correctly.

There is compelling evidence that this kind of reason-based, correctness by construction approach can both deliver a better product *and* reduce costs. The same study that showed the high proportion of time spent in integration and verification [7], also concluded that safety critical software cost no more than non-critical software. Their explanation is that critical systems are developed in a more rigorous manner with greater emphasis on getting things right during the early lifecycle stages. Non critical code is developed more informally and hits a bigger integration bottleneck later on. Why, as engineers, should we be surprised by the conclusion that doing things rationally and carefully is better and cheaper than doing them thoughtlessly?

8   Some Logical Successes

Two examples of the superiority of logic over magic follow. Both are SPARK[2] [12, 13, 14] based, not because SPARK can claim to be the world's only logic, but because it is the logic I am most familiar with. There are many similar success stories for which space cannot be found in this paper. Please note that the examples are not intended to suggest that SPARK itself is just a superior magic. SPARK was a *necessary* part of both these successful projects but it was certainly not *sufficient* to ensure success. Neither did SPARK make complexity and difficulty magically disappear; however, it did permit sufficiently skilled engineers to reason about and deal with that complexity.

8.1   The Lockheed C130J

The Lockheed C130J or Hercules II airlifter was a major updating of one of the world's most long-lived and successful aircraft. The work was done at the Lockheed company's own risk. Much of the planned improvement to the aircraft was to come from the completely new avionics fit and the new software that lay at its heart. The project is particularly instructive because it has some unusual properties which provide some interesting comparisons:
- Software sub-systems developed by a variety of subcontractors using a variety of methods and languages.
- Civil certification to DO-178B.
- Military certification to UK Def-Stan 00-55 involving an extensive, retrospective IV&V activity.

For the main mission computer software Lockheed adopted a correctness by construction approach well documented in [15, 16, 17]. The approach was based on:
- Semi-formal specifications using CoRE and Parnas tables.
- "Thin-slice" prototyping of high-risk areas.
- A template-driven approach to the production of similar and repetitive code portions.
- Coding in the unambiguous language SPARK with static analysis (but not code proof) carried out prior to formal certification testing; this combination was sufficient to eliminate large numbers of errors at the coding stage; before any formal review or testing began.

This logical approach brought Lockheed significant dividends. Perhaps their most striking observation was in the reduced cost of the formal testing required for DO-178B Level A certification: *"Very few errors have been found in the software during even the most rigorous levels of FAA testing, which is being successfully conducted for less than a fifth of the normal cost in industry"*. At a later presentation [18]

---

[2] Note: the SPARK programming language is not sponsored by or affiliated with SPARC International Inc. and is not based on SPARC™ architecture.

Lockheed were even more precise on the benefits claimed for their development approach:
- Code quality improved by a factor of 10 over industry norms for DO 178B Level A software.
- Productivity improved by a factor of 4 over previous comparable programs.
- Development costs *half* of that typical for *non safety-critical* code.
- With re-use and process maturity, a *further* productivity improvement of 4 on the C27J airlifter program.

These claims are impressive but they are justified by the results of the UK MoD's own retrospective IV&V programme which was carried out by Aerosystems International at Yeovil in the UK. The results of this study have been widely disseminated at briefings to programme participants and the MoD. It should be remembered that the code examined by Aerosystems had already been cleared to DO-178B Level A standards which should indicate that it was suitable for safety-critical flight purposes. Key conclusions of this study were:
- Significant, potentially safety-critical, errors were found by static analysis in code developed to DO-178B Level A.
- Properties of the SPARK code (including proof of exception freedom) could readily be proved against Lockheed's semi-formal specification; this proof was shown to be cheaper than weaker forms of semantic analysis performed on non-SPARK code.
- SPARK code was found to have only 10% of the residual errors of full Ada and Ada was found to have only 10% of the residual errors of code written in C. This is an interesting counter to those who maintain that choice of programming language does not matter and that critical code can be written correctly in any language: the statement is probably true in principle but clearly not commonly achieved in practice.
- No statistically significant difference in residual error rate could be found between DO-178B Level A and Level B code which raises interesting questions on the efficacy of the MC/DC test coverage criterion.

As well as being an outstanding technical achievement, perhaps this project also provides an answer to another prevalent problem: the recruitment and retention of staff with suitable skills. With productivity and quality gains of this magnitude perhaps the answer is paying the right kind of engineers enough to make logic more attractive than magic.

8.2   SHOLIS

A full description of SHOLIS[3] can be found in [19]. The system, with software produced by Praxis Critical Systems, was the first to meet all the principal requirements of UK Def Stan 00-55, in particular the requirements for a formal specification and code proof against that specification. The striking finding from this project was the tremendous efficiency gained by logical reasoning at an early stage in

---

[3] Ship Helicopter Operating Limits Information System

the development lifecycle. For example, the most cost-effective technique for error detection and elimination, by a considerable margin, was proof of properties of the formal, Z, specification. Two factors produced this strong gearing: the power of proof when applied to rigorous, formal descriptions; and the low cost of error correction since each corrected specification error resulted in the avoidance of wasteful re-work at some later development stage. This is the exact opposite of the vicious circle of late error detection coupled with expensive correction described earlier.

More surprisingly, code proof appeared to be substantially more effective than unit test in locating errors at the source code level. In fact unit test appears to be relatively ineffective, adding weight to the view that it is system integration that is the real challenge. The result is so convincing that Praxis has already chosen to reduce the effort allocated to unit test on subsequent SPARK projects where the relevant standard allows this flexibility. Another significant bonus from using an unambiguous programming language with suitable tool support was the feasibility of *proving* the entire SHOLIS software to be free from run-time exceptions.

The SHOLIS project shows the clear benefits of taking a disciplined, engineering approach to all lifecycle stages.

9   Conclusion

There is compelling evidence that, in its attempts to seize anything that promises to make life easier, the software industry is making its life harder. Many contemporary magics are just that: they are *not* "sufficiently advanced technology" appearing to be magic, they have no logical or mathematical underpinnings at all. The use of such magics is foolish in general but it is potentially catastrophic to adopt such technologies for high-integrity systems. Here we cannot tolerate concealed complexity which might emerge at some unexpected and inconvenient time in the future. Having reduced it to a minimum, we must confront and reason about the complexity that remains, as other engineering disciplines have done, using mathematics and clever people. For example, the mathematics of data and information flow have been well-documented since 1985 [20] yet industry practice still regards such analysis as best being achieved by manual methods, instrumented dynamic testing [21] and code walkthroughs.

Where development processes have been created which allow software to be reasoned about *throughout all phases of development*, as in the C130J and SHOLIS examples, striking quality and economic benefits accrue. To abandon such benefits for soft, non-technical reasons (such as mistakenly equating a facility with a particular tool or programming language with engineering skill or employing the fashionable in place of the appropriate because staff "want it on their CVs") is a self-defeating strategy that ensures that the bad will drive out the good.

In short: we must decide we want to be engineers not blacksmiths.

References

1. Dijkstra, Edsger: *Go To Statement Considered Harmful*. CACM Vol 11. No. 3 March 1968, pp 147-148.
2. RTCA-EUROCAE: *Software Considerations in Airborne Systems and Equipment Certification*. DO-178B/ED-12B. 1992.
3. Ives, Blake and Earl Michael: *Mondex International: Reengineering Money*. London Business School Case Study 97/2. See http://isds.bus.lsu.edu/cases/mondex/mondex.html
4. Littlewood, Bev; and Strigini, Lorenzo: Validation of Ultrahigh Dependability for Software-Based Systems. *CACM 36(11)*: 69-80 (1993)
5. Butler, Ricky W.; and Finelli, George B.: The Infeasibility of Quantifying the Reliability of Life-Critical Real-Time Software. *IEEE Transactions on Software Engineering*, vol. 19, no. 1, Jan. 1993, pp 3-12.
6. Littlewood, B: *Limits to evaluation of software dependability*. In Software Reliability and Metrics (Procedings of Seventh Annual CSR Conference, Garmisch-Partenkirchen). N. Fenton and B. Littlewood. Eds. Elsevier, London, pp. 81-110.
7. Private communication arising from a productivity study at a major aerospace company.
8. Carré, Bernard: *Reliable Programming in Standard Languages*. In High-integrity Software. RSRE Malvern, Chris Sennett (Ed). ISBN 0-273-03158-9, 1989.
9. Amey, Peter: *The INFORMED Design Method for SPARK*. Praxis Critical Systems 1999.
10. Barnes, John: *The SPARK Way to Correctness is Via Abstraction*. ACM SIGAda 2000
11. Professor C.A.R. Hoare, The 1980 Turing award lecture. *The Emperor's Old Clothes*. CACM Vol. 24. No.2 February 1981. pp 75-83
12. Finnie, Gavin et al: *SPARK - The SPADE Ada Kernel*. Edition 3.3, 1997, Praxis Critical Systems
13. Finnie, Gavin et al: *SPARK 95 - The SPADE Ada 95 Kernel*. 1999, Praxis Critical Systems
14. Barnes, John: *High Integrity Ada - the SPARK Approach*. Addison Wesley Longman, ISBN 0-201-17517-7.
15. Sutton, James and Carré, Bernard: *Ada, the Cheapest Way to Build a Line of Business"*. 1994
16. Sutton, James and Carré, Bernard: *Achieving High Integrity at Low Cost: A Constructive Approach*. 1995
17. Croxford, Martin and Sutton, James: *Breaking through the V&V Bottleneck*. Lecture Notes in Computer Science Volume 1031, 1996.
18. Sutton, James: *Cost-Effective Approaches to Satisfy Safety-critical Regulatory Requirements*. Workshop Session, SIGAda 2000.
19. King, Hammond, Chapman and Pryor: *Is Proof More Cost-Effective than Testing?*. IEEE Transaction on Software Engineering, Vol. 26, No. 8, August 2000, pp 675-686.
20. Bergeretti and Carré: *Information-flow and data-flow analysis of while-programs*. ACM Transactions on Programming Languages and Systems 1985.
21. Santhanam, Viswa; Wright, Peggy A.; Decker-Lindsey, Barbara: *Dataflow Coverage in the Boeing 777 Primary Flight Control Software*. Boeing 1995

Can Java™ Meet Its Real-Time Deadlines?

Benjamin Brosgol[1] and Brian Dobbing[2]

[1] Ada Core Technologies, Inc, 79 Tobey Road, Belmont,
MA 02478 United States of America
brosgol@gnat.com
[2] Aonix Europe Ltd, Partridge House, Newtown Road,
Henley-on-Thames, Oxon RG9 1EN, United Kingdom
brian@aonix.co.uk

Abstract. Ada has been-there, done-that, as regards meeting real-time programming requirements. The Ada95 revision addressed almost all the concerns that had plagued Ada83's real-time usability. But Java is currently flavor of the month, although its existing real-time features are totally inadequate. Two independent recent efforts have defined extensions to the Java platform that intend to satisfy real-time requirements. This paper summarizes the major features of these efforts, compares them to each other and to Ada 95's Real-Time Annex, and argues that they may serve to complement rather than compete with Ada in the real-time domain.

1 Introduction

Over the past several years the computing community has been coming to grips with the Java platform, a technology triad comprising a relatively simple Object-Oriented Language, an extensive and continually growing set of class libraries, and a virtual machine architecture and class file format that provide portability at the binary level. Java was first introduced as a technology that could be safely exploited on "client" machines on the Internet, with various levels of protection against malicious or mischievous applets. However, interest in Java's promise of "write once, run anywhere" has expanded the platform's application domain dramatically.

One area that has been attracting attention is real-time systems. On the one hand, that should not be completely surprising. The research project at Sun Microsystems that spawned Java was attempting to design a technology for embedded systems in home appliances, and embedded systems typically have real-time constraints. Moreover, Java is more secure than C and simpler than C++, and it has found a receptive audience in users dissatisfied with these languages. And unlike C and C++, Java has a built-in model for concurrency (threads) with low-level "building blocks" for mutual exclusion and communication that seem to offer flexibility in the design of multi-threaded programs. Parts of the Java API address some real-time application areas (for example `javax.comm` for manipulating serial and parallel devices), and

A. Strohmeier and D. Craeynest (Eds.): Ada-Europe 2001, LNCS 2043, pp. 68-87, 2001.

V1.3 of the Java Software Development Kit has introduced a couple of utility classes for timed events. Java therefore may seem a viable candidate for real-time systems, especially to an organization that has adopted Java as an enterprise language.

However, even a casual inspection of Java reveals a number of obstacles that interfere with real-time programming. In this introductory section we will summarize these issues and then briefly describe how they have been addressed.

1.1 Challenges

Thread Model. Although Java semantics are consistently deterministic for the sequential parts of the language (e.g. the order of expression evaluation is defined as left-to-right, references to uninitialized variables are prevented) they are largely implementation-dependent for thread scheduling. The Java Language Specification explicitly states ([1] Section 17.12):

"... threads with higher priority are generally executed in preference to threads with lower priority. Such preference is not, however, a guarantee that the highest priority thread will always be running, and thread priorities cannot be used to reliably implement mutual exclusion."

This flexibility makes it impossible to ensure that real-time threads will meet their deadlines. The implementation may or may not use priority as the criterion for choosing a thread to make ready when a lock is released. Even if it did, unbounded priority inversions could still occur since there is no requirement for the implementation to provide priority inversion avoidance policies such as priority inheritance or priority ceiling emulation. There is also no guarantee that priority is used for selecting which thread is awakened by a notify(), or which thread awakened by a notifyAll() is selected to run.

Other facets of the thread model also interfere with real-time requirements. The priority range (1 through 10) is too narrow, and the relative sleep() method is not sufficient: the standard idiom for simulating periodicity with this method can lead to a missed deadline if the thread is preempted after computing the relative delay but before being suspended.

A more detailed analysis of Java threads, with a comparison to Ada's tasking model, may be found in [2].

Memory Management. Despite its C-like syntax, Java belongs semantically to a family of Object Oriented languages including Simula, Smalltalk, and Eiffel: languages that provide no mechanism for programmers to reclaim storage but which instead are implemented with automatic memory reclamation ("Garbage Collection" or "GC"). The idea of garbage collection in a real-time program may sound like a contradiction in terms, but there have been a number of incremental and concurrent collectors that attempt to address the predictability problems of a classical mark-and-sweep strategy [3]. Nevertheless, efficient real-time garbage collection is still more a research topic than a mainstream technology. This is a particular issue for Java, since all objects (including arrays) go on the heap.

Dynamic Semantics. One of the main attractions of Java is its run-time flexibility. For example, classes are loaded dynamically, intraspection allows the run-time interrogation of a class's properties, and cutting-edge compiler technology allows optimized code to be generated during program execution. Unfortunately, all of these capabilities conflict with the traditional static environment ("compile, download, run") for real-time programs. Implementing Java with static linking is possible but difficult, and necessitates restrictions on the use of certain language features.

Asynchrony. A real-time program typically needs to respond to asynchronous events generated by either hardware or software, and sometimes needs to undergo asynchronous transfer of control ("ATC"), for example to time out if an operation is taking too long. The Java Beans and AWT event registration and listener model is a reasonable framework for asynchronous events but omits semantic details critical to real-time programs, such as the scheduling of event handlers. The `interrupt` method requires polling and thus is not an ATC mechanism. The methods related to ATC have either been deprecated (`stop`, `suspend`, `resume`) or are discouraged because of their proneness to error (`destroy`). Thus Java is rather weak in the area of asynchrony.

Object-Oriented Programming. OOP support is one of Java's most highly touted strengths, but the real-time community has traditionally been very conservative in its programming style and still views OOP with some skepticism. The dynamic nature of OOP (for example the dynamic binding of instance methods) interferes with static analyzability, and Garbage Collection introduces unpredictability or high latency.

Application Program Interface. Class libraries that are to be used in real-time programs need to be implemented specially in order to ensure that their execution time be predictable. This is partly a programming issue (e.g. choice of algorithms and data structures) and partly a JVM implementation issue (GC strategy).

Missing Functionality. With the goal of language simplicity, the Java designers intentionally omitted a number of features that might be useful in a real-time program, such as general unsigned integral types, strongly-typed scalars, and enumeration types. Other omissions impinge on programming in general, such as generic templates and operator symbol overloading. The language and API also lack system programming facilities for accessing the underlying hardware (such as "peek" and "poke" to access numeric data at physical addresses).

Performance. Although "real time" does not mean "real fast", run-time performance cannot be ignored. Java has several challenges in this area. The key to "write once, run anywhere" is the JVM and the binary portability of class files. But a software interpreter introduces overhead, and hardware implementations are not mainstream technology. GC and the absence of stack-resident objects have an obvious performance impact, and there is also the problem that array initialization is performed with executable code, versus having a ROMable image in the class file.

1.2   The NIST Requirements and the Two Real-Time Java Efforts

The problems with Java as a real-time technology are steep but not insurmountable. Given the potential market and the fascinating technical issues it is not surprising that real-time Java has been a topic of active investigation. Probably the earliest work was by Kelvin Nilsen in late 1995 and early 1996 [4]. Subsequently Lisa Carnahan from the National Institute for Standards and Technology in the U.S. (NIST) took the lead in organizing a series of workshops to identify the issues and to develop consensus-based requirements for real-time extensions to the Java platform. The culmination of this group's efforts, which ultimately included participation by 38 different entities, was a document titled "Requirements for Real-Time Extensions for the Java Platform", published in September 1999 [5].

The NIST-sponsored effort focused on defining the *requirements* for real-time Java extensions. That group made a conscious choice not to develop a *specification* for such extensions.

Two independent groups have undertaken to define such specifications. One is the Real-Time Java Working Group under Kelvin Nilsen from Newmonics; this group was formed in November 1998 and is under the auspices of a set of companies and individuals known as the J-Consortium. The other effort is from the Real-Time for Java Expert Group ("RTJEG") under Greg Bollella (then with IBM, now at Sun Microsystems). The RTJEG was established under the terms of Sun's Java Community Process; the product of this effort is a specification, a reference implementation, and a conformance test suite. As of early 2001, the first draft of the specification has been published [6], while the reference implementation and the test suite formulation are in progress.

The split into two efforts versus a single undertaking was motivated by business considerations rather than technical factors. Participation in the RTJEG required signing an agreement with Sun Microsystems that some organizations found problematic. However, the two efforts ended up taking technical approaches that are more complementary than duplicative. The J-Consortium has focused on defining real-time "core" facilities external to a JVM, similar to services provided by a traditional RTOS, whereas the RTJEG has defined an API that needs to be supported within a JVM implementation.

2   Real-Time Core Specification

2.1   Summary

In order to establish a foundation upon which its Real-Time Core Extensions to the Java platform specification [7] would be built, the J Consortium's Real-Time Java Working Group (RTJWG) established a number of clarifying principles to augment the full list of key requirements identified in the NIST requirements document for real-time extensions to Java [5]. These working principles follow. For purposes of this discussion, the term "Baseline Java" refers to the 1.1 version of the Java language, as it has been defined by Sun Microsystems, Inc, and "Core Java" refers to an implementation of the Real-Time Core Specification.

- The Core Java execution environment shall exist in two forms: the *dynamic* one that is integrated with a Java virtual machine and supports dynamic loading and unloading of Core classes, and the *static* one that is stand-alone and does not supporting dynamic class loading.
- The Core Java dynamic execution environment shall support limited cooperation with Baseline Java programs running on the same Java virtual machine, with the integration designed so that neither environment needs to degrade the performance of the other.
- The Core Java specification shall define distinct class hierarchies from those defined by Baseline Java.
- The Core Java specification shall enable the creation of *profiles* which expand or subtract from the capabilities of the Core Java foundation.
- The Core Java system shall support limited cooperation with programs written according to the specifications of these *profiles*, with the integration designed so that neither environment needs to degrade the performance of the other.
- The semantics of the Core Java specification shall be sufficiently simple that interrupt handling latencies and context switching overheads for Core Java programs can match the overheads in current C and C++ RTOS-based programs.
- The Core Java specification shall enable implementations that offer throughputs comparable to those offered by current optimizing C++ compilers, except for semantic differences required, for example, to check array subscripts.
- Core Java programs need not incur the run-time overhead of coordinating with a garbage collector.
- Baseline Java components and components written according to the specifications of profiles, shall be able to read and write the data fields of objects that reside in the Core Java *object space*.
- Security mechanisms shall prevent Baseline Java and other external profile components from compromising the reliability of Core Java components.
- Core Java programs shall be runnable on a wide variety of different operating systems, with different underlying CPUs, and integrated with different supporting Baseline Java virtual machines. There shall be a standard way for Baseline Java components to load and execute Core Java components.
- The Core Java specification shall support the ability to perform memory management of dynamic objects under programmer control.
- The Core Java specification shall support a deterministic concurrency and synchronization model comparable to current Real-Time Operating Systems.
- The Core Java specification shall be designed to support a small footprint, requiring no more than 100K bytes for a typical static execution environment.
- All Core Java classes shall be fully resolved and initialized at the point of load.

In summary, the Core Java execution environment either:

a)   is a plug-in module that can augment any Baseline Java virtual machine. This allows users of the Core Java execution environment to leverage the large technology investment in current virtual machine implementations, including byte-code verifiers, garbage collectors, JustInTime compilers, and dynamic loaders, or;

b)   can be configured to run without a Baseline Java virtual machine. This allows users of the Core Java execution environment to develop high performance kernels deployed in very small memory footprints.

2.2 Concurrency and Synchronization

Scheduling and Priorities. The Core Java specification supports a large range of priorities. Each implementation is required to support a minimum of 128 distinct values, with the highest N being used as interrupt priorities, where N is implementation-defined. In addition, the Core Java semantics require preemptive priority-based scheduling as defined by the *FIFO_Within_Priorities* policy. Alternative scheduling policies may be specified via profiles.

The Core task class hierarchy is rooted at `CoreTask`. A `CoreTask` object must be explicitly started via the `start()` method. There are two specialized extensions of `CoreTask`:

1. The `SporadicTask` class defines tasks that are readied by the occurrence of an *event* that is triggered either periodically or via an explicit call to its `fire` method.
2. The `InterruptTask` class defines tasks that are readied by the occurrence of an *interrupt* event, making them analogous to interrupt service routines.

Task Synchronization Primitives. Task synchronization is provided in the Core Java specification via a number of different features, a first group of which supports priority inversion avoidance and a second group of which does not.

In the first group, Baseline Java-style usage of `synchronized` code is supported and defines transitive priority inheritance to limit the effects of priority inversion. In addition, traditional POSIX-style *mutexes* are supported, and these also define transitive priority inheritance to be applied when there is contention for the lock. Finally there is support for Ada-style *protected objects* that are locked using priority ceiling protocol (via immediate ceiling locking as in Ada95), and that prohibit execution of suspending operations, e.g. `wait()`. An extension of the priority ceiling protocol interface, known as the *Atomic* interface, is defined for `InterruptTask work()` methods. This interface implies that all the code must be statically execution-time-analyzable. The intent is to be able to guarantee the static worst case execution time bounds on interrupt handler execution.

In the second group, POSIX-style counting and signaling semaphores are supported. There is no concept of a single owner of a semaphore and hence there is no priority inheritance on contention (and unbounded priority inversion may result). A counting semaphore may have *count* concurrent owners. A signaling semaphore is similar to Ada's *suspension object* except that multiple tasks can be waiting for the signal. A signal that occurs when there are no waiting tasks is a no-op.

2.3 Memory Management

Core Object Space. The Core Java requirements include the provision of security measures to ensure that the Baseline Java domain cannot compromise the integrity of Core objects in the dynamic Core execution environment. This is realized in the specification by segregating Core objects into their own object space that is quite separate from the Baseline Java heap.

However another requirement of the dynamic Core Java execution environment is to provide limited and controlled communication with the Baseline Java domain. This is achieved via the CoreRegistry class that includes a publish() method to publish the names of externally-visible Core objects. A lookup() method is also provided for the Baseline Java domain to obtain a reference to the published Core object. However the Baseline Java domain is only permitted to call special *core-baseline* methods that are explicitly identified within the published object, and so access to the Core object space is totally defined and controlled by these methods.

Garbage Collection. A key requirement of the Core Java specification is that the system need not incur the overhead of traditional automatic garbage collection ("GC"). This is intended to provide the necessary performance and predictability, avoiding overheads such as read/write barriers, object relocation due to compaction, stack/object scanning and object description tables, as well as avoiding the determinism problems associated with executing the garbage collector thread.

Core Object Allocation / Deallocation. A garbage collector is an essential component of a Baseline Java VM due to Java's object lifetime model, which does not provide an explicit deallocation operation, nor do the semantics provide known points for an implementation to perform guaranteed implicit deallocation. Hence the Core specification defines an alternative memory allocation and reclamation model under programmer control. This is achieved via the following:

- An object that is declared locally within a method can be explicitly identified as *stackable*, which asserts that the object lifetime is no greater than that of the enclosing method, as is the case for Ada's local variables. Restrictions are defined for stackable objects to prevent dangling references. Thus an implementation may allocate stackable objects on the runtime method stack as for Ada local variables. Stackable objects are not permitted to be published to the Baseline Java domain.

- A class called AllocationContext is defined in the Core specification that is somewhat analogous to Ada's Root_Storage_Pool type in that it provides a facility for declaring heap storage (including at a specific memory address) and the means to control it programmatically. Each task automatically allocates an allocation context upon creation, and this storage area is used by default for allocation of its non-stackable objects. Allocation contexts can also be used for collections of objects belonging to the same class, and for implementing *scoped* memory management, such as a mark / release capability. However it should be noted that use of the explicit release() method can result in dangling references, similar to Ada's Unchecked_Deallocation.

2.4 Asynchrony

Asynchronous interaction between Core tasks is achieved in the Core Java specification via *events*. There is also the abort() method to kill a task. Two event models are defined: the firing and handling of asynchronous events; and asynchronous transfer of control.

Asynchronous Events. Three kinds of asynchronous event are defined by the Core Java specification:

1. PeriodicEvent is defined to support periodic tasks. The event fires at the start of each period which causes the associated periodic event handler task to become ready to execute its work() method.
2. SporadicEvent is defined to support sporadic tasks that are triggered by software. The event is explicitly fired by a task which causes the associated sporadic event handler task to become ready to execute its work() method.
3. InterruptEvent is defined to support interrupt handling. The event can be explicitly fired by a task (to achieve a software interrupt) or implicitly fired by a hardware interrupt. This causes the associated interrupt event handler task to become ready to execute its work() method, which must implement the Atomic interface, as described in section 2.2.

Asynchronous Transfer of Control. This is supported in the Core Java specification by building upon the asynchronous event model. A special ATCEvent class is defined for the event itself. Each task construction may specify a handler for ATCEvent that is invoked whenever another task calls the signalAsync() method, unless the task is currently in an abort-deferred region. If the handler returns normally, the ATCEvent is handled without causing a transfer of control, i.e. the task resumes at the point at which it was interrupted. This is useful in situations such as ignoring a missed soft deadline.

Otherwise, if the handler returns by raising a special ScopedException object and the task is in an ATC-enabled execution scope, then the exception causes the transfer of control in the task. An ATC-enabled scope is created by constructing a ScopedException object and having a try-catch clause that includes a handler for that exception class.

The Core Java specification also defines certain abort-deferred regions that defer the transfer of control action, in particular Atomic scopes and finally clauses. Note however that once an ATC-enabled region has been entered, all method calls are susceptible to ATC other than the abort-deferred regions mentioned above (as in Ada95). Since the Core Java specification rules prevent a Core program from making direct method calls to the Baseline Java domain, an ATC cannot occur at any point within "legacy" Baseline Java code that was not designed to expect that eventuality.

The ATC construct can be used for several common idioms, such as preventing time budget overrun, and for mode change. Special rules apply to the handlers for ScopedException to ensure that nested ATC scopes can be created without the danger of an outer ATC exception being caught by an inner ATC catch clause.

2.5 Time

The Core Java specification defines a `Time` class that includes methods to construct times in all units from nanoseconds through to days. These are used to construct periodic events to trigger cyclic tasks or to timeout overrunning task execution.

In addition, the relative delay `sleep()` method and the absolute delay `sleepUntil()` method provide a programmatic means of coding periodic activity. In both cases, the time quantum can be specified to the nanosecond level.

There is also the method `tickDuration()` to return the length of a clock tick.

2.6 Other Features

The Core Java specification also includes a comprehensive low-level I/O interface for access to I/O ports, and a class `Unsigned` for unsigned operations.

2.7 Profiles of the Core Specification

Several Core profiles are under development. One of interest to the Ada community is the High Integrity Profile [8] which is designed to meet the requirements of:

- Safety Critical / High Integrity, for which all the software must undergo thorough analysis and testing, and be guaranteed not to be corruptible by less trusted code.
- High Reliability / Fault Tolerance, for which the code must be resilient enough to detect faults and to recover with minimal disturbance to the overall system.
- Hard Real-Time, for which the timing of code execution must be deterministic to ensure that deadlines are met.
- Embedded, for which a small footprint and fast execution are required.

These requirements are very similar to those that steered the definition of the Ravenscar Profile [9] and hence it is not surprizing that the high integrity profile provides similar functionality:

- The dynamic Core Java execution environment is not supported (i.e. no direct interaction with a JVM);
- All tasks are constructed during program startup;
- `sleepUntil()` is supported, but `sleep()` is not;
- Periodic, sporadic and interrupt event handler tasks are supported;
- Signaling semaphores are supported, but counting semaphores and mutexes are not
- Protected objects are supported;
- All synchronized code is locked using priority ceiling emulation;
- The scheduling policy is `FIFO_Within_Priorities`;
- Asynchronous abort is not supported;
- Asynchronous dynamic priority change is not supported;
- Asynchronous suspension is not supported;
- Asynchronous transfer of control is not supported.

This profile allows the construction of a very small, fast, deterministic runtime system that could ultimately be a candidate even for formal certification.

3 RT Java Expert Group Specification

3.1 Summary

Before setting out on the design of the real-time specification for Java ("RTSJ"), the RTJEG established the following guiding principles:

- *Applicability to particular Java environments.* Usage is not to be restricted to particular versions of the Java Software Development Kit.
- *Backward compatibility.* Existing Java code can run on any RTSJ implementation.
- *"Write Once, Run Anywhere".* This is an important goal but difficult to achieve for real-time systems, e.g. variation in critical timing on different platforms.
- *Current practice versus advanced features.* The RTSJ addresses current real-time practice and includes extensibility hooks to allow exploitation of new technologies.
- *Predictable execution.* This is the highest priority goal; performance or throughput may need to be compromised in order to achieve it.
- *No syntactic extension.* The RTSJ does not define new keywords or new syntax.
- *Allow variation in implementation decisions.* The RTSJ recognizes that different implementations will make different decisions (for example a tradeoff between performance and simplicity) and thus does not require specific algorithms.

The resulting specification consists of the `javax.realtime` package, an API whose implementation requires specialized support in the JVM. In summary, the design provides real-time functionality in several areas:

- *Thread scheduling and dispatching.* The RTSJ introduces the concept of a *real-time thread* and defines both a traditional priority-based dispatching mechanism and an extensible framework for implementation-defined (and also user-defined) scheduling policies. The RTSJ defines the concept of a *no-heap real-time thread* which is not allowed to reference the heap; this restriction means that such a thread can safely preempt the Garbage Collector.
- *Memory management.* The RTSJ provides a general concept of a *memory area* that may be used either explicitly or implicitly for object allocations. Examples of memory areas are the (garbage-collected) heap, *immortal* memory whose objects persist for the duration of an application's execution, and *scoped* memory that is used for object allocations during the execution of a dynamically determined "scope", and which is automatically emptied at the end of the scope.
- *Synchronization and resource sharing.* The RTSJ requires the implementation to supply one or more mechanisms to avoid unbounded priority inversion, and it defines two monitor control policies to meet this requirement: priority inheritance and priority ceiling emulation. The specification also defines several "wait free queues" to allow a no-heap real-time thread and a Baseline Java thread to safely synchronize on shared objects.
- *Asynchrony.* The RTSJ defines a general event model based on the framework found in the AWT and Java Beans. An event can be generated from software or from an interrupt handler. Event handlers behave like threads and are schedulable entities. The design is intended to be scalable to very large numbers of events and

event handlers (tens of thousands), although only a small number of handlers are expected to be active simultaneously. The RTSJ also defines a mechanism for asynchronous transfer of control ("ATC"), supporting common idioms such as timeout and thread termination. The affected code needs to explicitly permit ATC; thus code that is not written to be asynchronously interruptible will work correctly.

• *Physical and "raw" memory access.* The RTSJ provides mechanisms for specialized and low-level memory access. Physical memory is a memory area with special hardware characteristics (for example flash memory) and can contain arbitrary objects. Raw memory allows "peek" and "poke" of integral and floating-point variables at offsets from a given base address.

3.2 Concurrency and Synchronization

The basis of the RTSJ's approach to concurrency is the class `RealtimeThread`, a subclass of `Thread`.

Scheduling and Priorities. The RTSJ requires a base scheduler that is fixed-priority preemptive with at least 28 distinct priority levels, above the 10 Baseline Java levels. An implementation must map the 28 real-time priorities to distinct values, but the 10 non-real-time levels are not necessarily distinct.

Constructors for the `RealtimeThread` class allow the programmer to supply scheduling parameters, release parameters, memory parameters, a memory area, and processing group parameters. The scheduling parameters characterize the thread's execution eligibility (for example, its priority). A real-time thread can have a priority in either the real-time range or the Baseline Java range.

The release parameters identify the real-time thread's execution requirements (e.g. computation time, deadline) and properties (whether it is periodic, aperiodic or sporadic). Memory parameters identify the maximum memory consumption allowed and an upper bound on the heap allocation rate (used for Garbage Collector pacing). Processing group parameters allow modeling a collection of aperiodic threads with bounded response time requirements.

The programmer may supply overrun handlers to respond to two kinds of abnormality: overrunning the budgeted cost, and missing a deadline.

One of the RTSJ's distinguishing capabilities is a general-purpose extensible scheduling framework. An instance of the `Scheduler` class manages the execution of schedulable entities and may implement a feasibility analysis algorithm. Through method calls a real-time thread can be added to, or removed from, the scheduler's feasibility analysis; the release parameters are used in this analysis. The scheduler's `isFeasible()` method returns `true` if the existing schedulable entities are schedulable (i.e., will always meet their deadlines) and `false` otherwise.

The priority-based scheduler is required to be the default scheduler at system startup, but the programmer can modify this at run time (for example setting an Earliest-Deadline First scheduler, if one is supplied by the implementation). The priority-based scheduler implements *FIFO_Within_Priorities* policy and manages Baseline

Java threads as well as real-time threads. The priority-based scheduler is said to be fixed-priority since it is not allowed to modify thread priorities implicitly except for priority inversion avoidance; (schemes such as "priority aging" are not allowed).

Synchronization. An unbounded priority inversion in a thread synchronizing on a locked object can lead to missed deadlines. The RTSJ requires the implementation to supply one or more monitor control policies to avoid this problem. By default the policy is priority inheritance, but the RTSJ also defines a priority ceiling emulation policy. Each policy can be selected either globally or per-object and the choice can be modified at run time. An implementation can supply a specialized form of priority ceiling emulation that prohibits a thread from blocking while holding a lock, thus avoiding the need for mutexes and queues in the implementation.

The price for a consistent heap is extra latency, since it is possible for the Garbage Collector to inherit a priority in the no-heap real-time thread range. The RTSJ allows the programmer to avoid this latency through wait-free queues; Baseline threads and no-heap real-time threads can use such queues to communicate without blocking.

3.3 Memory Management

Perhaps the most difficult issue for the RTSJ was the question of how to cope with garbage collection. Requiring specific GC performance or placing constraints on GC-induced thread latency would have violated several guiding principles. Instead the opposite approach was taken: the RTSJ makes no assumptions about the GC algorithm; indeed in some environments there might not even be a garbage collector.

The key concept is the notion of a *memory area*, a region in which objects are allocated. The garbage-collected heap is an example of a memory area. Another memory area is *immortal memory*: a region in which objects are not garbage collected or relocated and thus persist for the duration of the program's execution. More flexibility is obtained through *scoped memory areas*, which can be explicitly constructed by the programmer. Each scoped memory area contains objects that exist only for a fixed duration of program execution. The heap and immortal memory can be used by any thread; scoped memory can be used only by real-time threads.

Common to any memory area is an `enter()` method which takes a `Runnable` as a parameter. When `enter()` is invoked for a memory area, that area becomes active, and the `Runnable` object's `run()` method is invoked synchronously. The memory area is then used for all object allocations through "`new`" (including those in methods invoked from `run()` whether directly or indirectly) until either another memory area becomes active or the `enter()` method returns. When `enter()` returns, the previous active area again becomes active.

A memory area may be provided to a real-time thread constructor; it is then made active for that real-time thread's `run()` method when the thread is started.

Memory areas may also be used for "one shot" allocation, through factory methods that construct objects or arrays in the associated area.

Scoped memory may be viewed as a generalization of a method's stack frame. Indeed, early in the design the RTJEG considered providing a mechanism through which objects allocated in a method would be stored on the stack instead of the heap, with automatic reclamation at method exit instead of garbage collection. Standard class libraries could then be rewritten with the same external specifications (public members, method signatures and return type) but with an implementation that used the stack versus the heap for objects used only locally. There would be compile-time or runtime checks to prevent dangling references. However, the reason that a simple stack-based object scheme was eventually rejected is that a reference to a local object could not be safely returned to a caller. Thus the goal of using specially-implemented versions of existing APIs would not be achievable.

Instead the RTSJ has generalized the concept of storing local objects on the stack. A scoped memory area is used not just for one method invocation but for the "closure" of all methods invoked from a `Runnable`'s `run()` method. The objects within the memory area are not subject to relocation or collection, and an assignment of a scoped reference to another reference is checked (in general at run time) to prevent dangling references. Scopes may be nested. When the `enter()` method returns, the area is reset so that it contains no objects. A common idiom is a `while` or `for` loop that invokes `enter()` on a scoped memory area at each iteration. All objects allocated during the iteration are effectively flushed when `enter()` returns, so there is no storage leakage.

The RTSJ also provides several more specialized kinds of memory area. Support for physical memory (i.e. memory with special characteristics) is offered through *immortal physical memory* and *scoped physical memory*. This is useful for example when the programmer needs to allocate a set of objects in a fast-access cache. The *raw memory access* and *raw memory float access* memory areas offer low-level access ("peek" and "poke") to integral and floating-point data, respectively.

3.4 Asynchrony

The RTSJ supplies two mechanisms relevant to asynchronous communication: asynchronous event handling, and asynchronous transfer of control.

Asynchronous Event Handling. The RTSJ defines the concepts of an *asynchronous event* and an *asynchronous event handler*, and the relationship between the two.

An async event can be triggered either by a software thread or by a "happening" external to the JVM. The programmer can associate any number of async event handlers with an async event, and the same handler can be associated with any number of events. Async event handlers are schedulable entities and are constructed with the same set of parameters as a real-time thread; thus they can participate in feasibility analysis, etc. However, there is not necessarily a distinct thread associated with each handler. The programmer can use a bound async event handler if it is necessary to dedicate a unique thread to a handler.

When an async event is fired, all associated handlers are scheduled. A programmer-overridable method on the handler establishes the behavior. If the same event is fired multiple times, the handler's actions are sequentialized. In the interest of efficiency and simplicity, no data are passed automatically from the event to the handler. The programmer can define the logic necessary to buffer data, or to deal with overload situations where not all events need to be processed.

The async event model uses the same framework as event listeners in Java Beans and the AWT but generalizes and formalizes the handler semantics with thread-like behavior.

Asynchronous Transfer of Control. Asynchronous Transfer of Control ("ATC") is a mechanism whereby a triggering thread (possibly an async event handler) can cause a target thread to branch unconditionally, without any explicit action from the target thread. It is a controversial capability. The triggering thread does not know what state the target thread is in when the ATC is initiated while, on the other side, the target thread needs to be coded very carefully if it is susceptible to ATC. ATC also imposes a run-time cost even for programs that do not use the functionality. Nevertheless, there are situations in real-time programs where the alternative style (polling for a condition that can be asynchronously set) induces unwanted latency, and the user community identified several situations (timing out on an operation, or mode change) where ATC offers the appropriate semantic framework.

A rudimentary ATC mechanism was present in the initial version of the Java language: the `Thread` methods `stop()`, `destroy()`, `suspend()` and `resume()`. Unfortunately a conflict between the ATC semantics and program reliability led to these methods' deprecation (`stop()`, `suspend()`, `resume()`) or stylistic discouragement (`destroy()`). If a thread is `stopped` while it holds a lock, the synchronized code is exited and the lock is released, but the object may be in an inconsistent state. If a thread is `destroyed` while it holds a lock, the lock is not released, but then other threads attempting to acquire the lock will be deadlocked. If a thread is `suspended` while it holds a lock, and the resuming thread needs that lock, then again a deadlock will ensue.

The problem is that Baseline Java does not have the Ada concept of an "abort-deferred region". The RTSJ has introduced this concept, together with other semantic constraints, in the interest of providing ATC that is safe to use.

Several guiding principles underlie the ATC design:

- Susceptibility to ATC must be explicit in the affected code.
- Even if code allows ATC, in some sections ATC must be deferred - in particular, in synchronized code.
- An ATC does not return to the point where it was triggered (i.e. it is a "goto" rather than a subroutine call), since with resumptive semantics an arbitrary action could occur at arbitrary points.
- If ATC is modeled through exception handling, the design needs to ensure that the exception is not caught by an unintended handler (for example a method with a catch clause for `Throwable`)

- ATC needs to be expressive enough to capture several common idioms, including time-out, nested time-out (with correct disposition when an "outer" timer expires before an "inner" timer), mode change, and thread termination.

From the viewpoint of the target thread, ATC is modeled by exception handling. The class AsynchronouslyInterruptedException (abbreviated "AIE") extends InterruptedException from java.lang. An ATC is initiated in the target thread by a triggering thread causing an instance of AIE to be thrown. This is not done directly, since there is no guarantee that the target thread is executing in code prepared to catch the exception. In any event there is no syntax in Java for one thread to asynchronously throw an exception in another thread[1].

ATC only occurs in code that explicitly permits it. The permission is the presence of a "throws AIE" clause on a method or constructor. ATC is deferred in methods or constructors lacking such a clause, and is also deferred in synchronized code.

The Timed class (a subclass of AIE) is provided as a convenience to deal with time out; the firing of the AIE is done by an implementation-provided async event handler rather than an explicit user thread.

3.5 Time and Timers

The RTSJ provides several ways to specify high-resolution (nanosecond accuracy) time: as an *absolute* time, as a *relative* number of milliseconds and nanoseconds, and as a *rational* time (a frequency, i.e. a number of occurrences of an event per relative time). In a relative time 64 bits (a long) are used for the milliseconds, and 32 bits (an int) for the nanoseconds.

The rational time class is designed to simplify application logic where a periodic thread needs to run at a given frequency. The implementation, and not the programmer, needs to account for round-off error in computing the interval between release points.

The time classes provide relevant constructors, arithmetic and comparison methods, and utility operations. These classes are used in constructors for the various release parameters classes.

The RTSJ defines a default real-time clock which can be queried (for example to obtain the current time) and which is the basis for two kinds of timers: a one-shot timer, and a periodic timer. Timer objects are instances of async events; the programmer can register an async event handler with a timer to obtain the desired behavior when the event is fired. A handler for a periodic timer is similar to a real-time thread with periodic release parameters but is likely to be more efficient.

3.6 Other Features

The RTSJ provides a real-time system class analogous to java.lang.System, with "getter" and "setter" methods to access the real-time security manager and the maximum number of concurrent locks. It also supplies a binding to Posix signal handlers (required only if the underlying system supports Posix signals).

---

[1] The functionality is present in Thread.stop(), but this method is now deprecated.

4 Comparative Analysis

4.1 The Two RT Java Specifications

The main distinction between the specifications is the execution environment models.

The Core Java approach is to build a Core program as a distinct entity from a Java virtual machine (JVM). The intent is for the Core Java specification to be used to build small, high performance stand-alone programs similar to those in C and C++ today. These Core programs can communicate with a JVM in a controlled way.

The RTSJ approach is to define an API with real-time functionality that can be implemented by a specially constructed JVM. The intent is for the RTSJ specification to be used to build predictable real-time threads that execute in the same environment as non-real-time threads within one virtual machine.

It is interesting to conclude that a system could be composed of sub-systems that are implemented using both specifications. For example, a system may require a high-performance micro kernel implemented using Core Java, executing in conjunction with a JVM that is executing some predictable real-time threads, as well as using a wide range of standard APIs within background threads.

This distinction in the execution environment models is also reflected in the goals and semantics of the specifications, for example:

- The RTSJ specification is more of a scalable framework that can be implemented by virtual machines with differing characteristics, and executing over a variety of operating systems. In contrast, the Core specification has more precise and fixed semantics that match the characteristics of traditional real-time kernels.
- The RTSJ specification retains security of operation, for example by preventing dangling references, and by ensuring that ATC is deferred in synchronized code. This is consistent with Java design philosophy and the safety model of JVMs. In contrast, the Core specification assumes that the Core programmer is a "trusted expert" and so provides more freedom and less safety; for example a dangling reference to an object can occur; an ATC can trigger immediately within a protected object; and the `stop()` method does not release held locks.
- The RTSJ specification concentrates on adding predictability to JVM thread operations, but does not aim to deal with memory footprint, performance, or interrupt latency. In contrast, the Core specification has been designed to optimize on performance, footprint and latency. Kelvin Nilsen has summarized this distinction as follows: "The RTSJ makes the Java platform more real-time, whereas the Core Java specification makes real-time more Java-like."

The other major distinction between the two specifications is in their licensing models. The RTSJ specification is an extension to the trademarked Java definition and hence is subject to Sun Microsystems, Inc licensing requirements. However the Core specification is independent of the trademark (and hence licensing requirements) and is being put forward as an ISO standard specification via the J Consortium's approval to be a submitter of ISO Publicly Available Specifications.

4.2 Comparison with Ada95

Similarity to Ada Real-Time Annex. Almost all new elements in one or other real-time Java specification can be found in either the Ada95 core language definition, or its Systems Programming or Real-Time Annex [10]. These include:

- A guaranteed large range of priority values;
- Well-defined thread scheduling policy including `FIFO_Within_Priorities`;
- Addition of Protected Objects to the existing Synchronized objects and methods, that prohibit voluntary suspension operations (in the Core Java specification), and that define Priority Ceiling emulation for the implementation of mutual exclusion;
- Addition of asynchronous transfer of control triggered by either time expiry or an asynchronous event;
- Allocation of, and access to, objects at fixed physical memory locations, or in the current stack frame;
- Suspend / Resume primitives for threads (c.f. suspension objects);
- Dynamic priority change for threads (c.f. `Ada.Dynamic_Priorities`);
- Absolute time delay (c.f. `delay_until` statement);
- Use of nanosecond precision in timing operations (c.f. `Ada.Real_Time.Time`);
- Definition of interrupt handlers and operations for static and dynamic attachment.

In addition, the High Integrity Profile of the Core Java specification has the same execution model as that of the Ravenscar Profile, as discussed in section 2.7.

Thus the real time extensions for Java are quite compatible with the Ada95 Real-Time Annex and Ravenscar Profile execution models, which encourages the view that both Ada and Real-Time Java languages could be used to develop parallel subsystems that execute in a common underlying environment.

Dissimilarity to Ada Real-Time Annex. The following design decisions were taken during the development of the Core Java specification that conflict with those taken for Ada95:

- Low-level POSIX-like synchronization primitives, such as mutexes and signaling and counting semaphores, are included as well as the higher-level of abstraction provided by synchronized objects, monitors and protected objects. Ada95 chose to provide only the higher level of abstraction such as the protected object and the suspension object. There is therefore greater scope for application error using the Core Java specification, such as accidentally leaving a mutex locked.
- More than one locking policy is present. Synchronized objects and semaphores require only mutual exclusion properties and so are subject to priority inversion problems. Mutex locks and monitors require priority inheritance to be applied in addition to mutual exclusion. Protected objects require instead the priority ceiling protocol to be applied as for *Ceiling_Locking* in Ada95. The requirement on the underlying environment to support both inheritance and ceiling locking was one that Ada95 chose not to impose.
- The only mutual exclusion region that is abort-deferred is the *Atomic* interface used by interrupt handlers. In particular, protected object and monitor operations are not abort-deferred regions. This removes the integrity guarantees that a designer may

well be relying on in a protected operation. Use of the *Atomic* interface introduces a number of coding restrictions that limit its general applicability (in particular all the code must be *execution-time analyzable*). In Ada95, all protected operations are abort-deferred and there is no restriction on the content of the code other than that it does not voluntarily suspend.

- There is no notion of *requeue* in the Core Java specification. Ada95 *requeue* has been found to be useful in designing scenarios such as servers that provide multi-step service.
- Asynchronous transfer of control includes the ability to resume execution at the point of interruption (i.e. effectively discarding the transfer of control) which could be useful for example to ignore an execution time overrun signal in certain context-specific situations. This option is not provided by Ada95.
- Dangling references to objects within allocation contexts can occur in the Core Java specification. Ada95 semantics were carefully crafted to prevent dangling references except via unchecked programming.

Some of the RTSJ design decisions that conflict with the Ada 95 core language and Real-Time Annex follow:

- The RTSJ has a more general view of scheduling and dispatching, with feasibility analysis, overrun and deadline miss handlers, rational time, etc.
- For the fixed-priority preemptive policy, the RTSJ does not dictate the scheduling rules for preempted tasks. In the Ada Real-Time Annex, this is deterministic.
- The RTSJ's priority ceiling emulation monitor control policy requires queuing in general, since a thread holding a priority ceiling lock can voluntarily suspend.
- There is no direct Ada analog to the RTSJ's async event model (in particular the many-to-many relationship between events and handlers).
- In the RTSJ, an ATC is not deferred in *finally* clauses because of lack of information at the bytecode level. In Ada, abort is deferred during finalization.

5 Looking Ahead

We can look back on the '90s as the decade of revolutionary communication for individuals and for business, primarily via the internet. Use of e-mail, the web, mobile phones, e-banking etc has become part of everyday life, and e-business is an extremely rapidly growing industry. The Java execution environment has been most prominent in the software part of this new technology, with its write-once-run-anywhere capability and its abundant highly practical and portable APIs. But many of today's Java applications do not have demanding size and performance constraints.

So what will the next decade bring us? The next revolution could well be in communicating embedded devices. Some have predicted a trillion communicating devices by 2025, affecting almost all aspects of our daily lives. In at least some of these cases, an embedded device application environment will have demanding size and performance constraints, and will also require high availability, high integrity and hard real time deadlines. A growing number of these systems may even have safety critical requirements.

The Real-Time Java initiatives presented in this paper illustrate that the Java community as a whole is taking real-time requirements and embedded system constraints very seriously, and is preparing Java, its JVMs and its APIs for the next revolution. So what of Ada95, or its next revision Ada0Y?

Ada enthusiasts can argue quite validly that Ada95 environments can already meet the stringent requirements of embedded systems better than any other, and that Ada's suitability for use in high integrity and safety critical is second to none. However it is clear that Ada did not figure in the communications revolution of the 90's, and does not enter the new millennium with an expanding community. So can Ada, with all its excellent reputation within high integrity and safety critical embedded systems, find a role in the new revolution as the battleground moves into Ada's own strongholds?

The key to Ada's successful future almost certainly lies in seamless co-operation with the Java environment, rather than in competing with it. It is interesting to see how the two language environments are starting to converge somewhat. This cross-fertilization could be known as the "*Jada* effect".

We have already seen in this paper that many of the new ideas for Real-Time Java have been borrowed from Ada, such as those needed for predictability and deterministic schedulability analysis. Baseline Java had already used Ada's exception model, and now we see that the real-time extensions have equivalents for protected objects, priority ceiling emulation, well-defined thread scheduling policies, absolute delay, high precision timers, suspension objects, dynamic priority change, interrupt handlers, asynchronous transfer of control, access to physical memory, abort-deferred regions etc. So Java is definitely evolving towards Ada in the real-time domain.

In similar fashion, Ada is evolving towards Java. The Ada95 revision already brought in support for a comprehensive object oriented programming model not dissimilar to that in Java, including single inheritance hierarchies, constructors and finalizers etc. The next revision of Ada (Ada0Y) may well see the addition of support for Java-style *interfaces*, thereby providing the same limited form of multiple inheritance as in Java (from one class plus any number of interfaces). Furthermore, Ada0Y may relax the rules that currently prevent mutually-dependent package specifications, via a new *with type* construct. This would allow mutually-dependent Java classes to be modeled as Ada packages that each define a tagged type plus its primitive operations, without having kludges to workaround circularities in the "with" dependencies. Finally there is even some discussion about whether to allow a Java-like OOP syntax for invoking the primitive operations of a tagged type. This could be used instead of the traditional procedure calling style that requires some rules to identify which parameter is the object that controls the dynamic dispatching, with an OOP style of *object'Operation(parameters)*.

So it seems that both Java and Ada are undergoing the *Jada* effect. However as well as language convergence, it is also very important to have execution environment convergence if the two are going to co-exist happily. We have already seen some worthy attempts at integration between Java and Ada execution environments. A few different approaches are mentioned below:

- Aonix *AdaJNI* [11] makes use of the Java Native Interface that is provided with the Java Development Kit. This approach allows Ada native programs to interact with Java classes and APIs that are executed by a local or remote JVM via Ada-style interface packages.
- Ada Core Technologies *JGNAT* [12] compiles Ada95 into Java bytecodes in standard class files. This approach allows JVM-based programs to comprise a mixture of Ada and Java. Again, there is also the capability for the Ada code to access Java classes and APIs via Ada-style interface packages.
- Ada ORB vendors (e.g. [13]) provide access to CORBA objects from Ada programs. This approach allows a logically distributed mixed-language (including Ada and Java) system to communicate using the CORBA client/server model.

If Ada is to gain any kind of foothold in the new generation of communicating devices, we must build on foundations such as these. The efforts of users and vendors alike within the Ada community need to be focused on developing and evolving Ada in ways that are compatible with the emerging requirements, not least a seamless co-existence with the new Real-Time Java execution environments, their JVMs and their APIs. If we can achieve this goal, this can give a whole new lease of life to Lady Ada. We may even want to rename her Lady Jada ☺.

References

1. Gosling J., Joy B., Steele G., and Bracha G.; *The Java Language Specification* (second edition); Addison-Wesley; 2000.
2. Brosgol B.; *A Comparison of the Concurrency and Real-Time Features of Ada and Java*; Proceedings of Ada U.K. Conference 1998; Bristol, U.K.
3. Jones R. and Lins R.; *Garbage Collection*; Wiley and Sons; 1997.
4. Nilsen K.; *Issues in the Design and Implementation of Real-Time Java*, July 1996. Published June 1996 in "Java Developers Journal", republished in Q1 1998 "Real-Time Magazine", http://www.newmonics.com/pdf/RTJI.pdf.
5. Nilsen K., Carnahan L., and Ruark M., editors. *Requirements for Real-Time Extensions for the Java Platform*. Published by National Institute of Standards and Technology. September 1999. Available at http://www.nist.gov/rt-java.
6. Bollella G., Gosling J., Brosgol B., Dibble P., Furr S., Hardin D., and Turnbull M.; *The Real-Time Specification for Java*; Addison-Wesley; 2000.
7. International J Consortium Specification, *Real-Time Core Extensions*, Draft 1.0.14, September 2nd 2000. Available at http://www.j-consortium.org.
8. Dobbing B. and Nilsen K., *Real-Time and High Integrity Extensions to Java™*, Embedded Systems Conference West 2000 Proceedings, September 2000.
9. Dobbing B. and Burns A., *The Ravenscar Tasking Profile for High Integrity Real_Time Programs*. In "Reliable Software Technologies – Ada-Europe '98", Lecture Notes in Computer Science 1411, Springer Verlag (June 1998).
10. *Ada95 Reference Manual*, International Standard ANSI/ISO/IEC-8652:1995, Jan 1995.
11. Flint S. and Dobbing B., *Using Java™ APIs with Native Ada Compilers,* In "Reliable Software Technologies - Ada-Europe 2000", Lecture Notes in Computer Science 1845, Springer Verlag (June 2000).
12. Ada Core Technologies, Inc; *JGNAT User's Guide*; 2000.
13. Objective Interface Systems, Inc, *ORBexpress*, http://www.ois.com

Parameter-Induced Aliasing in Ada

Wolfgang Gellerich[1] and Erhard Plödereder[2]

[1] IBM Deutschland Entwicklung GmbH
Schönaicher Strasse 220
71032 Böblingen, Germany
gellerich@de.ibm.com
[2] University of Stuttgart, Computer Science Department
Breitwiesenstrasse 20-22
70565 Stuttgart, Germany
ploedereder@informatik.uni-stuttgart.de

Abstract. Parameter-induced aliasing means that overlapping areas of memory are associated with different identifiers causing assignments to one of them to have the unexpected effect of also changing the other's value. The disadvantages of aliasing for most aspects of programming languages have been known for decades and it is reported that aliasing occurs quite often when programming in languages like C or Fortran. In contrast, our examination of 173 MB real-world Ada code with a total of 93690 subprogram calls revealed less than one alias pair per 10000 lines of code. Further code inspection showed that most alias pairs could have been avoided. The rare occurrence of aliasing may be one reason for the low error rate frequently reported for Ada programs. This paper presents the methods and results of our analysis. Further, it discusses two approaches to forbid aliasing by language rules and evaluates the usability of our alias-free "named container" model suggested earlier.

1 Introduction and Overview

The term *aliasing* means that two different names designate overlapping areas of memory. As a result, an assignment to one variable can have the unexpected effect of also changing another variable although its name has not been the target of an assignment. Aliasing interferes with data dependence analysis and is likely to cause program errors [Hoa89,Hor79,ASU86,GJ87,Wol95,Muc97,Mor98].

Sources of aliasing include declarations explicitly overlaying memory, parameter passing, and pointers. While pointer aliasing might reflect a property of the real-world problem being solved, parameter-induced aliasing is usually unintended. It can occur between two formal reference parameters or between a formal reference parameter whose actual is a variable also being accessed directly by the respective subprogram.

Procedure `reverse` shown in figure 1 is intended to reverse the order of elements in an array. Parameter `B` is passed by reference as its value is to be changed. It is common to pass `A` by reference, too, as passing by value is less efficient for arrays. However, a call like `reverse(x,x)` does not show the intended

A. Strohmeier and D. Craeynest (Eds.): Ada-Europe 2001, LNCS 2043, pp. 88–99, 2001.

```
TYPE Vec = ARRAY [1..N] OF REAL;        A: T;
...                                     PROCEDURE P(f: IN OUT T) IS
PROCEDURE reverse (VAR A, B: Vec);      BEGIN
VAR i: INTEGER;                           A:= Const2;
BEGIN                                   END P;
  FOR i:= 1 TO N DO                     ...
    B[i]:= A[N -i +1];                  BEGIN
  END;                                    A:= Const1;
END reverse;                            P(A);
```

Fig. 1. Two examples of parameter-induced aliasing in Modula-2 [Ack82] and Ada

behavior: an assignment to B[i] also changes A[i] so that the lower half of the array will be overwritten by values from the upper half. An alias pair like A and B could be propagated to other parts of the program by nested subprogram calls.

1.1   Ada's Parameter Passing

Ada has three formal parameter modes, IN, OUT, and IN OUT. This looks like an abstract approach, specifying the direction of data flow between caller and callee rather then describing parameter passing in implementation-related terms only, as most procedural languages do. However, the effect of parameter passing is partially defined in such terms, e.g., by distinguishing between by-reference types and by-copy types, and left undefined for some types [TD98].

When there is more than one access path to a variable, the result of program execution may depend on the actual passing method. For example, the value of A after calling P in figure 1 is Const2 if T is passed by reference, and Const1 in case of passing by copy-in/copy-out. This effect is classified as *bounded error* in Ada 95 [TD98], meaning that the effect of the program is not statically predictable but will nevertheless lie within certain bounds. In Ada 83 [Ada83], such programs were declared *erroneous*, implying completely undefined behavior.

Language semantics allows optimizing Ada compilers to rely on the absence of aliasing. However, this may be detrimental to program reliability because the absence of such effects is undecidable in general [Jok82]. An article entitled *How to Steal from a Limited Private Account* shows how knowledge about parameter passing can be used to destroy the consistency of the seemingly protected internal data of an abstract data type [Bak93].

To summarize, Ada pretends providing a high level of abstraction but its parameter passing rules are actually more annoying than those of languages like Modula-2: The behavior of reverse(x,x) might surprise the programmer, but at least the result is predictable from source code and will be the same for all implementations.

1.2   Overview

Section 2 presents our evaluation on how frequently and in what context aliasing occurs in real-world code. In section 3 we compare the results to data reported for other languages and then relate the differences to measured data for runtime performance and software reliability in section 4. Finally, section 5 addresses the question whether aliasing could be prevented by language rules.

2 Experimental Evaluation of Aliasing in Ada

Section 2.1 describes our tool for alias analysis and section 2.2 gives the statistic results. Section 2.3 explains the context where alias pairs were introduced.

2.1 An Alias Analysis Tool for Ada

We implemented an alias analysis algorithm developed by K.D. Cooper [Coo85]. Input to this algorithm is a program representation available via GNAT's ASIS interface [gna95]. Cooper's algorithm consists of two phases. The first phase recognizes newly introduced formal/formal and global/formal alias pairs. The second phase propagates these along the edges of the programs call graph.

The algorithm was designed for languages passing parameters by reference and only considers variables of scalar types. Our adaption lead to the following modifications and limitations:

- Although copy-in/copy-out prevents aliasing according to its formal definition, similar problems are caused nonetheless by creating more than one access path to variables, as was pointed out in section 1. To cover these cases and since the passing mechanism is left undefined for certain types, our tool assumes that *all* parameters are passed by reference.
- Aliasing involving an IN parameter is considered when the actual parameter is also passed as OUT or IN OUT parameter, or is actually assigned to locally or in any (transitively) called subprogram.
- For components of the same array variable and for pointers to the same data type, the intro-phase makes the conservative assumption that they form an alias pair. For scalar and record variables, exact solutions are used.
- The original algorithm recognizes global/formal alias pairs based on the information which variables are visible inside a certain subprogram. This causes false positives for variables that are visible but not accessed. In order to get more precise results, we implemented an inter-procedural may-modify analysis and consider the actually referenced variables only.
- Due to implementation problems with ASIS we were unable to analyze generic packages. We do, however, assume that the overall result is not affected by this omission since there is no reason why aliasing should occur significantly more or less frequently in such code.

2.2 Statistic Results

The analysis tool was applied to some Ada programs from a public source code repository [Que] which are a reasonably random sample. Figure 2 shows their

Program	kB	LOC	Pack-age	Sub-prog	Calls	total	prop	Ind	Ptr	form/form	glob/form	Comp
			Program Size				Alias Pairs					
StyleChck	334	9287	17	146	1237	0	0	0	0	0	0	0
AVL tree	6	1017	5	11	47	3	0	0	3	0	0	0
Datagen	387	11114	42	275	1487	1	0	0	0	0	1	0
Hoopla	866	26140	34	600	5869	13	7	1	5	0	0	0
Manpower	19	1390	5	5	178	0	0	0	0	0	0	0
Scanner	18	534	1	14	4	0	0	0	0	0	0	0
Redico	508	18496	25	423	2757	2	1	0	1	0	0	0
Stubber	109	3339	9	37	477	1	0	0	0	0	1	0
F77toAda	3261	58935	86	1563	12257	4	1	1	0	0	1	1
LexPars	140	4772	15	41	211	0	0	0	0	0	0	0
Pplaner	481	12771	20	213	1845	1	0	0	0	0	1	0
Testlog	27	1517	6	19	88	0	0	0	0	0	0	0
TabVerw	11	1146	6	12	56	1	0	0	1	0	0	0
Prop	616	21208	40	282	3342	2	0	2	0	0	0	0
Image	156	4105	20	52	297	0	0	0	0	0	0	0
Expert	32	1787	6	32	120	0	0	0	0	0	0	0
Plantool	170	9459	13	71	679	0	0	0	0	0	0	0
Web1	56	2056	10	30	431	3	0	0	0	0	3	0
Web2	56	2056	10	30	431	0	0	0	0	0	0	0
Network	1116	30855	95	607	3918	1	0	0	0	0	1	0
UnifName	191	2872	10	38	161	0	0	0	0	0	0	0
Gnat	8624	239732	160	4594	57097	11	4	1	0	0	6	0
total	17298	466314	639	9118	93690	43	13	5	10	0	14	1

Fig. 2. The size of and the alias pairs found in some real-world programs [Gel00]

sizes in kByte, in lines of code (LOC) "inclusive all", and the number of packages, subprograms and call sites. The second set of columns reports the result of our analysis. The "total" column contains the total number of alias pairs found. Obviously, aliasing is quite seldom in Ada programs. The average density is one alias pair per 10845 lines. An alias pair occurs in every 2179nd call.

Column "prop" gives the number of pairs yielded by propagation. These are approximately one third of all pairs. A theoretical statement about the alias problem suggests the danger that alias pairs might be propagated along call chains, thereby endangering almost any part of the program. We could not observe this effect in any of the programs that we analyzed.

2.3 The Context of Aliasing

The remaining columns of Figure 2 detail how the alias pairs are introduced. We examined each of them by hand in order to get information about their origin in the particular program.

Column "Ind" contains alias pairs that consist of two indexed components of the same array variable. For "HOOPLA" and "F77toAda", there was no real aliasing since the index expressions were unequal constants.

Column "Ptr" is the number of alias pairs caused by passing dereferenced pointers to compatible types in the same call. The program "AVL tree" has a real alias pair. We happened to know the history of this program, an earlier version of which actually fell prey to the aliasing effect and had to be fixed to explicitly check for the existence of aliasing. In all other cases, the pointers referred to different nodes of trees.

The next two columns give the number of formal/formal and formal/global alias pairs involving scalar variables or complete variables of structured types. The alias pair in "Stubber" occurs because a record variable named `Token` is passed to a procedure `ADD_ON` which calls another procedure accessing components of `Token` directly. Since `Token` is passed in *every* call of `ADD_ON`, the alias pair could have been avoided. Aliasing in this program neither causes an error nor is it necessary to achieve some intended effect. Similar statements hold for all other global/formal pairs.

Finally, "Comp" gives the number of alias pairs consisting of a complete, structured variable and one of its components. This case occurred one time when the complete variable was passed as `IN` parameter while a component was passed as `OUT` parameter.

3   Aliasing in Other Languages

Measurements about aliasing seem to be published rarely. We found, however, data for C and Fortran programs.

3.1   Aliasing in Fortran

Fortran 77 follows an approach similar to Ada by disallowing assignments to dynamically aliased variables, but "such assignments are common practice and tolerated by most compilers" [ZC92] which "painstakenly avoid using register optimization on global variables or call-by-reference formal parameters to ensure that aliased variables behave in the expected fashion" [Coo85]. A study concerning parallelization of real-world Fortran code [MW93] revealed that the sets of potentially aliased names determined by compile-time analysis contain 4.4 variables on average. The largest alias set contained 55 variables, while only 39.7% of all parameters were un-aliased. Reasons for the frequent occurrence of aliasing include that by-reference is the *only* passing mechanism in Fortran 77, and that Fortran programmers seem to use rather long parameter lists [MW93].

3.2   Aliasing in C

Except for vectors, all parameters are passed by value in C. Passing results from the callee to the caller via parameters requires applying the address operator to the arguments and explicitly dereferencing the formal parameter inside the function's body. Discovering parameter-induced aliasing is thus relegated to a general pointer analysis, whose results are generally much weaker. Explicit pointer usage for parameter passing is a weakness of C as this task can be handled by the compiler in a much safer and ultimately more efficient manner.

A study about pointer analysis in a vectorizing compiler covering the *whole* C language [LMSS91] and applied to real-world programs yielded that the number of variables potentially referred to by a certain pointer could only be reduced in 31,4% of all dereferentiations. For the remaining 68,6% it had to be assumed that pointers might reference any variable. For one program, the set of potentially referenced variables could not be reduced at all. The set of variables referenced by a pointer had an average size of 15,3 elements, the maximum was 158 variables. Note that these values include both the equivalent of parameter-induced aliasing and general pointer aliasing. For this reason, these numbers are not directly comparable to our results. They do, however, indicate the difficulties that the C idiom for by-reference parameters creates for compile-time analysis and human reasoning about the absence of parameter-induced aliasing in C programs.

Some papers about pointer analysis algorithms report much better, but unrealistic results. These are caused by significant simplifications such as ignoring type casts or unions, which would weaken the results. Furthermore, optimistic assumptions about pointer arithmetic are made: accessing individual elements of an array or any dynamically created objects of a given type is considered as access of a *single* variable.

4   Effects of Aliasing

The numbers given in sections 2 and 3 indicate that aliasing occurs considerably less frequently in Ada programs. We tried to find out whether this result is correlated to effects usually cited as problems caused by aliasing.

4.1   Effects on Compiler Optimization

J. Stare from Tartan, Inc., a company selling C and Ada compilers, reports that Ada usually outperforms C for real-time applications on digital signal processors [Sta94]. D. Syiek examined the execution of 13 benchmark programs available in both languages using Tartan's compilers and found that the Ada versions are 28% faster on average [Syi95]. He gives a detailed analysis of what language features make compiler optimizations more successful for Ada than for C. Major reasons include more precise program-wide data dependence analysis where C's excessive usage of pointers "reduces compile-time information".

Our finding of a low rate of aliasing in Ada programs presumably is not a factor in Ada outperforming C, given that Ada compilers are effectively allowed to ignore parameter-induced aliasing. It does, however, imply that doing so is unlikely to cause problems, and that alias analysis in an Ada compiler could eliminate nearly all penalties on code quality that arise when aliasing is taken into account. It also implies that language support and coding idioms in Ada are vastly superior to C, in terms of both safety and code quality.

The problems of dealing with pointers are also stated in a study about the quality of vectorizing and parallelizing C-compilers [Smi91] and in a report about the development of such a compiler [AJ88]. M. Wolfe summarizes in his book on parallelizing compilers [Wol95] that aliasing and other details of Fortran and C "hinder advanced analysis and optimization".

Two experimental studies show the effect of aliasing in isolation. D.W. Wall traced the execution of programs and examined how the average degree of instruction-level parallelism depends on the precision of alias information [Wal91]. He considers four levels: no alias information, perfect information, little information based on the local context of instructions, and good information as would be yielded by global alias analysis at compile-time. Changing from no information to perfect information increases the degree of parallelism by factors of 2.55 to 17.7 with an average of about 8. Local information yields values nearly as bad as with no information while good information is close to the perfect case.

S. Horwitz and M. Shapiro [HS97] compare the precision of four different algorithms for alias analysis in C and examine its effects on three different data-flow analyses making use of points-to information. The precision of alias analysis, i.e., the alias set sizes, are good predictors for "transitive" effects like the size of live variable sets. For example, using alias sets twice as large compared to sets yielded by a more precise algorithm led to an increase of about 70% in the size of sets resulting from global modification side effect analysis.

4.2   Effects on Program Reliability and Error Rates

A study conducted in 1991 for the U.S. Air Force [Air91] found that the error rate in Ada programs is 27% lower than it is for other languages, measured during integration test. For the final product, the rate is 67% lower. Similar values are also reported by R. Lebib's study comparing Ada and Cobol for the implementation of management information systems [Leb93].

A very detailed examination of error rates in C and Ada projects was made by the Rational Software Corporation [Zei95]. Their study also gives a detailed analysis regarding the comparability of software, including statements about automatically generated code, re-use, and programmers' skills. The sample consists of commercial software developed since 1983 with a total size of over 1.5 million SLOC C and over 1.2 million SLOC Ada code. For Ada, the rate of errors detected by tests performed during development is approximately half of the value for C, no matter if program size is measured in SLOC or in Function Points. The rate of post delivery errors in Ada code was 86% lower than for C.

Another analysis of error rates for different languages is presented by Reifer [Rei96]. The sample consists of 190 software projects, ranging from 25 to 3000 kSLOC in size. The rate of post-delivery errors in Ada programs is up to 70% lower than it is for programs written in other languages.

M. Eisenstadt analyzed the types and methods of locating errors and asked people to send him descriptions of their bugs [Eis97]. He received 39 stories with 41 bugs and made them public available. J.W. McCormick found that 24 bugs were outside of the program. However, 15 out of 17 errors that required debugging in other languages would have been detected automatically if Ada had been used [McC97].

The advantages of Ada with respect to program reliability are also supported by some comments. The Nippon Telegraph and Telephone Corporation prefers Ada "because it is more reliable and easier to maintain" [Tan91]. K. Hines from Motorola states about their experience with changing from C to Ada as implementation language for hardware control software [Hin90]: "Also, the system was less likely to fail due to Ada's checking mechanisms and the ability to handle extraneous error conditions".

Unfortunately, none of these studies states how many errors were due to aliasing. It is, however, plausible that the rare occurrence of aliasing contributes to the reliability of Ada programs.

5   Programming Languages Rules to Prevent Aliasing

Language rules to prevent parameter-induced aliasing would completely eliminate this source of programming errors, and it would simplify a compiler's program analysis, lead to more precise results in data dependence analysis and thus support code optimization and parallelization.

The question is, however, what language rules might be appropriate to achieve this effect. While a rule preventing direct formal/formal aliasing is quite obvious, global/formal aliasing and propagation require inter-procedural analysis. In section 5.2 we discuss an approach where this is done by the compiler, while the rules suggested in section 5.1 only require local compiler checks, leaving all program-wide considerations to the programmer. Section 5.3 discusses aliasing due to passing dynamically selected components of data structures as parameter, a problem common to both approaches. A survey of other approaches to prevent parameter-induced aliasing is given in [GP97,Gel00].

5.1   Local Compiler Checks

One approach to allow checking for the absence of aliasing in local context is to add access attributes to variables and to formulate associated rules. For local variables, it is only necessary to specify whether local subprograms can access them directly or may receive them as actual parameter, but not both. For static variables, however, a more flexible approach is needed.

Approach. The global name space is split into *levels*. A *level number* $l(V)$ is associated with every static variable V. This is a positive number chosen by the programmer. An *access level* $a(P)$ is chosen for any subprogram P declared at global level. This number is treated as part of the subprogram's signature and is implicitly valid for any of its local subprograms. A subprogram P may directly access a variable V only if $l(V) \leq a(P)$. A variable V fulfilling $l(V) > a(P)$ can occur as an actual (IN) OUT parameter. Thus, level numbering ensures that adverse formal/global aliasing effects cannot occur. Figure 3 shows an example, using the symbol @ to specify level numbers. From this approach, a set of legality

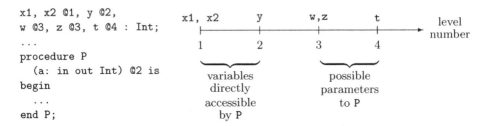

```
x1, x2 @1, y @2,
w @3, z @3, t @4 : Int;
...
procedure P
   (a: in out Int) @2 is
begin
   ...
end P;
```

Fig. 3. Using Level Numbers

rules concerning subprogram calls, parameter passing, and handling subprogram parameters is derived. Details are given in [GP97,Gel00].

Theoretical Evaluation. An examination of the effects that this approach has on programming revealed that many well-known concepts are special cases, i.e., can be characterized by level numbers [GP97,Gel00]. These cases include *pure* subprograms and packages (these have no state and thus no side effects), initialization parts of packages (these have no parameters), as well as some classes of packages introduced by G. Booch [Boo87], i.e., packages for abstract data types, for grouping related subpropgrams, and for abstract state machines (accessing static variables local to the abstraction).

Finding appropriate access and level numbers for a given program requires to consider all global subprograms and variables and can be done using a certain graph representation. There is no upper limit for level numbers and examples exist where program-wide re-assignment of levels becomes necessary after adding a single subprogram.

Experimental Evaluation. To gain practical experience, we implemented the new model as an extension to GNAT and rewrote existing Ada programs to meet the new rules [Gel00]. Our prototype implementation offered keywords **pure** and **state** to implicitly declare levels associated with a package so that they fulfill the requirements of a pure package or a state machine, respectively.

We began rewriting with short programs from a lecture about algorithms and finally rewrote a scanner generator and a compiler for a research language. Most packages could be declared as **pure** or **state**. None of the programs required more level numbers than 0, 1, and 2. The low number of levels needed can be explained by the fact that global variables are used rarely in Ada programs. An examination of 265609 variable accesses revealed that only 5.1% of all accesses were made to global variables [GG96].

However, program-wide assignment of appropriate numbers turned out to be a lot of work. This, and the somewhat difficult rules will limit the practical application of our model.

5.2   Global Compiler Checks

This approach is quite simple as it can be achieved with existing algorithms for analyzing parameter-induced aliasing. Using Cooper's algorithm, only the intro-phase is needed, as detected alias pairs will result in an error message but need not to be propagated. Two important implementation issues are the efficiency of checking and the handling of libraries.

Efficiency. Several implementations indicate that the analysis of parameter-induced aliasing is not overly time consuming. One Fortran compiler spends 1.1 % of its total compile time to analyze aliasing caused by parameters and by EQUIVALENCE declarations [OE92]. For another Fortran compiler, analyzing parameter-induced aliasing takes 4.6 %, which includes "detailed text output traces" [MW93]. In a compiler for Euclid (a Pascal-descendent with added rules that forbid parameter-induced aliasing), alias prevention contributes less than 0.4 % of total CPU time for the compilation [Cor84].

Section 5.1 suggests that the description of packages as state and pure not only improve the self-documentation of source code but also reduce the effort for alias-prevention. A pure declaration is available as pragma in Ada 95. It could be expanded to be applicable to subprograms also.

Libraries. A global re-analysis can be avoided if the library interfaces describe the exported subprograms' access to global variables. This information could be stored in the compiled library interfaces.

5.3 Dynamically Selected Components as Actual Parameters

Components of the same array variable are only allowed as actual parameter if they do not introduce an alias pair. Unfortunately, this may be undecidable at compile-time since index expressions can include arbitrary variables. There are several ways to handle this problem:

1. Index expressions are checked at compile time using array dependence tests developed for parallelizing compilers [ZC92,Wol95]. These algorithms have proven to be quite powerful and are aided by two empirical observations: Most variables occurring in index expressions are quantified by the ranges of surrounding loops. Also, most index expressions found in real-world programs have a quite simple structure and take a form that can be handled by dependence tests [CTY94]. However, index expressions that can not be analyzed at compile time would have to be forbidden, so this approach is likely to be considered overly restrictive.
2. The compiler generates run-time tests when aliasing cannot be excluded by compile-time analysis. This approach offers more flexibility to the programmer and guarantees that aliasing will not go undetected. A disadvantage is, however, the need to handle errors at run-time.
3. Another possibility is to allow potential aliasing only if its absence is asserted with a pragma. This would clearly document all dangerous cases in the source code and allow for checking them with reviews or formal verification techniques. In addition, the compiler could perform static checks as suggested above and generate run-time tests when dependence tests are not applicable.

Similar approaches can be used to handle aliasing caused by dereferenced pointer variables that occur as actual parameters, where points-to analysis would be applied instead of index dependence tests.

6   Summary and Conclusions

Our analysis of a large sample of Ada programs conclusively shows that aliasing rarely occurs in real-world Ada programs, which may well be a contributing factor to the reliability of Ada programs. The results justify to some extent the language design decision allowing compilers to ignore the effects of parameter-induced aliasing for the purposes of code generation, as conservative assumptions about aliasing would have significant impact on code quality. However, this is little consolation to the program analyst who needs to ensure the error-free operation of the software. Our experience and the results reported in the literature also show that an automated alias analysis can be very efficient. Combined with a low frequency of potentially dangerous alias situations in Ada, such analysis allows the manual examination of the few remaining danger spots to ensure the proper functioning of the software. Lastly, we presented alternative language rules, by which aliasing can be minimized or entirely prevented.

References

[Ack82]   W.B. Ackerman. Data Flow Languages. *IEEE Computer*, 15(2):14–25, Feb 1982.

[Ada83]   *The Programming Language Ada Reference Manual*. LNCS vol. 155. Springer, 1983.

[Air91]   Ada and C++: A Business Case Analysis. U.S. Air Force, Jul 1991.

[AJ88]   R. Allan and S. Johnson. Compiling C for Vectorization, Parallelization and Inline Expansion. In *Proceedings of the SIGPLAN '88 Conference on Programming Language Design and Implementation*. ACM, 1988.

[ASU86]   A.V. Aho, R. Sethi, and J.D. Ullman. *Compilers*. Addison-Wesley, 1986.

[Bak93]   H.G. Baker. How to Steal from a Limited Private Account. *ACM Ada Letters*, XIII(3):91–95, May 1993.

[Boo87]   G. Booch. *Software Engineering with Ada*. Benjamin/Cummings, 1987.

[Coo85]   K.D. Cooper. Analyzing aliases of reference formal parameters. In *Conference Record of the Twelfth Annual ACM Symposium on Principles of Programming Languages*, pages 281–290. ACM, 1985.

[Cor84]   J.R. Cordy. Compile-Time Detection of Aliasing in Euclid Programs. *Software – Practice and Experience*, 14(8):744–768, Aug 1984.

[CTY94]   D.K. Chen, J. Torellas, and P.C. Yew. An Efficient Algorithm for the Runtime Parallelization of DOACROSS Loops. In *Proceedings of Supercomputing'94*, pages 518–527. ACM and IEEE, 1994.

[Eis97]   M. Eisenstadt. My Hairiest Bug War Stories. *Comm. ACM*, 40(4):30–37, Apr 1997.

[Gel00]   W. Gellerich. *Ein datengesteuertes Ausführungsmodell für Programmiersprachen mit mehrfacher Wertzuweisung (A data-driven execution model for programming languages with multiple assignment)*. PhD thesis, Universität Stuttgart, (available from Shaker Verlag, Postfach 1290, 52013 Aachen, Germany, www. shaker. de), 2000. ISBN 3-8265-7900-3.

[GG96]   J.P. Goodwin and E.F. Gehringer. Optimizing Procedure Calls in Block-structured Languages. *Software Practice and Experience*, 26(12):1385–1414, 1996.

[GJ87]   C. Ghezzi and M. Jazayeri. *Programming Language Concepts*. John Wiley and Sons, 1987.

[gna95]   Gnu ada translator (gnat) documentation, 1995. cs.nyu.edu: /pub/gnat.

[GP97]   W. Gellerich and E. Plödereder. Parameter-induced aliasing and related problems can be avoided. In *Reliable Software Technologies – Ada-Europe 1997*, volume 1251 of *LNCS*, pages 161–172. Springer, 1997.

[Hin90]   K. Hines. Ada Impacts On A Second Generation Project. In *Proceedings TRI-Ada '90*, pages 488–492, Dec 1990.

[Hoa89]   C.A.R. Hoare. Hints on Programming Language Design (reprint). In *Essays in Computing Science*. Prentice Hall, 1989.

[Hor79]   J.J. Horning. A Case Study in Language Design: Euclid. In G. Goos and J. Hartmanis, editors, *Program Construction*, LNCS vol. 69. Springer, 1979.

[HS97]   S. Horwitz and M. Shapiro. The effects of the precision of pointer analysis. In *Static Analysis 4th International Symposium*. Springer, 1997.

[Jok82]   M.O. Jokinen. The Effect of Parameter Passing and Other Implementation Dependent Mechanisms is Undecidable. *ACM SIGPLAN Notices*, 17(9):16–17, Sep 1982.

[Leb93]   R. Lebib. The Impact of Ada on MIS applications. In *Proceedings of the 12th Ada-Europe International Conference*, pages 54–63, Paris, Jun 1993.

[LMSS91]   J. Loeliger, R. Metzger, M. Seligman, and S. Stroud. Pointer target tracking. In *Proceedings of Supercomputing '91*, pages 14–23, 1991.

[McC97]   J.W. McCormick. Don't Forget Ada. *Comm. ACM*, 40(8):30, Aug 1997.

[Mor98]   R. Morgan. *Building an Optimizing Compiler*. Butterworth-Heinemann, 1998.

[Muc97]   S.S. Muchnik. *Compiler Design and Implementation*. Morgan Kaufmann Publishers, 1997.

[MW93]   H.G. Mayer and M. Wolfe. Interprocedural Alias Analysis: Implementation and Empirical Results. *Software Practice and Experience*, 23(11):1202–1233, Nov 1993.

[OE92]   K.J. Ottenstein and S.J. Ellcey. Experience Compiling Fortran to Program Dependence Graphs. *Software Practice and Experience*, 22:41–62, Jan 1992.

[Que]   www.informatik.uni-stuttgart.de/ifi/ps/ada-software/ada-software.html, ftp.informatik.uni-stuttgart.de, ftp.uni-stuttgart.de.

[Rei96]   D.J. Reifer. Quantifying the Debate: Ada vs. C++, 1996. http://www.stsc.hill.af.mil/crosstalk/1996/jul/quantify.html.

[Smi91]   L. Smith. Vectorizing C compilers: How good are they? In *Proceedings of Supercomputing '91*, pages 544–553, 1991.

[Sta94]   J. Stare. Ada for DSP. Technical report, Tartan, Inc., 1994. http://www.adahome.com/Ammo/Stories/Tartan-Realtime.html.

[Syi95]   D. Syiek. C vs Ada: Arguing Performance Religion. *Ada Letters*, 15(6):67–69, Nov/Dec 1995.

[Tan91]   K. Tanaka. Using Ada at NTT. *Ada Letters*, 11(1):92–95, Jan/Feb 1991.

[TD98]   S.T. Taft and R.A. Duff. *Ada 95 Reference Manual*. Springer, 1998.

[Wal91]   D.W. Wall. Limits of instruction-level parallelism. In *Proc. ASPLOS-IV, Santa Clara, CA*, pages 176–188. ACM, 1991.

[Wol95]   M.J. Wolfe. *High-Performance Compilers for Parallel Computing*. Addison-Wesley, 1995.

[ZC92]   H. Zima and B. Chapman. *Supercompilers for Parallel and Vector Computers*. Addison-Wesley, 1992.

[Zei95]   S.F. Zeigler. Comparing Development Costs of C and Ada, Mar 1995. http://www.rational.com/sitewide/support/whitepapers/.

Slicing Tagged Objects in Ada

Zhengqiang Chen[1], Baowen Xu[1*], and Hongji Yang[2]

[1]Department of Computer Science & Engineering, Southeast University, China
State Key Laboratory of Software Engineering, Wuhan University, China

[2]Department of Computer Science, De Montfort University, England

Abstract. This paper presents an approach to representing dependencies for object-oriented (OO) Ada 95 programs. This new approach distinguishes sub-components for different objects and represents the effects of polymorphism and dynamic bindings. Based on this model, we developed approaches to slicing subprograms, packages/types and hierarchies of types. Our slicing algorithm is more efficient because most of the results can be reused, and inter-subprogram slicing is transformed to intra-subprogram slicing.

1. Introduction

Program slicing is an effective technique for narrowing the focus of attention to the relevant parts of a program. It was originally introduced by Weiser [1]. The slice of a program consists of those statements of a program that may directly or indirectly affect the variables computed at a given program point. The program point s and the variable set V, denoted by <s; V>, are called a slicing criterion. Program slicing has been widely used in various software engineering activities such as program understanding, testing, debugging, maintenance, and complexity measurement [2, 3, 4, 5, 6].

Ada [7] is a concurrent and object-oriented programming language designed to support the construction of long-lived, highly reliable software systems. It includes facilities to define packages of related types, objects and operations. The types may be extended to support the construction of libraries of reusable, adaptable software components. The operations may be implemented as subprograms using conventional sequential control structures, or as entries that include synchronisation of concurrent threads of control as part of their invocation. Techniques for analysing concurrency issues have already been developed [8], [9], [10], [11], [12]. In this paper, we focus on slicing tagged objects in Ada 95 programs.

---

* This work was supported in part by the National Natural Science Foundation of China (NSFC).

A. Strohmeier and D. Craeynest (Eds.): Ada-Europe 2001, LNCS 2043, pp. 100-112, 2001.
© Springer-Verlag Berlin Heidelberg 2001

Several approaches have been developed to slice OO programs. Most of these approaches are based on graphs extended from the system dependency graph (SDG) which was first developed by Horwitz [13] to compute inter-procedural slices. Larsen and Harrold introduced the class dependency graph [14] to represent object-oriented features. One limitation of this approach is that it cannot distinguish data members of different objects instantiated from the same class; thus, the resulting slices may be imprecise. Tonella [15] improved Harrold's method by passing all data members of an object as actual parameters when the object invokes a method. In fact, only a part of data members is used in a method. Liang [16] used a more efficient representation by taking the object parameter as a tree in which an object is the root and data member are leaves. But this approach, based on C++, cannot directly be applied to Ada 95 programs because of the different object-oriented facilities between C++ and Ada 95. Also there are several areas to be improved for the approaches on SDG, in terms of representation and efficiency.

This paper presents a new approach to representing OO Ada 95 programs and it is different from the existing SDG based approaches [13, 14, 16]. Subprograms can interact with each other by the interfaces — dependencies among parameters and the dependencies among inner data and statements are invisible outside. This new program dependency graph (PDG) consists of a set of PDGs of subprograms and packages. The PDG of a package consists of a set of PDGs of the subprograms encapsulated in the package. Each PDG is an independent graph and does not connect to any other PDGs. Based on these PDGs, we developed an efficient algorithm to slice tagged objects in Ada 95.

The rest of the paper is organised as follows. Section 2 briefly introduces the slicing algorithm based on SDG. Section 3 discusses our dependency analysis approach and presents the program dependency graph. Section 4 shows how to compute static OO program slices in our model. Concluding remarks are given in Section 5.

2. Slicing Using SDG

A *system dependency graph* (SDG) [13] consists of a set of program dependency graphs each representing a subprogram. A *program dependency graph* (PDG) [4] represents a subprogram as a graph in which nodes are statements or predicate expressions and edges represent control dependency or data dependency. For two statements s_1 and s_2, if the execution of s_1 influences the execution of s_2, then s_2 is *control dependent* on s_1; if s_1 defines a variable and s_2 uses it, then s_2 is *data dependent* on s_1. Each subprogram dependency graph contains *entry* and *exit* nodes that represent entry and exit of the procedure.

To represent parameter passing, an SDG associates each subprogram entry node with formal-parameter nodes. There are three kinds of formal parameters: *in, in out* and *out*. If the parameter can only be read in the subprogram, it is an *in* parameter; else if it can only be written, it is an *out* parameter; otherwise it is an *in out* parameter. Each *in* parameter of the subprogram corresponds to a *formal-in* node; each *out* parameter corresponds to a *formal-out* node; and each *in out* parameter has both a *formal-in* node and a *formal-out* node.

An SDG associates each callsite with a *call* node and a set of actual-parameter vertices: an *actual-in* node for each actual parameter at the callsite; an *actual-out* node for each actual parameter that may be modified by the called procedure. A SDG connects procedure dependency graphs at call-sites. A *call* edge connects a call node to the entry node of the called subprogram's dependency graph. Parameter edges represent parameter passing: *parameter-in* edges (*parameter-out* edges) connect *actual-in* and *formal-in* vertices (*formal-out* and *actual-out* nodes). A *summary edge* connects an *actual-in* node and an *actual-out* node if the value associated with the *actual-in* node may affect the value associated with the *actual-out* node.

Horwitz [13] computes inter-procedural slices by solving a graph reachability problem on an SDG. The slicing algorithm consists of two passes. In the first step, the algorithm traverses backward along all edges except parameter-out edges, and marks the reached nodes. In the second step, the algorithm traverses backward from all nodes marked in the first step along all edges except call and parameter-in edges, and marks reached vertices. The result slice is the union of the vertices marked in the two steps.

3. Dependency Analysis

3.1 OO Programming in Ada 95

Ada 95 supports object-oriented programming through two complimentary mechanisms: tagged types and class-wide types. Tagged types support inheritance by type extensions and class-wide types support run-time polymorphism via dispatching operations.

A record type or private type that has the reserved word tagged in its declaration is called a tagged type. User-written subprograms are classed as primitive operations if they are declared in the same package specification as the type and have the type as parameter or result. When deriving from a tagged type, additional components and primitive subprograms may be defined, and inherited primitive subprograms may be overridden.

Class-wide programming is the technique that enables programs to manipulate hierarchies of types. For each tagged type T, T's class comprises all the types that are in the hierarchy of types starting at T. Calling a primitive operation with an actual parameter of a class-wide type results in dispatching: that is the runtime selection of the operation according to the tag. A tagged type can be declared as abstract and can have abstract primitive subprograms. An abstract subprogram does not have a body but concrete derived classes need to supply such bodies. An abstract type provides a foundation for building specific types with some common protocols.

As an example (see Fig. 1), suppose we wish to define various kinds of geometrical objects to form a hierarchy. All objects will have a position given by their x and y co-ordinates. Each object has an Area. So we can declare the root of the hierarchy as shown in Fig. 1. The other types of geometrical objects will be derived (directly or indirectly) from this type. In this example we have a derived type Circle. The type Circle then has the three components: X, Y and R. It inherits the two co-ordinates from the type Point and the component R is added explicitly. A new function Area overrides the inherited function Area by the type Circle.

3.2 PDGs for Subprograms

In Ada 95, a subprogram is a program unit or intrinsic operation whose execution is invoked by a subprogram call. There are two forms of subprogram: procedures and functions. The primitive operations of a tagged type are subprograms. Thus, to represent a tagged type, subprograms must be represented first. A subprogram can be represented by a PDG.

In Ada 95, parameters can be passed by mode *in*, *in out*, *out* or *access*. The access parameters can be transformed into parameters in other modes by points-to analysis [15, 17, 18]. The non-local variables are treated as parameters. Whether the non-local variable is converted to an *in*, *in out* or *out* parameter is determined by its usage in the subprogram. The return value of a function is treated as an *out* parameter, whose name is the same as the function name.

In this paper, we use the *inter-parameter dependency set* to describe the dependencies among parameters (in SDG, the summary edges present these dependencies).

Informally, let ParaO be an *out* or *in out* parameter of a subprogram P, if the value of the ParaO is directly or indirectly dependent on a parameter ParaI, ParaO has an inter-parameter dependency on ParaI. All the parameters on which ParaO depends are denoted by DP(P, ParaO). In the example shown in Fig. 1,

DP(Points.Area, AreaP) = Φ, DP(Circles.Area, AreaC)={C}, DP(MA, AO)={O}.

For the sake of brevity, we illustrate our approach omitting the refinement of objects to their data components, i.e., we use "C" in lieu of "C.R". The extension to components is straightforward.

As mentioned above, the dependencies among inner data and statements are invisible outside the subprogram. Subprograms can interact with each other only by dependencies among parameters. To a subprogram call statement s, we map the dependencies among formal parameters to actual parameters: if a statement includes subprogram calls, nodes are added to represent their *out* and *in out* parameters. Such nodes are control-dependent on the call statement.

```
        package Points is
          type Point is tagged
          record
            X: Float;
            Y: Float;
          end record;
          procedure Area(P: Point; AreaP: out Float);
        end Points;

        package body Points is
          procedure Area(P: Point; AreaP: out Float) is
1         begin AreaP := 0.0; end;
        end Points;

        with Points; use Points;
        package Circles is
          type Circle is new Point with
          record
            R: Float;
          end record;
          procedure Area(C: Circle; AreaC: out Float);
        end Circles;

        package body Circles is
          procedure Area(C: Circle; AreaC: out Float) is
2         begin AreaC := 3.14*C.R*C.R; end;
        end Circles;
        with Points, Circles; use Points, Circles;
        with Text_IO; use Text_IO;
        procedure Main is
          P: Point := (1.0,1.0);
          C: Circle :=(1.0, 1.0, 20.0);
          A: Float;
          Condition: Character;
          package myFloat is new Text_IO.Float_IO (Float);
          use myFloat;
          procedure MA (O: Point'class; AO: out Float) is
3         begin  Area(O, AO); end;
        begin
4         Get(Condition);
5         if Condition = 'p' then
6           MA(P, A);
          else
7           MA(C, A);
          end if;
8         Put(A);
        end Main;
```

Fig. 1. An example with tagged objects

For a node s that represents a parameter x of P, let A be the corresponding actual parameter to x, Def(s) represents the variables defined at s, and Ref(s) represents the variables referred to at s, then Def (s)={A}, Ref (s)={A_i| F_i belongs to DP(P, x) and A_i is the corresponding actual parameter of F_i }.

Using these conversions, subprogram call statements are as easy to handle as other statements without calls. Inter-subprogram dependency analysis is converted to intra-subprogram analysis and a map from formal to actual parameters.

3.3 Representation for OO Programs

In this subsection, we present an approach for representing the OO features of Ada 95 including package, inheritance and object. Polymorphism will be discussed in the next subsection.

In Ada 95, packages are the mechanism for encapsulation. A tagged type and its primitive subprograms are encapsulated in a package. Thus, in our representation, a "package" encapsulates a set of PDGs, each representing a primitive subprogram in the package. Note that the PDG of each primitive subprogram is the "original" PDG, i.e., parameter passing and dynamic binding are not considered when constructing a package's dependency graph. This is the main difference from the SDG. In our representation, each PDG of a primitive subprogram is independent. In Ada 95, inheritance is supported by tagged type extensions. When constructing the PDG of a package that encapsulates a derived type, the parent package's PDG is not reconstructed. The derived type just "inherits" its parent's PDG. Thus, in this representation, each primitive subprogram has only one copy of a PDG that is shared by all the objects of the type and its derived type.

An object can be regarded as a state machine with an internal state that remembers the effects of operations. To obtain more precise information, an object represents not only the object itself but also its inner states (components). In our representation, as in [16], the object is represented as a tree: the root of the tree represents the object; the children of the root represent the object's components; and the edges of the tree represent the data dependencies between the object and its components. This can represent nested objects clearly. The purpose is to distinguish components from different objects. In our representation, each component has an object signature. Thus, an object parameter is also represented as a tree. The interparameter dependency represents not only the object but also its components.

In all, our representation is more "object-oriented" than previous approaches. The package's dependency graph set maps the package from source code to graphs. The hierarchies of PDGs are coincident with the hierarchies of types and packages.

3.4 Dependency Analysis for OO Programs

Although the concepts of polymorphism and dynamic binding extend the capability of OO programming, they also increase the difficulties to analyse such programs. In this subsection we will show how to analyse dependencies with dynamic binding.

In Ada 95, polymorphism is supported by class-wide programming. Objects whose tag is determined during execution are called polymorphic objects. When we construct a PDG for a package, we should record all the subprogram calls that accept class-wide parameters. Such subprograms are called *polymorphic subprograms*.

In previous approaches [14, 16], a polymorphic object is represented as a tree: the root represents the polymorphic object and the leaves represent the object in its various possible types. When the root object receives a message, each possible object has a call-site.

Ada 95 is a statically typed OO language. The possible types of an object can be determined statically [19]. In our representation, because the PDG of the whole program is not a connected graph, we use a different approach in which the polymorphic dependencies are represented by the interparameter dependency set. To distinguish the set for different types, the interparameter dependency set has a type signature. When a polymorphic subprogram is called, then the interparameter dependencies are the union of dependencies in all possible types.

For the example shown in Fig. 1, the "O" in statement 3 has type Circle or Point. Its type is determined during execution. Fig. 2 shows the SDG of the example and Fig. 3 is our PDGs (In the two figures we omits the dependencies on the initialisations. The inter-parameter dependency sets are listed in Section 3.2, so we do not repeat them here.). In our representation, the PDG of a package or subprogram is independent. We can see that Fig. 3 is cleaner and easier to understand.

4. Program Slicing

In the previous sections, we have introduced the control dependency and data dependency and have built the program dependency graph. This section will discuss how to slice tagged objects in Ada 95 programs based on this model.

A slice will be divided into three levels [20]: (1) subprogram slicing which computes the slices of a single subprogram or subprograms interacting with each other (this being the basis of other slicing algorithms), (2) package/type slicing which determines which subprograms of a package or which primitive subprograms of a tagged type might influence the slicing criterion, and (3) slicing of hierarchies of types which determines which types might influence the slicing criterion. The whole program slice includes all these three kinds of slices.

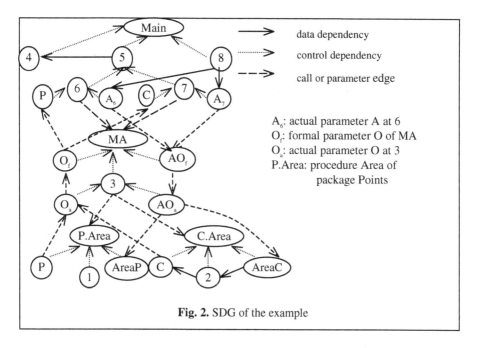

Fig. 2. SDG of the example

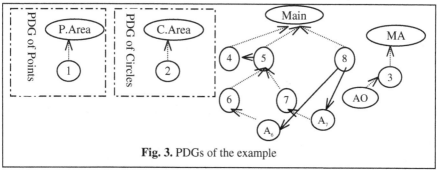

Fig. 3. PDGs of the example

4.1 Slicing Subprograms

Based on the PDG of a subprogram, slicing a single subprogram is a graph-reachability problem as the previous approaches [13, 16], and the details are not presented here.

When computing inter-subprogram slices, we developed a different approach, in which a special kind of slice is introduced. Such slices are called *slices on parameters* and are defined as follows.

Let x be an *out* or *in out* parameter of P and s_{exit} the exit node of P. P's slice on x is the slice in P on the slicing criterion $<s_{exit}, x>$.

In our slicing algorithm, the inner dependencies are invisible outside, and there are no edges to connect formal parameters and corresponding actual parameters. Therefore, when analysing statements with procedure calls, the slices on actual parameters should be converted to slices on the corresponding formal parameters. The slice on parameters can be obtained while analysing the inter-parameter dependencies. It is a graph reachability problem.

The main task of inter-subprogram slicing is to decide the slicing criterion to slice the called subprograms. That is, it needs to establish on which *out* or *in out* parameters to base the slice, because only the *out* or *in out* parameters might affect the caller. Thus the slice of a called subprogram is converted to slices on parameters. Such slices can be obtained while analysing inter-parameter dependencies. The algorithm can reuse the results for each call. After these analyses, the inter-subprogram slicing is converted to a set of independent single slices of subprograms.

In fact, when we construct the PDG of a program, all PDGs of subprograms have already been constructed. Based on these PDGs, we can get the inter-subprogram algorithm. In our slicing algorithm, each subprogram is sliced independently. It computes inter-subprogram slices in two steps: firstly, taking the subprogram call statement as a common statement, the algorithm computes the slice for the single subprogram, simultaneously determining the slicing criterion of the called subprograms; secondly, the algorithm computes the corresponding slices of the called subprograms. The final slice is the union of the two steps.

The main purpose of program slicing is to identify the interesting parts of a large system. In various software engineering activities including program understanding, testing, debugging, maintenance and complexity measurement, users might focus attention on a part of the program at a time. For incomplete system or components from third parties without source codes, we could not analyse the whole system. For such cases, completely slicing a whole program is impossible. Therefore, we provide *partial slicing*. Informally, given a slicing criterion $<s, v>$ where v is a variable defined or used at s, the *partial slicing* only slices the interesting parts of the program. The algorithm shown in Fig. 4 is our slicing algorithm.

In this algorithm, W is the current work-list and the node set Dep_S saves the statements included in the slice. PL is a set each element of which has the form (P, x), where P identifies a subprogram and x is a parameter of P. The `repeat` ... `until` structure in the algorithm computes the slice of a single subprogram, and the rest computes slices of the called subprograms.

In the algorithm shown in Fig. 4, we do not take aliased parameters into account. If a procedure call statement has aliased parameters, the inner dependencies might be changed. For such cases, another pass is needed to analyse the procedure by replacing the formal parameters with actual parameters.

4.2 Slicing Packages/Types

In Ada 95, a tagged type and its primitive operations are encapsulated in a package. Package/type slicing is to determine which subprograms of a package or which primitive subprograms of a tagged type might influence the slicing criterion. It is mainly used for tasks like debugging and program understanding. The user would like to focus attention on one type at a time.

```
Input: PDGs of program P, and slicing criterion <s₀, v>.
Output: The slice on <s₀, v>: Dep_S.
Init: W={s₀}; Dep_S = {s₀}; PL = Φ;
Algorithm:
  repeat
    Remove a node s from W;
    for all edges <s, s'> which are not marked do
    Mark <s, s'>;
    W = W ∪ {s'};
      Dep_S = Dep_S ∪{s'};
      if s' calls a function F then
        PL = PL ∪ {(F, F)};
      end if;
      if s' represents an actual parameter of P then
        Let y' be the corresponding formal parameter.
        PL = PL ∪ {(P, y')};
      end if;
    end for;
  while W is not empty;
  while PL ≠ Φ do
    Remove an element (P, x) from PL
    if P is interesting or P calls any interesting
    subprogram
directly or indirectly then
      if P's slice on x has not been computed then
        Compute P's slice on x;
      end if;
      if P is interesting then
        Dep_S = Dep_S ∪ P's slice on x;
      end if;
      if P's slice on x includes Mᵢ's slice on z then
        PL=PL∪{(Mᵢ, z)};
      end if;
    end if;
  end while;
```

Fig. 4. Partial slicing algorithm

In our dependency analysis method, the PDG of a package is shared by all objects of the tagged type declared in the package. When given a slicing criterion, the statements in a subprogram identified by a slicing algorithm includes statements in different instances of the subprogram. To slice a type, the slicing criterion is changed to <s, v, Type>. Informally, given a slicing criterion <s, v, Type>, type slicing identifies the primitive operations of the type that might affect the slicing criterion <s, v>.

To slice a type T, suppose the set PL has been computed using the partial slicing algorithm. While PL is not empty, remove an element (P, x) from PL, if P is a primitive operation of T, get P's slice on x and mark P; else if P calls any primitive operation of T directly or indirectly, get P's slice on x. The final result is the union of the operations marked.

In fact, type slicing is a special partial slicing. If only the identified subprograms of a type are considered, it can help the designers to check the interfaces of the type or reconstruct the type and its operations. If the statements are considered, it can help the programmers to understand the type more clearly according to its functions.

4.3 Slicing Hierarchies of Types

Hierarchies of types are tree structures introduced by type extensions. As products of the design phase, hierarchies of types are important structures of OO systems. Also they are complicated structures which are hard to construct and often need to be reorganised. Analysing these structures is a necessary step to understand OO systems in reverse engineering and reengineering activities. Slicing hierarchies will give a clearer view of the system structures.

Informally, slicing of hierarchies of types is to distinguish the types that might influence the slicing criterion from those that do not influence the criterion and to remove the latter.

Using the algorithms above, it is easy to determine which types might influence the slicing criterion. If any statement in any primitive subprogram of a type might influence the slicing criterion, the type will remain in the hierarchies. Another way is to integrate the above decision process into the dependency analysis by defining dependency between objects and their types. For each type or object specification add a node in the PDG. Let O be an object of type T, then the node specifying O depends on the node specifying T. Any statement referring to O depends on the node specifying O. The inner components depend on the units including them.

5. Conclusion

In this paper, we have presented a new approach to slicing OO Ada 95 programs. In this approach, the program dependency graph (PDG) of different subprograms is not connected. This is different from the traditional system dependency graph (SDG) which connects all PDGs of subprograms. More precise slices can be obtained by distinguishing components belonging to different objects.

In our slicing algorithm (assuming that the slicing criterion is given), if the needed subprograms have not been analysed, the algorithm analyses these methods and saves the independent information (dependency graph, slices on parameters) into the libraries, else reuses the previous results. Thus it is more efficient.

The main benefits of this algorithm are listed as follows.
  a. Each PDG is independent. This scales well for larger programs.
  b. It is easy to be reused. In our representation, a "package" consists of a set of PDGs. It can be reused by other packages. In our slicing algorithm, when the slicing criterion changes, most PDGs need not be traversed, because we can reuse the previous results that are saved on disk.
  c. The inter-subprogram dependency analysis and slicing can be converted to intra-subprogram analysis.

In this paper, we also present partial slicing, package/type slicing and hierarchies of types slicing. Partial slicing can make users pay attention to the interesting parts of the program, and slice incomplete programs or components from third parties without source codes. Type slicing can help designers to modify the operations of types and design efficient types. And hierarchies slicing can help the designers to specify the dependencies, especially inheritance and use relations.

References

1. Weiser, M., Program Slicing, *IEEE Trans. Software Engineering*, Vol. 16, No. 5, 498-509, 1984.
2. Xu, B., Reverse Program Dependency and Applications, *Chinese J. Computers*, Vol. 16, No. 5, 385-392, 1993.
3. Tip, F., A Survey of Program Slicing Techniques, *Journal of Programming Languages*, Vol. 3, No. 3, 121-189, 1995.
4. Ferrante, J. and et al., The Program Dependence Graph and its Use in Optimization, *ACM Trans. Programming Languages and Systems*, Vol. 9, No. 3, 319– 349, 1987.
5. Gallagher, K. B. and J. R. Lyle., Using Program Slicing in Software Maintenance, *IEEE Trans. Software Engineering*, Vol. 17, No. 8, 751–761, 1991.
6. Gupta, R. and et al., Program Slicing Based Regression Testing Techniques, *Journal of Software Testing, Verification, and Reliability*, Vol. 6, No. 2, 83-112, 1996.
7. ISO/IEC 8652:1995(E), *Ada Reference Manual-Language and Standard Libraries*.
8. Chen, Z., Xu, B. and Yang, H., An Approach to Analysing Dependency of Concurrent Programs, *APAQS'2000*, 39-43, 2000.
9. Chen, Z. and Xu B., Detecting All Pairs of Statements in Parallel Programs, *NCYCS'2000*, 265-269, 2000.
10. Cheng, J., Dependency Analysis of Parallel and Distributed Programs and Its Applications, *Int. Conf. on Advances in Parallel and Distributed Computing*, 370-377, 1997.

11. Zhao, J., Slicing Concurrent Java Programs, *7th IEEE International Workshop on Program Comprehension*, 126-133, 1999.
12. Krinke, J., Static Slicing of Threaded Programs, *ACM SIGPLAN Notices*, Vol. 33, No. 7, 35-42, 1998.
13. Horwitz, S. and et al., Interprocedural Slicing Using Dependency Graphs, *ACM Trans. Programming Languages and Systems*, Vol. 12, No. 1, 26-60, 1990.
14. Larsen, L. and Harrold, M. J., Slicing object-oriented software, *18th International Conference on Software Engineering*, 495–505, 1996.
15. Tonella, P. and et al., Flow insensitive C++ Pointers and Polymorphism Analysis and its Application to Slicing, *19th International Conference on Software Engineering*, 433–443, 1997.
16. Liang, D. and et al., Slicing Objects Using System Dependence Graphs, *International Conference on Software Maintenance*, 358-367, 1998.
17. Johmann, K.R. and et al., Context-dependent Flow-sensitive Inter-procedural Dataflow Analysis, *Software Maintenance: Research and Practice*, Vol. 7, No. 5, 177-202, 1995.
18. Yong, S.H., Horwitz, S. and Reps, T., Pointer Analysis for Programs with Structures and Casting, *ACM SIGPLAN Notices*, Vol. 34, No. 5, 91-103, 1999.
19. Chatterjee, R. and et al., Scalable, Flow-Sensitive Type Inference for Statically Typed Object-Oriented Languages, *Technical Report DCS-TR-326*, Rutgers University, 1994.
20. Li, B. and et al., An Approach to Analyzing and Understanding Program ----Program Slicing, *Journal of Computer Research & Development*, Vol. 37, No. 3, 284-291, 2000.

OASIS - An ASIS Secondary Library for Analyzing Object-Oriented Ada Code

Alexei Kuchumov[1], Sergey Rybin[1], Alfred Strohmeier [2]

[1] *Scientific Research Computer Center*
Moscow State University, Vorob'evi Gori
Moscow 119899, Russia
mailto:rybin@alex.srcc.msu.su

[2] *Swiss Federal Institute of Technology in Lausanne*
Software Engineering Lab, Department of Computer Science
1015 Lausanne EPFL, Switzerland
mailto:alfred.strohmeier@epfl.ch

Abstract: ASIS has proven to be an effective platform for developing various program analysis tools. However, in many cases ASIS, as defined in the ASIS ISO standard, appears to be at a very low-level of abstraction compared to the needs of the tool developer. Higher-level interfaces and common libraries for specific needs should therefore be developed. The paper describes a ASIS secondary library providing abstractions and queries for analyzing object-oriented Ada code.

Keywords: Ada, Ada Semantic Interface Specification, ASIS, Object-Oriented Programming, GNU Ada Compiler, GNAT, ASIS-for-GNAT.

1   Introduction

The Ada Semantic Interface Specification (ASIS) [1] [2] is an interface between an Ada environment [3] [4] and any tool or application requiring statically-determinable information from this environment.

The set of the basic ASIS abstractions closely corresponds to the basic notions used in the Ada Standard [4], called RM 95 for Reference Manual: an ASIS Context represents an Ada environment, an ASIS Compilation_Unit represents an Ada compilation unit, and an ASIS Element models a syntactic construct, e.g. a declaration, a statement, an expression, etc. [5]. Operations on these types and the results of their calls are called "queries" in ASIS terminology.

One of the primary ASIS design goals was to provide a minimal complete set of abstractions which would allow tools to get all the static syntax and semantic properties of Ada code. "Completeness" means that any syntax or semantic property defined in RM 95 should be either directly retrievable by some ASIS query or it should be possible to derive it from the results of other queries. "Minimal set" means that ASIS tries to avoid any duplication of functionality and that it provides directly only "basic" information about the Ada code, letting the tool compute "higher-level" properties of the Ada code.

For many tools, however, the set of abstractions and queries directly provided by ASIS is at a level too low. Tool developers therefore often create first a higher-level library based on the standard ASIS abstractions and that better suits the tool's needs. Such a

A. Strohmeier and D. Craeynest (Eds.): Ada-Europe 2001, LNCS 2043, pp. 113–122, 2001.

library is called an ASIS secondary library, and abstractions and queries defined in a secondary library are called secondary abstractions and secondary queries. The tool is finally built on top of ASIS and such a secondary ASIS library.

In [6] we presented the general idea of OASIS - the ASIS secondary library providing a set of abstractions for analyzing properties of object-oriented Ada code. This paper provides an overview of the design and implementation of OASIS and demonstrates how its use simplifies the development of tools performing object-oriented specific analysis of Ada components.

2   ASIS terminology and the object-oriented model

We will start by defining the terminology used in the rest of the paper.

2.1. ASIS terminology

Most of the ASIS terms we will need were already mentioned in the previous section. We briefly repeat them here, with some additions and extra precision:

- *Primary queries* and *abstractions* are subprograms and types defined in the ASIS standard; an abstraction represents some syntax or semantic notion.

- A *secondary query* is a query providing some useful syntax or semantic information from the Ada environment and implemented as a combination of primary and other secondary queries. A *secondary ASIS library* defines a set of secondary queries and *secondary abstractions*. For each secondary abstraction, there should be some mapping to primary ASIS abstractions. No secondary queries and abstractions are defined by the ASIS standard.

The set of primary ASIS abstractions includes:

- *Context* is the abstraction for an Ada compilation environment, as defined in RM 95, 10.1.4. In most cases, a Context can be viewed as a set of ASIS Compilation Units.

- *Compilation Unit* is the abstraction for an Ada compilation unit, as defined in RM 95.

- *Element* is the abstraction for a syntax construct of a (legal) Ada compilation unit. Besides some minor technical details, we can say that an ASIS Element can represent any syntax component as defined by the syntax of Ada in RM 95. An ASIS Element can also represent an implicit declaration, such as an inherited record component, or an inherited or predefined operation. Finally, Elements can also represent the results of generic instantiations.

2.2. Object-Oriented terminology

When using technical terms for Ada, we will conform to the RM 95.

Object-oriented terminology varies widely with the language, and Ada is not an exception. Because the Unified Modeling language UML [7] is an industry standard widely used for object-oriented analysis and design, we will use its terminology when comparing with Ada.

In UML, the most important basic concept is that of a class. A class groups together objects, called its instances, having common properties. Basically, there are two kinds of properties, attributes that encapsulate the state of an object, and operations that implement its behavior, including its interaction with other objects.

A class can be derived from another class by specialization, or inheritance; in this generalization-specialization relationship, the derived class is often called the child class, and the other class is called the parent class. The child class inherits the attributes and components of the parent class. It might add new attributes and operations. It might also redefine some operations.

In Ada 95, a class is realized by a tagged type or to a type extension together with its primitive operations. The attributes of the class are the components of the record type, and the operations are its primitive operations (sic!). To be a primitive operation or not is defined by special rules and syntactically they do not belong to the definition of the type. To the contrary of other object-oriented programming languages, like C++ and Java, Ada therefore does not have a specific syntax construct for a class (in the sense of UML). Inheritance is realized in Ada by type derivation. Instead of speaking of the child class, Ada will therefore say "the derived type". Primitive operations are inherited by the derived type, and the implementation of such an operation can be redefined, or overridden as Ada says.

Ada 95 defines the notion of a (derivation) class (RM 95, 3.4.1(1)). This concept corresponds to the inheritance hierarchy rooted at some tagged type. A class-wide type in Ada is the way to denote such a hierarchy, but the hierarchy itself does not correspond to a specific syntax construct. The "closest" construct is the declaration of the tagged type or the type extension that is at the root of the hierarchy.

An important feature of object-oriented programming is dynamic binding of an operation to one of its implementations. The idea is that within an inheritance hierarchy an operation might have different implementations, and the right one is chosen only at run-time when the class, as UML would say, or the specific type, as Ada would say, of the object that executes the operation is known. In Ada, the choice between static and dynamic binding, the latter being called dispatching, is made when writing a call to the operation. This is in contrast to other languages: in Java, a call is always dynamically bound, and in C++, the decision is made when declaring the operation, i.e. the member function. To come back to Ada, dynamic binding only takes place when an actual parameter of the call is of a class-wide type.

Finally, Ada has the concept of a class-wide operation. One or several formal parameters of such an operation are of a class-wide type. When calling the operation, any actual belonging to the derivation class can be passed. Class-wide operations are not primitive operations, and therefore they are not inherited. They can be defined at any level of the inheritance hierarchy.

In the rest of the paper, we will use Ada's view on the object-oriented world. We will use the term *derivation item* to represent tagged type or a type extension together with all its components and all its primitive operations; a derivation item corresponds therefore to the concept of a class in UML terminology. We will use the term *derivation class* to represent a derivation hierarchy rooted at some derivation item.

3   Using ASIS for analyzing object-oriented properties of Ada code

ASIS' view of an Ada compilation unit is based on its syntax structure. All syntax constructs are mapped to so called ASIS Elements, and such an Element carries both the syntactic and the semantic properties of the corresponding Ada construct. Individual Elements are quite natural and sufficient when only syntactical information is needed. However the approach is very limited when it comes to semantic information. Indeed, by the very nature of the approach, a semantic property about some Element must be returned and represented by some *other* Element or set of Element(s). For example, if Element is an expression, a query about its type will return the Element representing the corresponding type declaration. Also, if Element represents a subprogram call, ASIS can inform about the called subprogram by providing the Element representing the declaration of the subprogram.

This "Element-based" approach works well when the tool needs only semantic information formulated for a single specific construct, e.g. the type of an expression, the definition of a name, the declaration of a called subprogram etc. But when the information of interest is about sets of Elements which are in some specific relation with each other, ASIS provides very limited capabilities, and the tool has to compute most of the information itself.

This is certainly the case for tools performing analysis of object-oriented Ada code.

Consider the following simple example of object-oriented Ada code:

```ada
package Pack1 is
   type A is tagged record
      Comp : Integer;
   end record;

   procedure P1 (X : A);
   procedure P2 (X : A);

   type A1 is new A with record
      Comp1 : Integer;
   end record;
end Pack1;

with Pack1; use Pack1;
package Pack2 is

   procedure P3 (X : A);

   type A2 is new A with record
      Comp2 : Integer;
   end record;

   procedure P1 (X : A2);

end Pack2;
```

From the point of view of ASIS, the code consists of two Compilation Units, both defining syntax Elements such as tagged type declarations, type extension declarations and subprogram declarations. When analyzing the code with ASIS primary queries, we can traverse its structure, either manually or by using some instantiation of the ASIS Traverse_Element generic procedure. By using the ASIS Element classification queries, we can easily detect the tagged types, record components, type extensions and subprograms.

In contrast, from the point of view of the object-oriented paradigm, the code defines a hierarchy of three classes, in classic object-oriented terminology, and a derivation hierarchy containing three derivation items in our terminology. Each derivation item has a position in the hierarchy, and a set of components and a set of primitive, inheritable operations. The derivation item at the root is the tagged type A with its derivable component Comp and the primitive operations Pack1.P1 and Pack1.P2; notice that Pack2.P3 is not a primitive operation of this type, and therefore does not belong to the derivation item.

To perform this kind of analysis of object-oriented code, an ASIS tool must first create abstractions for the concepts of a derivation item and a derivation class. It then has to use non-trivial combinations of standard "Element-based" queries to collect and to assemble all the needed information. Let's outline a possible approach, based on primary queries only.

A derivation item is linked to an ASIS Element representing the declaration of a tagged type or a type extension. The full set of components of a derivation item corresponding to a type extension is the union of the inherited components and of the components that are member of the extension part. The tool can retrieve the inherited components with the query Asis.Definitions.Implicit_Inherited_Declarations.

To get the set of operations of a derivation item, i.e. the set of primitive operations of the corresponding type, the tool must traverse the package declaration enclosing the corresponding type declaration. During this traversal, for each encountered subprogram declaration, including the implicit declarations of inherited subprograms, it must check if the subprogram is a primitive operation of the type. To find the derivation class rooted at some derivation item, e.g. the one associated with Pack1.A, the application must traverse (almost) the whole Context and collect all the derivation items related to types derived directly or indirectly from the root type.

4   Presentation of OASIS - an ASIS secondary library for object-oriented analysis

4.1. Design goals of OASIS

We suspect that most ASIS-based tools analyzing object-oriented Ada code share similar abstractions, i.e. data types and operations, to represent basic properties of such code. There is therefore a need for an ASIS secondary library defining and implementing such abstractions. For Ada programmers, usability of these abstractions is increased if they are based on Ada's view of object-oriented concepts. The OASIS project is an attempt to satisfy these needs.

Providing a set of high-level abstractions for the analysis of object-oriented Ada code was one design goal of OASIS. Another one was to integrate these abstractions with the "Element based" approach used in "core" ASIS. In other words, the goal was not to create a completely new model for extracting object-oriented information, but to extend in a natural way existing ASIS functionality.

The current version of OASIS is the result of a university research project. We are expecting some changes in the interface, such as repackaging and extending the functionality. But the first experiments of using OASIS have shown that OASIS is a great foundation for developing ASIS tools performing object-oriented analysis of Ada code.

4.2. Interface of OASIS

The main idea behind OASIS is to provide direct support for the main concepts of Ada's object-oriented programming concepts. The basic OASIS abstractions are the derivation item and derivation class.

An OASIS derivation item is related to the declaration of a tagged type or a type extension. In contrast to such a declaration, the basic properties of a derivation item include the complete lists of components and primitive operations of the corresponding type, together with the position of the type in the "enclosing" derivation class.

A derivation item associated with a tagged type is a root derivation item. Otherwise stated, a derivation item is called a root item, if it is not derived from some other derivation item. An OASIS derivation class is the hierarchy of all the OASIS derivation items that are derived directly or indirectly from a root derivation item.

OASIS defines its own specific abstractions to represent a basic property of a derivation item - a component or a primitive operation. These abstractions are based on the corresponding syntax constructs: a component declaration and a subprogram declaration. In OASIS, these abstractions have additional basic properties: a reference to the derivation item the component or primitive operation belongs to, and a reference to the derivation item that explicitly declares the component or operation.

To represent information about dynamic binding, OASIS defines two abstractions, one for a class-wide operation and one for a dispatching call.

OASIS is structured as a hierarchy of Ada packages rooted at the package named OASIS. The root OASIS package contains the definition of the types Derivation_Item, Component and Primitive. Each of the child packages contains type declarations and queries needed for one piece of the OASIS functionality: working with derivation classes, working with components, working with class-wide operations, etc. OASIS therefore follows ASIS' philosophy for packaging the interface.

The following list provides an overview of the functionality offered by the current version of OASIS:

- For each OASIS abstraction, there are queries for mapping OASIS concepts onto basic ASIS abstractions. It is therefore possible to "convert" an OASIS-defined entity into its corresponding ASIS Element, i.e. the syntax construct on which it is based, and to "convert" an ASIS Element into an OASIS entity, if any;

- It is possible to retrieve a list of all the root derivation items within a given construct. i.e. within an ASIS Element, within a given ASIS Compilation Unit or within a whole Context;
- For any root derivation item, it is possible to get the derivation class rooted at this item;
- For any derivation item, be it a root or not, it is possible to get the derivation class containing this item; the result can be limited to a given Element or a given Compilation Unit;
- For a derivation item, it is possible to get the list of all its ancestor items and the list of all descendants;
- For two derivation items, it is possible to find the nearest common ancestor item, if any;
- For a derivation item, it is possible to get the list of all its components and the list of all its primitive operations;
- It is possible to distinguish between "public" and "private" components, possible in Ada with private tagged types and private type extensions;
- For a primitive operation, it is possible to distinguish between an inherited and an explicitly declared operation;
- For a derivation item, it is possible to get the list of all the dispatching calls that could take this derivation item as an actual parameter;
- For a dispatching call, it is possible to get the list of primitive operations that can be invoked at run-time depending on the actual parameter;
- For a derivation item, it is possible to get the list of class-wide operations defined for it and for all its ancestors;
- OASIS defines its own generic list and tree data structures. Their instantiations are used for various OASIS abstractions, e.g. a derivation class is implemented as an instantiation of the generic tree. OASIS also defines traversal procedures for its generic lists and trees, used e.g. for traversing a derivation class.

4.3. Implementation of OASIS

From the very beginning, the OASIS project was based on the public version of the GNAT ASIS technology [8] [9] [10].

Two different implementation approaches can be considered: 1. Implement OASIS using only the standard ASIS functionality; 2. Implement it using the internal GNAT data structure, the Abstract Syntax Tree - AST. Choosing between these two approaches is not obvious - each of them having pros and cons.

Implementing OASIS directly on the AST simplifies the implementation of many OASIS queries, because semantic information is often available in the AST, but is not reflected by primary ASIS queries. E.g. in the AST, a boolean flag marks a controlling formal parameter in a subprogram specification. Also when implementing OASIS on top of standard ASIS, all kinds of unnecessary data structure transformations and checks must take place, leading eventually to poor performance. On the other side, working directly with the AST leads to a non portable implementation; also, and even when staying within the GNAT technology, the maintenance effort is higher since the structure of the AST may change with new GNAT versions.

Taking into account the research nature of the OASIS project and the fact that the main developer is not a specialist in the internals of GNAT, we chose to implement OASIS on top of ASIS, i.e. as a secondary library. The current version makes some use of the ASIS-for-GNAT specific Asis.Extensions package, which contains queries extending the standard ASIS functionality and is implemented directly on GNAT's internal data structures. However, the use of these non-portable extensions is quite limited, and only a temporary solution, we plan to get rid of in a near future.

We are not quite happy with the performance, but consider it as acceptable for a research project, especially since we have not yet investigated optimization possibilities. The OASIS-based sample tools (see Section 5) run quite fast on small Ada examples. The OASIS-based program that prints out all the derivation classes in a given Context takes several minutes to process the Booch components. This library consists in 146 Ada compilation units, contains more then 21'000 source lines of code, and defines 6 derivation classes that contain 99 derivation items altogether.

5   Examples of using OASIS

In this section, we will show how the use of OASIS simplifies the development of tools that analyze object-oriented Ada code.

5.1. Class browser

A class browser is a tool that allows one to navigate through class hierarchies, in the sense of basic object-oriented terminology. For Ada, class browsers are of special importance because the language does not have a specific syntax construct to represent a "class", e.g. a data structure together with applicable operations. In OASIS, a Derivation Item fulfills this need, since it corresponds to the classic concept of a class. Furthermore, the OASIS query All_Roots returns the list of all root Derivation Items defined in either a Context, a Compilation Unit or an Element, depending on the actual parameter. A class browser could therefore start by extracting this list for the whole Context:

```
Root_List := All_Roots (My_Context);
```

For any Derivation Item, even if it is not a root item, it is possible to retrieve with the query Derivation_Class the transitive closure of the derivation hierarchy this Derivation Item is contained in. It is also possible to retrieve for any Derivation Item the subtree of which it is the root by calling the query Derivation_Subtree. To traverse a derivation hierarchy, the tool can use an instantiation of the generic traversal procedure Full_Traverse_Tree.

5.2. Detecting non overridden operations

In object-oriented code, not overriding an inherited operation is a potential source of errors, especially when new components are added to the derived type. For example, consider a hierarchy derived from the predefined type Ada.Finalization.Controlled; whenever a new component is added by a type extension, it is most likely that at least some of the primitive operations Initialize, Adjust and Finalize for this type should be overridden. We therefore think that a tool which detects non overridden operations in the presence of additional components might be useful.

The outline for such a tool is the following:

1. Get the list of all the derivation items used in the given program. This part is similar to the class browser problem.

2. Select all derivation items which are not root, for which there is at least one new component and for which at least one primitive operation is inherited "as is" from the direct ancestor. Compared with standard ASIS, this is easy to implement with OASIS, since we need exactly one OASIS query to get the complete list of components of a derivation item and exactly one OASIS query to get the complete list of its primitive operations.

3. Print out the selected derivation items together with the non overridden primitive operations.

5.3. Ideas for other tools

It might also be interesting to have a tool that finds all NON primitive operations of all tagged types and type extensions. Indeed, it happens quite often that a programmer thinks a subprogram is a primitive operation while it is not, because "placing" and freezing rules are not trivial in Ada.

A reverse-engineering tool that generates UML class diagrams out of object-oriented Ada code would also benefit from OASIS.

6   Conclusions

We think that the current version of the OASIS - the ASIS secondary library for getting the object-oriented-specific information about Ada code - is a good starting point for developing an industry-quality version of such a library. Even though OASIS is currently a university research prototype, first experiences in developing tools analyzing object-oriented properties of Ada code have shown that OASIS significantly simplifies the structure of the tools' code and cuts down the effort needed for their development.

References

[1]   Ada Semantic Interface Specification (ASIS); International Standard ISO/IEC 15291 1999 (E).

[2]   Currie Colket et all; Architecture of ASIS: A Tool to Support Code Analysis of Complex Systems; ACM Ada Letters, January 1997, vol. XVII, no.1, 1997, pp 35-40.

[3]   John Barnes (Ed.); Ada 95 Rationale: The Language, The Standard Libraries; Lecture Notes in Computer Science, vol. 1247; Springer-Verlag, 1997; ISBN 3-540-63143-7.

[4]   S. Tucker Taft, Robert A. Duff (Eds.); Ada 95 Reference Manual: Language and Standard Libraries, International Standard ISO/IEC 8652:1995(E); Lecture Notes in Computer Science, vol. 1246; Springer-Verlag, 1997; ISBN 3-540-63144-5.

[5]   Sergey Rybin, Alfred Strohmeier; Ada and ASIS: Justification of Differences in Terminology and Mechanisms; Proceedings of TRI-Ada'96, Philadelphia, USA, December 3 - 7, 1996, pp 249-254.

[6]   Sergey Rybin, Alfred Strohmeier, Vasiliy Fofanov, Alexei Kuchumov; ASIS-for-GNAT: A Report of Practical Experiences - Reliable Software Technologies - Ada-Europe'2000 Proceedings, Hubert B. Keller, Erhard Ploedereder (Eds), LNCS (Lecture Notes in Computer Science), vol. 1845, Springer-Verlag, 5th Ada-Europe International Conference, Potsdam, Germany, June 26-30, 2000, pp. 125-137.

[7]   James Rumbaugh, Ivar Jacobson, Grady Booch; The Unified Modeling Language Reference Manual; Addison-Wesley, 1999.

[8]   Sergey Rybin, Alfred Strohmeier, Eugene Zueff; ASIS for GNAT: Goals, Problems and Implementation Strategy; Proceedings of Ada-Europe'95, Toussaint (Ed.), LNCS (Lecture Notes in Computer Science) 1031, Springer, Frankfurt, Germany, October 2-6 1995, pp. 139-151.

[9]   Sergey Rybin, Alfred Strohmeier, Alexei Kuchumov, Vasiliy Fofanov; ASIS for GNAT: From the Prototype to the Full Implementation; Reliable Software Technologies - Ada-Europe'96: Proceedings, Alfred Strohmeier (Ed.), LNCS (Lecture Notes in Computer Science), vol. 1088, Springer, Ada-Europe International Conference on Reliable Software Technologies, Montreux, Switzerland, June 10-14, 1996, pp. 298-311.

[10] Alfred Strohmeier, Vasiliy Fofanov, Sergey Rybin, Stéphane Barbey; Quality-for-ASIS: A Portable Testing Facility for ASIS; International Conference on Reliable Software Technologies - Ada-Europe'98, Uppsala, Sweden, June 2-8 1998, Lars Asplund (Ed.), LNCS (Lecture Notes in Computer Science), Springer-Verlag, 1998, pp. 163-175.

Building Modern Distributed Systems

Laurent Pautet, Thomas Quinot, and Samuel Tardieu

École Nationale Supérieure des Télécommunications
Networks and Computer Science Department
46, rue Barrault
F-75634 Paris Cedex 13, France
{pautet,quinot,tardieu}@enst.fr
http://www.infres.enst.fr/

Abstract. Ada 95 has been the first standardized language to include distribution in the core language itself. However, the set of features required by the Distributed Systems Annex of the Reference Manual is very limited and does not take in account advanced needs such as fault tolerance, code migration or persistent distributed storage.

This article describes how we have extended the basic model without abandonning the compatibility in GLADE, our implementation of the Distributed Systems Annex. Extensions include restart on failure, easy code migration, hot code upgrade, restricted run time for use on embedded systems with limited processing as well as distributed storage capabilities and persistent storage handling.

1 Introduction

It is generally admitted that Ada 83 had a strong focus on real-time, mission-critical systems. But Ada 83 has been criticized from a number of standpoints, one of them being its lack of cooperation with foreign programming languages and with the outside world in general. To fix those defects, new features were added in the latest major revision of Ada, called Ada 95 [1]. Moreover, Ada 95 was the first internationally standardized OO language (ANSI/ISO/IEC-8652:1995). It is also the first internationally standardized language including distribution features.

A great effort was led by Ada Core Technologies (ACT) to provide the Ada community with a free high-quality Ada 95 compiler called GNAT. This compiler, which implements the core Ada 95 language as well as all its optional annexes, belongs to the GCC family and shares its back-end with the C and C++ compilers. As with the other compilers from the GCC suite, GNAT supports many native and cross configurations.

In collaboration with ACT, we have been developing GLADE [2], an implementation of the Distributed Systems Annex of the language, as found in the Ada 95 reference manual. GLADE, which is available under the same free license as GNAT, has been designed for this particular compiler, but should be portable to any Ada 95 compilation environment with minimal efforts. We also worked

A. Strohmeier and D. Craeynest (Eds.): Ada-Europe 2001, LNCS 2043, pp. 123–135, 2001.

on proposing new extensions to the original Ada 95 model for distributing Ada programs, which is described in section 2.

Those extensions, whose goal is to allow the use of modern distribution paradigms while maintaining total compatibility with the basis model describe in the Distributed Systems Annex, have been inspired by other middlewares such as CORBA [3] or by user needs and remarks. The first extension, presented in section 3, removes the single point of failure often found in distributed systems. Section 4 focuses on restarting parts of a distributed systems after a failure, which may have been scheduled (in case of code migration or upgrade) or not. Section 5 concentrates on shared and persistent data storage.

In section 6, we present other useful features such as encryption or data compression. We then conclude and present our current and future research work in the last section.

2   Distribution in Ada

In this section we present the distribution model of Ada 95, then analyze its intrinsic limitations as well as the ones present in older GLADE releases.

2.1   Distribution Model

Ada 83 lacked distribution facilities. Every compiler vendor had to provide its own proprietary solution for letting users build distributed applications. This led to situations where a program could not easily be ported to another compiler[1], which went against Ada's implicit rule of "as soon as it is written in Ada, it will work the same way with every conforming Ada compiler". In fact, there were so many different solutions that a comparative study had already been made in 1985 [4].

The designers of Ada 95 chose to solve this problem by adding distribution features right in the language. This led to the "Distributed Systems Annex" of the Reference Manual [1, Annex E]. This annex describes how an application can be split into different **partitions** (as described in [5]). Partitions can be **active**, in which case they can contain threads of control and packages with code, or **passive**, meaning that they only hold passive packages, containing variables. The annex also defines how particular packages belonging to the application can be categorized using **categorization pragmas**. Those pragmas identify the packages playing a special role in a distributed application; they come in addition to regular categorization pragmas such as Pure and Preelaborate. The additional pragmas are:

Remote_Call_Interface: subprograms declared in a Remote_Call_Interface package will not be replicated on all the partitions where they are used. Each such package is placed on only one active partition in the distributed

---

[1] To be honest, this problem could have been solved in an elegant way if Ada 83 had a standardized way of interfacing with other languages, which was not the case.

application. When calling a subprogram declared in a Remote_Call_Interface package, a remote call takes place transparently if the package has been placed on a partition different from the one of the caller.

Remote_Types: types declared in a Remote_Types package are guaranteed to be transferable from one partition to another. Notably, those types have global semantics; for example, pointers are good examples of type whose semantics are only local, since it makes no sense to transport them on another machine. At the opposite, integers have the same meaning on every partition.

Shared_Passive: variables declared in a Shared_Passive package can be accessed from several partitions. Simple variable assignments and reads can be used to exchange data between partitions. Shared_Passive packages can be placed on either active or passive partitions.

As soon as a package holds the Remote_Call_Interface pragma, the subprograms present in its declarative part can be called remotely. When necessary, the compiler will generate stubs and skeletons to make a remote call; categorization dependency rules guarantee that this will be doable.

This model allows to switch from the monolothic model to the distributed one (and vice-versa) very easily, thus easing the debugging of distributed applications. However, the Reference Manual does not say anything about the way a distributed application gets built, just as it does not describe the compiler comand line options in the case of a regular program. In GLADE, we chose to create an external tool called GNATDIST, described in [6] and [2]. This tool takes a configuration file written in an Ada-like language and produces one executable per active partition; it shares code with GNATMAKE, GNAT's tool for building non-distributed programs.

GNATDIST allows the designer of a distributed application to apply pragmas and attributes on partitions. Using them, it is possible to set properties on partitions, such as their behaviour when a service becomes temporarily unavailable, as is described in section 4.

2.2 Limitations

The Ada 95 model for distributing applications has been a big win over Ada 83, but is still very limited with regards to today's needs. We strongly feel that important features and network protocols should also have been standardized, to increase Ada 95 interoperability. To take an example, a validated implementation does not have to support heterogeneous systems, when Intel-based and SPARC-based machines are involved in the same distributed program[2]. Also, an implementation made by a compiler vendor will probably not be compatible with an implementation made by another vendor.

Also, the behaviour of a distributed application in case of a partition's failure is undefined. This is consistent with the non-distributed model conception, where the disappearance of a part of the code from memory is not taken in account; it just cannot happen on a working hardware with a working operating system.

---

[2] Note that GLADE fully supports heterogeneous systems.

More advanced concepts such as safety and integrity of the communication have not been integrated in the annex either. It is generally assumed that the network and the computers are under complete control, and that no attacker can snoop or alter data packets (our solution for precisely this limitation can be found in section ??).

Former versions of GLADE also had limitations. For example, some versions had a single point of failure, called the **boot server**; it was the main partition of a distributed application, and the only entry point for new partitions. Its disappearance made it impossible to add new partitions to the running distributed program. As explained in sections 3 and 4, this limitation has been removed in the last version of GLADE. Also, another limitation that has been recently reduced and will be detailed in section 6 was that every partition contained the whole run time; this was a real problem in embedded systems where memory and processing power are both expensive and constrained.

3   Removing the Single Point of Failure

As we have seen in section 2.2, the boot server is the weakest part of the distributed application; if it dies, no more partition will be able to join the running distributed system. For this reason, we have added to GLADE the capability of having more than one boot server, using what we call **boot mirrors**.

A ring of boot mirrors connected together act as a replicated boot server. Tree-like structures could have been used instead of a ring; we chose a ring because it was easier to reconfigure in case of a partition failure.

A partition wishing to join a running distributed application needs to know the address of one of the boot mirrors and connects to it. The boot mirror will then propagate data about the new partition to the whole distributed program, and it will also provide the new partition with all the needed information to become an integral part of the distributed system.

Note that the presence of boot mirrors does not obsolete the boot server: one of the boot mirrors is considered to be the boot server. Its role is to launch the global wave-based termination detection algorithm similar to the one found in [7] and refined in [2].

While a single boot server can take all the decisions such as assigning a Partition_ID[3] for the new partition by itself, the various boot mirrors have to negotiate to avoid possible race conditions. One potential problem is if two instances of the same partition try to connect simultaneously to two different boot mirrors. Each of them will check that the partition is not already present in the distributed system, which will be the case. However, only one of the two partitions must be accepted, and the other one must be disconnected soon enough not to have received any request from third-party partitions. To solve this issue, different startup algorithms are used in this boot mirrors ring. One of them handles

---

[3] A Partition_ID is an integer used to identify a partition in a running distributed system [1, E.1(8)].

Partition_ID allocation, and another one with the Remote_Call_Interface package declaration and version check. The interested reader will find descriptions of those algorithms using the high-level Petri nets formalism in [2].

The boot mirrors ring can reconfigure itself dynamically, and can be extended or shrunken. When a new boot mirror wants to join the distributed application, it connects as any other partition does by contacting an existing boot mirror. Once it has been fully added to the running distributed application, it can insert itself in the ring and from there act as a boot mirror. If a boot mirror disappears, its predecessor and successor connect to each other and form a shrunken ring. All the partitions who previously chose the now-dead boot mirror contact another one from the last list of boot mirrors they got. Also, a new boot server is elected among the set of existing boot mirrors.

To prevent early death of the only boot mirror, a new attribute **Mirror_Expected** has been introduced in GNATDIST. Its presence prevents the distributed application from starting remote procedure calls until at least two boot mirrors are present, so that one of them can die without compromising the liveness of the whole distributed application.

However, when a partition offering an active service (such as through a Remote_Call_Interface package) dies, it may make the whole distributed application useless. The next section shows how a dead partition can be restarted or upgraded dynamically.

4   Fault Tolerance and Code Migration

There are several reasons why a partition must be restarted:

1. A failure occurred and the machine on which the partition was running is no longer reachable.
2. The administrator of the distributed systems decided that the machine on which the partition was running could not afford the load anymore; the partition is then stopped and must be restarted on a new node (this is also called **code migration**).
3. Errors or inefficiencies have been detected in the implementation of the services offered by the partition, or new services have been implemented. The old code will be replaced by the new one (**hot code swapping**).

In any case, the distributed application as a whole must be notified that a service has become unusable; decisions must be taken regarding the behaviour to adopt when this situation arises, depending on whether the service is supposed to be restarted or not, and whether the service is strictly necessary for the good health of the distributed program.

In section 4.1, we show how a partition can be restarted. Section 4.2 describes the various behaviours that can be adopted by the other partitions of the distributed application.

4.1   Restarting a Partition

The Distributed Systems Annex does not say anything about the name of a partition. A partition is known only through its Partition_ID, which must be unique in the distributed application at any time. This Partition_ID is obtained through the attribute of the same name applied to packages or subprograms, and it can only be used for comparaison with other such attributes. However, nothing in the Reference Manual forces the value of this attribute to stay the same during the whole life of the distributed program.

This facility has been used in GLADE to implement service restarting. When a partition offering a service becomes unavailable, its Partition_ID will not be reused at any later time. However, this service can be restarted on a new partition, which will get its own new Partition_ID.

The only constraint put on a service being restarted is to keep the same Version, that is to have the same declarative part as the one it replaces. It can be restarted on another machine with another architecture, or have a totally different implementation. Two direct consequences are that code migration and hot code swapping can be achieved very easily by using the right reconnection policy, as described in the next section. State data about the service can be kept using methods described in section 5.

4.2   Failure Handling Policy

A client using a service can adopt different behaviours when the service goes away. We have implemented three different behaviours, chosen through the Reconnection attribute of GNATDIST:

Reject_On_Restart: this policy is the strictest one. Once a service has been started, there is no way it can be replaced if it dies. This ensures that no inconsistency can be introduce by loss of data or incomplete transactions. Any call to such a service after its death will raise Communication_Error, even if it tries to start again.

Wait_Until_Restart: this policy makes any attempt to call the remote service blocking until the service has been revived. From the client point of view, no call to the service will ever fail, except when a call is in progress while the service is being disconnected. However, there is no guarantee that the client will not hang forever.

Fail_Until_Restart: this policy is a compromise between the two others. While the service is absent, Communication_Error will be raised. When it comes back, clients will be served again as if nothing happened. This allows a client to use a service when possible, or to use a fallback one if the main service is unavailable without blocking forever.

We have been recently proposed a fourth failure handling policy, whose descriptive name could be Wait_Until_Restart_Or_Timeout. We prefer the use of the "select ... then abort ... end select" construct in conjunction with the Wait_Until_Restart policy to get the same result.

5 Preserving Partition State

It is useful to be able to revive a dead partition. It is even better if the partition can restart with a meaningful consistent state. One of the ways to achieve this is to preserve the state of the partition at some specific points on a persistent data store to be able to restore it later.

Preserving the state of a partition can be performed at different programming levels. For example, the user can manually save all the pertinent partition data on a persistent storage object such as a file-system. This is error-prone as no automatic mechanism can ensure that the whole state has been saved.

A more transparent solution consists in using Shared_Passive packages. These categorized packages contain the declaration of shared variables: global data can be shared between active partitions, providing a repository similar to a shared memory, a shared file-system or a database. Entry-less protected objects offer safe concurrent access and update of shared objects. This feature is orthogonal to the notion of distributed objects, which are only accessed through their exported methods. Shared_Passive packages can be configured on both active and passive partitions. An active partition comprises one or more threads of control, whereas a passive partition must be pre-elaborated and may not perform any action that requires run time execution[4]. Typically, a passive partition can be seen as a global address space shared by several active partitions.

5.1 Shared_Passive Packages Implementation

In the GLADE /GNAT model, each partition that includes a Shared_Passive package has its own local copy of the package data. This local copy can have an initial state if the data storage used for this partition is persistent. In GNAT's implementation, this property is achieved by maintaining a set of files, in a dedicated directory. GLADE's implementation provides this particular storage along with additional ones.

Each variable v from a Shared_Passive package p gets its own file named after the fully qualified name of the variable, here "$p.v$". When a partition needs to read the value of variable v, it checks for the existence of this file. If it does not exist, the in-memory value of v is used, which corresponds to the initial value (if any) given at variable declaration time. If the file exists, the value stored in the file is used. Assigning a new value to v will create or update the content of the file. Therefore, this model automatically provides persistence assuming the underlying storage support lifetime is longer than the one of the program execution. It is up to the persistent storage interface to choose when the data is really committed to the persistent store. An easy choice could be at "Shared_Var_Close" time.

---

[4] In fact, those limitations only apply to user code and a compiler is free to add any code deemed necessary to perform the expected operations. However, it is against the spirit of passive partitions to embed code in them, as they should be placeable on strictly passive nodes such as a pure memory area.

Gnat Implementation Issues. For each shared variable v of type T, a read operation "vR" is created whose body is given in figure 1. The function Shared_Var_ROpen in package System.Shared_Storage either returns null if the storage does not exist, or returns a Stream_Access value that references the corresponding shared storage in which the current value will be read.

```
procedure vR is
   S : Ada.Streams.Stream_IO.Stream_Access;
begin
   S := Shared_Var_ROpen ("p.v");
   if S /= null then
      T'Read (S, v);
      Shared_Var_Close (S);
   end if;
end vR;
```

Sample 1: Read expansion

Each read operation of v is preceeded by a call to the corresponding "vR" procedure, which either leaves the initial value unchanged if the storage does not exist, or reads the current value from the shared storage if it does. In addition, for each shared variable v, an assignment procedure is created whose body is given in figure 2. The function Shared_Var_WOpen in package System.Shared_Storage returns a Stream_Access value that references the corresponding shared storage, ready to write the new value.

```
procedure vA is
   S : Ada.Streams.Stream_IO.Stream_Access;
begin
   S := Shared_Var_WOpen ("p.v");
   T'Write (S, v);
   Shared_Var_Close (S);
end vA;
```

Sample 2: Assignment expansion

Each assignment operation to v is followed by a call to the corresponding "vA" procedure, which writes the new value to the shared storage.

The call to procedure Shared_Var_Close indicates the end of a read or assignment operation. When a read operation and an assignment operation occur at the same time on the same partition, as the same stream is used simultaneously, both operations can terminate abruptly by raising an exception. Such a fatal error may occur when the stream has been opened in read mode (call to "vR") and then in write mode (call to "vA") and at least used by the read operation (call to T'Read). To avoid this unfriendly behaviour, we introduced an additional mutual exclusion at the partition level. This GNAT expansion always takes place, whether the user works in the distributed environment of GLADE or in the non-distributed environment of GNAT.

Glade Implementation Issues. GLADE provides a data representation based on XDR [8]. As GNAT's expansion is based on streams, heterogeneity is not a problem even for Shared_Passive packages shared between partitions running on different architectures.

Like a Remote_Call_Interface package, a Shared_Passive package has to be unique in the overall distributed system [1, E.2.1(10) and E.2.3(17)]. Moreover, a version check has to be performed to ensure that the package specification used at execution time is consistent with the one used at compilation time [1, E.3(6)]. In the GLADE environment, a Shared_Passive package like a Remote_-Call_Interface package has to register to the boot server during its elaboration code in order to declare its partition location.

For these reasons, GLADE generates specific elaboration code for the client stubs and the server skeleton. The server skeleton of a Shared_Passive package P registers information about itself onto the boot server, and then checks that it has been correctly registered by performing a request concerning itself. The client stubs retrieve information about the package and check the result against the information concerning the package specification as known at compile time.

5.2   Passive Partition Implementation

An interesting problem is raised by passive partitions, because they are not able to perform any action at run time, as they have no thread of control of their own. Therefore, active partitions that have visibility on Shared_Passive packages configured on passive partitions have to act in place of those partitions. Multiple registrations problems are solved by requiring that each passive partition in a distributed program has a unique name. For the same reason, Shared_Passive packages configured on such a partition are registered by the active partitions. The first registration of a Shared_Passive package is assumed to be authoritative; any further registration will be checked for consistency against this first registration.

5.3   Various Shared Storage Support

GLADE has a modular, layered and object-oriented architecture [9] which makes it easy to add new communication protocols. The important modules in this context are the core of GARLIC, called *Heart*, and the protocols. The protocol layers know nothing concerning the format of the data they convey, and the high-level layers will work on any protocol. All protocols inherit from a common abstract protocol class. To implement a new protocol, the developer overrides abstract methods of the base protocol class.

GLADE uses the same architecture for storages; every storage inherits from a common abstract storage class, whose methods will be redefined. Existing storage supports include GNAT's file-systems support, but also two other ones that have been recently added. One of them is based on a distributed shared memory algorithm, and the other one uses a fault-tolerant distributed database manager.

The user can configure the Shared_Passive packages and passive partitions by using GNATDIST. To support the configuration of passive partitions and storage supports, GNATDIST introduces two new attributes **Passive** and **Data_Location**.

The Passive attribute must be applied to a partition to indicate that this partition is passive. GNATDIST checks that it only holds Shared_Passive packages. GNATDIST allows to configure the network location of an active partition through the **Self_Location** attribute. This location contains the protocols with their internal data to use to communicate with this partition. It is also possible to configure the storage supports with their internal data to use to get access to shared objects from Shared_Passive packages configured on an active or passive partition through the **Data_Location** attribute. For instance, a developer using the GNATDIST configuration language could write the following representation clause.

for Partition'Data_Location **use** *"dfs://dir"*

This clause configures all the partitions storage supports to "dfs" which stands for Distributed File System; the directory used by the underlying storage support (probably NFS) is "dir".

5.4   Distributed File-System Storage

The basic storage support is based on a distributed file-system storage support. To safely share files among several partitions, the user must ensure that the partitions that reference shared objects have access to an operating system service such as NFS [10]. Also, some distributed file systems do not allow that two processes open the same file for writing at the same time; this can cause priority inversion problems, as various tasks with different priorities may be unblocked at the OS discretion.

5.5   Distributed Shared Memory Storage

This storage support provides an implementation of a distributed memory based on the well-known algorithm of Li and Hudak [11] [5].

Many algorithms have been proposed to maintain a strong memory coherence in a distributed shared memory. In the most basic algorithm, an object server is present on every partition of the distributed system and the servers are in charge of maintaining the consistency of the distributed shared memory. When a partition wants to access an object, it contacts its local server and two situations can occur: the object is available or it is not. If the object is unavailable, the server makes a read/write object fault in order to get the object from the others.

In a first approach, a server devoted to an object centralizes write and read operations. It receives these requests, executes them and sends acknowledgements or object copies. Naturally, the object server (or the object owner) may be overloaded by too many write requests especially when the object locality is

---

[5] The study of an Ada implementation of this algorithm can be found in [12].

not adequate. Thus, another strategy allows the object to migrate to the last client which becomes the new object owner. Read request bottleneck has a more flexible answer since the uniqueness of the object in read-mode is not required. Therefore, object replicas may be delivered by the object owner to several clients as long as the object is not modified. An invalidation protocol ensures that any write operation invalidates all object replicas.

GLADE's distributed shared memory is based on this algorithm with object migration and read-only replicas. This algorithm is very efficient in terms of network activity but does not provide fault-tolerance properties. Therefore, we plan to implement another algorithm for distributed memory which provides full object replicas [13].

5.6   Fault-Tolerant Database Storage

We have implemented one more back-end for Shared_Passive package, based on an existing soft real-time fault-tolerant distributed database manager, called Mnesia. Mnesia is written in Erlang[6], a language used primarily for building telecommunication switches [14].

Just as Ada, Erlang integrates distribution features right in the language. More exactly, the Erlang model is based on inter-process communication, but without any consideration about the physical location of the target process, which can be located on another Erlang node. The Mnesia database system allows an Erlang application to store any term and retrieve it with a $O(1)$ complexity in a read-only table[7]. Data can be accessed transparently from any Erlang node, and can be replicated on one or more nodes and with a reasonable complexity in more complicated cases.

We wrote this back-end with the assumption that a crash in an Ada distributed application was due to a network or a hardware failure, not to a fault in the application. Also, Erlang nodes are robust and not likely to crash, as the Erlang virtual machine takes care of all memory allocations and deallocations without letting the user manipulate pointers at all. Erlang even offers the programmer with automatic supervision, and can restart important threads if they die unexpectedly. Of course, an hardware failure will also affect an Erlang node, which is why Erlang keeps its databases replicated. We have then chosen to associate one local Erlang node to each Ada partition: an Ada partition P_i and its associatiated Erlang node E_i are located on the same machine.

Note that not all the Erlang nodes need to have a copy of the database holding the Shared_Passive state. However, to survive k simultaneous failures, at least $k + 1$ replicas of the database must exist.

6   Other Useful Features

The loose requirements of the Distributed Systems Annex over the internal behaviour of the distribution run time allowed us to implement additional features

---

[6] See http://www.erlang.org/ for more information on Erlang.

[7] A read-only table does not need exclusive access, as opposed to a read-write one.

while staying fully compatible with the Reference Manual. Some of those features have already been described in details in other articles; they will only be briefly summarized here for completeness.

Data Filtering: Incoming and outgoing data can go through a user-defined filter in order to provide services such as encryption or authentication [15];

Termination Policies: GLADE extends the classical termination model and allows for example clients to terminate while servers keep running [2];

Light Run-Time: in some particular configurations, GLADE can detect that a partition does not need to embed the whole distribution run-time. For example, if it can decide that a partition has a single-threaded client-only behaviour, then it can choose to include a light run-time that will not use any tasking.

7   Conclusion and Future Work

In this paper, we have shown how fault tolerance, code migration and data persistence have been added without giving up the compatibility with the language concepts described in the Reference Manual.

We are currently pursuing our research work in two directions:

1. We are extending the list of platforms that GLADE supports; support for JGNAT [16] is on its way, and will support distributed applications made of native and bytecode partitions.
2. We are working on bridges between the Distributed Systems Annex and other middleware, such as CORBA. We have already released ADABROKER[8], a free software CORBA implementation written in Ada. Our goal is to eventually use a common network layer and communication stack in both ADABROKER and GLADE. This could lead to the choice of IIOP, CORBA's standardized communication protocol for the Internet, as the underlying GLADE protocol.

Our goal is to continue to extend the range of domains that can be reached by Ada 95 distributed systems as much as possible.

References

1. ISO, *Information Technology – Programming Languages – Ada.* ISO, Feb. 1995. ISO/IEC/ANSI 8652:1995.
2. S. Tardieu, *GLADE – Une impl mentation de l'annexe des syst mes r partis d'Ada 95.* PhD thesis, École Nationale Sup rieure des T l communications, Oct. 1999. PhD advisor was L. Pautet.
3. L. Pautet, T. Quinot, and S. Tardieu, "CORBA & DSA: Divorce or Marriage?," in *Proceedings of AdaEurope'99*, (Santander, Spain), June 1999.
4. J. W. Armitage and J. V. Chelini, "Ada software on distributed targets: a survey of approaches," *ACM SIGADA Ada Letters*, vol. 4, pp. 32–37, Jan./Feb. 1985.

---

[8] ADABROKER is available at http://adabroker.eu.org/.

5. A. Gargaro, S. J. Goldsack, C. Goldthorpe, D. Ostermiller, P. Rogers, and R. A. Volz, "Towards distributed systems in Ada 9X," in *Proceedings of the Conference for Industry, Academia and Government*, (New York, NY, USA), pp. 49–54, ACM Press, Nov. 1992.

6. Y. Kermarrec, L. Nana, and L. Pautet, "GNATDIST: a configuration language for distributed Ada 95 applications," in *Proceedings of Tri-Ada'96*, (Philadelphia, Pennsylvania, USA), 1996.

7. F. Mattern, "Algorithms for distributed termination detection," *Distributed Computing*, vol. 2, no. 3, pp. 161–175, 1987.

8. Sun Microsystems, *xdr – library routines for external data representation*. Unix systems manual page.

9. Y. Kermarrec, L. Pautet, and S. Tardieu, "GARLIC: Generic Ada Reusable Library for Interpartition Communication," in *Proceedings Tri-Ada'95*, (Anaheim, California, USA), ACM, 1995.

10. J. Corbin, *The Network File System For System Administrators*. Mountain View, Californie, USA: Sun Microsystems, Inc., 1993.

11. K. Li and P. Hudak, "Memory coherence in shared virtual memory systems," *ACM Transactions on Computer Systems*, vol. 7, pp. 321–359, November 1989.

12. Y. Kermarrec and L. Pautet, "A Distributed Shared Virtual Memory for Ada83 and Ada9X Applications," in *Proceedings of TriAda'93*, (Seattle, Washington, USA), Sept. 1993.

13. K.-L. Wu, K. Fuchs, and J. Patel, "Error recovery in shared memory multiprocessors using private caches," *IEEE Transactions on Parallel and Distributed Systems*, vol. 1, pp. 231–239, April 1990.

14. J. Armstrong, M. Williams, and R. Virding, *Concurrent Programming in Erlang*. Englewood Cliffs, NJ: Prentice-Hall, 1993.

15. L. Pautet and T. Wolf, "Transparent filtering of streams in GLADE," in *Proceedings of Tri-Ada'97*, (Saint-Louis, Missouri, USA), 1997.

16. C. Comar, G. Dismukes, and F. Gasperoni, "Targeting GNAT to the Java Virtual Machine," in *Proceedings of the TRI-Ada'97 Conference, November 9–13, 1997, St. Louis, MO* (ACM, ed.), (New York, NY 10036, USA), pp. 149–164, ACM Press, 1997.

Reliable Communication in Distributed Computer-Controlled Systems

Luís Miguel Pinho[1] and Francisco Vasques[2]

[1] Department of Computer Engineering, ISEP, Polytechnic Institute of Porto,
Rua Dr. António Bernardino Almeida, 431, 4200-072 Porto, Portugal
lpinho@dei.isep.ipp.pt
[2] Department of Mechanical Engineering, FEUP, University of Porto,
Rua Dr. Roberto Frias, 4200-465 Porto, Portugal
vasques@fe.up.pt

Abstract. Controller Area Network (CAN) is a fieldbus network suitable for small-scale Distributed Computer Controlled Systems, being appropriate for transferring short real-time messages. However, CAN networks are also known to present some reliability problems, which can lead to an inconsistent message delivery, thus to an unreliable behaviour of the supported applications. In this paper, a set of atomic multicast protocols for CAN networks is presented, preventing the occurrence of such unreliable behaviours. The proposed protocols explore the CAN synchronous properties to minimise its run-time overhead, and to provide a timely service to the supported applications. The paper also presents conclusions drawn from the implementation of the protocols in the Ada version of Real-Time Linux.

1   Introduction

Currently, there is a trend to incorporate Commercial Off-The-Shelf (COTS) components in the development of Distributed Computer-Controlled Systems (DCCS). Using COTS components as the systems' building blocks provides a cost-effective solution, and at the same time allows for an easy upgrade and maintenance of the system. However, the use of COTS implies that specialised hardware can not be used to guarantee the reliability requirements. As COTS hardware and software do not usually provide the confidence level required by reliable real-time applications, reliability requirements must be guaranteed by a software-based fault-tolerance approach. It is obvious that the reliability of a DCCS lies, in a great extent, in its communication infrastructure, hence, the use of COTS networks poses new problems to the reliability of DCCS.

Controller Area Network (CAN) [1] is a fieldbus network suitable for small-scale DCCS, being appropriate for sending and receiving short real-time messages at speeds up to 1Mbit/sec. Several studies on how to guarantee the real-time requirements of messages in CAN networks are available (e.g. [2] [3]), providing the necessary pre-run-time schedulability conditions for the timing analysis of the supported traffic, even for the case of a network disturbed by temporary errors.

A. Strohmeier and D. Craeynest (Eds.): Ada-Europe 2001, LNCS 2043, pp. 136–147, 2001.
© Springer-Verlag Berlin Heidelberg 2001

CAN networks have extensive error detection/signalling mechanisms. The node that firstly detects an error sends an Error Frame, which leads to an automatic message retransmission. However, it is known that these mechanisms may fail when an error is detected in the last but one bit of the frame [4]. This problem occurs since the point of time at which a message is taken to be valid is different for the transmitter and the receivers. The message is valid for the transmitter if there is no error until the end of the transmitted frame. If the message is corrupted, a retransmission is triggered according to its priority. For the receiver side, the message is valid if there is no error until the last but one bit of the frame, being the value of the last bit treated as 'do not care'. Thus, a dominant value in the last bit does not lead to an error, in spite of violating the CAN rule stating that the last 7 bits of a frame are all recessive.

Receivers detecting a bit error in the last but one bit of the frame reject the frame and send an Error Frame starting in the following bit (last bit of the frame). As for receivers the last bit of a frame is a 'do not care' bit, other receivers may not detect the error and will accept the frame. However, the transmitter re-transmits the frame, as there was an error. As a consequence, some receivers will have an inconsistent message duplicate. The use of sequence numbers in messages can easily solve this problem, but it does not prevent messages from being received in different orders, thus not guaranteeing total order of atomic multicasts. However, if the transmitter fails before being able to successfully retransmit the frame, then some receivers will never receive the frame, which causes an inconsistent message omission. This is a more difficult problem to solve, than in the case of inconsistent message duplicates.

In [4], the probability of message omission and/or duplicates is evaluated, in a reference period of one hour, for a 32 node CAN network, with a network load of approximately 90%. Bit error rates were used ranging from 10^{-4} to 10^{-6}, and node failures per hour of 10^{-3} and 10^{-4}. For inconsistent message duplicates the results obtained were from 2.87×10^{1} to 2.84×10^{3} duplicate messages per hour, while for inconsistent message omissions the results ranged from 3.98×10^{-9} to 2.94×10^{-6}. These values demonstrate that for reliable real-time communications, CAN built-in mechanisms for error recovery and detection are not sufficient.

The following Section discusses the issue of atomic multicasts in CAN, and presents the considered failure assumptions. The proposed atomic multicast protocols are then presented in Section 3 (their specification is presented in Annex), where it is also shown how these protocols fulfil atomic multicast properties. Finally, Section 4 draws some considerations on the implementation of the protocols using the Ada version of Real-Time Linux [5].

2   Atomic Multicasts in CAN

In the considered system model, a hard real-time application is constituted by several tasks, which combined together perform the desired service. These processing tasks are distributed over the nodes of the system. To guarantee the reliability requirements of applications, some of its components must be replicated to tolerate individual faults. In order to have the same consistent state in the replicas, there must be a guarantee that they have the same input messages, and in the same order. That is, communication mechanisms must be used which ensure the atomic multicast properties. Multicast messages must be delivered by all (or none) of the replicas of a component, and they must be delivered only once. Also, they must be delivered in the same order in all replicas.

Therefore, in order to support hard real-time applications, the communication infrastructure must provide atomic multicast protocols. Based on [6], an atomic multicast has the following properties:

- Validity: If a correct node multicasts a message m, then all correct nodes deliver m.
- Agreement: If a correct node delivers message m, then all correct nodes deliver m.
- Integrity: For any message m, every correct node delivers m at most once, and only if m was previously multicast by *sender(m)*.
- Total Order: If correct nodes p and q both deliver message m and m', then p delivers m before m' if and only if q delivers m before m'.

CAN error detection and recovery mechanisms ensure the validity property, since when the sender is correct, all nodes will receive the message. Note that the network can be referred as a fail-consistent bus [7], since there is no possibility for different nodes to receive the message with different values. CAN error detection and recovery mechanisms are not, however, sufficient to guarantee the agreement and integrity properties [4]. In fact, it is possible for a correct node to receive a message not received by some other correct node (inconsistent message omission), and it is also possible that some node receives the same message more than once (inconsistent message duplicate). Total order is also not guaranteed, since new messages can be interleaved with retransmissions of failed messages, inducing nodes to receive messages in different orders.

Thus, the use of CAN to support reliable real-time communications must be carefully evaluated and appropriate mechanisms must be devised. In [4], a set of fault-tolerant broadcast protocols is proposed, which solve the message omission and duplicate problems. However, such protocols do not take full advantage of the CAN synchronous properties, therefore producing a greater run-time overhead under normal operation. For instance, in the best-case (data message with 8 bytes), the overhead of the total order protocol (TOTCAN) is approximately 150%. The problem is that, in order to achieve ordered multicasts, each receiver must re-transmit an ACCEPT message, even if there is no error. Other protocols in the set do not guarantee total order.

Another approach would be to use hardware-based solutions, such as the one described in [8]. This approach is based in a hardware error detector, which automatically retransmits messages that could potentially be omitted in some nodes. Although this approach solves the inconsistent message omission problem of CAN it does not provide solution to total order, as duplicates may occur. In order to achieve order, it is necessary to complement this mechanism with an off-line analysis approach. In this, messages must be separated in hard real-time and soft real-time. Only hard real-time messages have guaranteed worst-case response time inferior to the deadline, but it is necessary to use fixed time slots, off-line adjusting these messages to never compete for the bus.

2.1   Failure Assumptions

The proposed protocols only aim to tolerate network-related faults (including nodes' network interface faults). Application faults are masked by replication. Therefore, for the purpose of simplicity, from now on nodes will be used referring to their network interface. The protocols assumes that:

– System nodes either behave correctly or crash after a given number of failures. This behaviour is guaranteed by the CAN protocol, since in the case of multiple errors, the faulty node is disconnected from the network.
– During a time T, greater than the worst-case delivery time of any message, at most one single inconsistent message omission occurs. Considering the existence of 3.98 x 10^9 to 2.94 x 10^{-6} inconsistent message omissions per hour [4], the occurrence of a second omission error in a period T of, at most, several seconds has an extremely low probability.
– There are no permanent medium faults, such as the partitioning of the network. This type of faults must be masked by appropriate network redundancy schemes.

3   Middleware for Atomic Multicasts in CAN

The provided middleware for atomic multicasts in CAN (Figure 1) presents several protocols, with different failure assumptions and different behaviours in the case of errors. The Filtering layer allows that only nodes registered to receive a particular message stream will process messages related to that stream. This layer also decreases the number of messages in the bus in error situations. The *Unreliable* protocol provides only a simple multicast mechanism, giving no guarantees whatsoever to the streams that use it. The *IMD* protocol provides an atomic multicast that just addresses the inconsistent message duplicate problem. The *2M* protocol provides an atomic multicast addressing both inconsistent message duplicates and omissions, where messages are not delivered in an error situation (a previous version of this protocol is presented in [9]). The *2M-GD* protocol is an improvement of the *2M* protocol, which guarantees the message delivery, if at least one node has correctly received it.

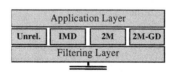

Fig. 1. Middleware for atomic multicasts in CAN

These atomic multicast protocols provide the system engineer with the possibility of trading efficiency by assumption coverage. The *IMD* protocol uses less bandwidth, but can lead to the violation of failure assumptions causing incorrect system behaviour. However, the use of protocols with higher assumption coverage may introduce unnecessary overheads in the system. Thus, it is possible to use different protocols for different message streams. Hence, streams with higher criticality may use protocols with higher assumption coverage, while streams with smaller criticality may use lighter protocols.

Relying on CAN frames being simultaneously received in every node, the protocols are based in delaying the deliver of a received frame for a bounded time. This behaviour is exploited to achieve atomic multicasts with the minimum number of exchanged messages. The approach is similar to the Δ-protocols [10], where, to obtain order, delivery is delayed for a specific time (Δ). However, in the proposed approach, delays are evaluated on a stream by stream basis, increasing the throughput of the system, since messages are delayed accordingly to their worst-case response times.

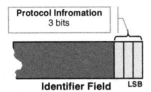

Protocol Bits	Message Type	
0 0 0	Data Msg.	2M-GD Protocol
0 0 1	Confirmation Msg.	
0 1 0	Retrans. Msg.	
0 1 1	Data Msg.	2M Protocol
1 0 0	Confirmation Msg.	
1 0 1	Abort Msg.	
1 1 0	IMD Protocol	
1 1 1	Unreliable Protocol	

Fig. 2. Identifier field and protocol information

The protocols use the less significant bits of the frame identifier to carry protocol information (Figure 2), identifying the type of each particular message and allowing the simultaneous use of different protocols. As the protocol information uses the less significant bits of the frame identifier, then more critical messages can use any type of protocol (even the Unreliable one), without loosing their criticality.

3.1   *IMD* Protocol

The *IMD* protocol (Figure 3) provides an atomic multicast that just addresses the inconsistent message duplicate problem. In order to guarantee that the duplicates are correctly managed, every node, when receiving a message marks it as unstable, tagging it with a $t_{deliver}$ (current time plus a $\delta_{deliver}$). If a duplicate is received before $t_{deliver}$, the duplicate is discarded and $t_{deliver}$ is updated (since in a node not receiving the original message $t_{deliver}$ refers to the duplicate).

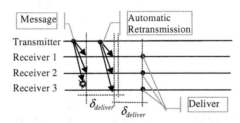

Fig. 3. *IMD* protocol behaviour: inconsistent message duplicate

For the transmitter (if it also delivers the message), since the CAN controller will only acknowledge the transmission when every node has received it correctly, there will be only one received message, even if there are duplicates. This message refers to the last duplicate sent, thus the transmitter can deliver the message after its $\delta_{deliver}$.

3.2   2M Protocol

The *2M* protocol (Figure 4) addresses both the inconsistent message duplicates and inconsistent message omissions guaranteeing that either all or none of the receivers deliver the message. For the latter, not delivering a message is equivalent to a transmitting node crash before sending the message.

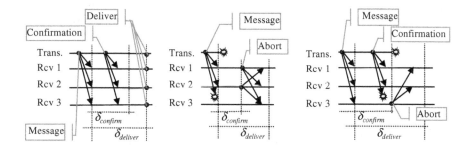

Fig. 4. *2M* protocol behaviour: error free situation (left), inconsistent message omission while sending the message (centre) and while sending the confirmation (right)

In the *2M* protocol, a node wanting to send an atomic multicast transmits the data message, followed by a confirmation message, which carries no data (*2M*: two messages). A receiving node before delivering the message, must receive both the message and the confirmation. If it does not receive the confirmation before $t_{confirm}$, it multicasts the related abort frame. This implies that several aborts can be simultaneously sent (at most one from each receiving node that is interested in that particular message stream). A message is only delivered if the node does not receive any related abort frame until after $t_{deliver}$ (a node receiving the message but not the confirmation does not know if the transmitter has failed while sending the message, or while sending the confirmation).

When a message is received, the node marks it as unstable, tagging it with $t_{confirm}$ and $t_{deliver}$. A node receiving a duplicate message discards it, but updates both $t_{confirm}$ and $t_{deliver}$. As the data message has higher priority than the related confirmation, then all duplicates will be received before the confirmation. Duplicate confirmation messages will always be sent before any abort (confirmation messages have higher priority than related abort messages), thus they will confirm an already confirmed message.

The advantage of the *2M* protocol is that in a fault-free execution there is only one extra frame (without data) per multicast. Only in the case of an error (low probability), there will be more protocol related messages in the bus, inducing a higher bandwidth utilisation. Note that the transmission of an abort is only necessary if there is a previous failure of the transmitter. Therefore, from the failure assumptions (there is no second inconsistent in the same period T), this abort will be free of inconsistent message omissions.

The transmitter can automatically confirm the message, since if it does not fail, every node will correctly deliver the message and the confirmation. The situation is the same as for the *IMD* protocol, since if the transmitter remains correct and delivers the message, then it will re-transmit any failed message.

3.3   *2M-GD* Protocol

The *2M* protocol can be modified to guarantee the delivery of a transmitted message to all nodes, if it is correctly received at least in one node. In the *2M-GD* (guaranteed delivery) protocol (Figure 5), nodes receiving the message but not the confirmation, retransmit the message (instead of an abort). This protocol is however less efficient than the *2M* protocol (in error situations), since messages are retransmitted with the data field. To guarantee order of delivery, it is necessary to use a $t_{deliver\_after\_error}$ to solve inconsistent retransmission duplicates.

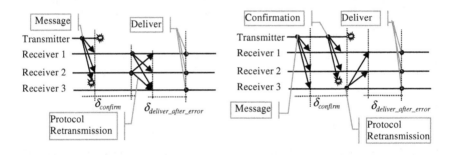

Fig. 5. *2M-GD* protocol behaviour: inconsistent message omission while sending the message (left) and while sending the confirmation (right)

3.4   Guaranteeing Atomic Multicast Properties

Atomic multicast properties (Section 2) are guaranteed by the protocols, since:

– Validity: A correct node is defined as one that does not fail while a multicast is in progress, that is until the multicast is correctly received by every node. As the CAN built-in mechanisms guarantee that any message will be automatically retransmitted, in the case of either a network or a receiving node failure, then the Validity property is guaranteed.
– Agreement: For the *IMD* protocol, if the transmitter does not fail, the CAN built-in mechanisms guarantee that every correct node will receive the message. Thus, they will all deliver it. For the *2M* protocol, a correct node only delivers a data message after receiving the related confirmation message and knowing that it will not receive any abort from other correct nodes. Therefore it knows that all correct

nodes will also deliver the message. In the *2M-GD* protocol the behaviour is the same, except in error situations, where if a correct node receives the message it will retransmit it, thus every correct node will receive and deliver it.

- Integrity: As the delivery of the message is delayed, duplicates are discarded and the Integrity property is guaranteed. On the other side, the CAN built-in mechanisms guarantee that a message is from the actual sender, since an error in the identifier field is detected with a sufficiently high probability [1].
- Total Order: The CAN network guarantees that correct messages are received in the same order by all nodes. However, the existence of duplicates and omissions may preclude messages from being orderly delivered. The use of the $t_{deliver}$ parameter guaranteed the total order of message delivery.

3.5   Evaluation of the Proposed Protocols

It is clear that when using the proposed atomic multicast protocols the worst-case delivery time of messages will be significantly increased. Due to the lack of space, the reader is referred to [11] for a presentation of the model and assumptions for the evaluation of the message streams' delivery time considering the proposed protocols.

Also in [11] an example is presented, allowing to conclude that although worst-case delivery time of message streams is increased, the predictability of message transfers is still guaranteed. It is obvious that the *IMD* protocol is the one that introduces smaller delays, while the *2M-GD* protocol is the one with the higher delays. The system's engineer can use this reasoning to better balance reliability and efficiency in the system. Moreover, the protocols increase network utilisation by less than 50%, since protocols-related retransmissions only occur in inconsistent message omission situations. Although this load increase is still large, it is much smaller than in other approaches, and it is the strictly necessary to cope with inconsistent message omissions using a software-based approach.

4   Implementation Considerations

The concept of using a real-time version of Linux as a platform for Distributed Computer-Controlled Systems is gaining an increased attention. Real-Time Linux provides a solution in which applications with real-time requirements can execute, whilst allowing interconnection with non real-time applications, thus connecting (in a controlled manner) real-time applications to other levels of the system.

Predictability is still an open issue in the (several) Real-Time Linux variants, manly due to both the PC architecture and the support to background Linux applications, and the lack of consolidated studies is impairment for applications with safety requirements. However, Real-Time Linux presents an easy to use solution, which tied together to the current open source movement, makes it a strong contender for a DCCS platform. Furthermore, small-scale DCCS can be easily supported due to the availability of support to CAN networks.

Therefore, it is pertinent to consider the viability of using Ada and Real-Time Linux together for the programming of Distributed Computer-Controlled Systems.

Thus, the middleware has been implemented in a platform of PCs running the Ada version of Real-Time Linux [5], connected through a CAN network (for a more detailed description of implementation details the reader is referred to [9]). Currently, the Ada version of Real-Time Linux provides a tasking kernel underneath the Linux kernel, implementing the low-level tasking mechanisms that are used to support Ada concurrency constructs. However, there is still no compiler targeting this platform, thus these mechanisms must be directly used. Furthermore, the full set of mechanisms is not implemented, lacking, for instance, the capability for interrupt handling.

In the implementation, these two issues came up. First, the available implementation of the Ada executive does not provide the high level mechanisms of Ada for concurrency and to control shared resources (e. g. tasks, protected objects). It only provides the low-level primitives for task and lock managing, which are used to program such mechanisms. Thus, the implementation had to rely on such low-level mechanisms, instead of using the higher level Ada constructs.

Interrupt handling services are also not available. Therefore, an interface to the available Real-Time Linux kernel interrupt services was created. However, as the Real-Time Linux kernel patch (version 1.2) used by the Ada version does not allow handlers to receive the interrupt number, it was not possible to implement a generic mechanism for interrupt handling. Therefore, interrupt handlers are created in a one-by-one basis, and are only used to wakeup a task, which is the proper handler.

It is, undoubtedly, possible to build DCCS applications using the Ada version of Real-Time Linux. However, although the presented problems were solved in this specific implementation, the attained solutions make no use of Ada's advantages for real-time programming. In this case, programming is as error prone as with other languages (e. g. C), not taking advantage of Ada's full programming power. Furthermore, the solutions are specific to the considered problem, thus they may not be appropriate for other applications.

It is important for Ada to be widely considered suitable for this platform, since it is a platform that is increasingly being used for real-time applications, a domain where Ada (still) has some influence. However, the lack of proper tools is impairment for Ada, since it is difficult to justify its use in preference to other languages.

5   Conclusions

This paper proposes a set of protocols for the support of atomic multicasts in CAN networks, providing both a timely and reliable service to the supported applications. In the proposed approach, atomic multicasts are guaranteed through the transmission of just an extra message (without data) for each message that must tolerate inconsistent message omissions. Only in case of an inconsistent message omission (low probability) there will be more protocol-related retransmissions. Inconsistent message duplicates are solved with a protocol that does not require extra transmissions, guaranteeing total order. Moreover, atomic multicast properties are achieved without more overheads than the strictly needed for a reliable multicast. These protocols explore the CAN synchronous properties to minimise its run-time overhead, and thus to provide a reliable and timely service to the supported applications.

The paper also draws some considerations on the platform used for implementation: PCs, running the Ada version of Real-Time Linux, connected through a CAN network. It is noted that, although this platform may be considered for Distributed Computer-Controlled Systems, currently the use of Ada does not present a significant advantage, and it is difficult to justify its use in preference to other languages.

Acknowledgements. The authors would like to thank the anonymous referees for their helpful comments. This work was partially supported by FCT (project DEAR-COTS 14187/98).

References

1. ISO 11898. (1993). Road Vehicle - Interchange of Digital Information - Controller Area Network (CAN) for High-Speed Communication. ISO.
2. Tindell, K., Burns, A. and Wellings, A. (1995). Calculating Controller Area Network (CAN) Message Response Time. In *Control Engineering Practice*, Vol. 3, No. 8, pp. 1163-1169.
3. Pinho, L., Vasques, F. and Tovar, E. (2000). Integrating inaccessibility in response time analysis of CAN networks. In *Proceedings of the 3rd IEEE International Workshop on Factory Communication Systems*, pages 77–84, Porto, Portugal, September 2000.
4. Rufino, J., Veríssimo, P., Arroz, G., Almeida, C. and Rodrigues, L. (1998). Fault-Tolerant Broadcasts in CAN. In *Proc. of the 28th Symposium on Fault-Tolerant Computing*, Munich, Germany, June 1998.
5. Shen, H. and Baker, T. (1999). A Linux Kernel Module Implementation of Restricted Ada Tasking. In *Proc. 9th International Real-Time Ada Workshop*, Ada Letters, Vol. XIX, N. 2, June 1999.
6. Hadzilacos, V. and Toueg, S. (1993). Fault-Tolerant Broadcasts and Related Problems. In Mullender, S. (Ed.), *Distributed Systems*, 2nd Ed., Addison-Wesley, 1993.
7. Powell, D. (1992). Failure Mode Assumptions and Assumption Coverage. In *Proc. of the 22nd Symposium on Fault-Tolerant Computing*, Boston, USA, July 1992.
8. Kaiser, J. and Livani, M. Achieving Fault-Tolerant Ordered Broadcasts in CAN. In *Proc. of the 3rd European Dependable Computing Conference*, Prague, Czech Republic, September 1999, pp. 351-363
9. Pinho, L., Vasques, F. and Ferreira, L. (2000). Programming Atomic Multicasts in CAN. In *Proc. of the 10th International Real-Time Ada Workshop*, Avila, Spain, September 2000.
10. Cristian, F., Aghili, H., Strong, R. and Dolev, D. Atomic Broadcast: From Simple Message Diffusion to Byzantine Agreement. In *Information and Control*, 118:1, 1995.
11. Pinho, L. and Vasques, F. Timing Analysis of Reliable Real-Time Communication in CAN Networks. Technical Report HURRAY-TR-0026, December 2000.

Annex: Protocol Specifications

IMD Protocol

Transmitter

```
1:     atomic_multicast (id, data):
2:          send (id, data)

3:     when sent_confirmed (id, data):  -- if it is registered for this message
4:          received_messages_set := received_messages_set ∪ msg(id,data)
5:          t_deliver(id) := clock + δ_deliver(id)

6:     deliver:
7:          for all id in received_messages_set loop
8:                  if t_deliver(id) < clock then
9:                          state(id) := delivered
10:                 end if
11:          end loop
```

Receiver

```
1:     when receive (id, data):
2:          if id ∉ received_messages_set then
3:                  received_messages_set := received_messages_set ∪ msg(id,data)
4:                  state(id) := unstable
5:          end if
6:          t_deliver(id) := clock + δ_deliver(id)

7:     deliver:
8:          for all id in received_messages_set loop
9:                  if state(id) = unstable and t_deliver(id) < clock then
10:                         state(id) := delivered
11:                 end if
12:          end loop
```

2M Protocol

Transmitter

```
1:     atomic_multicast (id, data):
2:          send (id, message, data)
3:          send (id, confirmation)

4:     when sent_confirmed (id, message, data):
5:          received_messages_set := received_messages_set ∪ msg(id,data)
6:          state(id) := confirmed
7:          t_deliver(id) := clock + δ_deliver(id)

8:     deliver:
9:          for all id in received_messages_set loop
10:                 if state(id) = confirmed and t_deliver(id) < clock then
11:                         state(id) := delivered
12:                 end if
13:          end loop
```

Receiver

```
1:     when receive (id, type, data):
2:          if type = message then
3:                  if id ∉ received_messages_set then
4:                          received_messages_set := received_messages_set ∪ msg(id,data)
5:                          state(id) := unstable
6:                  end if
7:                  t_deliver(id) := clock + δ_deliver(id)          -- duplicate update
8:                  t_confirm(id) := clock + δ_confirm(id)
9:          elsif type = confirmation then
10:                 state(id) := confirmed
11:          elsif type = abort then
```

```
12:                     if id ∈ received_messages_set then
13:                         received_messages_set := received_messages_set - msg(id)
14:                     end if
15:              end if

16:     deliver:
17:              for all id in received_messages_set loop
18:                     if state(id) = confirmed and t_deliver(id) < clock then
19:                         state(id) := delivered
20:                     elsif state(id) = unstable and t_confirm(id) < clock then
21:                         send (id, abort)
22:                         received_messages_set := received_messages_set - msg(id)
23:                     end if
24:              end loop
```

2M-GD Protocol

Transmitter

```
1:     atomic_multicast (id, data):
2:              send (id, message, data)
3:              send (id, confirmation)

4:     when sent_confirmed (id, message, data):
5:              received_messages_set := received_messages_set ∪ msg(id,data)
6:              state(id) := confirmed
7:              t_deliver(id) := clock + δ_deliver(id)

8:     deliver:
9:              for all id in received_messages_set loop
10:                    if state(id) = confirmed and         t_deliver(id) < clock then
11:                        state(id) := delivered
12:                    end if
13:             end loop
```

Receiver

```
1:     when receive (id, type, data):
2:              if type = message then
3:                     if id ∉ received_messages_set then
4:                         received_messages_set := received_messages_set ∪ msg(id,data)
5:                         state(id) := unstable
6:                     end if
7:                     t_deliver(id) := clock + δ_deliver(id)
8:                     t_confirm(id) := clock + δ_confirm(id)
9:              elsif type = confirmation then
10:                    state(id) := confirmed
11:             elsif type = retransmission then
12:                    if id ∉ received_messages_set then
13:                        received_messages_set := received_messages_set ∪ msg(id,data)
14:                    end if
15:                    state(id) := confirmed
16:                    t_deliver(id) := clock + δ_deliver_after_error(id)
17:             end if

18:     deliver:
19:             for all id in received_messages_set loop
20:                    if state(id) = confirmed and t_deliver(id) < clock then
21:                        state(id) := delivered
22:                    elsif state(id) = unstable and t_confirm(id) < clock then
23:                        send (id, retransmission, data)
24:                    end if
25:             end loop

26:     when sent_confirmed (id, retransmission, data):  -- if message was retransmitted
27:             state(id) := confirmed
28:             t_deliver(id) := clock + δ_deliver_after_error(id)
```

Building Robust Applications by Reusing Non-robust Legacy Software*

Francisco Guerra Santana, Javier Miranda González,
José Miguel Santos Espino, and José Carlos Rodríguez Calero

Instituto Universitario de Microelectrónica Aplicada (IUMA)
University of Las Palmas de Gran Canaria. Canary Islands, Spain.
fguerra@cma.ulpgc.es
jmiranda@cma.ulpgc.es
jomis@dis.ulpgc.es

Abstract. We propose a methodology for building robust Ada applications by reusing legacy software that we replicate among the nodes of a distributed system in order to increase fault tolerance of the service provided by the reused software. This methodology consists of writing an Ada interface which makes the binding to the legacy library. This interface forwards client requests to a group of remote servers, each one executing a copy of the legacy library. Dependability and consistency issues are solved inside the new interface code. In order to provide continuous service when adding new members, we propose techniques which prevent the server group from stopping service during state transfer. As an example of this methodology we present a robust database.

Keywords: Distributed Systems, Fault-Tolerant Systems, Continuous Service, Robust Database.

1 Introduction

Ada 95 facilitates the binding to libraries written in other languages [8]. If the library implements a deterministic behaviour we can go a step ahead and provide an Ada interface which not only makes a binding to the legacy library, but it also provides fault-tolerant operation. In particular, the interface forwards client requests to a group of replicated remote servers which behave like a single member. Each server runs a copy of the library code. For this purpose we need some additional software which provides reliable group communication.

Group_IO [5,6] is a library written in Ada which facilitates the construction of fault-tolerant distributed applications based on the active replication paradigm [15]. Compared with the primary-backup approach, the active replication technique offers the additional advantage that it allows for continuous service in the

---

* This work has been partially funded by the Spanish Research Council (CICYT), contract number TIC98–1032–C03–02.

A. Strohmeier and D. Craeynest (Eds.): Ada-Europe 2001, LNCS 2043, pp. 148–159, 2001.

presence of failures. Group_IO offers a simple interface to the implementation of reliable, atomic, causal, and uniform multicast. The work on Group_IO was initially motivated by our experience with Isis [2] and similar reliable multicast frameworks. The library allows also client-server interactions where the client is a group—interaction not supported by Isis— and it relies on an own consensus protocol [3,4] to implement uniform broadcast protocols. Current protocols inside Group_IO assume the fail-silent model [14]. Group_IO is the base on which the programming language Drago [1,11,12,13] has been implemented; however, Group_IO does not require Drago for its use.

In this paper, we propose a methodology for building robust applications from non-robust legacy applications. This methodology also provides a technique for the dynamic addition as well as replacement of replicas. We will use a real-life example to discuss this methodology in detail: a robust database implemented from an existing non-robust database named mSQL [10].

This paper is structured as follows. In the next section we present a short description of the Group_IO library. In Section 3 we present our proposed methodology for building robust applications by reusing existing applications. In Section 4 we present our example (the robust database) and discuss the problem of dynamic addition and replacement of members to the robust group. We close with conclusions and references.

2   Group_IO

Group_IO [5,6] is a library written in Ada which facilitates the construction of fault-tolerant distributed applications based on the active replication paradigm [15]. The initial version of Group_IO was static; this means that group membership could only change when any member failed. In the current version, Group_IO [7] provides support for the incorporation of new members to a group without being necessary to temporarily stop the application.

Group_IO provides two models for the incorporation of a new member: with and without state exchange. In both models the new member initially acts as a remote client and it sends to the group a *Join* or a *Join_And_Send* request.

In the first model, when the *Join* request is accepted and processed by the group the caller becomes a new member of the group. After this step, the new member receives exactly the same sequence of remote calls as the other replicas do. Therefore, this model ensures that the new member joins the group in a virtually synchronous order [2].

In the second model, when the new member sends to the group a *Join_And_Send* request it also includes state data. This state can be used to register any special information in all replicas. For example, "my process id is 2344", "my process name is S2", "my current state is ...". Each member gets this state information and sends a reply back to the new process. The reply contains the sender's current state. The state included in the *Join_And_Send* request and the state included in the corresponding reply must be short enough to be sent in a single message. After the full exchange of information between the new member and the current members, the new member can process subsequent requests to the group in the same way as its colleagues.

Let us examine this process in detail. The *Join* request is transparent to the code implemented for the replicas. However, the *Join_And_Send* request delivers the caller state to the replicas in a virtually synchronous ordering. Once the replicas process the *Join_And_Send* request, the new member will receive the same remote requests as its colleagues do. However, it will also receive the states of each one of the members. Group_IO does not oblige the new member to block until it receives the state of the other group members. Depending on the application semantics, the programmer can decide whether the new member must wait or must not wait for these states (in some cases this information is not critical, so the new member can process these messages later).

Group_IO could also be used to extend the semantics of the Ada 95 Distributed Systems Annex [8]. There would be no need to change the specification of System.RPC, nor the compiler or the language itself, only rewrite the implementation of System.RPC so that it calls Group_IO when needed, that is, when the actual remote call is directed towards a procedure of a replicated partition. Whether a certain partition is replicated or not would be decided at configuration time (after compile time and before link time) and that information could be stored in a configuration file, from where the code of System.RPC would retrieve it at run-time. However, the Ada 95 Distributed Systems Annex does not define how to pass the state to the incoming replica.

3   The Proposed Methodology

We propose to write a server which makes the binding to the existing deterministic library. This deterministic behaviour means that given an input X and a state Y, the library always returns the output Z; therefore, from a global view we can see the full software as a state machine [15]. This server is then replicated on several nodes and fed with group remote calls. As all the servers are assumed to be deterministic, they do exactly the same work, thus the remote client only needs to wait for the first reply to get the (valid) response for the service. If N-version programming is also required (implemented by means of several equivalent legacy libraries), the programmer can implement a voting mechanism on the client side [9].

3.1   First Stage: Build an Ada Interface

Most current standard software is written in other languages than Ada. However, it is simple to bind to such software from Ada 95 [8]. Therefore, if we need to build our robust application by reusing an existing legacy library, we must first write the corresponding Ada binding.

To provide remote access to the legacy library, we add a server which receives remote calls from clients. In order to tolerate hardware failures, this client-server software must handle them. If the legacy library provides remote access, the corresponding legacy client and legacy server are both placed on the same node to tolerate hardware failures [15], together with our server that binds to the legacy client. If the legacy library does not provide remote access, our server directly binds to it.

3.2 Second Stage: Add Group Semantics

We can also go a step ahead and, instead of providing a common Ada binding, we modify the body of our interface to do some additional work. In particular, the client side implementation of this Ada library can forward client requests to a group of remote servers which execute copies of the legacy library. This task can be easily done by means of Group_IO. The remote servers introduced in the previous section receive remote calls through Group_IO and they do the binding to their local copy of the legacy code.

This work is remarkably simple if we view the interaction with legacy software as a stream exchange. Our server does not need to analyze the data transferred in the legacy application from the client to the server side. Our client-side library just sends a byte stream to the group. Each remote server receives this byte stream and feeds its local copy of the legacy library. When the server has the reply, it sends back the corresponding byte stream to the remote client.

3.3 Third Stage: Support Dynamic Member Joins

Previous steps make the software robust, but they do not consider the issue of the dynamic join of a new member to the server group. This is especially required for non-stop applications where a member must be replaced because it has failed, or because software has been upgraded.

The incorporation of a new member in a replicated process group introduces one interesting problem. The full state of the running processes must be transferred to the new replica. While state transfer is going on, the impact on service performance must be minimum, both on throughput and latency. This problem will be discussed in the following section using the example of a robust database.

4   Example: A Robust Database

We have developed an example which helps to understand the state transfer problems: a robust database. We have applied the previously described methodology to build a fault-tolerant replicated database from mSQL [10] binaries. We first explain the overall methodology, and then we concentrate on the state transfer problem and several solutions we propose for this.

4.1   mSQL

mSQL [10] (Mini SQL) is a commercial database developed by *Hughes Technology* which is free for academic use. The first version was designed to handle small data sets in a fast and efficient way. The initial philosophy was to develop a simple and fast database engine which did not require special hardware nor too much memory. These features have made it very popular. In the second version mSQL keeps these features but also provides support for processing large amounts of data.

The mSQL implementation uses the client-server paradigm (Figure 1). On the client side, mSQL provides a C library named *libmsql.a*; on the server side it provides a daemon named *msql2d* which receives multiple SQL requests, serializes and processes them and sends back to the remote clients their corresponding replies.

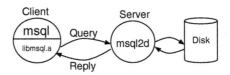

Fig. 1. mSQL Architecture

4.2   The Methodology in Practice

First Stage. We implemented an Ada library for the client side which receives mSQL queries and forwards them as group remote calls to a group of servers. Messaging is done by the Group_IO library. Each server is placed on a different node of the network. Each server runs a *msql2d* executable and works on a local copy of the database contents (Figure 2).

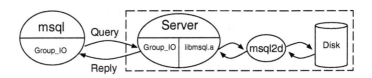

Fig. 2. Remote access to mSQL after first stage

Second Stage. To add group semantics to this architecture is quite simple, since Group_IO is used as the communication module. Group_IO protocols ensure that all servers receive exactly the same sequence of remote calls in the same order. As long as legacy software is deterministic, consistency is preserved in database contents (Figure 3).

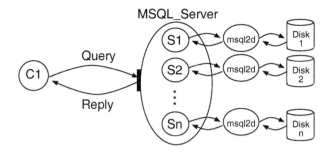

Fig. 3. Fault-tolerant access after second stage

Third Stage. Suppose we wish to add a new server to a working group. First of all, this new member must receive a copy of the database from the other servers, before it will be able to process client requests.

While the new server is receiving the database, some client can request a service which modifies the database contents. This must be taken with care, since there is a risk of inconsistency between the group database and the new member's one. One simple solution is to block all client requests to the group until the new member has completed its state transfer. This approach leads to unacceptable delays: the database may contain millions of registers, so the state transfer can take several minutes.

Our aim is to build a solution which attains to *continuous service*, that is, clients can make succesful requests even while state transfers are running.

For simplicity, we will consider a replicated group composed of two processes (S1 and S2) which executes requests made by two remote clients (C1 and C2). The state of S1 and S2 consists of one variable (*Dump_Id*) associated to the number of state transfers already done, and the contents of the database. We will also consider another process (S3) which must join the group and attain for the same state than S1 and S2 have: the current value of *Dump_Id* and the database contents.

mSQL has a utility called *msqldump* which generates a file containing all the required SQL commands to regenerate the database. We use this tool to implement the state transfer of the replicated database to the new replica. When each member of the *MSQL_Server* group receives the *Join_And_Send* request sent by the incoming member, it executes this utility. Each replicated dump file is given a unique name (a fixed prefix and the current value of *Dump_Id*). The new member then requests this replicated dump file and regenerates the database. The dump file is usually too big to be sent in a single message. Therefore, the new member must make multiple calls to get the whole file.

In the following sections, we describe some alternatives to attain continous service.

4.3   State Transfer: First Solution

In a simple solution S3 could make the state transfer in three steps. First, it sends a *Join_And_Send* request to the *MSQL_Server* group using its name, S3. When all members receive this request, they register the new member, dump their database into a unique file, and associate the dump file to the new member. Once completed, all group members send back their local state to the new member (its name and the current value of *Dump_Id*). This information is used by the new member to achieve the same local state as its peers (Figure 4).

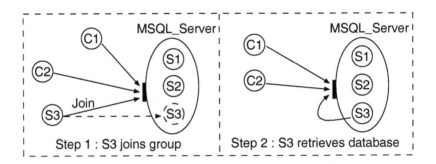

Fig. 4. First solution to state transfer

Once the *Join_And_Send* request has been processed, S3 is already a member of the database group. This implies that S3 will receive every remote call issued by C1 and C2.

However, although the state exchange is complete, the state transfer is not. Before processing the remote requests S3 must of course receive the dump file and rebuild its local database. In a second step, instead of accepting remote calls, S3 repeatedly sends requests to the group to receive chunks of its dump file. These requests are received by all group members: S1, S2 *and S3*, but Group_IO allows S3 to send back a null reply. Once S3 has received the whole dump file, it rebuilds the database and starts accepting all its queued remote calls.

Apparently it is a good solution. S3 does not block the remote callers C1 and C2 because, due to the database replication, C1 and C2 do not need to wait for S3 to process their remote calls. They can continue working as soon as they receive a reply from S1 or S2. Note that after S3 has retrieved the database, it must process these requests and reply them, too. The reasons for this are:

- The remote requests can modify the database.
- S1 and S2 may fail, thus S3 may be the only server able to serve client requests.

However, this solution has an important drawback. A parameter in Group_IO (*Max_Async*) specifies the maximum number of asynchrony between group members. This value fixes the size of several buffers; if this limit is reached the process will not accept any further remote call. If C1 and C2 send too many remote calls while S3 is requesting the database (requests which are also received by itself because it is already a member of the *MSQL_Server* group) and the *Max_Async* limit is reached, S3 blocks. It will not be able to process its own requests to the group to get its dump file. The main problem is the value of *Max_Async*, which can not be estimated easily (the database can contain millions of registers).

4.4   State Transfer: Second Solution

The problem stated above rises the need of a separate channel to transfer the database to the new member, different from the channel used in common client/server messaging. This channel can be built by means of a second group, called *MSQL_Transfer*, intended to transfer database contents. Such a group has the same membership as *MSQL_Server* in order to tolerate crash failures while at least a copy of the database remains available in the system.

Every process is member of these two overlapped groups: *MSQL_Server* to process database client requests, and *MSQL_Transfer* to process state transfers to new members. Group_IO provides mechanisms to know the destination group of every remote request. In addition, Group_IO has got mechanisms to easily bind one Ada task to each group message queue. This way, one Ada task can process remote calls for the *MSQL_Server* group and another Ada task can process the remote calls for *MSQL_Transfer*.

The new member behaves as follows. First, similarly to the previous solution, it sends a *Join_And_Send* request to the *MSQL_Server* group. Every member dumps the database and the caller becomes a new member of the *MSQL_Server* group. Second, the new member connects to the *MSQL_Transfer* group to retrieve a dump file (the database contents). Once completed, the member sends a *Join* request to *MSQL_Transfer* to become a new member of this group, too. Third, the new member builds the database and starts processing all its queued remote requests, that is, all remote requests that were received by the *MSQL_Server* group while the new member was retrieving the group state (Figure 5).

This solution has some problems. Let us consider the following scenario. Two clients *C1* and *C2* continuously issue requests to our robust database which initially is composed of a single member *S1*. Two processes *S2* and *S3* simultaneously try to join the server group to make it really fault-tolerant.

Group_IO serializes all requests. Let us assume S2 is served first. S1 generates a database dump file and associates it to S2. Next, S1 sends back its state to S2 which starts the database retrieval via *MSQL_Transfer*. Next, the group (now composed of S1 and S2) accepts S3's request to join the group. S1 dumps the database and sends back its state but S2 can not do the same, since it has to regenerate its own database first.

S2 and S3 are now simultaneously retrieving the database. Let us further assume S3 is faster than S2. Suppose that S1 fails when S3 has received the full database but S2 has not finished yet. In this case, the group becomes composed

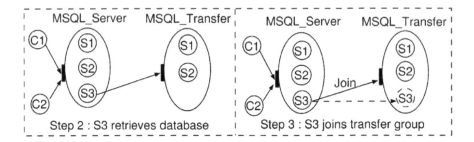

Fig. 5. Second solution to state transfer

of two servers with different state (S3 has the full database and S2 has an incomplete database). This inconsistent state can be avoided if, immediately after a server failure, we force every server which has not received the full database to leave the group and re-join again. However, it is not a good solution: the time required for transferring the full database must be as short as possible because it is a critical issue and simultaneous database transfers to new members increase this time (Figure 6).

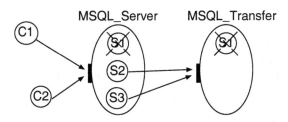

Fig. 6. S2 and S3 are retrieving the database from S1 when it fails

A more efficient approach is to serialize new member joins. This can be done if we force every new member to wait for all replies (the replies associated with the *Join_And_Send* request) before it connects to the *MSQL_Transfer* group to retrieve the database. In the case that there is an existing member which is still retrieving its database, this member is not able to serve any client requests, including the new member join request, which thereby is stopped. The consequence of this is that every new member blocks other processes which are trying to join the group until the new member is fully operational.

Figure 7 shows the sequence in detail. Bold vertical lines indicate that a process is a fully operational server. S2's request to join the group is accepted at time T2 (when the group is only composed by S1). S3's request is accepted

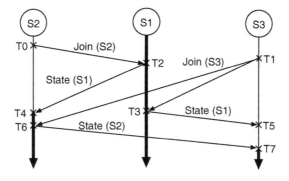

Fig. 7. Example sequence diagram for the join serialization solution

at T3 (when the group is composed by S1 and S2). Therefore, S2 waits for S1's reply only, but S3 must wait for the replies of S1 and S2. In this way, S3 waits until S2 completes its state transfer before it starts its state transfer.

The main disadvantage of this solution is that multiple dump files can be simultaneously generated (therefore consuming too much disk space). We are also slowing down the group performance because the new servers are receiving all new requests although they can not process these requests (because they must first receive the whole database). Therefore, it is again probable to reach the *Max_Async* value and block the whole group during state transfer.

4.5 State Transfer: Final Solution

In order to solve all these problems we can create another overlapped group named *Join_Sequencer* which serializes the requests to join the *MSQL_Server* group. Before joining *MSQL_Server*, each new server must first enter the *Join_Sequencer* group and wait for all replies. A member of *Join_Sequencer* does not reply any *Join_And_Send* requests until it has built its database and it has succesfully joined the *MSQL_Transfer* group (Figure 8).

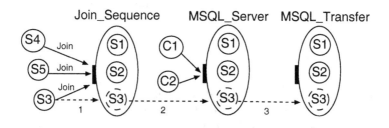

Fig. 8. Serialized joins of new members

This solution has an additional advantage. It reduces the number of operations required to retrieve the group state because, as we have already seen, each server must not only receive the full database; but it must also process all pending remote calls (remote calls which have been processed by its colleagues while it was receiving the whole database).

4.6   Optimizing the Proposed Solution

We have already seen that the task of transferring the whole database to a joining server is a critical issue. We have ensured the database availability by means of an overlapped, replicated group (*MSQL_Transfer*). However, we have also noted that the database can be composed by millions of registers. Therefore the overlapped group will make every member create its own dump file and to process all requests from the joining member asking for dump file chunks.

Group_IO not only provides support for group communication. It also provides support for the communication with a single member of the group. We can use this feature to optimize our algorithm for transferring the database as follows. First, a new member sends a *Join_And_Send* request to *MSQL_Server* group. Every member of *MSQL_Server* generates its own dump file. Second, instead of sending a request to all members of *MSQL_Transfer*, the new member selects one single member of this group and asks him to send the dump file. In this way, only one member does the transfer job. The following steps remain unmodified (the new member joins the *MSQL_Transfer* group, rebuilds its database and starts processing remote requests made by remote clients).

There is no trouble if the selected process fails before the state transfer is completed, as the other members of *MSQL_Transfer* have dump file copies and they are ready to resume state transfer. The new member just selects another (alive) member and database reception continues. When the new member finally joins *MSQL_Transfer*, the other members can delete their dump file copy.

4.7   Dynamic Software Updates

This methodology can also be applied to replace the running servers or update the application while it is running. If we get a new version of the legacy library which is compatible with the currently used one, we can just recompile the server program, launch new servers on our system nodes (so they get the group state) and finally terminate the old servers.

5   Conclusions

A methodology has been presented for building robust Ada applications by reusing non-robust legacy software. This methodology consists of writing an Ada interface which binds to the existing software and makes some additional work. This interface sends client requests to several remote servers which execute a copy of the legacy software. In order to provide continuous service we have also discussed a technique for the addition of new members to this server group without the need to temporarily stop the servers. We have analyzed various solutions for the state transfer and we have proposed a solution based on overlapped groups. As an application of this methodology, we have shown how to build a robust database from MSQL commercial software. This methodology can yield additional benefits such as dynamic software updating.

References

1. Arévalo, S., Álvarez, A., Miranda, J. and Guerra, F.: A Fault-tolerant Programming Language Based on Distributed Consensus, *Cabernet'94 Workshop*, Dublin (March 1994)
2. Birman, K., R. Cooper, T. Joseph, K. Marzullo, M. Makpangou, K. Kane, F. Schmuck, and M. Wood. The Isis System Manual. Version 2.1. September 1990.
3. Guerra, F., Arévalo, S., Álvarez, A., and Miranda, J. A Distributed Consensus Protocol with a Coordinator. *International Conference on Decentralized and Distributed Systems ICDDS'93*. IFIP, Palma de Mallorca (Spain). September 1993.
4. Guerra, F., Arévalo, S., Álvarez, A., and Miranda, J. A Quick Distributed Consensus Protocol. *Microprocessing and Microprogramming 39* (1993) pp.111–114.
5. Guerra, F. 1995. *Efficient Consensus Protocols for Distributed Systems*. Doctoral Dissertation. Technical University of Madrid. (In Spanish.)
6. Guerra, F. and Miranda, J. and Álvarez, A. and Arévalo, S. *An Ada Library to Program Fault-Tolerant Distributed Applications*. Reliable Software Technologies. Ada-Europe'97. 1997. pp.230–243.
7. Guerra, F. and Miranda. *The Group_IO Interface v3.0*. Technical Report (in spanish) *http://www.cma.ulpgc.es/users/gsd/*
8. Intermetrics, Inc. 1995. *Ada 95 Language Reference Manual*. Intermetrics, Inc., Cambridge, Mass. (January).
9. Lyu, M. R., ed. Software Fault Tolerance. Chichester, England: John Wiley and Sons, Inc., 1995.
10. Hughes Technologies Tye Ltd. *http://www.Hughes.com.au/*
11. Miranda, J., Álvarez, A., Guerra, F. and Arévalo, S. *Drago: A Language for Programming Fault-Tolerant and Cooperative Distributed Applications*. Reference Manual. *http://www.cma.ulpgc.es/users/gsd/*
12. Miranda, J., Álvarez, A., Arévalo, S. and Guerra, F. *Drago: An Ada Extension to Program Fault-Tolerant Distributed Applications*. Reliable Software Technologies. Ada-Europe'96. 1996. pp.235–246.
13. Miranda, J., Guerra, Martín, J. and González, A. *How to Modify GNAT Frontend to Experiment with Ada Extensions*. Reliable Software Technologies. Ada-Europe'99. 1999. pp.226–237.
14. Powell, Bonn, Seaton, Verísimo and Waeselynck, *The Delta-4 approach to Dependability in Open Distributed Computing Systems*, Digest of papers, FTC-18, 1988.
15. Schneider, F.B. Implementing Fault-tolerant Services Using the State Machine Approach: A Tutorial. *ACM Computing Surveys*, **22**(4), December 1990.

New Developments in Ada 95 Run-Time Profile Definitions and Language Refinements

Joyce L. Tokar

400 N 5th Street, Suite 1050
Phoenix, AZ 85004
USA
jlt@ddci.com

Abstract. The Ada 95 Programming Language [1] was designed to meet the needs of a variety of programming domains. The Ada 95 Special Needs Annexes provided the standard definition of the facilities required for special areas of use such as Systems Programming, Real-Time and Safety Critical domains. As the user community began to put the profiles defined in these Annexes to use, the need for new profiles emerged. The first such profile, Ravenscar, was defined as part of the work conducted at the 8th and 9th International Real-Time Ada Workshop (IRTAW-8 and IRTAW-9). This paper will present the latest refinement to the Ravenscar profile as modified at the IRTAW-10. Additional proposals for enhancements to Ada 95 to meet other needs of the real-time community will be described briefly. The concluding comments will provide some insight into the future of the Ada Programming Language with respect to support for special needs in the domains of real-time and high-integrity programming.

1 Introduction

The Ada 95 Programming Language [1] was designed to meet the needs of a variety of programming domains. Some of these areas require special definition of additional features or restrictions to the language that were beyond the core language specification. The Ada 95 Special Needs Annexes provided the standard definition of the facilities required for special areas of use such as Systems Programming, Real-Time and Safety Critical domains.

As the user community began to put the profiles defined in the Special Needs Annexes to use the need for new ones emerged. The first such profile, Ravenscar, was defined as part of the work of the International Real-Time Ada Working Group 8 (IRTAW-8). This group has refined the definition at IRTAW-9 based upon the preliminary findings in early implementations of the profile. This paper will present the latest definition of the Ravenscar profile as modified at the IRTAW-10. This definition of the profile is to be submitted for consideration for inclusion in the next revision of the Ada Standard.

The paper will begin with a brief review of the domain specific support that is defined in Ada 95. It will continue with a discussion of run-time profiles. A short section will follow to present some of the work on enhancements beyond run-time profiles. Finally, there will be a short summary of the standardization of the profiles presented herein.

A. Strohmeier and D. Craeynest (Eds.): Ada-Europe 2001, LNCS 2043, pp. 160-166, 2001.
© Springer-Verlag Berlin Heidelberg 2001

2 Background

Ada 95 is divided into two sections: the Core Language and the Annexes. The Core contains the definition of all of the syntax of the language along with most of the semantics. One of the key features described in the Core Language that is used throughout the specification of run-time profiles is the **pragma** Restrictions. This **pragma** is provided to facilitate the construction of simpler run-time environments.

The Annexes are refined further into the Predefined Language Environment, Interfaces to Other Languages and the Special Needs Annexes. The Special Needs Annexes define the semantics of features that are required to meet the needs of specific domains. The areas described are Systems Programming, Real-Time Systems, Distributed Systems, Information Systems, Numerics, and Safety and Security. The execution profiles described in this paper will focus primarily on the Systems Programming, Real-Time Systems, and Safety and Security domains.

The Systems Programming Annex specifies system level features such as the access to the underlying hardware, interrupt handling, access to shared variables, and task identification. The Real-Time Systems focuses on those features that are required for the development of real-time applications.

Included in the Real-Time Systems Annex are the definition of the run-time model, the definition of the priority model, dispatch scheduling models, execution time restrictions and other characteristics of the tasking model. This annex defines several run-time profiles that were well understood at the time of standardization: ceiling locking policy, FIFO or priority queuing policies, and FIFO within priority dispatching policy. These capabilities are defined in such a way to support extensions to the definition either by a vendor or by additional standardization at some time in the future.

Other domains addressed by the Special Needs Annexes include Numerics, Distribution, Information Systems, and Safety and Security. The Safety and Security Annex makes use of the **pragma** Restrictions to further restrict the execution profile to eliminate features that are considered high risk in the safety critical domain.

3 Run-Time Profiles

A run-time *profile* is defined to be a set of restrictions and behaviors specified to satisfy the needs of an operational domain. Hence, the features defined in the Special Needs Annexes may be combined by users or implementers to meet the demands of operational environments. Such a combination of features is considered to be a run-time profile.

3.1 Implementer Defined Profiles

An *implementer defined profile* is a definition of a run-time profile provided by an Ada vendor that uses **pragma** Restrictions and other characteristics of the Special Needs Annexes to refine the behavior of the Ada Execution Environment to meet the needs of a specific domain. Such a system generally results in an Ada Run-Time System (RTS) that is optimized to meet the requirements specified.

For example, DDC-I offers four different run-time profiles that may be specified using **pragma** Restrictions to provide the user with a variety of options to use when developing a bare board application. These options include:

1. Tasking with FIFO queuing, heap management, and exception handling
2. Tasking with Priority queuing, heap management, and exception handling
3. No tasking, no heap management, and exception handling
4. No tasking, no heap management, and no exception handling

Option 4 provides the user with the smallest operational run-time system. Such a system is often suitable for applications that are executing with very limited memory space.

3.2 User Defined Profiles

A *user defined profile* specifies an execution profile where an Ada user selects characteristics of the Special Needs Annexes along with restrictions enforced by **pragma** Restrictions to refine the behavior of the Ada Execution Environment to meet the needs of their specific domain. In this case, the user expects that a vendor supplying such a system will include an Ada RTS that is optimized to meet the requirements specified.

When a user defined profile defines an execution environment that meets the needs of a large domain of users, the user community expects common implementations of such a profile from all vendors. To achieve this goal, the user community unites to define an agreed upon profile and then publishes such a profile for adoption by the larger community and the vendors. The Ravenscar profile [2] is an example of such a profile.

The Ravenscar Profile. The Ravenscar profile [4] was the result of the work of a number of individuals at the 8th International Real-Time Ada Workshop. The profile was initially defined to be the minimum set of run-time functionality for use in high-integrity real-time systems that included the Ada tasking model based on fixed-priority preemptive scheduling. At the 9th International Real-Time Ada Workshop, the profile was finely tuned based on findings from the first implementation of the profile. This version of the profile is considered to be a *de facto* standard and is referenced in the ISO Technical Report Guide for the Use of the Ada Programming Language in High Integrity Systems" [5].

A brief summary of the Ravenscar profile may be described by the following set of restrictions:

```
No_Task_Hierarchy
No_Abort_Semantics
No_Task_Allocators
No_Dynamic_Priorities
No_Asynchronous_Control
No_Calendar
```

```
No_Relative_Delay
No_Protected_Type_Allocators
No_Local_Protected_Objects
No_Requeue
No_Select_Statements
No_Task_Attributes
No_Task_Termination
Simple_Barrier_Variables
Max_Task_Entries => 0
Max_Protected_Entries => 1
Max_Asynchronous_Nesting => 0
Max_Tasks => N -- fixed by the application
Max_Entry_Queue_Depth => 1
```

Several papers ([6], [7], [8], [9], [10], [11], [12]) were presented at the 10th International Real-Time Ada Workshop based on user experiences with various implementations of the Ravenscar profile. Based on the lessons learned that were presented at the Workshop and much discussion during the Workshop, several additional refinements have been suggested for the profile.

While the original profile was silent on exceptions, there are some occasions when raising an exception is the predefined behavior of the language. There were discussions at the workshop about what should happen when a bounded error occurs for example, when calling a potentially blocking operation from a protected object. This discussion led to the following recommendation: While executing within a protected object, a Ravenscar compliant implementation shall raise Program_Error for all potentially blocking operations. The only exception to this is if a subprogram call is to a foreign language domain (via **pragma** Import). In this case it may not be possible to detect the error.

Another area of interest was in the area of dynamic interrupt handlers. The original profile did not specify what the behavior should be although there are a number of instances in the high-integrity and real-time domain where the presence of dynamic handlers has compromised certification. Therefore, the following is recommended: The Ravenscar Profile should only support the static attachment of interrupt handlers via a new restriction - No_Dynamic_Interrupt_Handlers. When using this restriction, the programmer cannot use any of the subprograms defined in the package Ada.Interrupts. Therefore, an implementation may provide null bodies for these routines or raise Program_Error.

The next item of consideration was the use of dynamic storage and, in particular, storage pools. The group agreed that a Ravenscar compliant implementation shall make no implicit use of the heap in the RTS. The implementation shall not use the storage pool other than for the execution of allocations. Hence, the restriction No_Implicit_Heap_Allocations is added to the Ravenscar restrictions. The recommendation is to remain silent on the use of allocators and storage pools at the application level. Note that the application is free to use program-defined storage pools.

The research on scheduling theory had demonstrated that a range larger than the predefined range of 31 priorities is useful in developing efficient scheduling algorithms. The consensus of the group at the 10th IRTAW was not to make any recommendations on extending the range of priority since the Ravenscar profile is focused on restrictions not extensions.

Another item considered for inclusion in the profile was restricting the use of floating-point numbers in tasks. The view was that the task switching time could be significantly faster if the RTS did not need to consider floating point registers in the switch. It was decided that this was not an appropriate restriction for the Ravenscar profile and that many vendors already provide optimizations that address this issue.

Finally, there was considerable discussion about elaboration control of an application. In some instances the Ada 95 language rules for elaboration result in the possibility of code executing prior to the completion of the initiation of the execution environment. It was agreed that the Ravenscar profile should allow a user to specify if such elaboration should be delayed until the execution environment is initialized.

A number of ideas were presented for future extensions to the Ravenscar profile. For example, it would be nice to require an implementation to specify the length of time that an atomic operation is non-preemptible.

Other topics for future consideration include:

- What should be done about exceptions?
- Should the `No_Nested_Finalization` restriction be required by the Ravenscar profile?
- Could dynamic priorities be included in the profile? Dynamic priorities are needed to implement earliest deadline first scheduling.
- Could library level task creation and destruction be included in the profile? Library level access types and dynamic arrays of tasks are interesting features that are often considered to be useful in applications.
- Would it be possible to extend the profile to include multiple protected object entries and multiple elements in the entry queue?
- Should conditional entry calls be included? What about timed entry calls?
- When should dynamic protected objects be added to the profile?

The next step in the development of the Ravenscar profile is to present the proposed definition to the Ada Rapporteur Group for consideration for inclusion in the next revision of the Ada Language Reference Manual that is scheduled to occur in the next five years. The proposal recommends that a new configuration **pragma** be introduced that specifies the run-time profile to be used.

4 Additional Proposals for Language Refinement and Extension

Beyond the Ravenscar profile, there are a number of areas of interest to the real-time community regarding modification and use of various language features.

4.1 Extensible Protected Types

Combining the object-oriented features of Ada 95 with the real-time features is an area that has had extensive research over the past few years [13]. One of the primary developments from this work is a proposal for an extension to the definition of the protected type that would allow protected types to be extended in much the same manner as is done for tagged types.

One of the key areas of investigation to date has been in the area of protected entry barrier conditions. As a protected object is extended, the barrier condition on an entry that overrides a parent entry must strengthen the parent's entry barrier condition. A child can call a parent's entry as a special procedure to avoid being a potentially suspending operation.

In the current proposal for extensible protected types, the parent barrier is not evaluated when a call is made from a child. There is some interest in revising the model to check the parent's barrier, and raise `Program_Error` when there is a failure in the evaluation of the barrier when called from an extended child.

Similarly, there is some question as to what should be done in the post processing phased of a requeue to a parent's entry call. Presently, the model forbids post processing.

Moving to abstract protected entries there is some question as to whether these entries may have guards, should have guards, or shall not have guards. The current definition of extensible protected objects forbids guards on abstract protected entries.

More investigation and definition is needed in the areas of:

- Generics and mix-ins
- Integration with the features in the Real-Time Systems, Systems Programming, and Safety and Security Annexes
- Interrupt handlers
- The priority model

4.2 Alternative Scheduling Paradigms

There are a number of other interesting areas of research underway with respect to refining the real-time characteristics of Ada 95. These topics range from a proposal to support dynamic ceiling priorities to a variety of task dispatching and scheduling policies.

For example, a profile that supports dynamic ceiling priorities would provide an effective method to implement mode changes. The challenge here is to define a model that behaves predictably when used with all of the other features of Ada 95. To ensure efficiency, the model must not require an additional runtime lock. The profile must minimize the potential for priority inversion. It must be consistent with the dynamic task priorities and should result in minimum impact on the existing semantics for requeue, tasking, and the rest of the language features.

Generic formal task types would be useful to support the implementation of dynamic systems. Alternative scheduling paradigms are of interest in the development of a variety of real-time applications. Some of the candidates for inclusions are:

- Round-Robin Scheduling
- Sporadic Server Scheduling
- Non-preemptive, FIFO within priority

The proceedings of the 10th IRTAW [3] present some of the current positions on these topics and a more detailed summary of the Workshop discussions.

5 Relationship to the ISO/ANSI Standard

One final point for consideration is the standardization of the ideas proposed above. Presently, the ISO working group on Ada, WG 9, has put forth a Technical Corrigenda to the ISO community for approval and standardization. This document addresses a number of deficiencies that were found in the standard since its inception in 1995.

The next stage will be to propose addenda to the language through the Ada Rapporteur Group (ARG). The Ravenscar Profile was submitted to the ARG in November 2000. It is now under review and is expected to be modified slightly to conform to the entire language. This process will be monitored by the ARG. When complete, the profile will be included in the next submission to ISO as part of the continuing maintenance of the Ada language standard. Please contact the author of this paper if you have interest in contributing ideas and comments to the ARG.

References

1.   Ada95 Reference Manual, International Standard ANSI/ISO/IEC-8652:1995, January 1995.
2.   Burns, Alan, "The Ravenscar Profile," Ada Letters, Volume XIX, Number 4, December 1999.
3.   González Harbour, Michael (Editor), "Proceedings of the 10th International Real-Time Ada Workshop," Ada Letters, Volume XXI, Number 1, March 2001.
4.   Baker, Ted and Tuillio Vardanega, "Session Summary: Tasking Profiles," Ada Letters, Volume XVI.
5.   "Guide for the Use of the Ada Programming Language in High Integrity Systems," ISO/IEC TR 15942, 1999.
6.   de la Puente, Juan A., Juan Zamorano, José Ruiz, Ramón Fernández, and Rodrigo García, "The Design and Implementation of the Open Ravenscar Kernel," Ada Letters, Volume XXI, Number 1, March 2001.
7.   Dobbing, Alan, "The Ravenscar Profile for High-Integrity Java Programs," Ada Letters, Volume XXI, Number 1, March 2001.
8.   Asplund, Lars and Kristina Lundqvist, "Exceptions in Ravenscar - Complexity in the Formal Modeling," Ada Letters, Volume XXI, Number 1, March 2001.
9.   Michell, Stephen, "Position paper: Completing the Ravenscar Profile," Ada Letters, Volume XXI, Number 1, March 2001.
10. Vardanega, Tullio and Gert Caspersen, "Using the Ravenscar Profile for Space Applications: the OBOSS Case," Ada Letters, Volume XXI, Number 1, March 2001.
11. Audsley, Neil, Alan Burns and Andy Wellings, "Implementing a High-Integrity Executive using Ravenscar," Ada Letters, Volume XXI, Number 1, March 2001.
12. Audsley, Neil and Andy Wellings,"Issues with using Ravenscar and the Ada Distributed Systems Annex," Ada Letters, Volume XXI, Number 1, March 2001.
13. Wellings, A. J., B. Johnson, B. Sanden,J. Kienzle, T. Wolf, and S. Michell, "Extensible Protected Types: Proposal Status," Ada Letters, Volume XXI, Number 1, March 2001.

Complex Task Implementation in Ada

Alfons Crespo, Patricia Balbastre, and Silvia Terrasa

Universidad Politécnica de Valencia (Spain)
Camino Vera s/n; 46072 Valencia
alfons@disca.upv.es

Abstract. Control applications require defining several parallel activities to model the environment. Periodic tasks model the activities to be executed at periodic instants of time. While the process of control design is focused on obtaining the regulator, later on translated into an algorithm, the software design is focused on producing pieces of software that will be executed concurrently under a scheduler. Nowadays, more and more applications require complex computation and the use of complex algorithms that can compromise the response time of the system. The activities involving a control loop task can be structured in some parts: data acquisition, computation of the control action, optional activities and output of the control action. This decomposition is useful to improve the control performance and reduce delays due to the scheduler. This paper shows how to implement complex real-time control applications by means of periodic tasks in Ada, using a task decomposition.

1 Introduction

Real-time control applications are usually structured as a set of periodic and sporadic tasks which interact with the environment by reading the sensor values and sending actions to external devices. While the process of control design is focused on obtaining the regulator, later on translated into an algorithm, the software design is focused on producing pieces of software that will be executed concurrently under the supervision of a scheduler. The software designer has to ensure that all the tasks meet their deadlines, i.e., the system is schedulable. Nowadays, more and more applications require complex computation and the use of complex algorithms that can compromise the response time of the system. The activities involving a control loop task can be structured in the following parts [6]:

1. Data acquisition. Data from external sensor is acquired.
2. Computation of the control action. It is mandatory and should be executed as soon as possible. At the end of this part, the basic control action is ready to be sent to the actuators.
3. Solution improvement. During this time, an algorithm or method is able to improve the answer obtained in the first part. This computation may be based on an iterative technique or on other methods (knowledge based methods, progressive reasoning, etc.). At the end or in between, this second part, an improved solution is available to be sent to the actuators. This part can be considered optional.

A. Strohmeier and D. Craeynest (Eds.): Ada-Europe 2001, LNCS 2043, pp. 167-178, 2001.
© Springer-Verlag Berlin Heidelberg 2001

4. Output the control action. Must be done either as soon as possible or within a fixed time interval.

The control computation can be divided into a main part (mandatory) and one or more optional parts. The mandatory part gives a first solution to the control problem. Optional parts try to improve the solution. For the purpose of this work, it will only be considered the first four parts of a task. The following figure (Figure 1) illustrates the activity parts:

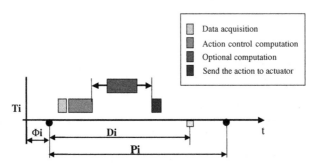

Fig. 1. Parts of a control activity.

This decomposition method is used to reduce jitter variation defining a Data Acquisition Interval (DAI) and Control Action Interval (CAI) under priority based scheduling [6]. The scheduling analysis of this new set of tasks is proposed for both static and dynamic scheduling policies in [6] and [3]. In [1] a methodology to find the appropriate scheduling to minimize the degrading of the control performances is proposed. The used task decomposition could be implemented as a single task with internal delays and priority changes. Although this alternative solution saves memory, context switches and synchronization mechanism, the integration of optional parts presents strong difficulties and has to be implemented as a separated task. However, this work have educational purposes and the task decomposition is cleaner than the single task solution and allows to experiment with different mechanisms.

This paper shows how to implement real-time control applications by means of periodic tasks in Ada. In Section 2 a periodic task scheme is presented. In Section 3 the model is improved in order to reduce the variance of the final parts. Section 4 explains how to include optional parts in the periodic tasks. In Section 5 the complete model, with initial, optional and final parts is presented. An example is shown in Section 6, and, finally, Section 6 ends with some conclusions.

2 Periodic Task Scheme

The design of a control system involves the definition of several control loops (each one is a task) that have to be executed under the operating system scheduler. Therefore, periodic tasks are the main components in the design of real-time control applications, performing the actions at regular intervals of time. The periodic scheme is a well known model and there are several methods and techniques for the design, analysis and validation of this systems. [4]

A periodic activity is defined by means of a set of characteristics as period, deadline, offset and worst case computation time (*wcet*). Priority based scheduling has been studied and applied in the real-time community. There is a strong work done related to design, analysis and validation. Ada tasking provides a preemptive priority based scheduler to execute tasks [5]. The priority assignment can be done using Rate Monotonic (RM) [8] or Deadline Monotonic (DM) [7]. In both cases there are analytical methods to determine the system schedulability. The execution of several periodic tasks under a priority based scheduling involves the execution of these activities considering the priority assigned. Tasks with higher priority can preempt lower priority tasks.

The periodic task set has a common initial time that requires some initial synchronization among them. To synchronize all tasks a mechanism based on protected objects, like a Barrier, is used:

```
package Barriers is
   protected type Barrier is
      entry Wait;   --tasks wait UNTIL flag is true
      procedure Go;   --sets the flag to true
   private
      Flag: Boolean:=False;
   end Barrier;
end Barriers;
```

All periodic tasks wait in the Barrier until the time reference is taken and then the Go procedure to start all the periodic tasks is called.

The definition of a periodic task requires the parameters to create a periodic activity and the procedures to define the initial time and start and finish the periodic activities. The following package presents the task type Periodic_Task and its interface.

```
with Ada.Real_Time; use Ada.Real_Time;
package Periodic_Tasks  is
   task type P_Task (Id : Integer; Prio: Integer;
           Wcet, Period, Deadline, Offset : Natural) is
      pragma Priority(Prio);
   end P_Task;
   procedure Set_Initial_Time(It : Time);
   procedure Start;
   procedure Finish;
end Periodic_Tasks;
```

To define a periodic task it is required a task identifier, a priority, the computation time, the period, the deadline and the offset. The parameters connected to time (computation time, period, deadline, and offset) will be defined as Natural and considered as milliseconds. A more appropriated type should be Time_Span but the task discriminants must have a discrete type For the purpose of this paper, tasks only will execute irrelevant code to consume the *wcet*. In a real time control application other parameters should complete the periodic task definition such as sensor identifier, kind of regulator and parameters, actuator identifier and so on. The implementation of the package `Periodic_Tasks` is:

```
with Ada.Real_Time;use Ada.Real_Time;
with Barriers; use Barriers;
package body Periodic_Tasks is
    Initial_Time : Time;
    Stop : Barrier;
    Finished : Boolean := False;
    Pragma Atomic(Finished);

    procedure Compute(N : Integer ) is separate;
    procedure Set_Initial_Time(It : Time) is
    begin
        Initial_Time := It;
    end Set_Initial_Time;
    procedure Start is
    begin
        Stop.Go;
    end Start;
    procedure Finish is
    begin
        Finished := True;
    end Finish;

    task body P_Task is
        Per  : Time_Span;
        Next : Time;
    begin
        Stop.Wait;
        Per  := Milliseconds(Period);
        Next := Initial_Time + Milliseconds(Offset);
        delay until Next;
        loop
            Compute(Wcet);
            Next := Next + Per;
            delay until Next;
            exit when Finished;
        end loop;
    end P_Task;
end PeriodicTasks;
```

3 Delaying Final Parts

Different factors have strong influence in the termination time of a task. It varies in each activation due to:
- Data delays
- Computation variation
- Preemption of higher priority tasks

The jitter term in real time systems refers to this variation. It can have some important effects in the control performance because introduce variable delays at action computation time. [1] In some cases, it is better to have a large fixed but known than an unknown delay. As mentioned before, one of the possible solutions is to split the control task in two parts: data acquisition and action computation (main part) and the final part. The final part takes care of sending the computed action to the actuator. The final part can be delayed an offset from the beginning of the period to reduce the effects of the jitter problem. It can be implemented defining two different tasks: main task and final task. Both tasks have some characteristics in common such as: period, initial offset and deadline. Specific parameters are: the *wcet* for both tasks and the offset of the final part.

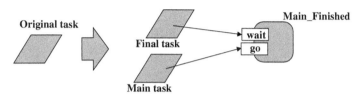

Fig. 2. Task decomposition: a main task and a final task with a synchronization mechanism

To avoid the introduction of additional jitter in the final parts, final tasks will have a higher priority than the main parts [6]. Assuming a priority assignation for the original tasks based on the deadline monotonic. Once the priorities are assigned, the task decomposition will generate two tasks (main task and final task) for each original task. The task priorities is organised in bands. All tasks from a higher band will have a priority higher than any task from a lower band. If the corresponding original task has a *k* priority level, the main task will have the same *k* priority level in the lower band and the final task will have *k* priority in the higher band. Both tasks are synchronised using a Barrier.

```
with Ada.Real_Time; use Ada.Real_Time;
package MF_Tasks is
    task type P_MF_Task (Id : Integer; Prio: Integer;
         Wcet_Main, Period, Deadline, Offset,
         Wcet_Final, Offset_Final : Integer) is
      pragma Priority(Prio);
    end P_MF_Task;
    procedure Set_Initial_Time(It : Time);
    procedure Start;
    procedure Finish;
end MF_Tasks;
```

The P_MF_Task task body defines an internal Final_Task task sharing some parameters defined in the instantiation.

```
with Ada.Real_Time;use Ada.Real_Time;
with Barriers; use Barriers;

package body MF_Tasks is
    Initial_Time : Time;
    Stop : Barrier;
    Finished : Boolean := False;
    Pragma Atomic(Finished);
```

```
task body P_MF_Task is
   Per  : Time_Span;
   Next : Time;
   Main_Finished: Barrier;

   task Final_Task is  pragma Priority(Prio_Final);
   end Final_Task;

   task body Final_Task is
      Next : Time;
   begin
      Stop.Wait;
      Next := Initial_Time + Milliseconds(Offset) +
              Milliseconds(Offset_Final);
      delay until Next;
      loop
         Main_Finished.Wait;
         compute(Wcet_Final);
         Next := Next + Per;
         delay until Next;
         exit when Finished;
      end loop;
   end Final_Task;

begin
   Stop.Wait;
   Per  := Milliseconds(Period);
   Next := Initial_Time + Milliseconds(Offset);
   delay until Next;
   loop
      Compute(Wcet_main);
      Main_Finished.Go;
      Next := Next + Per;
      delay until Next;
      exit when Finished;
   end loop;
end P_MF_Task;

end MF_Tasks;
```

4 Tasks with Optional Parts

The inclusion of optional parts in control system algorithms allows the use of the remaining CPU time to improve the response to some control demands. From the control system point of view, a task can determine a first solution and, if there is enough time, to improve it using more sophisticated algorithms or more information. The control action computation can be structured as:

1. Computation of the control action. It is mandatory and should be executed as soon as possible. At the end of this part, the basic control action is ready to be sent to the actuators.

2. Solution improvement. During this time, an algorithm or method is able to improve the answer obtained in the first part. This computation may be based on an iterative technique or on other methods (knowledge based methods, progressive reasoning, etc.). At the end, or in the middle of this second part, an improved solution is available to be sent to the actuators. This part can be considered as optional.

Optional parts cannot be considered as a part of the mandatory ones neither be executed at the same priority level. The execution of optional parts will be determined by the availability of remaining time and the demand for soft sporadic load. Several approaches to include optional computation in real time systems can be found in the literature [2]. From the point of view of this paper, we consider a simple solution. The requirements for the execution of optional parts are:
- Have to be executed in remaining time
- Have to be executed after the main part has finished and before the final part
- Can be aborted when the deadline for solution improvement has finished. Partial results are considered by the final part.

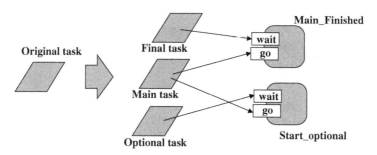

Fig. 3. A task is split in three tasks: Main, Final and Optional

Taking into account these requirements, a control task is split in three tasks with a priority task assignment following the a three band scheme: the priority of the final tasks are assigned to the higher band, main tasks are assigned to the intermediate band and the optional tasks to the lower band.

An asynchronous transfer control to control the execution time of the optional task is considered.

```
With Ada.Real_Time;use Ada.Real_Time;
package MOF_Tasks is

    task type P_MOF_Task (Id : Integer;
         Prio: Integer;
         wcet_Main, Period, Deadline, Offset, Id_Optional,
         wcet_optional, Wcet_Final, Id_Final, Prio_Final,
         wcet_Final, Offset_Final : Integer) is
      pragma Priority(Prio);
    end P_MOF_Task;
    procedure Set_Initial_Time(It : Time);
    procedure Start;
```

```
      procedure Finish;
   end MOF_Tasks;
```

The implementation of the previous package is the following:

```
with Ada.Real_Time;use Ada.Real_Time;
with Barriers; use Barriers;

package body MOF_Tasks is
   Initial_Time : Time;
   Stop : Barrier;
   Finished : Boolean := False;
   Pragma Atomic(Finished);

   task body P_MOF_Task is
      Per, Dead : Time_Span;
      Next,Optional_Deadline  : Time;
      Main_Finished, Start_Optional: Barrier;

      task Final_Task is  pragma Priority(Prio_Final);
      end Final_Task;
      task Optional_Task is  pragma Priority(Prio_Optional);
      end Optional_Task;

      task body Final_Task is
         Next : Time;
      begin
         Stop.Wait;
         Next := Initial_Time + Milliseconds(Offset) +
                 Milliseconds(Offset_Final);
         delay until Next;
         loop
            Main_Finished.Wait;
            Compute(Wcet_Final);
            Next := Next + Per;
            delay until Next;
            exit when Finished;
         end loop;
      end Final_Task;
      task body Optional_Task is
      begin
         Stop.Wait;
         loop
            Start_Optional.Wait;
            select
               delay until Optional_Deadline;
            then abort
               Compute(Wcet_Optional);
            end select;
            exit when Finished;
         end loop;
      end Optional_Task;

   begin
      Stop.Wait;
```

```
      Per  := Milliseconds(Period);
      Dead := Milliseconds(Offset_Final);
      Next := Initial_Time + Milliseconds(Offset);
      delay until Next;
      while not Finished loop
         Compute(Wcet_Main);
         Main_Finished.Go;
         Optional_Deadline := Next + Dead;
         Start_Optional.Go;
         Next := Next + Per;
         delay until Next;
      end loop;
   end MOF_Task;
end P_MOF_Tasks;
```

5 Task with Initial, Optional, and Final Parts

The model can be completed isolating initial part of the task to decrease the variance
of the data acquisition part. Following the same scheme proposed before, parts in a
task can be split in four components (Figure 4):

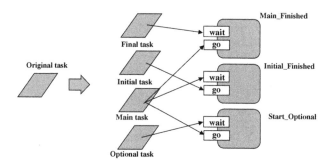

Fig. 4. A task split in four parts

```
with Ada.Real_Time;use Ada.Real_Time;
package IMOF_Tasks is
   task type P_IMOF_Task (Id : Integer; Prio: Integer;
      Wcet_Main, Period, Deadline, Offset : Integer;
      Id_Initial, Prio_Initial, Wcet_Initial, Id_Optional,
      Prio_Optional, Wcet_Optional, Id_Final, Prio_Final,
      Wcet_Final, Offset_Final : Integer)  is
   end P_IMOF_Task;
   procedure Set_Initial_Time(It : Time);
   procedure Start;
   procedure Finish;
end IMOF_Tasks;
```

The implementation of P_IMOF_Tasks package is:

```
with Ada.Real_Time;use Ada.Real_Time;
with Barriers; use Barriers;
package body IMOF_Tasks is
  Initial_Time : Time;
  Stop : Barrier;
  Finished : Boolean := False;
  ...
  task body P_IMOF_Task is
    Per, Dead : Time_Span; Next,Optional_Deadline  : Time;
    Main_Finished, Start_Optional, Initial_Finished: Barrier;
    task Final_Task is  pragma Priority(Prio_Final);
    end Final_Task;

    task Initial_Task is   pragma Priority(Prio_Initial);
    end Initial_Task;

    task Optional_Task is
       pragma Priority(Prio_Optional);
    end Optional_Task;

    task body Final_Task is ... -same code as MOF tasks
     task body Initial_Task is
     begin
       Stop.Wait;
       Per := Milliseconds(Period);
       Dead := Milliseconds(Offset_Final);
       Next := Initial_Time + Milliseconds(Offset);
       delay until Next;
       loop
          Compute(Wcet_Initial);
          Initial_Finished.Go;
          Optional_Deadline  := Next + Dead;
          Next := Next + Per;
          delay until Next;
          exit when Finished;
       end loop;
     end Initial_Task;
     task body Optional_Task is ... -same code as MOF tas
    begin  -- code of the main task
       Stop.Wait;
       loop
          Initial_Finished.Wait;
          Compute(Wcet_Main);
          Main_Finished.Go;
          Start_Optional.Go;
          exit when Finished;
       end loop;
    end P_IMOF_Task;
end IMOF_Tasks;
```

6 Example of Mixed Tasks

The following example shows the definition of three tasks with different behavior. T1 has four components: initial, main, final and optional; T2 has been split in two tasks: main and final; T3 has three parts: main, final and optional.

The main procedure is the following:

```
with Ada.Text_Io; use Ada.Text_Io;
with Ada.Real_Time;use Ada.Real_Time;
with All_Tasks;   use All_Tasks;
procedure Example is
   Initial_Time : Time;
   T1 : P_IMOF_Task(5,6,6,100,100,0,4,7,1,8,3,60,1,10,1,50);
   T2 : P_MF_Task(6, 5, 8, 150, 120, 0, 2, 9, 2, 70);
   T3 : P_MOF_Task(7,4,12,170,170,0,9,60,2,3,8,2,110);
begin
   Initial_Time := Clock + Milliseconds(2000);
   Set_Initial_Time(Initial_Time);
   Start;
   ......
   Finish;
end Example;
```

The package All_Tasks offers all the task types described above. The chronogram of this set task execution is shown in the figure 5.

7 Conclusions

This paper describes how to implement real-time applications using the decomposition method presented in [6]. With this decomposition, a real-time application can be modeled as a set of periodic tasks. Each of these tasks are divided in mandatory and optional parts, and this allows to reduce the jitter variation as it has shown in [6]and [3]. To implement this method it has been used Ada. In this implementation every part of a task (mandatory or optional) is represented as a task inside the main task. Barriers have been used to synchronized the different parts of each task and priorities allow mandatory parts to have more importance than optional parts. It also has been presented a monitor in order to verify the whole system.

References

[1] Albertos P., Crespo A., Ripoll I., Vallés M., Balbastre P., "RT control Scheduling to reduce control performance degrading". 39th IEEE Conference on Decision and Control CDC2000. December 12-15. Sydney.
[2] Audsley N.C., Burns A., Richardson M.F., Tindell K.W., Wellings A.J., "Applying New Scheduling Theory to Static Preemptive Systems". Sowtfare Engineering Journal 8 (5) pp. 284-292, 1993

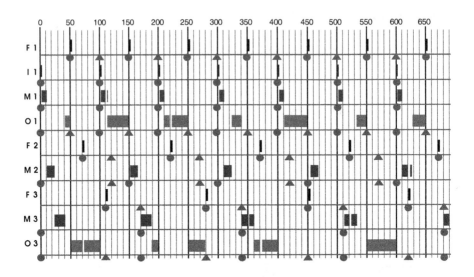

Fig. 5. Task execution of three mixed tasks

[3] Balbastre P., Ripoll I., Crespo A., "Control Tasks Delay Reduction under Static and Dynamic Scheduling Policies" 7th International Conference on Real-Time Systems and Applications (RTCSA 2000) 12-14 December 2000 Cheju Island, South Korea.

[4] A. Burns and A. Wellings, Real-Time Systems and their Programming Languages (2nd Edn), Addison-Wesley, 1996.

[5] A. Burns and A. Wellings, Concurrency in Ada, Cambridge University Press, 1995.

[6] Crespo, A., Ripoll I., and P. Albertos. " Reducing Delays in RT control: the Control Action Interval" IFAC World Congress, Beijing 1999.

[7] Leung J., Whitehead J., "On the Complexity of Fixed-Priority Scheduling of Periodic, Real-Time Tasks", Performance Evaluation, Vol. 2(4), pp. 237-250, December 1982.

[8] Liu C. L., Layland J. W., "Scheduling Algorithms for Multiprogramming in a Hard Real-Time Environment". Journal of the ACM, vol. 20, no. 1, pp. 46-61, 1973.

Implementing a Flexible Scheduler in Ada

Guillem Bernat and Alan Burns

Real-Time Systems Research Group
Department of Computer Science
University of York, UK

Abstract. Much of the research on flexible scheduling schemes is prevented from being used in practice by the lack of implementations that provide the necessary abstractions. In this paper we show how Ada's tasking facilities do enable such schedulers to be constructed. A case example is given that shows that the combination of existing language features is sufficient to program the required functionality. Only the lack of budget time management causes difficulty.

1   Introduction

Over the last decade a considerable volume of literature has been produced which addresses the issues and challenges of flexible scheduling. The focus of much of this research has been on how to effectively support a mixture of periodic and non-periodic, hard and non-hard activities. This work is seen as an enabling technology for a wide range of applications from multi-media to robust control. Notwithstanding the quality of individual contributions, it is unfortunately true that applications have not, in general, taken up these results. There are a number of reasons for this, including the normal inertia associated with technical change, but we would highlight the following.

- Inconsistency in the literature - no single technique has emerged as being widely applicable, indeed there is not even any consensus over the right simulation models to use for evaluation.
- Limitations of the scheduling models - too many models have unrealistic assumptions such as ignoring run-time overheads or assuming that the WCET is known for all tasks (or not recognising that actual execution times can be much smaller than WCET values).
- Difficulty of implementation - often the scheduling scheme will require operating primitives that are not available on any commercial platform.
- Lack of computational model - the scheduling results are not tied back to realistic models that applications can use to construct systems.
- Lack of computational algorithms - the seminal work on imprecise algorithms[15,10,12] (and anytime algorithms[7,19,13,20]) has not lead to the development of application-specific instantiations of these generic schemes.

The focus of this paper is on the third of these problems. We will show how the facilities available in the Ada tasking model do allow implementations to

A. Strohmeier and D. Craeynest (Eds.): Ada-Europe 2001, LNCS 2043, pp. 179–190, 2001.
© Springer-Verlag Berlin Heidelberg 2001

be programmed. The aim of this, and related work, is to define a framework that will have wide applicability and utility. The framework is given the name *Jorvik*. Of course we would not argue that the framework will be effective in all situations. This is not the aim. Rather, we contend that it is possible to deliver, with today's technology, a general purpose platform that will enable flexible scheduling schemes to be exploited in a range of application domains.

The challenges of flexible scheduling are easy to (informally) define: hard deadlines must always be met, and any spare capacity (typically CPU resource) must be used to maximise the utility of the application. The 'extra' work that could be undertaken typically exceeds the spare capacity available, and hence the scheduler must decide which non-hard task to execute at any time. As processors become more complex and the analysis of worst-case execution time more pessimistic the amount of spare capacity will increase. Indeed the utilisation of the hard task will often be less than 50%. There is continuing pressure on applications to minimise their use of hard tasks and to exploit flexible scheduling to deliver dynamic behaviour. The framework presented in this paper will facilitate these application requirements.

There are several examples which are suitable for this scheduling framework. One of them is based on providing real-time guarantees to artificial intelligence problems like real-time machine learning. These problems are characterised by the fact that no reasonable WCET can be determined as the execution time depends on the characteristics of the set of clauses that define the knowledge domain. Mandatory components provide an initial result with guaranteed minimum quality while the firm components run the non predictable code and improve this initial solution.

The rest of the paper is structured as follows. In the next section the process model in which Jorvik is based is presented. Section 3 analyses the problem of scheduling firm tasks. The core of the paper is in section 4 where the code for the scheduler is shown. The last section presents the future work and conclusions.

2   Process Model

We consider a general model in which an application is made up of a set of tasks (periodic or sporadic) which are made up by (potentially) two jobs. One initial mandatory (and therefore *hard*) job which upon completion releases an optional job. The task has an end-to-end deadline, D. All mandatory jobs must be guaranteed to finish by D, whereas all optional jobs are *firm*. Firm jobs are assigned (statically) a 'value', V [11,3,1,5,8]. This is the utility that will be generated by the job if it completes by the deadline, but there is no value in executing it beyond its deadline – no extra value will accrue. Another important attribute of all jobs is their execution time, C. Minimum, average and worst-case measures may all be available.

The model presented here is not constrained and allows an easy generalisation to include, for instance, a sequence of firm jobs in a task, or tasks with only one component (the hard one or the firm one).

3 Scheduling Firm Tasks

Given some mechanism for managing spare processing capacity, the resulting spare resource time must be assigned efficiently to the incoming firm tasks. A number of results in the literature form a boundary to this problem:

- if there is no overload then EDF (Earliest Deadline First) is an optimal scheme, but if there is an overload EDF performs poorly due to the known domino effect [4],
- with a pure value based scheme, scheduling according to V/C is the most effective [11].

The entity V/C, which we denote as W, gives the value that will accrue per unit of execution. It is optimal if a system is heavily loaded. These two observations have lead to a general scheduling structure which consists of two mechanisms. An *admissions policy* (that keeps the load from exceeding the capacity of the resource) and a *scheduling policy* (for the jobs that are admitted). If the admissions policy is effective then overloads are prevented and hence EDF is an effective scheduling policy. The difficulty with the admissions policy is that any near optimal scheme has very high overheads [16,14,9].

The scheme that Jorvik adopts is based on the following observations:

- it is wasteful to start a task that has little chance of completing and that would therefore be aborted (as zero value is obtained after the deadline). However, some level of aborts can be tolerated if it leads to better performance overall,
- in a busy system the state of the available resources as predicted when a task arrives is a poor indicator of the actual state when the task first gets to run,
- the 'optimal' best effort scheme [11] has extremely high overheads [17,18] and is only effective if exact execution times are known and delivered at run-time.

The algorithmic behaviour of Jorvik is as follows.

1. Each application task consists of a *mandatory* (hard) job and an *optional* (firm) job[1]. The mandatory job always executes first. Both jobs *should* finish by the deadline - the hard one *must*.
2. When a firm job arrives it has known value V and minimum and required computation time.
3. Upon arrival all jobs are put into an EDF queue.
4. When a job gets to the front of the queue for the first time, a decision is made to either accept it (execute it) or revoke it.
5. If the job is revoked it is removed from the queue and never executes (for this invocation).
6. If the job is accepted it executes; a budget may be assigned and the job may be aborted at its deadline.

---

[1] Some tasks may have no mandatory job, and others many have no optional job - however for these discussions we assume all tasks have both

By postponing the decision to execute until this late stage, the data of relevance is as timely as possible; although it is still based on estimates of the resources needed by the jobs in the EDF queue.

As all hard and firm jobs are placed in the EDF queue it will become overloaded. Jorvik implements what might be called a *lazy* admissions policy; jobs are only revoked immediately before they would otherwise start executing, rather than when they arrive.

The decision embodied in stage 4 has two components. One concerns the jobs itself, the other the load in the EDF queue. In the following description non-preemptive execution for the EDF jobs is assumed.

To ensure that hard jobs always meet their deadlines, but that the maximum spare capacity is made available for the firm jobs, the dual priority scheme is employed[6,12,2]. With this scheme a hard job (task) starts its execution at a lower priority but has its priority raised 'just in time' so that it meets its deadline (by preempting the current EDF job). While at the lower priority firm tasks can execute in preference. With the algorithm used in this paper the hard jobs are initially placed in the EDF queue. They will either execute as they come to the front of this queue, or they will have their priorities raised so that they execute in preference to the current EDF job.

Some of the published approaches to scheduling firm jobs assign a budget to the job and expect the underlying operating system to stop the job once the budget is exhausted. We will note below that this is not possible in Ada.

It is important to note that the emphasis of this paper is on the construction of a flexible scheduler in Ada - the motivation for the particular scheme chosen is less significant (for this paper).

4   Programming the Scheduler in Ada

Ada's task facilities provide an expressive set of facilities from which to construct a flexible scheduler. In this section these features are illustrated via the construction of a value-based scheduler for Jorvik.

Figure 1 gives an overview of the proposed scheme. In the figure a single client (there would of course be more in a complete system) calls the Sch protected object to either lodge a mandatory or optional execution request. Note Sch is a passive entity, it only executes when invoked by the client or by the Controller task.

The principal characteristic of the scheduler is that all management of the dispatching process is undertaken by manipulating priorities.

- Clients call in at their normal priority but then have their priorities dropped.
- The promoter task raises the priority of the client to ensure the mandatory part is completed.
- When an execution request gets to the head of the EDF queue (and is accepted for execution) its priority is raised.
- The priority of 'controller' is chosen so that it only executes if the current 'EDF' job has completed.

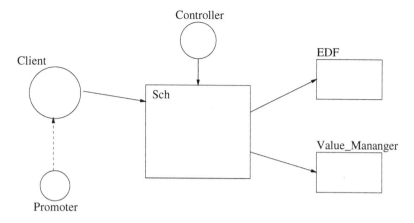

Fig. 1. Overview of Proposed Scheme.

These relationships are embedded in the following package:

```
package Program_Priorities is
   Hold : constant System.Priority :=
                   System.Priority'First + 1;
      -- priority of all task with jobs on EDF queue
   Controller_Pri : constant System.Priority := Hold + 1;
   Running : constant System.Priority := Hold + 2;
      -- priority of running task, i.e. job just
      -- removed from EDF queue
   Pro_Pri : constant System.Priority := System.Priority'Last;
      -- promoter tasks' priority
   subtype Promoted_Priorities is System.Priority range
                   Hold + 3 .. System.Priority'Last - 1;
      -- priority of tasks executing hard jobs (after promotion)
end Program_Priorities;
```

The `Sch` protected object makes use of the two 'queues': one holds all jobs in EDF order, the other manages the optional jobs using V and C.

First some general type definitions are needed:

```
package Specific_Parameters is
   type Value is range 0 .. 10; -- say
   type Load is new Float range 0.0 .. Max_Load_Factor; -- say
      -- load is a measure of current EDF work load
   Threshold : Load := 0.8; -- say
end Specific_Parameters;
```

The EDF package has a procedure for removing a mandatory job that has executed anyway (if it is found a Boolean flag is set). The `Controller` (via `Sch`) will call `Extract` to get the next job (i.e. the job with the shortest deadline). This routine also returns the current load on the EDF queue. If this load factor is greater than a threshold then an overload is assumed.

```
package Edf is
  procedure Add(Id : Task_Id);
  procedure Remove(Id : Task_Id; Found : out Boolean);
  procedure Extract(Id : out Task_Id; L : out Load);
end Edf;
```

The Value_Manager allows jobs to be added and removed. If there is an overload then the routine would perform a check to see whether the job has a value density above a threshold 'cut' value. This cut value is the value density of the jobs in the queue with a total load not greater than 1.0 (or an arbitrary load Ld). This is an approximation of the best-effort queue reordering method of Locke [11] but with the benefit that it has a very low running cost, only of $O(log\ n)$ where n is the number of firm jobs in the queue. The 'current' job is thus either admitted or not. Either way it is removed from the value queue.

```
package Value_Manager is
  procedure Add(Id : Task_Id);
  procedure Remove(Id : Task_Id);
  procedure Cut(Id : Task_Id; Ld : Load; Admit : out Boolean);
end Value_Manager;
```

To pass scheduling parameters between the client task, its promoter and the scheduler, task-attributes are used:

```
package Task_Info is
  type Task_Information is
  record
    Deadline : Time := Time_Last;
    Val : Value := Value'First;
    Comp_Min, Comp_Req : Time_Span := Time_Span_Zero;
    Man_Fin : Boolean := False;
  end record;

  Default : Task_Information;
  -- default object is needed in definition of task attributes

  package Scheduling_Parameter is new
    Ada.Task_Attributes(Task_Information, Default);
end Task_Info;
```

The promoter task is of a general structure for all clients. A rendezvous is used to pass the static timing parameters to the promoter

```
task type Promoter is
  entry Set_Times(Start_T : Time; Hp : Priority;
                  Period,R_Deadline,R_Pro : Time_Span);
  pragma Priority(Pro_Pri);
end Promoter;
```

```
type Pro is access Promoter;

task body Promoter is
  My_Period : Time_Span;
  Pro_Time : Time_Span;
  Rel_Deadline : Time_Span;
  Tp : Task_Information;
  High : Priority;
  Client : Task_Id;
  Epoch : Time;
begin
  accept Set_Times(Start_T : Time; Hp : Priority;
                   Period,R_Deadline,R_Pro : Time_Span) do
    My_Period := Period;
    Epoch := Start_T;
    High := Hp;
    Pro_Time := R_Pro;
    Rel_Deadline := R_Deadline;
    Client := Set_Times'Caller;
  end Set_Times;
  loop
    delay until Epoch + Pro_Time;
    Tp := Scheduling_Parameter.Value(Client);
    if not Tp.Man_Fin then
      Set_Priority(High,Client);
    end if;
    delay until Epoch + Rel_Deadline;
    Set_Priority(High,Client);
    Epoch := Epoch + My_Period;
  end loop;
end Promoter;
```

The client task necessarily has a number of internal data definitions:

```
task type Example_Client(My_Priority : Promoted_Priorities) is
  pragma Priority(My_Priority);
end Example_Client;

task body Example_Client is
  Start : Time;
  Period : Time_Span := ...
  Rel_Deadline : Time_Span := ...
  Abs_Deadline : Time;
  Rel_Promotion_Time : Time_Span := ...
  Mandatory_Finished : Boolean;
  Self : Task_Id;
  Quality : Value;
  Timing_Error : exception;
  Minimum_Comp_Man : Time_Span := ...
  Required_Comp_Man : Time_Span := ...
```

```
   Minimum_Comp_Opp : Time_Span := ...
   Required_Comp_Opp : Time_Span := ...
   P : Pro := new Promoter;
begin
   ...
end Example_Client;
```

Note that this example is for a periodic client. A sporadic client can also be constructed following a straightforward template.

The body of the task uses a select-then-abort construct to ensure that the deadline is not overrun. If it was, and the mandatory part had not completed, then this would be an error.

```
begin
  Start := Clock;
  Self := Current_Task;
  P.Set_Times(Start, My_Priority, Period, Rel_Deadline,
              Rel_Promotion_Time);
  loop
    Mandatory_Finished := False;
    Abs_Deadline := Start + Rel_Deadline;
    select
      delay until Abs_Deadline;
      if not Mandatory_Finished then
        raise Timing_Error;
      end if;
    then abort
      Quality := Value'Last;
      Scheduling_Parameter.Set_Value((Abs_Deadline, Quality,
          Minimum_Comp_Man, Required_Comp_Man,
          Mandatory_Finished));
      Sch.Register_Mandatory(Self);
      -- Mandatory Job
      Mandatory_Finished := True;
      Sch.Remove_Mandatory(Self);
      Quality := ... -- not Value'Last
      Scheduling_Parameter.Set_Value((Abs_Deadline, Quality,
          Minimum_Comp_Opp, Required_Comp_Opp,
          Mandatory_Finished));
      Sch.Register_Optional(Self);
      -- Optional Job
    end select;
    Start := Start + Period;
    delay until Start;
  end loop;
exception
  when ...
end Example_Client;
```

Ideally a budget could be assigned to the optional job and another select-then-abort statement used to terminate the optional execution when the budget is exhausted. Unfortunately, Ada does not provide access to an execution time clock and so budget timing cannot be supported. During the Ada 9X development process, a budget timer was considered (as an optional part of the Real-Time Annex) but it was not incorporated into the final language definition.

The scheduler protected object (Sch) is the more complex entity:

```
protected Sch is
  entry Release_New;
  procedure Register_Mandatory(Cl : Task_Id);
  procedure Remove_Mandatory(Cl : Task_Id);
  procedure Register_Optional(Cl : Task_Id);
  pragma Priority(Pro_Pri);
private
  Num_On_Edf : Natural := 0;
end Sch;
```

The entry is called by the controller task, which only executes when a job has finished (via the judicious setting of the priority levels):

```
task Controller is
  pragma Priority(Controller_Pri);
end Controller;

task body Controller is
begin
  loop
    Sch.Release_New;
  end loop;
end Controller;
```

If there are no current jobs then the controller will block on the entry.

For clarity of presentation two different register procedures are given (although it would be easy to roll them into one). The Remove_Mandatory routine is needed to cover for a job that has executed anyway (due to the dual priority being invoked). The protected procedures are straightforward.

```
protected body Sch is
  entry Release_New when ...
  end Release_New;

  procedure Register_Mandatory(Cl : Task_Id) is
  begin
    Edf.Add(Cl);
    Num_On_Edf := Num_On_Edf + 1;
    Set_Priority(Hold,Cl);
  end;

  procedure Remove_Mandatory(Cl : Task_Id) is
    Found : Boolean;
  begin
```

```
      Edf.Remove(Cl,Found);
      if Found then
        Num_On_Edf := Num_On_Edf - 1;
      end if;
    end;

    procedure Register_Optional(Cl : Task_Id) is
    begin
      Edf.Add(Cl);
      Num_On_Edf := Num_On_Edf + 1;
      Value_Manager.Add(Cl);
      Set_Priority(Hold,Cl);
    end;
  end Sch;
```

The call of the entry is what causes a new EDF job to be selected:

```
  entry Release_New when Num_On_Edf > 0 is
    Id : Task_Id;
    Ld : Load;
    Tp : Task_Information;
    Run_It : Boolean;
  begin
    Edf.Extract(Id,Ld);
    Num_On_Edf := Num_On_Edf - 1;
    Tp := Scheduling_Parameter.Value(Id);
    if Tp.Val = Value'Last then -- mandatory part
      Set_Priority(Running,Id);
      return;
    end if;
    if Clock + Tp.Comp_Min > Tp.Deadline then
      Value_Manager.Remove(Id); -- not worth starting
      requeue Release_New;
    end if;
    if Ld <= Threshold then  -- no overload
      Value_Manager.Remove(Id);
      Set_Priority(Running,Id);
      return;
    end if;
    Value_Manager.Cut(Id,Ld,Run_It); -- overload
    if Run_It then
      Set_Priority(Running,Id);
    else
      requeue Release_New; -- find another task
    end if;
  end Release_New;
```

Note the use of requeue to find another job (if the current one with the shortest deadline is not acceptable).

5   Conclusion

The focus of this paper has been on the construction of a flexible scheduler using the facilities of Ada. In doing this, the expressive power of the language has been demonstrated. As well as tasks and protected objects themselves, use is made of dynamic priorities, task attributes, select-then-abort and requeue.

The one area in which Ada is deficient is in its control of execution time. It is not possible to set a computation time budget and then stop a computation when the budget is exhausted. It is to be hoped that a future version of the Real-Time Annex will rectify this shortcoming.

Future work will aim to evaluate an implementation of this scheme. To do this a full and effective implementation of Ada is required. A number of such systems will be assessed in order to identify one that will provide the right characteristics for an evaluation framework.

References

1. S. Baruah, G. Koren, D. Mao, B. Mishra, A. Raghunathan, L. Rosier, D. Shasha, and F. Wang. On the competitiveness of online real-time task scheduling. *Real-Time Systems*, 4(2):124–144, 1992.
2. G. Bernat and A. Burns. Combining (n m)-hard deadlines with dual priority scheduling. In *Proceedings of 18th IEEE Real-Time systems symposium. San Francisco, CA*, December 1997.
3. S. Biyabani, J.A. Stankovic, and K. Ramamritham. The integration of criticalness and deadlines in scheduling real-time tasks. In *Proceedings of the 9th IEEE Real-Time Systems Symposium*, pages 152–169, 1988.
4. G. Buttazzo, M. Spuri, and F. Sensini. Value vs. deadline scheduling in overload conditions. In *Proceedings of the IEEE Real-Time Systems Symposium*, 1995.
5. G. Buttazzo and J. Stankovic. RED : A robust earliest deadline scheduling algorithm. In *Proceedings of the 3rd International Workshop on Responsive Computer Systems, Austin*, 1993.
6. R.I. Davis and A. J. Wellings. Dual priority scheduling. In *Proceedings Real-Time Systems Symposium*, pages 100–109, 1995.
7. T.L. Dean and M. Boddy. An analysis of time-dependent planning. In *Proceedings of the Seventh National Conference on Artificial Intelligence*, pages 49–54, 1988.
8. E.D. Jensen, C.D. Locke, and H. Tokuda. A time driven scheduling model for real-time operating systems. In *Proceedings IEEE Real-Time Sytems Symposium*, pages 112–122, 1985.
9. Y.S. Kim. An optimal scheduling algorithm for preemptive real-time tasks. *Information Processing Letters*, 50(1):43–48, 1994.
10. J.W.S. Liu, K.J. Lin, W.K. Shih, A.C.S. Yu, J.Y. Chung, and W. Zhao. Algorithms for scheduling imprecise computations. *IEEE Computer*, pages 58–68, 1991.
11. C.D. Locke. Best-effort decision making for real-time scheduling. CMU-CS-86-134 (PhD Thesis), Computer Science Department, CMU, 1986.
12. R. Oliveira and J. Fraga. Scheduling imprecise computation tasks with intra-task/ inter-task dependence. In *Proceedings of the 21st IFAC/IFIP Workshop on Real-Time Programming, WRTP'96*, pages 51–56, 1996.

13. S.J. Russell and S. Zilberstein. Composinng real-time systems. In *Proceedings of the Twelfth International Joint Conference on Artificial Intelligence*, pages 212–217, 1991.
14. K. Schwan and H. Zhou. Dynamic scheduling of hard real-time tasks and real-time threads. *IEEE Transactions on Software Engineering*, 18(8):736–748, 1992.
15. W. K. Shih, J. W. S. Liu, and J. Y. Chung. Algorithms for scheduling imprecise computations with timing constraints. In *Proc. IEEE Real-Time Systems Symposium*, 1989.
16. M. Silly, H. Chetto, and N. Elyounsi. An optimal algorithm for guaranteeing sporadic tasks in hard real-time systems. In *Proceedings 2nd IEEE Symposium on Parallel and Distributed Systems*, pages 578–585, 1990.
17. H. Tokuda, J.W. Wendorf, and H.Y. Wang. Implementation of a time-driven scheduler for real-time operating systems. In *Proceedings of IEEE Real-Time Systems Symposium*, pages 271–280, 1987.
18. J.W. Wendorf. Implementation and evaluation of a time-driven scheduling processor. In *Proceedings of IEEE Real-Time Systems Symposium*, pages 172–180, 1988.
19. S. Zilberstein. Resource-bounded sensing and planning in autonomous systems. *Autonomous Robots*, 3:31–48, 1996.
20. S. Zilberstein. Using anytime algorithms in intelligent systems. *AI Magazine*, 17(3):73–83, 1996.

Expression Templates in Ada

Alexandre Duret-Lutz

EPITA Research and Development Laboratory
14-16 rue Voltaire, F-94276 Le Kremlin-Bicêtre cedex, France
http://www.lrde.epita.fr/
Alexandre.Duret-Lutz@lrde.epita.fr

Abstract. High-order matrix or vector expressions tend to be penalized by the use of huge temporary variables. *Expression templates* is a C++ technique which can be used to avoid these temporaries, in a way that is transparent to the user. We present an Ada adaptation of this technique which — while not transparent — addresses the same efficiency issue as the original. We make intensive use of the *signature* idiom to combine packages together, and discuss its importance in *generic programming*. Finally, we express some concerns about *generic programming* in Ada.

1 Introduction

One of the strongest requirements on source code is its *maintainability*, which essentially means that the program should be easy to understand and adjust. To avoid cluttering the actual algorithms with low-level details, current programming schemes promote *abstractions*. For instance, object oriented programming makes it possible to define and use high order operations on objects. For example, given an `Integer_10x10_Matrix` type and its accompanying operations, one could write the following expression.

```
declare
   A, B, C : Integer_10x10_Matrix;
begin
   [...]
   A := B * 5 + C;
   [...]
end;
```

While easier to read and maintain, this expression has a significant drawback over a hand-crafted loop over the matrices elements: it uses matrix-sized temporary variables to hold subexpressions. The penalty incurred by these temporary matrices can be a serious annoyance when such expression appears in speed critical subprograms.

There are various means to avoid temporary expressions, the most straightforward being a hand-crafted loop:

A. Strohmeier and D. Craeynest (Eds.): Ada-Europe 2001, LNCS 2043, pp. 191–202, 2001.
© Springer-Verlag Berlin Heidelberg 2001

```
declare
   A, B, C : Integer_10x10_Matrix;
begin
   [...]
   for Row in Integer_10x10_Matrix'Range (1) loop
      for Col in Integer_10x10_Matrix'Range (2) loop
         A (Row, Col) := B (Row, Col) * 5 + C (Row, Col);
      end loop;
   end loop;
   [...]
end;
```

The expression now uses integer-sized temporaries (which can fit in registers) instead of matrix-sized temporaries (requiring memory usage). It is much faster but less readable, and can get cryptic when the expression become complex.

Other alternatives provide both efficiency and conciseness. *Domain Specific Languages* extend the underlying language, and "compilers" convert programs from the extended syntax to the native language; this however require an external tool. *expression templates* technique described below makes only use of the existing C++ languages features.

Since templates were introduced to C++, and more significantly since the introduction of STL [16,15], the C++ community developed a set of programming techniques globally referred to as *meta-programming* (for they abuse the compiler to perform computation or transformations at compile time) [11,12]. Most of these techniques are rather C++ specific because they rely on template specialization, a construction which is not available in Ada (see section 5.4). However this article presents an *attempt* to adapt one of these techniques to Ada.

In 1995, the C++ *generic programming* community introduced the *expression templates* [18,7,4]. *Expression templates* is a C++ programming technique which allows expressions like the first example of this section to be compiled like the second, *i.e.*, preventing the need for temporary variables. This is a powerful technique that allows to write fast and readable *user* code; the library, on the other hand, is significantly more complex (mostly because the way template functions are checked, see section 5.2).

In short, the idea is to build a type that represents the expression to assign, and an instance of that type which keeps references to the various subexpressions of the expression. The operators of the expression don't perform any computation, they simply return an object whose type represents the expression (for instance `plus<plus<vector<int>,vector<int> >,vector<int> >`). The actual computation is delayed until the assignment. This technique is transparent to the user, because the type construction is done by *implicit* template instantiations.

This paper tackles the adaptation of *expression templates* to Ada. Section 3 illustrates our solution with matrix computation, which rely heavily on the use of signatures recalled in section 2, and whose speed is compared to other approaches in section 4. Finally, we express some concern about the usage of Ada for *generic programming* [11] in section 5.

2   Expressing Concepts with Signatures

Ada 95 allows generic packages to be used as generic formal parameters. The Rationale [8] shows one use — also known as *signature* — of this possibility: characteristics of an abstraction are grouped using the formal parameters of a generic empty package.

This feature plays a significant role in *generic programming*. The STL documentation uses the term *concept* to designate a set of requirements (types or function definitions, behaviors), but these concepts have no mapping in the C++ syntax: concepts exist only in the documentation, the compiler is unaware of them and therefore it cannot help the programmer. When U. Erlingsson and A. Konstantinou adapted the STL to Ada [3,9], they found that *signatures* was the natural way to express *concepts*.

We will use *signatures* to express the concept of matrix type and matrix expression. In our matrix expression code, we want to let the user supply his own matrix type. For simplicity, we assume that matrices are always stored as double arrays[1]. Therefore we define the *matrix type* concept as a type of values, two ranges, and an array type. An instance of `Matrix_Type` will then be used everywhere matrix specifications are needed. The `Matrix_Expression` concept, for example, is defined by a matrix type and a function which can return elements from the matrix expression.

```
generic
   type Values is private;
   type Height_Range is range <>;
   type Width_Range is range <>;
   type Array_Type is array (Height_Range, Width_Range) of Values;
package Matrix_Type is end Matrix_Type;

with Matrix_Type;
generic
   with package Matrix_Spec is new Matrix_Type (<>);
   with function Get_Value (At_Row : in Matrix_Spec.Height_Range;
                            At_Col : in Matrix_Spec.Width_Range)
      return Matrix_Spec.Values;
package Matrix_Expression is
   procedure Assign (To : out Matrix_Spec.Array_Type);
end Matrix_Expression;
```

`Matrix_Expression` additionally declares the procedure `Assign` which is defined as follows. It will be used to evaluate a matrix expression while assigning the result to the target matrix.

```
package body Matrix_Expression is
   procedure Assign (To : out Matrix_Spec.Array_Type) is
   begin
      for Row in To'Range (1) loop
         for Col in To'Range (2) loop
            To (Row, Col) := Get_Value (Row, Col);
         end loop;
      end loop;
   end Assign;
end Matrix_Expression;
```

---

[1] Supporting other kind of storage is a matter of adding `Get_Value` and `Set_Value` in `Matrix_Type` and making `Array_Type` private.

Intuitively, `Assign` represents the loop we would have written manually, and `Get_Value` is used to evaluate the expression at the matrix cells level. Our objective is to build this function by combining generic packages.

3   Building Expressions

`Matrix_Expression` is the base building block for our matrix expressions. Our aim is to build a matrix expression from other matrix expressions. For example, given two instances of `Matrix_Expression` we want to apply a binary operator (element-wise). This is naturally done using a generic package `Matrix_Operators.Binary` parameterized by two matrix expressions and one operator function. Because this package can itself be seen as a matrix expression, it defines an instance of `Matrix_Expression`.

```
with Matrix_Expression;
generic
   with package Left_Expr is new Matrix_Expression (<>);
   with package Right_Expr is new Matrix_Expression (<>);
   with function Operator (Left : in Left_Expr.Matrix_Spec.Values;
                           Right : in Right_Expr.Matrix_Spec.Values)
      return Left_Expr.Matrix_Spec.Values;
package Matrix_Operators.Binary is

   function Get_Value (At_Row : in Left_Expr.Matrix_Spec.Height_Range;
                       At_Col : in Left_Expr.Matrix_Spec.Width_Range)
      Return Left_Expr.Matrix_Spec.Values;
   pragma Inline (Get_Value);

   -- Instances of Binary can be seen as a Matrix Expression:
   package Expr is
      new Matrix_Expression (Left_Expr.Matrix_Spec, Get_Value);

end Matrix_Operators.Binary;
```

The supplied operator is actually applied whenever `Get_Value` is called.

```
package body Matrix_Operators.Binary is
   function Get_Value (At_Row : in Left_Expr.Matrix_Spec.Height_Range;
                       At_Col : in Left_Expr.Matrix_Spec.Width_Range)
      return Left_Expr.Matrix_Spec.Values
   is
      -- we need to convert At_Row and At_Col to
      -- the range types used by the right expression.
      subtype Rh is Right_Expr.Matrix_Spec.Height_Range;
      subtype Rw is Right_Expr.Matrix_Spec.Width_Range;
   begin
      return Operator (Left_Expr.Get_Value (At_Row, At_Col),
                       Right_Expr.Get_Value (Rh (At_Row), Rw (At_Col)));
   end Get_Value;
end Matrix_Operators.Binary;
```

So far, we are able to compound matrix expressions with binary operators. Unary operators or other specialized operation (e.g. matrix multiplication) can be done likewise. The next step is to build atomic matrix expressions (i.e., matrices). Because a matrix expression is a package, we need a mean to convert a matrix (double array) to a package. This can be done via a generic package which takes the matrix array as a generic parameter.

```
with Matrix_Type;
with Matrix_Expression;
generic
   with package Matrix_Spec is new Matrix_Type (<>);
   Object: in out Matrix_Spec.Array_Type;
   use Matrix_Spec;
package Matrix_Instance is

   -- read values from Object
   function Get_Value (At_Row : in Height_Range;
                       At_Col : in Width_Range) return Values;
   pragma Inline (Get_Value);

   package Expr is new Matrix_Expression (Matrix_Spec, Get_Value);

end Matrix_Instance;
```

We have now all the tools required to build and evaluate an expression. The following code creates the expression **Res_Expr** which can be used to compute B*5+C.

```
declare
   -- the user construct his own matrix type
   type Range3 is range 0 .. 2;
   type Matrix33 is array (Range3, Range3) of Integer;

   -- then he build a specification package for his matrix,
   -- this package will be used later when building high order
   -- operations on matrices.
   package Matrix33_Spec is new Matrix_Type (Values => Integer,
                                             Height_Range => Range3,
                                             Width_Range => Range3,
                                             Array_Type => Matrix33);

-- Define two dummy matrices.
B : Matrix33 := ((1, 0, 0), (0, 1, 0), (0, 0, 1));
C : Matrix33 := ((0, 1, 0), (0, 0, 1), (1, 0, 0));

-- Instanciate a package for the B matrix
-- (we map an object to a package)
package B_Inst is new Matrix_Instance (Matrix33_Spec, B);
-- the above package can the be used as a Matrix_Expression,
-- it defines a Expr subpackage for this purpose.
package B_Expr renames B_Inst.Expr;

-- idem with the second matrix
package C_Inst is new Matrix_Instance (Matrix33_Spec, C);
package C_Expr renames C_Inst.Expr;

-- Build the expression B*5
package B5_Inst is new Scalar_Binary (B_Expr, 5, "*");
package B5_Expr renames B5_Inst.Expr;

-- Build the expression B*5+C
package Res_Inst is new Binary (B5_Expr, C_Expr, "+");
package Res_Expr renames Res_Inst.Expr;
```

The resulting expression, `Res_Expr` can now be assigned to a matrix variable using the `Assign` function aforementioned. This assignment will actually evaluate the expression.

```
   A : Matrix33; -- where the result will be stored
begin
   [...]
   Res_Expr.Assign (To => A);
end;
```

It is important to note that the B and C matrices can be modified and that successive calls to `Res_Expr.Assign` will take these new values into account (this is a consequence of the `in out` mode used for the `Matrix_Instance.Object` parameter). By combining packages, we have built a function which fills a matrix according to the contents of B and C.

As this example shows, a somewhat large programming overhead is required to write an expression as simple as `B*5+C` using expression templates. This is to the point that the resulting code seems even more cryptic and less maintainable than the hand-crafted loop. However, it is interesting to see that this technique success in achieving good performance and might therefore be worth to consider in other fields than linear algebra; and as a C++ technique adaptation, it permits some comparison between the two languages for *static* component oriented programming.

4   Benchmark

Figure 1 gives the timing of the evaluation of the expression Y = A + B + C using different size of matrix and different expressions representations.

hand-crafted loop
   The expression is computed using a double loop as shown in section 1.
package-built expression
   The expression is built using packages, as described in section 3.
package-built expression (without inline)
   Same as above, with the `-fno-inline` compiler option added.
standard expression
   The expression is evaluated as-is, using the classical OO definition for the operator "+" which generate temporary variables in expressions.
abstract expression
   Instead of using packages and signatures, we use tagged types and abstract tagged types (respectively) to build the expression. This correspond to the more classical object-oriented way to represent an expression (e.g. in a parser): `Expression` is an abstract tagged type which is derived into `Addition`, `Multiplication`, etc.

As it can be seen from the results, the timings of the package-built expression are equivalent to those of the hand-crafted version. Both are twice faster than expression computation using temporaries.

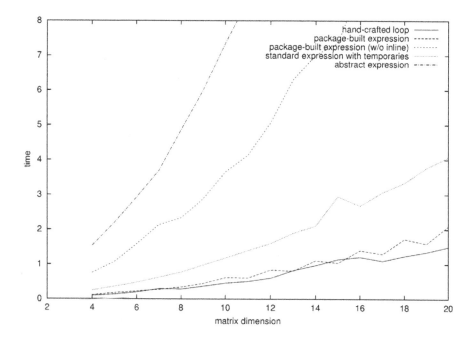

Fig. 1. Time required for the evaluation of expressions of the form `Y = A + B + C` The timing account only for the evaluation of the expression, the the building of the expression (when it is needed) is not accounted. The expression was evaluated 100000 times. The code, available from `http://www.lrde.epita.fr/download/`, was compiled with `gnat 3.13p` and run on an K6-2 processor. The compiler options used were `-gnatfvpnwuwl -O3. -fno-inline` option.

It is interesting to make a parallel between generic packages and tagged types. Generic packages have instances, as tagged types have, and signatures are the counterparts of abstract tagged types. Expression templates could be built using tagged types more easily, however tagged type suffer two performance loses: they hinder inlining, and add some overhead to handle dispatching calls. The comparison between the abstract expression and the non inlined package-built expression give an idea of that latter overhead. The main speedup obtained by using generics over tagged types is thus due the inlining calls allowed by these formers.

5   Critique of Ada

We have adapted a C++ technique to Ada (the converse is also possible, e.g. mixin inheritance is not well known in C++). Such conversion makes it possible to compare both languages and exhibit their weaknesses. Here, we focus on the issues we encountered in our attempts to adapt some C++ techniques to Ada.

5.1   Implicit Instantiation

Ada and C++ behave differently with respect to generic entities. C++ templates are instantiated implicitly the first time they are refered to. Ada generics need to be instantiated explicitly. This actually is a source of tediousness when using expression templates.

C++ implicit instantiation, though a source of errors, simplify the expression templates usage because the instantiations to perform are deduced from the expression itself.

5.2   Semantic Analysis

In C++, the semantic analysis (and in particular the type checking) of a function or class template is only performed after the template has been instantiated. In Ada, this analysis is done prior to any instantiation: the developer is therefore required to declare all the functions or types used (for instance one cannot use the "+" operator on a parameter type without declaring that this operator actually exists). This is definitely a better behavior because it allows errors to be caught earlier. C++ code can be wrong or make wrong assertions about the parameters, any error will only be revealed when the template is first instantiated, i.e., when it is first used (if it ever is).

The strong typing system of Ada is therefore a real help for the developer of a generic library, for it enforces the expression of requirements: the entities used by a generic package or subprogram must be listed in or deduced from the generic formal parameters list.

However, the difficulties arise when you start to parameterize a generic with several generic packages.

5.3   Additional Constraints on Package Parameters

The use of generic packages as formal parameters is a really powerful feature as far as *generic programming* is concerned, because it can factor requirements, allowing to express concepts (something really desired by the C++ *generic programming* community [14,10]). Still, as generic parameters get more complex, the need for constraints between parameters grows.

For instance, though the package `Matrix_Operators.Binary` allows to combine two instances of `Matrix_Expression`, it does not ensure that these two packages declare matrices of equal dimensions. Accesses to values out of the matrices ranges will throw a `Constraint_Error` at run-time, but it would be better to prevent the instantiation of `Binary` when the two operand-packages are not of equal dimensions, because this can be known at compile-time. Basically we want to ensure that `Left_Expr.Matrix_Spec.Array_Type` is the same type as `Right_Expr.Matrix_Spec.Array_Type`.

One way to constrain two non-limited types parameters to be equal is to require the availability of an equality operator for that type. For example the `Matrix_Operators.Binary` parameter list would become as follow.

```
generic
   with package Left_Expr is new Matrix_Expression (<>);
   with package Right_Expr is new Matrix_Expression (<>);
   with function Operator (Left : in Left_Expr.Matrix_Spec.Values;
                           Right : in Right_Expr.Matrix_Spec.Values)
      return Left_Expr.Matrix_Spec.Values;
   -- constraint
   with function "=" (Left : in Left_Expr.Matrix_Spec.Array_Type;
                      Right : in Right_Expr.Matrix_Spec.Array_Type)
      return Boolean is <>;
[...]
```

If `Left_Expr.Matrix_Spec.Array_Type` differs from `Right_Expr.Matrix_Spec.Array_Type`, the `"="` function *probably* does not exists and an instantiation attempt will lead to a compile-time error. Yet, this solution is not perfect: it won't work on limited types, or if the user has defined the checked `"="` function. Moreover the compiler is likely to complain about the absence of matching `"="`, which is not the best error message one would expect. Finally even if, to a certain extent, this can ensure the equality of two types, this does not make this equality explicit: the developer of the body still has *two* types to deal with and must perform conversion when needed because the compiler is unaware that the two types are equal.

A nice extension to Ada would be the addition of a whole sub-language to allow the expression of such constraints. E.g.

```
generic
   with package Left_Expr is new Matrix_Expression (<>);
   with package Right_Expr is new Matrix_Expression (<>);
   -- constraint (this is NOT Ada 95)
   where Left_Expr.Matrix_Spec.Array_Type
      is Right_Expr.Matrix_Spec.Array_Type;
```

Among the same lines, bounded genericity [1] on package parameters of generics would be useful. One doesn't always want to parameterize a generic with a single type of package, but for a whole set of package featuring a common interface: the present solution is to use a signature to express this interface and instantiate this signature in each package, however this is painful and hinder reusability. Being able to qualify formal package parameters with an interface would actually simplify expression templates implementation and usage a lot.

5.4   Template Specialization

Template specialization is among the most powerful features of C++, as far as *generic programming* is concerned. A fairly good number of *generic programming* techniques and idioms rely on template specialization. Ada does not support it (and this doesn't appear to be a trivial extension), therefore we list below some common use of template specialization in C++ and give hints about how it can be worked around in Ada.

Its primary use is to provide a better implementation of a generic entity for a given set of parameters. For example the minimum of a list can be computed more quickly when the list's elements are booleans, therefore C++ allows you to specialize your `min` function to the `list<bool>` case.

```
// generic minimum function for any (non-empty) list
template<typename T>
T min (const std::list<T>& l) {
  T m = std::numeric_limits<T>::max (); // maximum value for type T
  for (std::list<T>::const_iterator i = l.begin(); i != l.end(); ++i)
    if (*i < m)
      m = *i;
  return m;
}

// specialized version for lists of booleans
template<>
bool min (const std::list<bool>& l) {
  for (std::list<bool>::const_iterator i = l.begin(); i != l.end(); ++i)
    if (*i == false)
      return false;
  return true;
}
```

The C++ user will call `min` on a list without special care, and the compiler will implicitly instantiate the more specialized function for that particular kind of list. In Ada, since explicit instantiations are required anyhow, the Ada programmer would write two functions, say `Generic_List_Min` and `Bool_List_Min`, and left to the user the responsibility to choose the best implementation. However, this is not always practical: consider the writing of a generic package which should instantiate a `Min` function for one of it's type parameters, the appropriate implementation cannot be chosen unless `min` is actually a generic parameter of that package too.

As far expression templates are concerned, template specialization can be used to perform pattern matching on matrix expressions to call the corresponding BLAS[2] operations[20].

The second common use of template specialization is the building of traits classes [13,19]: traits classes are kind of static databases built using the type system. `numeric_limits` as used in the example above is a traits class defined in the C++ standard, the definitions of its members (e.g. `max()`) are specialized for the different type `T` available. Traits classes can be seen as an associative arrays between a type, and a signature-like class. Such associative array cannot be done in the Ada type system, therefore the associated signature has to be passed as another generic formal argument by the user.

Last, template specialization allows recurring templates, i.e. templates which instantiate themselves recursively and stop when they reach a specialized case. This is mostly used in *meta-programming*, where you force the compiler to compute some values at compile-time, or to perform loop unrolling [17]. Unfortunately, we did not found any work-around for this in Ada.

6   Conclusion

We have tackled the adaptation of expression templates to Ada. While our adaptation addresses one important issue covered by the original technique — the

---

[2] The *BLAS* (Basic Linear Algebra Subprograms) library provide optimized (and non generic) building block for matrix operations.

elimination of temporary variables — it is neither as powerful not practicable in Ada as it is in C++ where implicit instantiation makes it invisible to the user.

However, this paper shows one intensive use of the *signature* construction. This idiom is essential to generic programming, since it allows to work on *static abstractions* (i.e., abstractions resolved at compile-time, without any run-time cost), and is worth using when both high-order design and performance are required. Most of Gamma's design patterns [6] can be adapted to *generic programming* using *signatures* instead of abstract classes. In a previous work [2] we have shown such adaptations in C++; we also did some similar work in Ada, but it is still unpublished.

Last, we have combined packages to build a function (`Assign`). The small size of the building blocks used in matrix expression make the construction of such function a rather painful process comparatively to writing the same function manually. This technique deserves more experimentation too see how well it can serve in contexts were building blocks are larger.

References

1. Luca Cardelli and Peter Wegner. On understanding types, data abstraction, and polymorphism. *Computing Surveys*, 17(4):471–522, December 1985.
2. Alexandre Duret-Lutz, Thierry Géraud, and Akim Demaille. Design patterns for generic programming in C++. In *Proceedings of the 6th USENIX Conference on Object-Oriented Technologies and Systems (COOTS'01)*, San Antonio, Texas, USA, July 2001. To appear.
3. Ulfar Erlingsson and Alexander V. Konstantinou. Implementing the C++ Standard Template Library in Ada 95. Technical Report TR96-3, CS Dept., Rensselaer Polytechnic Institute, Troy, NY, January 1996.
4. Geoffrey Furnish. Disambiguated glommable expression templates. *Computers in Physics*, 11(3):263–269, May/June 1997. Republished in [5].
5. Geoffrey Furnish. Disambiguated glommable expression templates. *C++ report*, May 2000.
6. Erich Gamma, Richard Helm, Ralph Johnson, and John Vlissides. *Design patterns – Elements of reusable object-oriented software*. Professional Computing Series. Addison Wesley, 1995.
7. Scott W. Haney. Beating the abstraction penalty in C++ using expression templates. *Computers in Physics*, 10(6):552–557, Nov/Dec 1996.
8. Intermetrics, Inc., Cambridge, Massachusetts. *Ada 95 Rationale*, January 1995.
9. Alexander V. Konstantinou, Ulfar Erlingsson, and David R. Musser. Ada standard generic library. source code, 1998.
10. Brian McNamara and Yannis Smaragdakis. Static interfaces in C++. In *First Workshop on C++ Template Programming, Erfurt, Germany*, October 10 2000.
11. David R. Musser, editor. *Dagstuhl seminar on Generic Programming*, SchloßDagstuhl, Wadern, Germany, April-May 1998.
12. David R. Musser and Alexandre A. Stepanov. Generic programming projects and open problems. 1998.
13. Nathan C. Myers. Traits: a new and useful template technique. *C++ Report*, 7(5):32–35, June 1995.

14. Jeremy Siek and Andrew Lumsdaine. Concept checking: Binding parametric polymorphism in C++. In *First Workshop on C++ Template Programming, Erfurt, Germany*, October 10 2000.
15. Alex Stepanov. Al Stevens Interviews Alex Stepanov. *Dr. Dobb's Journal*, March 1995.
16. Alex Stepanov and Meng Lee. *The Standard Template Library*. Hewlett Packard Laboratories, 1501 Page Mill Road, Palo Alto, CA 94304, October 1995.
17. Todd Veldhuizen. Using C++ template metaprograms. *C++ Report*, 7(4):36–43, May 1995. Reprinted in C++ Gems, ed. Stanley Lippman.
18. Todd L. Veldhuizen. Expression templates. *C++ Report*, 7(5):26–31, June 1995.
19. Todd L. Veldhuizen. Using C++ trait classes for scientific computing, March 1996.
20. Todd L. Veldhuizen. Arrays in blitz++. In *Proceedings of the 2nd International Scientific Computing in Object-Oriented Parallel Environments (ISCOPE'98)*, Lecture Notes in Computer Science. Springer-Verlag, 1998.

A Design Pattern for State Machines and Concurrent Activities

Bo I. Sandén

Colorado Technical University
4435 N. Chestnut Street
Colorado Springs, CO 80907-3896
Phone: (719) 590-6733
bsanden@acm.org
http://www.coloradotech.edu/~bsanden

Abstract. State machines are used to design real-time software controlling anything from household devices to spacecraft. They are also a standard way of describing the life of an object in object-oriented analysis and design. This paper presents a pattern for the implementation of state machines and associated activities by means of tasks and protected objects. It is a refinement of earlier work on a state-machine pattern and part of a set of concurrent design patterns based on the entity-life modeling design philosophy.

Keywords: State Machines, Entity-Life Modeling, Design Patterns, Protected Objects.

1 Introduction

Patterns have become a popular way to capture lessons learned in software design. A design pattern is a generic solution to a design problem in a given context. A pattern should be generally accepted rather than novel. The intention is not to teach old hands at software new tricks but rather to transfer design experience to novices. The design pattern community feels that a particular literary style [4] is an important part of pattern definition. I loosely follow their canonical format.

In a series of papers, I have endeavored to document a set of patterns for interacting tasks. Of these, the *resource task* and the *resource-user task* are dual patterns for the sharing of single resources. They give the designer a choice: Either you represent each resource as a task that successively handles requests, or you let the resource users be tasks and represent resources by means of protected objects [10].

A second design situation involves simultaneous, exclusive access to multiple shared resources. In this case, the usual solution includes a resource-user task. Deadlock is a concern in this type of problems, but resource-user tasks can often be designed according to a programming convention such as a locking order that prevents them from forming a circular wait chain [11].

A. Strohmeier and D. Craeynest (Eds.): Ada-Europe 2001, LNCS 2043, pp. 203-214, 2001.
© Springer-Verlag Berlin Heidelberg 2001

A third pattern concerns the implementation of a state machine and associated activities. The state machine is implemented as a protected object. An earlier version of the state machine pattern implemented the machine as a task if it included timing events [8, 12]. (A timing event is the event that x seconds have passed since some other event.) This meant that the implementation would have to be changed if a timing event were introduced at a late stage. The version of the pattern presented here instead implements timing events by means of timer tasks.

1.1 Design Philosophy: Entity-Life Modeling

A set of patterns can define a design philosophy. The state machine pattern reflects the *entity-life modeling* design approach (*ELM*), presented fully elsewhere [6, 7, 9, 11]. It combines two objectives. First, it is a modeling approach that describes how the thread architecture of software can be patterned on concurrent structures in the problem. Second, it promotes a restrictive use of concurrency that aims to eliminate unnecessary threads and context switches. Each event in the problem environment that the software has to deal with is generally handled by a single task.

Object orientation can be called a modeling approach to design in that classes and objects found in the analysis of the domain "seamlessly" carry into design and implementation, which are also based on the concepts of classes and objects. In ELM, concurrent features of the domain are carried into the design. For example, if the domain contains resource contention, the design may contain tasks corresponding to the resource users in the domain and protected objects that represent the resources. The resource users' wait for a resource is then modeled by means of the task queues provided by the Ada syntax.

In general, ELM looks for independent processes in the problem domain, such as multiple phone operators for a catalog business running transactions against a database, or customers executing transactions at the different ATM machines of a bank. Inanimate entities such as the elevators in a multi-elevator control system can also have their independent processes. The term "entity-life modeling" suggests that each task is made to model the behavior over time of an entity in the problem environment, such as an operator or an elevator.

ELM can model the thread architecture of software on the problem domain at two levels. At the basic level it models tasks on *event threads*, which are sequences of events in the problem. This principle is very general and typically results in many possible thread architectures for a given problem. Additional rules of thumb identify the preferred solutions. The higher level is where a thread architecture is modeled directly on patterns identified in the problem as already mentioned.

Level 1: Identifying Event Threads. At a basic level, tasks are based on event threads in the problem. The analyst identifies the threads by partitioning the events occurring in the problem domain according to the following *partitioning rule*:

1. Create an imaginary *trace* by putting all the events a software system has to serve along a time line.

2. Partition the events in the trace into event threads such that the following holds:

Each event belongs to exactly one thread

The events in each thread are separated by sufficient time for the processing of each event.

The result is a *thread model* of a problem, defined as a set of event threads accounting for all relevant events in the problem. A thread model generally leads to a software design with a task per event thread. (One exception is where events are dealt with entirely by interrupt handlers.)

The partitioning rule does not limit the number of threads so in the extreme, each event can have its own thread and consequently its own task. To avoid this, we need a notion of independent threads that can be busy at the same time, while other, dependent threads must wait. A notion of *coincidental simultaneity* has proven useful to capture the intuition of independent threads. The idea is that event threads are independent if occasionally all happen to have an event at the same time.

Strictly speaking, the likelihood of instantaneous events occurring at the same time is zero. For a more careful definition, we shall say that two threads *co-occur* if an arbitrarily short time interval can be found where they both have an event. An *optimal* thread model is one where all threads co-occur. It contains a minimum number of threads. A thread model does not have to be optimal in order to be useful, however. A designer may choose a model with additional threads for various reasons, often to separate concerns or to design for change.

Level 2: Patterns. Many problems include standard types of entities or exhibit common concurrent patterns that are easy to spot. You can often base an entire thread architecture on such patterns without applying the partitioning rule directly. The patterns are a way to arrive at thread models in standard cases without going back to the first principles of Level 1. At Level 2 these principles reduce to the following checklist against which you can test a candidate thread model:

1. Do the entities and threads account for all events in the problem? If not, additional entities and threads are needed.

2. Do all simultaneous events belong to different threads? If not, the candidate entities must be partitioned.

3. Is the solution close to optimum? If not, are the redundant threads justified, or could they be eliminated?

2 The State Machine Pattern

State machines are included in UML and most other approaches to object-oriented analysis and are used to describe the behavior over time of the instances of a class. At each point in time, each instance exists in one of a number of *states*. State transitions occur as a result of events, which can also cause instantaneous *actions*.

In a real-time system, an object whose dynamic behavior is described by a single state machine typically controls an electro-mechanical or electronic device that can be described as a finite automaton. At one end of a spectrum are everyday devices such as a toaster, an automated garage door, an answering machine, or a cruise control system or a window elevator for a car. At the other end are large real-time systems that control satellites or aircraft and have major modes of operation such as "airborne". A state machine allows a programmer to model the logic of a program on the reality to a remarkable degree: Once you have captured the behavior of a device as a state machine, you have essentially designed a program that controls the device.

2.1 Motivating Examples

I will use two devices, an odometer and a weather buoy, to illustrate the pattern.

Odometer. A particular bicycle odometer has four states: Distance, Speed, Mileage and Time. In each state, it repeatedly displays one quantity: distance traveled, speed, total mileage and elapsed time, respectively, each with its own frequency. The odometer has two buttons, A and B. By pressing A, the biker changes the odometer's state cyclically from Distance to Speed, etc., back to Distance. Pressing B in the Distance or Time state resets a reference distance and a reference time, respectively. B has no effect in the other states [9].

Buoy. A number of free-floating buoys provide navigation and weather data to air and ship traffic at sea. Under normal circumstances, each buoy makes a *regular transmission* of current wind, temperature and location information every minute on the minute. A passing vessel may request a *history transmission* of all data collected over the last 24 hours. This long transmission takes precedence over the regular transmission. Furthermore, a sailor in distress who reaches the buoy may engage an emergency switch and initiate an *emergency transmission*, which continues until explicitly reset and takes precedence over the other transmissions [1, 5, 7, 9].

2.2 Participants

The state-machine pattern has two kinds of participants: The *state machine*, implemented as a protected object, and zero or more *activity tasks*.

State Machine Protected Object. Events and actions in a state machine are conceptually instantaneous, but a software implementation must deal with actions that are *approximately* instantaneous. These are performed within the event reporting procedures of the protected object, which are discussed below.

Activity Tasks. Any event response that is not approximately instantaneous is called an *activity* and requires a task. It may consist of a lengthy computation, an operation on a contested resource for which the task may have to wait, or a set of actions that depend on timing. The sampling of some quantity in order to detect a change in value is an example of a timed activity. A sampling activity is often defined for a superstate that encompasses some or all of the states in a given system.

2.3 Collaborations

Activity tasks interact with the state machine by calling operations of the following kinds:

Event Reporting Procedure. A task calls an event-reporting procedure to register the occurrence of an event. The procedure performs any necessary state transition and associated actions. An event reporting procedure may be an interrupt handler.

Examples. The odometer has the handlers A_Int and B_Int for the interrupts from buttons A and B. A_Int performs a state transition, while B_Int resets the reference distance or time. The buoy has procedures such as History_Req, which is called when a request for a history broadcast is received.

State Query Function. A state query function returns the current state or superstate. For example, the odometer has a Get_State function that returns the current state.

State Wait Entry. A state wait entry blocks a task until a certain state or superstate is entered. It is often the subject of a timed entry call or an asynchronous transfer of control (ATC; see 2.4). For example, the odometer has the entry State_Change.

Parameter Query Function. The state machine object may contain private variables that are given values by actions. A parameter query function returns such a value. For example, the odometer has the functions Rel_Dist and Rel_Time, which return the current distance and time, respectively.

State Dependent Action Procedure. A state-dependent procedure performs actions depending on the current state. This is useful when an activity must continue at a given periodicity independent of state but take effect only in certain states.

Example. In the buoy, an activity task, Regular, produces output every 60 seconds, but the output is suppressed during history and emergency broadcasts. For this, the task calls Regular_Msg, which either transmits or suppresses the output.

Note. An event reporting procedure normally does not communicate with an activity task. Instead, the activity task finds out about state transitions through state query functions or state wait entries. This assumes that activity tasks are generally created at program initialization. If a task must be created when a state is entered, this may have to be done in an event reporting procedure.

2.4 Implementation

State Machine Protected Object. The state is represented by means of a private variable, which typically appears in various conditional expressions. Event reporting procedures can be implemented in two simple ways:

1. A single state-transition procedure that takes the event as a parameter. It contains a case statement over states and within each state, a case statement over event types. Its advantage is that it faithfully models a flat state diagram.

2. A procedure for each event. This implementation is often more efficient, but the translation from a state diagram is indirect and potentially error prone. The procedures of the odometer and the buoy are all of this type.

Activity Tasks. In an optimum model according to ELM, all activity tasks must co-occur. This means that separate tasks are warranted whenever one activity is defined for a superstate and another for a substate or where the activities run in partly overlapping superstates. To some degree, additional tasks may be justified for separation of concerns. There is reason to be restrictive, however. When, for example, a cyclic executive is translated into a concurrent solution, there may be a tendency to make every frame a task. This can be counter-productive, especially if the tasks share data and need synchronization. Synchronization might also be needed when there is a state change. The overhead for any state change protocol will penalize all the tasks.

State Change. In the simplest case, an activity task queries the state periodically. This is particularly simple with periodic tasks, which typically query the state upon return from a delay. An example where this is inadequate is when the periodicity itself must be changed. If a task takes action every 60 seconds and the period is changed to 2 seconds, the 60-second suspension must be broken. This is solved by means of a timed call to a state wait entry as in the Odometer example:

```
select Odo.State_Change;
or delay until Next;
end select;
```

ATC provides a solution in case a lengthy computation must be interrupted. The activity task uses the call to a state wait entry as the trigger in a asynchronous select statement as follows: (The delay statement is intended to cover any time between the end of the computation and the next periodic activation.)

```
select FSM.State_Change;
then abort
     <computation>;
     delay until Next;
end select;
```

Timer Tasks. In general, a timing event is implemented by means of a task that calls an event reporting procedure after a delay. Often the timing event is intended to time out some other event, and not supposed to occur if that event occurs first. This calls for a more complex interaction of task and protected object, where the timer task may be as follows:

```
task body Timer is
begin
  loop
     FSM.Hold_Timer;        -- Wait for right state(s)
     select
        FSM.Stop_Timer;     -- Cancel timer
     or delay T;
        FSM.Time_Out;       -- Create timing event
     end select;
  end loop;
end;
```

Hold_Timer and Stop_Timer are state wait entries in the FSM protected object. Their respective barriers become True when timing must start and when the timer has to be canceled. Time_Out is the reporting procedure for the timing event.

2.5 Sample Programs

The odometer and buoy examples illustrate two approaches to state change. In the odometer, all activities are concentrated in a single task, which calls a state query function and a state wait entry. The task is dependent on a single resource, the display, and is similar to a resource task. Separate tasks for each kind of output would only complicate the state change. The buoy, on the other hand, relies on different activity tasks controlled by state dependent action procedures and state wait entries.

Odometer. The protected unit Odo and the body of the activity task Displayer are shown below. Wheel is a protected unit that handles wheel revolution interrupts. Wheel.Dist and Wheel.Speed return the current distance and speed, respectively.

```
protected Odo is
   function Get_State return State_Type;
   entry State_Change;
   function Rel_Dist return Display_Type;
   function Rel_Time return Display_Type;
private
```

```
   procedure A_Int;
   procedure B_Int;
   Ref_Dist     : Distance_Type := 0;
   Ref_Time     : Time := Clock;
   New_State    : Boolean := False;
   State        : State_Type := Distance;
end Odo;

protected body Odo is
-- Event reporting procedures
procedure A_Int is
begin
   if State = Tyme then State := Distance;
   else State := State_Type'Succ (State);
   end if;
   New_State := True;
end A_Int;
procedure B_Int is
begin
   if State = Distance then
      Ref_Dist := Wheel.Dist;
   elsif State = Tyme then
      Ref_Time := Clock;
   end if;
end B_Int;
-- State query function
function Get_State return State_Type is
begin
   return State;
end;
-- State wait entry
entry State_Change when New_State is
begin
   New_State := False;
end;
-- Parameter query functions
function Rel_Dist return Display_Type is
begin
   return Wheel.Dist - Ref_Dist;
end Rel_Dist;
function Rel_Time return Display_Type is
begin
   return Display_Type(Clock - Ref_Time);
end Rel_Time;
end Odo;

task body Displayer is
State : State_Type;
Next : Time;
Display_Value : Display_Type;
Delay_Array : constant array (State_Type) of Duration :=
```

```
begin
  loop
    State := Odo.Get_State;
    Next := Clock + Delay_Array (State);
    case State is
      when Distance => Display_Value := Odo.Rel_Dist;
      when Speed    => Display_Value := Wheel.Disp_Speed;
      -- etc
    end case;
    Display (Display_Value);
    select
        Odo.State_Change;
    or
        delay until Next;
    end select;
  end loop;
end Displayer;
```

Buoy. The buoy state machine is represented as the protected object Reporter, shown below. There are three tasks, Regular, History and SOS, as follows:

Regular prepares a regular transmission every 60 seconds, then calls Reporter.Regular_Msg, which sends the message if the buoy is in the state Regular.

History blocks on Reporter.Hold_History waiting for a history request, then repeatedly calls Reporter.History_Msg with history data messages until the relevant history information has been exhausted. It then again blocks on Hold_History. History_Msg transmits history messages only as long as the buoy is in the History state.

SOS repeatedly produces an SOS message and calls Reporter.SOS_Msg, whose barrier blocks it except in the Emergency state.

```
protected Reporter is
  procedure History_Request;
  procedure Reset;                -- Emergency reset
  entry Hold_History;             -- Parking for History_Task
  entry SOS_Msg (....);           -- Send SOS message
  procedure Regular_Msg (...);--  Send regular message
  procedure History_Msg (..; Stop : out Boolean);
                                  -- Send history message
private
  procedure Switch;               -- Switch flipped
  State : State_Type := Regular;
end Reporter;
protected body Reporter is
-- Event reporting procedures
procedure History_Request is
begin
  if State = Regular then State := History; end if;
end;
```

```
procedure Switch is
begin State := Emergency; end;
procedure Reset is
begin
  if State = Emergency then State := Regular; end if;
end;
-- State wait entries
entry Hold_History when State = History is
begin
  null;
end;
entry SOS_Msg (....) when State = Emergency is
begin <send message> end;
-- State-dependent actions
procedure Regular_Msg (....) is
begin
  if State = Regular then <send message > end if;
end;
procedure History_Msg (..; Stop : out Boolean) is
begin
  if State /= History then Stop := True;
  elsif <end of messages> then
    State := Regular; Stop := True;
  else <send message>; Stop := False;
  end if;
end;
end Reporter;
```

2.6 Alternative Solutions

The main alternative is to implement a state machine as a task. This is reasonable if the entity modeled by the machine is a resource user. Perhaps multiple instances of a resource user type vie for access to various shared resources [11].

A more questionable solution is based on dataflow tasking. With dataflow tasking, each input is handled by one task after another. The tasks are connected by queues. Such a solution to a cruise control problem is given in [2]. In a similar solution to the odometer problem, the interrupt handlers insert event records in a queue implemented as a protected object. A task implementing the state-machine retrieves the records and performs any state transitions and actions.

If a queue of unhandled event records really builds up in front of a state-machine task, something is wrong with the state machine model. It is the nature of a state machine to be able to keep up by only performing approximately instantaneous actions. If no queue forms, the queue manipulation and context switching represent unnecessary overhead.

2.7 Related Pattern

The pattern does not preclude a more sophisticated, polymorphic implementation of a state machine as long as it provides the activity tasks with the interface given here, and the overhead is acceptable in a real-time environment. The State pattern [4] allows you to build a new state machine incrementally by extending an existing one.

2.8 High-Integrity Implementations

Many systems where a state machine is central are hard real-time systems. Lately, safe subsets of Ada such as the Ravenscar profile [3] have been defined for high integrity systems. The pattern violates the following Ravenscar requirements:

> *An entry barrier must be a Boolean variable or literal.* In the pattern, barriers are often of the form "S = Value" where S is a state variable. While this seems innocent enough, the Ravenscar requirement can be met by letting the event reporting procedures update various Booleans used for barriers in addition to updating the state variable.

> *A protected object can have at most one entry.* This is clearly violated in the Buoy example. The Ravenscar solution seems to be multiple protected objects that call each other's event reporting procedures and state query operations, which appears to be a dubious advantage.

> *No ATC.* The pattern uses ATC to implement a state change during a lengthy computation. The alternative solution is to insert state query calls with sufficient frequency during the computation. Nonetheless, recent thinking on extensions of the profile (10th International Real-Time Ada Workshop, Sept. 2000) acknowledges the need for a mechanism that times out a computation.

> *No select statements.* The pattern uses timed entry calls to implement state changes while a task is suspended. Any other mechanism that times out a computation could be used for this, however.

3 Conclusion

The purpose of this pattern is to provide a single template for implementing state machines in a real-time environment. When such templates are used, the resulting programs become easier to understand and maintain. In order to make this pattern complete, I challenge the reader to come up with cases that are not covered.

Acknowledgment. I am grateful for the anonymous reviewers' insightful comments. One review in particular prompted me to restructure the paper in a way that hopefully makes it much more useful.

References

1. G. Booch, *Object-oriented development*. IEEE TSE, 12(2), Feb. 1986, 211-221.
2. D. Budgen, Software Design. Addison-Wesley 1993
3. B. Dobbing, A. Burns, *The Ravenscar tasking profile for high integrity real-time programs*, Proc. SIGAda '98, Ada Letters XVIII:6 (Nov./Dec. 1998) 1-6
4. E. Gamma, R. Helm, R. Johnson, J. Vlissides. Design Patterns: Elements of Reusable Object-Oriented Software, Addison-Wesley 1995
5. B. I. Sandén, *The case for eclectic design of real-time software*, IEEE TSE 15 (March 1989), 360 - 362.
6. B. I. Sandén, *Entity-life modeling and structured analysis in real-time software design - a comparison.* CACM, 32:12 (Dec. 1989) 1458-1466.
7. B. I. Sandén, Software Systems Construction with Examples in Ada. Prentice-Hall, 1994.
8. B. I. Sandén, *The state machine pattern.* Proc. TRI-Ada, Philadelphia, PA, Dec. 1996, 135-142.
9. B. I. Sandén, A course in real-time software design based on Ada 95, ASSET repository, 1996, http://www.coloradotech.edu/~bsanden/DISA
10. B. I. Sandén, *Concurrent design patterns for resource sharing.* Proc. TRI-Ada, St. Louis, MO, Nov. 1997, 173-183.
11. B. I. Sandén, *Modeling concurrent software.* IEEE Software, Sept. 1997, 93-100.
12. B. I. Sandén, *Implementation of state machines with tasks and protected objects.* Ada User Journal 20:4 (Jan 2000), 273-288. [Also in Ada Letters 20, 2 (June 2000) 38-56]

Component Libraries and Language Features

Ehud Lamm

The Open University of Israel, Max Rowe Educational Center, P.O.B 39328
Ramat-Aviv, Tel-Aviv 61392, Israel
mslamm@mscc.huji.ac.il,
http://purl.oclc.org/NET/ehudlamm

Abstract. One major vehicle for reuse is the use of libraries of code. Reusability is the prime route to software reliability. In this work, we will use the term software component in its widest sense, including all kinds of self-contained libraries of code, including collection libraries, APIs (bindings), application frameworks etc. Abstraction boundaries are essential both for reuse and for reliability. We study language features that help overcome limitations imposed by abstraction boundaries (e.g., incomplete interfaces) without completely breaking abstraction. Language features discussed: type sytem features, object orientation, genericity and reflection.

The work presented is work in progress, preliminary results and observations will be shown and discussed.

1 Introduction

Software reliability, a fundamental goal of software engineering [5], is most often achieved by building up from reliable and reusable *software components*. Good software components provide useful *abstractions*, with good abstraction boundaries. Abstraction boundaries are assessed using such concepts as *information hiding* [32] and the notion of *interfaces*. The determining factor for the reliability of a software component is the quality of the interface (or interfaces) the component provides. Achieiving independence requires two things: encapsulation and specification [26]. It is important not to overlook another factor: the quality of the *glue* connecting the components [17]. This factor is, also, programming language dependent, and related to the quality of the components interfaces.

There are many types of software components, among them: abstract data types, collection libraries, class-hierarchies, bindings and application frameworks. There are also higher level concepts that attempt to capture design decisions that cannot be formalized as a concrete implementation of a software component in current programming languages, for example: patterns and architectural styles.

In a related work [23] I elaborate on the concept of software abstraction as related to the variety of software component styles, and discuss how to apply and refine the criteria for good software abstractions.

A large part of software engineering is a cycle of creating and breaking abstraction boundaries.

A. Strohmeier and D. Craeynest (Eds.): Ada-Europe 2001, LNCS 2043, pp. 215–228, 2001.

We attempt to study how language features effect software components. We concentrate on software components that provide good abstractions, by exporting explicit interfaces that hide implementation details. Producing software from abstractions is based on creating, composing and breaking abstractions. By abstraction breaking we mean any form of use that extends or bypasses the component interface. The mechanisms, and language features, used for creating abstractions have been the focus of software engineering research for many years [32,26,29]. Many, if not most, language features are abstraction mechanisms: routines, modules, types, inheritance, interfaces, information hiding mechanisms etc. In this work, we concentrate on situations that may require abstraction breaking, and the language features that support it.

We explore basic abstraction breaking faciltes. Reflection will be used as a cath-all mechanism that allows breaking all language enforced abstraction boundaries, as well as breaking the abstractions supplied by language features (e.g., procedure calls).

Finally we conclude with some remarks about specifying interfaces in typed object oriented languages (such as Ada95). This issue is related to typing and polymorphism. Based on these observations an outline of a theoretical line of research into software abstraction based on the study of universal abstraction breaking operators is presented.

2   Software Components

In some contexts the term *software component* is used to refer to an independent, executable and language neutral code package [15,37]. These *binary* distributed components are used in the framework of a *component architecture* such as Microsoft's COM. In essence they provide a language-independent package of software services. The differences between using a binary component and using a source level component are unfortunate, but currently unavoidable. In this paper, unless otherwise indicated, we use the term software component to refer both to source level and to executable software abstractions. Even when discussing source level components we consider *separate compilation* to be a very important factor.

The scope of software abstractions, and more acutely software components, is strongly related to the programming paradigms and features supported by different programming languages. As Gamma et al. put it, in the context of studying design patterns: *"...only examples of patterns can be embodied in code"* [12]. Indeed, it has been suggested that programming language features may be extracted from design patterns [13]. Some issues that arise from the use of binary components, such as versioning, may ultimately find their solution in the shape of programming language features.[1]

---

[1] The new language C#, for example, directly supports versioning

3   The Role of Abstraction Breaking

We may want to view software components as black boxes, accessed only via their interfaces. Alas, this view is simplistic. Aside from obvious limitations on the expressiveness of interfaces (e.g, providing complexity information), there are many situations in which the supplied interface isn't enough to achieve required functionality. Building a new component from scratch, when an existing component is close to meeting the requirements, is often too costly. Modifying the existing component requires project coordination and regression testing and may thus be impractical – especially when dealing with vendor supplied binary distributed components.

Other situations causing abstraction breaking:

- Maintenance (The component already in use doesn't support a new required functionality; a new version of a component breaks some hidden assumption of the user code; need to circumvent bugs discovered late in the lifecycle).
- Glueing problems (composing components requires exposing implementation details).
- System evolution: It may sometimes be better to carefully break and repackage an abstraction, even if it is possible to simply modify the code - provided the language features used to do this are safer to use.
- Performance: the component's performance may be inadequate for some specific use; a small optimization may make it usable. A special case is when the actual use is different from the component designer's expectations. It may be possible to use the public interface to achieve the required functionality, but at unacceptable performance.
- etc.

What usually happens in practice in such situations, is some kind of abstraction breaking. The worst method is, of course, creating a private version of the component. This is one of the dangers of source level abstractions: they may be copied and modified, creating a private and perhaps rogue version, with changes that may never be merged with the offical version. This method is, by its very nature, unstructured. When a new version of the component is released, it must be copied and the changes must be redone from scratch. This may be very difficult to do if there are major changes in the code. The result is, all too often, that projects continue to use their private, obsolete and unsupported versions of components.

Other, less catastrophic, methods of abstraction breaking exist. They ultimately depend on language mechanisms that allow modifying a component's behaviour, without modifying the component code itself. The most obvious such tool is *inheritance*. Using inheritance it is sometimes possible to extend an existing component, without modifying it. This is done by using the applicable code from the base class, and supplying new code when appropriate [28]. Alas, as we will see, this is not always possible to do without reengineering the inheritance hierarchy, with all the difficulties this entails.

Some software architectures are more prone to abstraction breaking than others. Consider *application frameworks*, that use callback routines. The callback routines are used to modify the behaviour of the framework, and usually require some method of gaining visibility to the framework's internal state. In some simple cases the callback routines can be viewed as parameterizations of the framework module, but more complicated frameworks usually expose at least some of their inner structure in the form of a visible inheritance hierarchy [22].

Real life reliability depends, in many cases, on breaking abstractions in a calculated manner - and repackaging the result as a new encapsualted software abstraction.

Some quality factors in abstraction breaking are:

- The result should be a software abstraction (i.e, specified via an interface and not by implementation details). This encourages a methodlgy based on *opening* and then *closing* the abstraction. The best scenario is when, of course, the interface need not be changed, and the changes are hidden behind the old interface, thus being invisible to clients. This approach is related to the *layered* architectural style.
- Structured. It is important to have some form of traceability of requirements. Single statement changes are usually not well documented. Scattering many related changes of this kind, usually produces hard to maintain code.
- Following the original component contract as much as possible, or extending it (i.e., being consistent with it) [29]. As much as possible, even abstraction breaking should follow the contract of the abstraction, and not be dependent on some coincidental implementation property, this can be ensured as long as the abstraction breaking code uses the component interface. [20] addresses the contract-consistency issue under the heading *consistent generic functions*.
- Reliance on compile-time checking as much as possible.

See [21] for related design principles in the context of metaobject protocols.

Since most languages do not offer explicit mechanisms for abstraction breaking, but rather rely on using lower level facilities to achieve the required results, it is important to establish how and to what extent these facilities should be used. The results should also influence the design of new language features for this purpose, and help create a taxonomy of kinds of abstraction breaking, and of abstraction breaking mechanisms. Using more expressive languages in general, and more expressive types systems in particular, may reduce the need for abstraction breaking, by allowing the creation of more flexible components. We touch briefly on these issues, which are mostly left for further research.

4   Reflection

Computational reflection is the activity performed by a computational system when doing computation about its own computation [27]. There are many approaches to achieving computational reflection, the most common is language-

and interpreter-based and involves the process of converting some component of the interpreter's state into a value that may be manipulated by the program, and the process of converting programmatically expressed values into components of the interpreter's state [36]. Examples of reflective computation are: to keep performance statistics, to keep information for debugging purposes, self-optimisation and self-modification [27].

The classic model for reflection is an infinite tower of interpreters, each interpreter being a program run by the interpreter one level above it. A program at level n is simply a data structure being interpretered at level $n + 1$. A reflective framework allows cross level access by supplying level shifting operators: a program at level n can look at its execution as viewed by the interpreter at $n + 1$, using the *reification* operation. The inverse operation is called *reflection*.

The analogy to abstraction levels in a layered architecture should be straightforward: obvsiously abstraction boundaries (i.e, information hiding) which limit the implementaion details the n level programmer can access are transparent to the $n + 1$ interpreter, that must run the level n program.

The above model assumes the languages themselves support abstraction boundaries (e.g., *private* declarations). This complicates the model. A more elegant translation between the reflective model and a model with information hiding is to view abstractions, which in the component model are exported from lower level components, as *primitives* supplied by the $n + 1$ level interpreter to the n level program. This, in a sense, implies two mirror image towers: the abstractions tower 'going up', from low level details; and the reflection tower 'going down' from an interpreter that uses only low level primitives, each level supplying the next with primitives implementing some abstraction.

Naturally, the reflection level-shifting operators, provide a universal method for abstraction breaking. This makes reflection a good yardstick against which abstraction breaking language facilites can be compared. Note, that reflection can be problematic as a programming approach both for efficiency reasons and for security reasons. Furthermore, it is inherently unstructured, since as described here, a level n program can change any *part* of an abstraction provided to it (as well as change everything else), without having to treat the abstraction as a whole. In our model the abstraction supplied interface is provided down the reflective tower in the form of primitive operations. More structure can be given to the system if related primitives are packaged together, perhaps even with explicit consistency properties (e.g., invariants).[2]

We choose not to restrict reflection in these ways, and to keep it as an ultimate and universal mechanism, through which we can define and model safer and more restricted abstraction breaking facilites.

A potentially more structured approach to reflection, in the context of object oriented programming languages was suggested by [27]. This approach is based on assigning each object a meta-object holding all the reflective information about the object. The meta-object has methods that specify how the object

---

[2] These properties may be modeled via the type system the level $n + 1$ interpreter supplies level n.

inherits information, how the object is printed, how a new instance of the object is made, etc.

Using metaobject protocols of this kind it is possible to customize hidden implementation details, even those that stem from the behaviour of the programming language. For example [21] discusses how the representation of fields in an object may be customized. An array approach which might be useful for a dense set of fields may be replaced by a hash table structure, for objects with a sparse set of used fields drawn from a large set of possibilities.

The object oriented approach is somewhat more localized than the original model of reflection. It allows *incremental definitions* using subclass specialization [21].

4.1   Uses in Theory and Practice

The most widely used language offering reflection is Java. Java supplies a reflection API, which is much more limited than the theoretical model of reflection. The Java reflection API allows the programmer to query and to some extent manipulate Java classes and objects at runtime. Contrary to the reflection tower approach, which allows arbitrary user code to run at the level of the interpreter, and the metaobject approach which allows customizing most object behaviours, the Java reflection API is quite limited in its scope. furthermore, the API's interface is not very rich. Most complicated uses can not be simple localized modifications (e.g., you can not simply redefine the way inheritance behaves).

Naturally, as opposed to the unlimited theoretical uses of reflection, most actual uses of reflection in Java fall into a few major classes.

We discuss the use of reflection to overcome programming language shortcomings and to break programmer supplied abstractions.

Reflection can be used to overcome language shortcomings, in which the programming language is, in effect, the abstraction boundary. This is an important case, as programming languages often preempt the programmer by imposing implementation restrictions (see the discussion in [21]).

It may be illuminating to distinguish between two types of language shortcomings that can be dealt with using reflection. The straightforward case involves situations requiring the customization of existing language behavior. Consider providing persistence to some objects in the system. A possible approach may be to customize the way storage handling is done for these objects.[3] Since memory handling is part of what the language does, it seems plausible that reflection would enable us to customize the way it is done. However, it seems that full-fledged reflection is not needed. Quite possibly a language may provide explicit hooks that allow customizing memory handling. The behavior customized is well defined and localized. We see, and this follows the previous observations, that instead of reflecton which may be too poweful as it can break most barriers, a

---

[3] We will blatantly ignore efficiency concerns, which must be dealt with in practice.

simple more localized approach can be found.[4] This is a result of the fact that we are considering customizing an existing, circumscribed, language behavior.

The second use of reflection, to overcome language shortcomings, involves bypassing language restrictions. Distinguishing between this and the previous case may sometimes be difficult, and a matter of personal taste. By language restrictions we mean language issues that are not well localized, and may reflect fundamental language design decisions.

A classic example is the use of reflection in Java to handle dynamic arrays. A generic routine for enlarging arrays with any kind of component that returns an array of the type `Object[]`, is unusable, since type information of the component is lost making the array unusable. It is possible to produce a working solution using Java's reflection facilites, which enable the routine to query and allocate specific array types [16].

Reflection allows us to bypass a language restriction on creating polymorphic routines. This example is quite telling. Reflection, with its obvious drawbacks (e.g., reliability) , is used to overcome a language abstraction problem. Furthermore, the Java reflection API is not powerful enough, so specific array handling facilites were added to it to overcome this spcific issue (i.e., java.lang.reflect.array). Compare this to the possibilities offered by languages with *generic programming* and *type inference*.

Generic programming (as in Ada's *generic units* and C++ *templates*) would allow generalizing the function over all types of arrays. As implemented in Ada, for example, generic programming will ensure type safety while allowing separate compilation of the generic unit.[5]

Consider a language the supports type inference, polymorphic functions and has the principal type property (i.e., it is possible to infer the most general polymorphic type of an expression). Without getting into specific details, these properties mean that the language interpreter (or compiler) may infer the most general type for the function, and that this type may contain type variables (i.e., be polymorphic). Essentialy it should be possible to deduce that the function type is $Array[T] \to Array[T]$ for any type T. This information can be inferred statically, and be used in the compilation and optimization processes.

Reflection was used, in the Java example, to solve a language limitation. Reflection is both too strong, thus allowing dangerous constructs, unstructured modifications, and runtime choices – and too weak, not allowing the language interpreter to deduce useful information at compile time, allowing type checking and optimization. As the example showed it is possible to introduce language features which are more limited in scope, but are more reliable and more efficient. As opposed to reflection these features have the desirable properties listed in section 3 above (e.g., they are structured).

---

[4] Storage pools in Ada are in effect following this course of action, though no to its full extent. Another example is 'tied' variables in Perl.

[5] Of course, the Ada model of arrays is different from the Java model, and there is usually no need for an Ada version of the Java routine. Also note that the Ada generic model requires explicit instantiation.

Still reviewing the uses of reflection in the programming language domain, it is possible to devise a method for foreign language interfacing utilizing reflection. Naturally, the foreign component will have to implement some reflection API. The discussion of this approach is beyond the scope of this work.

Reflection can, of course, also be used to infiltrate programmer-created abstraction boundaries. Using reflection for this purpose suffers from the general problems of using reflection as discussed above. The more refined tools shown (genericity and implicit polymorphism) can, some times, be used in this context too. They allow creating more *configurable* components (in the case of genericity) and more *general* components.

It is worth noting that though useful for designing software components, these tools address programming language issues (mostly related to typing). The connection is not surprising as programming languages are used for producing software components, and their limitations limit the solution space available to component designers (recall the discussion of *patterns* above). There are no equivalent, more specialized language tools, addressing the problem of breaking abstraction boundaries of components (i.e., encapsulation).

Some Empirical Results. One prominent use of reflection in Java is in the context of *Java Beans*. Beans are the Java approach to component oriented programming (i.e., what we termed 'binary' components). A bean (i.e., a component) can explicitly export its interface; if it does not, the interface can be deduced using reflection. This process is done by using clues about the meaning of various routines the component makes available. Essentialy this is done by relying on *naming conventions* coupled with routine signatures (e.g., a routine with a name starting with 'set' is a mutator). The drawbacks of this approach are obvious.

Preliminary results from opensource software reveals that most uses of reflection are indeed in the context of using beans. I was also able to find some libraries using reflection for things like logging. An extensive example of the former use can be found in the *Netbeans* IDE project[6]. A simple example of the latter can be found in the *Grace JavaLog* library.[7]

As both these uses are expected, the results are not surprising. It would be of interest to find out whether reflection is used for breaking programmer supplied abstractions, in the context of software maintenance. Alas, this may require exploring mature projects, far from their initial design. Systems of this sort are usualy not publically available.

5   Inheritance and Casting

Reflection is a general tool, applicable to any language based framework. We now turn to examine a more restricted language landscape consisting of typed

---

[6] http://www.netbreans.org
[7] http://www.homestead.com/javalog/

object oriented languages (e.g, C++, Ada, and Java). *Inheritance* can be used to modify and enhance software abstractions. Inheritance is a very powerful programming tool, and can be used for a variety of purposes [29]. It is used both for creating abstractions (e.g., by refinement) and for breaking abstraction (e.g., by overriding).

Abstraction and abstraction breaking in the context of object-oriented programming is discussed extensively in the literature [20,26,29,24]. Notions such as *design by contract* were proposed a mechanisms to enhance safety.

Casting (which is also used in non object-oriented contexts) can be used by *clients* of a component (i.e., class) for abstraction breaking purposes (e.g., injecting application specific classes into an application framework). In order to study the use of casting, it is not enough to examine libraries (i.e, components), it is essential to examine client code. In fact one might well say that in some designs casting is part of the component interface. It is described informally, and not part of the interface definition in the code, but it is most definitely part of the *protocol* used to comunicate with the component.

Some Empirical Results. Inheritance can play multiple roles and is not just used for specifying abstraction boundaries. In depth studies of its use are important (see [29,8,10]). Quantitive studies can reveal actual patterns of use. Alas, results in the literature are inconclusive, and more studies are needed ([4,9,14, 33]). These studies indicate that massive use of inheritance, especially resulting in large inheritance depth, may produce hard to maintain code. As layering, in and of itself, should not lead to this result, the data suggests viewing inheritance as too powerful a tool [7].

The C++ standard defined four casting forms, meant to refine the conventional C cast: `const_cast` is used to cast away constness; `dynamic_cast` is used to perform safe downcasting (casting down the inheritance hierarchy); `reinterpret_cast` is engineered for casts that yield implementation-dependent results and `static_cast` is used when none of the other forms is applicable.

Further studies measuring the breakdown between the different kinds of casts may help shed some light on the real-life uses of casting for abstraction breaking, and may help refine them toward safer abstraction breaking operators.

6   Interfaces and Abstraction Breaking in Ada

To show some possible relations between interfaces and abstraction breaking we use the Ada programming language and its abstraction facilities. Ada supports quite a few abstraction mechanisms, we concentrate on the major kinds, emphasizing those that allow the definition of interfaces by the programmer[8]:

---

[8] The description is not intended for Ada experts, but familiarity with Ada terminology is assumed.

1. Type families. Ada supports a rich set of types, organised into families by common interfaces (e.g, discrete, enumeration). The type classes can be found in [1] 3.2(12).
2. Routine signatures. Including parameter names and default values. Support overloading.
3. Package specifications. These include the client interface, and declarations visible only to the package implementation and child units (in the `private` part). Private types can have visibile discriminants that allow basic parameterization.
4. Generic Units (routines and packages). These include the generic parameters (i.e, the instantiation interface) and the unit's interface.
5. Generic packages without generic paraemeters. This special case of the above allows instantiating multiple copies of the package (useful for packages that have state: abstract data objects).
6. Task specifications. Include entry declarations.
7. Protected types specifications.
8. Tagged types. These are the Ada types supporting inheritance.
9. Abstract tagged types.
10. Generic Signature Packages. Used as generic formal package parameters (define only an instantiation interface).

The language also offers several features allowing different levels of abstraction breaking. These include: unchecked conversions, representation clauses, child units, and inheritance. Different abstraction breaking features are applicable to different kinds of abstractions (e.g, unchecked conversion can be used to break typing checks).

Naturally, overall language design restricts the types of abstractions, and since the desired goal after abstraction breaking is a new abstraction, it restricts the possible modifications of existing abstractions. Imagine a software component that represents a deterministic finite automaton (DFA), built as a generic Ada package and parameterized by $\Sigma, Q, q_0, \delta, F$. The package implements the DFA as an abstract data object (i.e, the automaton's current state is held by a variable declared in the package body). The package supports a basic interface which includes resetting the state, acting on single letter input, and checking if the automaton is in an accepting state. It is possible to extend the component, from the outside, using generic formal package parameters. For example it is possible to code a routine that applies an automaton to a string:

```
generic
    with package Automaton_To_Use is new Automaton(<>);
function Accepts_Word(S:String) return Boolean is ...
```

It this case it is possible to extend the functionality, without breaking the abstraction at all.[9] A more complicated case would have arisen if the demand required relying on implementation details. In such a case, it might have been

---

[9] Notice that the package specification need not be changed.

possible to extend the package using a child unit, *if* the state information would have been stored in the **private** part of the package specification and not inside the body. In such a case the ability to extend the abstraction, without having to modify it, depends on a design/coding decision that is made well before the new requirement is known. This is problematic, but is a common design concern.

We now consider a more complicated requirement. It is well known that any non-deterministic finite automaton (NFA) can be translated into an equivalent DFA. Given some representation of NFAs we want to create a routine that does the determinization, and returns the equivalent DFA, using the DFA representation above. However, packages (and generic packages) are not first class in Ada, and it is impossible to write a routine that returns an instantiation of the DFA package. Thus, to fulfill the requirement, the representation of DFAs must be changed. This will imply changing all clients. This costly process must be done, even if the core interface supplied by the DFA package does not need to change.

In other words, the strong coupling between the abstraction interface and implementation proves problematic. In fact, even other types of abstractions with less interface/implementation coupling, suffer from similar problems. An extreme approach to this problem is to impose complete separation between interfaces and implementation, by adding a connection-phase in which routines are attached to interface declarations (this is similar to the Modula-3 approach). This approach is perhaps too decoupled, since it looses the structuring effect of abstractions, the routines being independent of each other until attached to interfaces. Another issue is that if the attaching is static, and done only by explicit declarations, some powerful techiques are lost [11].

Suppose (following [11]) a set of collection interfaces: Enumerable - supporting iteration; Finite - supporting a **size** operation and Searchable - supporting a **contains** operation. It is possible to define the **contains** operation for any finite enumerable collection of elements supporting equality checking (finite is not realy necessary, but ensures termination). Instead of relying on the class heirarchy to reflect common functionality, which might require restructuring the system when new interfaces are needed, and may also require the use of multiple inheritance[10], it is possible to declare (via some form of logic programming) that any abstraction that supports the Finite and Enumerable interfaces also supports the Searchable interface. This connection can be done using the type system, and be modelled along the lines of Haskell *type classes* [11,38].

What we are suggesting, in essence, is to allow *implicit* connection between interfaces and implementations, while using the type system to ensure consistency. Connecting interfaces, as in the example above, explicitly and staticaly can be done using Ada generic programming faclities.[11]Since we value the flex-

---

[10] At the very least multiple *ineterface* inheritance.

[11] Ada generic formal package parameters are useful for this purpose. However they can be enhanced. Currently a parameter can impose no constraints on the actual (using <>), or specify the exact parameters of the generic actual. When connecting interfaces it is often desirable to specify only those constraints that tie the different interfaces together.

ibility offered by separating the interface relations from actual implementation needs, but also agree with Ada's philosophy of readability, we think that having the interface relations explicit (as proposed above), while allowing the *implements* relation to be inferred (via logical rules) strikes a good balance. A possible research approach is to use generic signature packages to define interface relations, and connect implementations with the supported interfaces via some form of automatic instantiation [35].

Another approach for having multiple interfaces, and separating implementation from interface is to add abstract interfaces (ike *interface* defintions in Java) to Ada as proposed by Ada Issue 251 (AI-251) [2]. This proposal does not deal with the inference approach discussed above. It is useful in that it refines the notion of inheritance.

Ada is not orthogonal in its treatment of interfaces. Interface relations, like the ones discussed in this section, must be designed on a case by case basis. Changing this situation requires a redesign of many basic elements of the language (the package specification being the fundamental method for defining ADT interfaces in the language). This does not seem to be justified or feasable.

7   Conclusions

Abstraction Breaking. Scanning source code, it is much easier to find explicit creation of software abstractions than to find abstraction breakings. This is because both programming languages and programming paradigms concentrate on the creation of abstraction.[12] Abstraction breaking is done implicitly, and most of it is not localized. This is problematic and unreliable. The best tool we have for ensuring correctness (i.e., programming languages) is not used.

To design and study abstraction breaking operators it is crucial to refine our notion of software abstractions, and specifically the notion of interfaces. This requires adding the notion of a logical theory to interfaces to capture the notion of specifications (cf. [7,29]). The obvious tool both for expressing interfaces and for studying them is the use of type systems. The specification and use of abstract data types can be expressed using strong enough type systems [31]. This approach can be integrated with work on data algebras [3] and on type classes [38]. Notice that we assume *explicit* interfaces. Type inference, should be incoorperated into the framework, being a powerful tool, but we agree with the emphasis on explicit interfaces, both for readability and for reliability [26].

Having a sound theory of interfaces allows work on relations between interfaces. Interface relations can be subtle, since they must take into account behaviour as ooposed to syntactic properties (e.g., stacks are not the same as queues). More interesting are relations that depend of implementation details, and thus on abstraction breaking (e.g., a letter by letter traversal protocol for a set of strings implemented by a trie).

Axiomatically defining these types of relations requires explicit specifications. To make the relations mechanically verifiable from code (e.g, to provide better

---

[12] One may note that the concept of 'refactoring' is related to abstraction breaking.

error messages) requires language evolution. A theory should capture the relations between interfaces and implementations, in order to be able to express interface relations that depend on implementation details.

On top of such a theory it should be possible to define universal abstraction and abstraction breaking operators (e.g, by following a reflection model for abstraction), with well understood properties. Language features can then be mapped to the generalized operators. Aside from the theoretical value, this work is likely to give insights and suggestions for new language features. However, abstraction breaking depends on the types of abstractions, which are also programming language dependent.

Final Comments. Abstraction breaking is part of the cycle of abstraction use. Software components specified as interfaces, may still require abstraction breaking by clients. Software engineering studies language features supporting abstraction in detail. It is important to study abstraction breaking mechanisms. This is also a way to refine our notion of abstraction.

The research on the semantics of abstraction should include a detailed study of abstraction breaking operators. Reflection can be used as a yardstick.

Both reflection, and unrestricted inheritance are too powerful as abstraction breaking operators. More refined operators are needed. A taxonomy of abstraction breaking operators, including their relation to inheritance is left for future research.

Strict abstraction boundaries are too limiting in practice. The good news is that one man's abstraction breaking is another's language feature.

Acknowledgements. Ed Schonberg provided comments on earlier drafts of this paper.

References

1. *Ada95 Language Reference Manual*, 1995, ANSI/ISO/IEC 8652:1995
2. *Ada95 Ada Issues*, available from *http://www.ada-auth.org/ acats/ais.html*
3. Backhouse R., Jansson P., Jeuring J., Meertens L., *Generic Programming — An Introduction*, Lecture Notes in Computer Science **1608**, Springer-Verlag, 1999
4. Bieman J. M., Zhoa J. X., *Reuse through Inheritance: A Quantative Study of C++*, 17th Intl. Conf. on Software Engineering, 1995
5. Booch G., *Software Engineering in Ada*, Benjamin/Cummings, 1983
6. Bosch J., Mitchell S. (Eds.) *Object-Oriented Technology, ECOOP'97 Workshop Reader* , Lecture Notes in Computer Science **1357**, Springer-Verlag, 1997
7. Canning P. S., Cook W. R., Hill W. L. and Olthoff W. G., *Interface for Strongly-Typed Object-Oriented Programming*, OOPSLA'89
8. Cook W. R., Hill, W. L., Canning P. S., *Inheritance is Not Subtyping*, POPL'90, 1990
9. Daly J., Brooks A., Miller J., Roper M., Wood M., *An Empirical Study Evaluating Depth of Inheritance on the Maintainability of Object-Oriented Software*, research report EFoCS-10-95, Department of Computer Science, University of Strathclyde, Glasgow 1995, available from
   http://www.cs.strath.ac.uk/research/EFOCS/abstracts.html

10. Day M., Gruber R., Liskov B., Myers A. C., *Subtypes vs. Where Clauses: Constraining Parameteric Polymorphism*, OOPSLA'95
11. De Volder K., De Meuter W., *Type Oriented Programming*, ECOOP'97. In [6]
12. Gamma E., Helm R, Johnson R., Vlissides J., Design Patterns, *Elements of Reusable Object-Oriented Software*, Addison-Wesley, 1995
13. Gil J., Lorenz D. H, *Design Pattens vs. Language Design*, ECOOP'97. In [6]
14. Harrison R., Counsell S., Nithi R., *Experimental Assessment of the Effect of Inheritance on the Maintainability of Object-Oriented Systems*, 3rt Intl. Conf. on Empirical Assessment and Evaluation in Software Engineering, 1999
15. Hopkins J., *Component Primer*, CACM, Vol. 43, No. 10, 2000
16. Hortsmann C. S., Cornell G., *Core Java, Volume I - Fundamentals*, Sun Microsystems Press, 1999
17. Hughes J.,*Why Functional Programming Matters*, in D. Turner, editor, *Research Topics in Functional Programming*, Addison-Wesley, 1990
18. Hutton G., *A Tutorial on the Universality and Expressiveness of Fold*, J. Functional Programming, **1**, 1993
19. Kernighan B. W., Ritchie D. M., *The C Programming Language, second edition*, Prentice Hall, 1988
20. Kiczales G., Lamping J., *Issues in the Design and Specification of Class Libraries*, OOPSLA'92, 1992
21. Kiczales G., *Towards a New Model of Abstraction in Software Engineering*, IMSA'92 Workshop on Reflection and Meta-level Architectures, 1992
22. Lamm E. *Building Frameworks in Ada95*, Ada-Belgium'99, Ada-Belgium Newsletter, Vol. 7, 1999
23. Lamm E. *The Little Abstractionist - A Cacaphony of Abstractions in Ada*, unpublished manuscript
24. Lamping J., *Typing the Specialization Interface*, OOPSLA'93, 1993
25. Liskov B., Guttag J., *Abstraction and Specification in Program Development*, MIT Press, 1986
26. Liskov B., *A History of CLU*, ACM *SIGPLAN Notices*, Vol. 28, No. 3, 1993
27. Maes P., *Concepts and Experiments in Computational Reflection*, OOPSLA'87, ACM *SIGPLAN Notices*, Vol. 22, No. 12, 1987
28. Martin R. C., *The Open-Closed Principle*, C++ Report, January, 1996
29. Meyer B., *Obejct Oriented Software Construction* 2nd edition, Prentice Hall, 1997
30. Meyers S., *Effective C++, Second Edition*, Addison-Wesley, 1997
31. Mitchell J. C., Plotkin G. D., *Abstract Types Have Existential Type*, ACM *TOPLAS* Vol. 10, No. 3, 1988
32. Parnas D. L., *On the Criteria To Be Used in Decomposing Systems into Modules*, *CACM*, Vol. 15, No. 12, 1972
33. Prechelt L., Unger B., Philippsen M., Tichy W. F., *A Controlled Experiment on Inheritance Depth as a Cost Factor for Maintenance*, submmited to IEEE Trans. on Software Engineering, March 200, Available from *http://wwwipd.ira.uka.de/EIR/*
34. Sethi R. *Programming Languages - Concepts and Constructs*, Addison-Weseley, 1996
35. Shen J., Cormak G. V., *Automatic Instantation in Ada*, Annual International Conference on Ada , 1991
36. Sobel J. M., Friedman D. P., *An Introduction to Reflection-Oriented Programming*, Reflection'96, 1996
37. Sparling M., *Lessons Learned - through six years of component based development*, *CACM*, Vol. 43, No. 10, 2000
38. Wadler P. L., Blott S., *How to Make Ad-Hoc Polymorphism Less Ad Hoc*, POPL'89, 1989

Using the SPARK Toolset for Showing the Absence of Run-Time Errors in Safety-Critical Software

Darren Foulger[1] and Steve King[2]

[1] BAE SYSTEMS, Brough, East Yorkshire, UK
darren.foulger@baesystems.com
[2] Department of Computer Science, University of York,
Heslington, York, YO10 5DD, UK
king@cs.york.ac.uk

Abstract. This paper reports the results of a study into the effectiveness of the SPARK toolset for showing the absence of run-time errors in safety-critical Ada software. In particular, the toolset is examined to determine how effective it is in finding run-time errors in a SPARK program, and how much of the process of proving freedom from run-time errors can be performed automatically. The study identifies areas where automatic run-time checks are not so effective and, where possible, gives recommendations about the design of the software so that the toolset is as effective as possible in automatically proving absence of run-time errors.

The results will be of interest to anyone contemplating the use of the SPARK toolset for ensuring the absence of run-time errors, both as guidance in planning the effort required, and for practical advice on making the best use of the toolset.

1 Introduction

While hardware engineers may design systems to fail-safe so that they stabilise in the least-damaging way when the system malfunctions, software systems typically continue to operate after a software error occurs and often do so in an unspecified and undesirable way. Many programming languages therefore provide appropriate run-time checks which guarantee that mis-applications of program operations are signalled as errors. As the program is running, an exception is generated if the check fails, giving the program the opportunity to take remedial action. Although this solution ensures that programs do not return random results, it is not completely satisfactory because errors are not signalled until run-time. A program written in such a language can only recover from potential malfunctions anticipated by the programmer. While such error-detection mechanisms may be sufficient in some applications, in many safety-critical applications, any software failure is undesirable. It is therefore essential to be able to guarantee in advance that a program will not cause any run-time error to occur.

A. Strohmeier and D. Craeynest (Eds.): Ada-Europe 2001, LNCS 2043, pp. 229–240, 2001.
© Springer-Verlag Berlin Heidelberg 2001

There are several methods to determine whether there is a possibility of run-time errors in a program. One such method is through testing (dynamic analysis). However, even systematic testing can only detect the presence of bugs in a program and not their absence. Therefore, while testing has its uses and provides confidence that the software behaves correctly, it cannot be used to verify that the program is free from all run-time errors. On the other hand, it is possible to make software more robust, and perhaps even make claims about the absence of run-time errors, through the use of static analysers or, as they are otherwise known, static debuggers or static checkers. For instance, in an Ada trustworthiness study [6], Saaltink recommends that for high integrity systems, static analysis is required for statement execution prediction, static object analysis, storage usage, etc., in order to show that run-time errors cannot occur.

Safety-related standards, such as UK Defence Standard 00-55 [4], require that, during development of safety-related software, evidence is obtained on the quality, correctness and robustness of software. Evidence is required for software of the higher safety integrity levels that the software is suitable for use in safety-critical applications. Safety-related standards now recognise that testing of safety-critical software is inadequate and that complementary methods, such as static analysis and formal proof, are required in order to provide sufficient verification and validation of software systems.

This paper discusses work undertaken as part of an initiative to investigate the introduction of automated static run-time checking into the safety-critical software development process within BAE SYSTEMS. As discussed above, there is a definite need for analysis for absence of run-time errors within safety-critical software applications. This is currently part of the manual code review within BAE SYSTEMS, and therefore it was necessary to identify a suitable tool that would support such analysis. The tool chosen needs not only to be dependable but also to be effective in identifying all areas in the software where potential run-time errors could occur. In analysing a given software product the tool should have a significant amount of automation. Manual analysis suffers from human error and the amount of software being developed for safety-critical software makes a manual analysis of software impractical. Therefore in order to be an effective toolset for use by BAE SYSTEMS, the chosen toolset must minimise the manual analysis required.

A toolset is therefore required that is effective in two ways:

1. in checking for all possible run-time errors such that a claim can be made that the software is free from run-time errors;
2. in ensuring that the checking and analysis process is mostly (if not entirely) automated, so that significant manual effort is not required — either in annotating the code or in performing in-depth manual analysis or proof.

The rest of this paper is structured as follows: the next section gives a brief overview of the SPARK language and toolset, explaining in particular which run-time errors can occur. We then describe the study itself and the results that were obtained. Finally, we draw some conclusions.

2   Run-Time Errors in SPARK

The SPARK language is a subset of Ada[1], augmented with annotations, some of which are mandatory and some optional. A detailed description of the subset can be found in [7], but it can be summarised as follows [8]:

- it includes packages, private types, functions returning structured values and the library system;
- the following language constructs are not permitted:
    - tasks, exceptions, generic units, access types;
    - use clauses, type aliasing, anonymous types;
    - goto statements
    - declare statements
    - default values in record declarations and default subprogram parameters
- overloading is avoided as much as possible;
- all storage constraints are statically determinable.

The full Ada language [5] allows the possibility of raising five predefined exceptions: CONSTRAINT_ERROR , NUMERIC_ERROR, PROGRAM_ERROR, STORAGE_ERROR or TASKING_ERROR. However, use of the SPARK language removes the possibility of many forms of run-time error, either because the language subset of SPARK does not include the Ada feature, or because the additional static semantic rules of SPARK allow the error to be detected before the program is executed. Thus the remaining potential run-time errors are:

- incorrect indexing of arrays,
- assignment to a variable of a value that is out of range of the type of the variable,
- division by zero, and
- overflow of a sub-expression that results in a value that exceeds the range of a variable's base type range.

The exceptions that can be raised in a SPARK program are therefore only CONSTRAINT_ERROR and NUMERIC_ERROR.

[8] describes how the SPARK language and toolset are currently applied in the development of safety critical software at BAE SYSTEMS. The SPARK Examiner [1] can be applied at various levels of analysis. It is currently used for *Lexical and Syntactic Analysis, Static Semantic Analysis* and *Data and Information Flow Analysis*. The additional levels of analysis that are possible are *Program Verification* and *Run-time Error Checking*. For each level of analysis, certain annotations need to be included in the SPARK program. These are formally Ada comments, preceded by the syntax "--#", and thus have no effect on the compilation of the program. Annotations are required for every package and subprogram, including the main program. Package annotations define a view of

---

[1] Throughout this paper, we deal with Ada83 and its associated language SPARK83, rather than Ada95 and SPARK95: this is simply because the software used for the study had been written in Ada83.

the state data declared within the package, and they may describe the state data in abstract terms at the specification level, hiding the implementation details within the package body. Subprogram annotations define the data that is accessed globally, rather than via the parameters of the subprogram, as well as the dependencies between the data being imported and exported by the subprogram. Optionally, subprograms can be annotated to allow program verification: by adding preconditions, postconditions, assert and check annotations, partial correctness can be shown.

Whichever level of analysis is chosen by the developer, the SPARK Examiner works on the program by examining compilation units. The source code is checked to ensure that it complies with the SPARK subset and appropriate Verification Conditions (VCs) are generated in a file. The next stage of the process involves invoking the SPARK Automatic Simplifier against these VCs. This is a Prolog tool which is used to discharge as many of the VCs as possible using symbolic manipulation. The main parts of the Simplifier are a contradiction hunter (which attempts to find contradictions among the hypotheses), a reduction unit (which attempts to discard redundant hypotheses) and various expression simplification and standardisation tools. These last tools are actually taken from the final component in the SPARK toolset, the Proof Checker. This is an interactive environment within which the developer can attempt to prove the VCs. It is a first-order predicate calculus tool, using a natural deduction system with a wide range of proof strategies such as proof by cases, contradiction and induction.

An overview of the SPARK toolset can be seen in Figure 1.

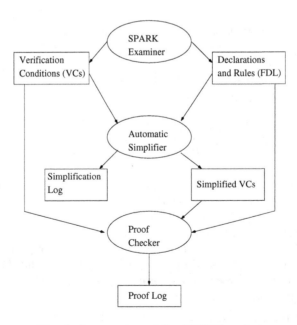

Fig. 1. An overview of the SPARK toolset

3   The Study

As mentioned above, the purpose of this study was to investigate extending the use of the SPARK toolset to perform run-time checks. The study used a sample of safety-critical code taken from the Eurofighter (EFA) and NIMROD avionics projects to show the practical effectiveness of the SPARK tools. The sample of avionics source code taken from these two projects was selected as typical of the types of safety-critical application software in avionics systems being developed at BAE SYSTEMS. The packages selected differ in nature in order to provide an assessment of the run-time check effectiveness over different types of software. They cover state-based functions, monitor and control functions and arithmetic functions. In total, 58 packages were examined, which break down into the areas identified below.

EFA Fuel	Number of packages
Fuel Manager (FUM)	27
Fuel Gauging (FUG)	21
Fuel Calcs (FCG)	1
NIMROD USUMS	**Number of packages**
FPS	1
IRP	1
IRW	1
DCP_POWER	6

Each of the packages chosen was annotated with the mandatory SPARK annotations and had undergone Lexical and Syntactic Analysis, Static Semantic Analysis and Data and Information Flow Analysis. By selecting source code across two different projects the study can draw some general conclusions about the effectiveness of the SPARK run-time checking that are independent of a particular project.

The SPARK toolset offers two levels of VC generation for run-time errors: the first level generates VCs for index check, range check and division check, while the second level also generates VCs for overflow check. Some experiments were carried out with using just the first level of VC generation to see whether how much extra effort was involved in generating and proving the overflow VCs. It was found that, although more VCs were generated for overflow checks, the conclusions tended to be a repeat of other VCs generated and so little extra effort was needed to prove them. Thus the second level of checks was applied throughout the study.

The process followed for each package was as follows: first the VCs were generated. This did not involve any additional annotations, since the starting point was a well-formed SPARK program that was free from data-flow errors. A bottom-up strategy was followed, starting at the bottom of the Ada package calling hierarchy and working up until the main program was reached. The

Simplifier was then applied to the generated VCs. Those VCs that were not discharged completely by the Simplifier were simplified as far as possible, and this simplified form was then examined, to see whether the VC should be provable with further annotations, or perhaps manually provable with the Proof Checker. Alternatively, it might be a potential run-time error.

If there did not seem to be enough information in the hypotheses to make all of the conclusions provable, then manual inspection might reveal a problem: if the conclusions refer to entities that do not appear at all in the hypotheses, the most likely cause is the presence of loops in the code. When the Examiner encounters a loop in the source code it will automatically insert a virtual cut point into the loop — if there is no cut point identified already — to allow it to develop VCs for the loop. This virtual cut-point is a default *assert* annotation of the form `--# assert true`. Such default *assert* annotations are usually not strong enough to generate hypotheses capable of automatically proving VCs. Hence a VC not proven by the Simplifier is typically as a result of a loop in the source code. In such situations, annotations are required that will allow VCs to be generated with the required information. The VC and source code should be examined together in order to determine what further annotations can be added to provide information that would aid in the proof of the VC. Having performed the above steps, further constraints will have been established for the existing annotations.

Once the annotations have been added or strengthened, the process described above is repeated until an optimum state is reached, i.e. a situation where most VCs are simplified away and what is left is either provable or a potential run-time error.

4   The Results of the Study

The study has shown that the SPARK approach is effective in finding and identifying run-time errors in source code. We summarise below the potential run-time errors found during analysis of the sampled code. Only one definite run-time error was revealed during the run-time checking of the sampled code. In addition several potential run-time errors were revealed but it is likely that such potential errors would never happen in the context of the system and its operating environment. Given that the sampled code had been produced using safety-critical software development practices, it is not surprising that the Examiner detected very few run-time errors. However, what the study has shown is that with only a little effort, evidence can be provided to show the absence of run-time errors in this safety-critical software. Such evidence is currently provided by the manual code review stage in the safety-critical software development practices of BAE SYSTEMS: automation of at least part of this process would be beneficial.

The study reveals that the SPARK toolset is effective on all types of software but is particularly effective on moding and control software. The statistics arising from the study — some of which are shown below, while the remainder can be found in the more detailed reports [2,3] — show that the SPARK toolset is very effective in providing automated evidence of the absence of run-time errors. These results suggest that the standards currently in use by BAE SYSTEMS in developing safety-critical software are generally suitable in producing code that can be readily analysed by the Examiner. However, as we shall see, there are a number of design features that if adopted can improve the SPARK toolset's ability to automatically prove absence of run-time errors and significantly reduce the amount of effort required for manual proof using the Proof Checker. The loop structure is an area that sometimes requires extra manual effort, where further annotations need to be added as described above.

The run-time error checking can be less effective than anticipated in certain known areas. The SPARK toolset highlights these areas by issuing warning messages. Other issues that impact on the effectiveness of run-time error checking include the use of defensive programming techniques and real arithmetic that are discussed below.

Degree of Automated Proof. A sample of the numerical results is given in Figure 2: here we have recorded, for one of the EFA modules, the number of conclusions in the VCs, (i.e. the number of things that have to be proved), together with the number of conclusions solved by the Simplifier, (i.e. the number automatically proved). This gives an indication of the effectiveness of the automation of the run-time checks. (Package names have been disguised.)

FUG from EFA FUEL				
Package Name	Notes	No. of operations	conclusions gen-erated	conclusions solved by Simpli-fier
CONTS_1	(1) (2) (3) (5) (6)	25	2807*	2744
CONTS_2		11	11	All
CONTS_3		8	8	All
CONTS_4_L	(1) (4)	28	2003	1993
CONTS_4_R	(1) (4)	28	1834	1826
DENS_1	(1)	3	121	108
FLOW_1	(1) (7)	7	384	370
FUEL_1	(1)	7	112	106
FUEL_2	(1) (4) (7) (8)	13	579	525
FUG_1		19	21	All
FUG_2		16	20	All
FUG_3		6	16	All
FUG_4		6	104	All
FUG_5		16	1414	All
LVL_1	(1) (2) (7) (9)	6	278	267
PROBE_1	(1) (2) (7) (9)	9	982	922
PROPS_1	(1) (2) (7) (9)	7	203	183
REF_1		3	38	All
TANK_1		24	527	All
TOT_1		3	91	All
WARN_1		3	241	All
Sub-total (FUG sub-system)		248		97.8%

* annotations added to generate acceptable VCG file

(1) Requires manual proof using Proof Checker.
(2) Loop requires annotations.
(3) Potential run-time error detected in type range.
(4) Potential run-time errors detected.
(5) Lack of information due to no real RTCs selected.
(6) Rounding rules required in order to solve manually.
(7) Extra checks for overflow that require manual proof that they are within base type range. Can be done using RLS file.
(8) Definite run-time error detected.
(9) Restructuring code with internal operations to ease manual proof.

Fig. 2. Numerical results for one of the samples of EFA code

In terms of automatic discharge of proofs, the results in Figure 2 are slightly better than the overall results, since the overall figure is that more than 95% of the conclusions generated in the VCs were proven automatically. Of course, the interest really lies in the remaining 5% of conclusions that could not be automatically proved. Investigation of these revealed one definite bug that could have resulted in a run-time error, and several cases where there was a potential for an error. It is however unlikely that these potential errors would ever happen in the context of the system and its operating environment. The vast majority of the conclusions that could not be automatically proved were discharged using the Proof Checker: this involved making additional annotations in the code and providing additional rules. In particular, loop structures are an area where extra manual effort is required to ensure absence of run-time errors. (The current use of SPARK within BAE SYSTEMS does not involve performing correctness proofs, so precondition, postcondition and loop invariant assertions are not normally required.)

Less Effective Areas. There are certain areas where the SPARK Examiner generates warning messages to indicate that the tool cannot guarantee absence of run-time errors. These include expressions involving real number arithmetic (where the Examiner does not generate VCs at all), and complex expressions where the order of evaluation might affect the possibility of overflow (the Examiner assumes left-to-right evaluation, but warns that a compiler might differ). A warning is also issued whenever the *hide* annotation is encountered. These warnings emphasise the fact that SPARK run-time checking needs to be accompanied by further verification activities targeted at the areas where the SPARK tools cannot achieve analysis, where the potential for run-time errors remains.

Defensive Programming. One of the interesting results from the study was in the area of defensive programming: this is a standard technique used in safety-critical software, so it was worrying to find that use of defensive programming could 'mask' run-time errors, so that they would not be detected by the Examiner. The consequence of writing defensive programming code is that during analysis the SPARK toolset believes this defensive programming to contain paths through the code that cannot ever be traversed, i.e. non-executable code. The SPARK toolset will therefore not even attempt to detect any software errors in these paths and so run-time errors will not be detected. For example, in the following extract of code, X is defined as an import variable of X_Type, but it is required to be protected against possible corruption, i.e. defensive programming is required:

```
if X in X_Type then
        path 1
else
        path 2
end if;
```

In this example, the Examiner would generate VCs for both path 1 and 2. In generating hypotheses for path 2, the Examiner first indicates that the imported value of X is within its type range. This is an initial assumption always made by the Examiner:

```
H1:      x_type__first <= x.
H2:      x <= x_type__last.
```

However in order to traverse path 2, the variable X must be outside the type range:

```
H3:      not ((x_type__first <= x) and (x <= x_type__last)).
```

The Simplifier would recognise this as a contradiction in the hypotheses: the variable X must be within its type range X_Type and must also be outside its type range X_Type. Any contradictions found within the hypotheses will result in the VC being reduced to true, i.e. the VC is automatically proven since the path is non-executable.

Some proposed work-arounds, involving additional *assert* annotations are given in the full report [2,3], but the general advice is to examine carefully all code where VCs have been proved by the Simplifier through a contradiction in the hypotheses.

Other Design Issues. The detailed write-up of this study [2,3] includes a discussion of ways to improve the effectiveness of SPARK run-time checking, in terms of the amount of automation of proofs, by adopting various 'good practices' in the design of software. These practices include the use of:

- low coupling of packages: this eases data flow and makes VCs easier;
- small packages: these give easier and more manageable VCs;
- small subroutines: these generate fewer VCs that are often easier to prove automatically;
- simple implementations: a less complex implementation gives simpler VCs;
- well-defined interfaces that use subtypes to define imported and exported data ranges;
- data hiding: this reduces the information needed in hypotheses, which is desirable because accessing global data in Ada specifications can cause extremely large VCs that exceed the capacity of the Examiner.

The good design practices listed above will generally improve the effectiveness of the run-time checks performed by the SPARK toolset. Software designers should aim to achieve the above attributes as they will aid in generating simpler VCs that can be more easily proved automatically by the Simplifier.

A software designer should design the software such that the number of paths through a subprogram is low. The number of VCs generated for a subprogram is directly related to the number of paths through the code. Thought should be given to the creation of further internal subprograms in order to reduce code that has a significant number of paths.

Implementations performing state-based behaviour are easier to analyse than implementations performing numerical algorithms, while implementations using real arithmetic are even more difficult to analyse. Where possible, functionality using arithmetic, particularly real arithmetic, should be isolated and put into self-contained subprograms that can be analysed separately from the more easily analysable state-based behaviour.

5   Conclusions

We have shown that the SPARK approach is generally effective in finding and identifying run-time errors in source code. The study showed that the SPARK Examiner generates VCs for each of the required checks where run-time errors can occur in a SPARK program. The results of the study identified one definite run-time error and several potential run-time errors in a sample of source code that had been through a safety-critical software development process. From these results, we can see that the SPARK toolset can be used to provide evidence of an absence of run-time errors in a program. Had time allowed, it would have been interesting to inject faults, i.e. run-time errors, into the software to determine if they were detectable by the SPARK toolset.

The study sampled a range of software covering state machines, arithmetic calculations, moding and control software modules. It revealed that the SPARK toolset was very effective in automatically proving the majority of VCs generated for all these differing types of software. A figure of 95% of conclusions generated in the run-time error checking VCs are proven automatically by the Simplifier. This figure represents a very effective automated approach to run-time error checking, although this effectiveness has in part been achieved because the SPARK language has been designed to contain only those parts of the Ada language that can be effectively analysed.

Applying changes to the software design can improve the effectiveness of the toolset when it performs run-time error checking. Employing general good design practice assists in generating simpler VCs that increase the effectiveness of the Simplifier in automatically proving the VCs. In some areas, the code generates run-time check VCs that are more difficult to prove and the study has identified ways of restructuring the code so that it generates VCs that are simpler to prove. It is clear that restructuring techniques such as use of internal procedures can significantly reduce the complexity of VCs and make manual proof of such VCs easier to accomplish.

Some 5% of conclusions in VCs generated by the Examiner from the sampled code remained unproven. These VCs are ones that the toolset cannot prove automatically, potential run-time errors and definite run-time errors. These unproven conclusions in VCs are where manual effort is required in the proof of the VCs or in the justification of the "errors" through rigorous argument. This small percentage recorded by the study allows us to conclude that the SPARK toolset does minimise the manual effort required to be applied to the run-time checking of a program, but that the process is not fully automated. Indeed the study has found that some cases involve an iteration of the analysis process in order to generate VCs that can be proved. (It would be interesting to know the relationship between the 5% of unproven VCs and some measure of complexity or criticality; unfortunately, this data is not available.)

The study has identified occasions where further annotations are required to be added to the code in order to improve the effectiveness of the proof of run-time check VCs. For instance, *assert* annotations are often required within loops to constrain the loop variable and generate hypotheses with suitable information that allows VCs to be proved.

It has been shown that manual proof of the remaining simplified VCs can generally be accomplished through use of existing predefined rules within the Proof Checker and subprogram specific rules generated automatically by the Examiner. We have seen that there are a number of typical VC proofs that keep cropping up in run-time checking VCs. Examples of these are:

- run-time error check VCs of constant arrays,
- VCs with conclusions containing base type expressions,
- VCs containing round() expressions resulting from real to integer type conversions.

These can be proved using the Proof Checker.

It can be concluded that the SPARK toolset can detect most run-time errors in a SPARK program and it minimises the manual effort required to prove absence of run-time errors. However in specific areas the toolset does not meet these aims and so it must be concluded that the SPARK toolset does not provide complete coverage of *all* run-time errors in *all* instances.

The study revealed that there were areas where the run-time checks were not effective. Investigations found that use of *defensive programming* might result in run-time errors being hidden in the code and remaining undetected from the SPARK toolset. It is therefore recommended that manual inspection is undertaken on areas where VCs have been proved by the Simplifier through proof by contradiction. Further areas where the SPARK toolset is not effective at detecting run-time errors are highlighted as warnings to the programmer. Raising the awareness of these areas allows the programmer to target other verification activities at these areas, specifically aimed at gathering evidence that the risk of a run-time error in these areas is low enough to be acceptable. The conclusion of the study is that the SPARK toolset must be used alongside other activities, such as IV&V and testing, to provide an effective approach to run-time error checking. The SPARK toolset on its own does not provide a complete solution for all types of software but provides a significant contribution to the overall claim for absence of run-time errors in a safety-critical software program.

The work undertaken in run-time error checking and described in this report is not only beneficial to others undertaking run-time checking but will also benefit programmers who are looking at program verification using the SPARK toolset. Many of the issues discussed during the study are equally applicable to program verification as they are to run-time checks.

The findings discussed in this report will assist programmers in adopting the run-time checking of the SPARK toolset. As experience is gained in using the SPARK toolset on projects, it is predicted that further beneficial software design strategies and proof rules will be discovered to assist in the proof of absence of run-time errors and so add to the knowledge gained and described in this report.

One of the obstacles to using program verification in safety-critical projects is the perceived difficulty and expense in undertaking proof. The step from proof of absence of run-time errors to program proof is a small one. The process, using the SPARK toolset, is very similar. It is expected that development of skills in proof for run-time checks will assist in the move towards applying program verification at a later date.

In conclusion, this study provides valuable evidence from an extensive study of the application of a particular static analysis tool. The data on numbers of conclusions generated and automatically proved should be of use to anyone considering or planning the introduction of proofs of absence run-time checks to a development process. Similarly, the experiences and advice should be of use in the actual application of such techniques.

Acknowledgements. We are grateful for comments on earlier drafts to: Phil Thornley, Tullio Vardanega and the Ada Europe 2001 referees.

References

1. J. Barnes. *High integrity Ada: The SPARK approach.* Addison-Wesley, 1997.
2. D.M. Foulger. *Evaluation of the SPARK toolset in checking for run-time errors in safety-critical software.* MSc report, University of York, Heslington, York, UK, 2000.
3. D.M. Foulger. Results of study into run-time checks of SPARK programs. Technical Report BAe-BSY-RP-GEN-000008, Issue 1, BAE SYSTEMS, Brough, E. Yorkshire, July 2000.
4. MOD. *The procurement of safety related software in defence equipment.* UK Ministry of Defence, August 1997. DEF STAN 00-55 (Part 1: Requirements and Part 2: Guidance).
5. K.A. Nyberg, editor. *The annotated Ada Reference Manual.* ANSI, 1983. ANSI/MIL-STD-1815A-1983.
6. M. Saaltink and S. Michell. Ada95 trustworthiness study: guidance on the use of Ada95 in the development of high integrity systems. Technical Report TR-97-5499-04a, Version 2.0, Department of National Defence, Ottawa, Canada, March 1997.
7. *SPARK — The SPADE Ada Kernel.* Praxis Critical Systems, August 1997. Edition 3.3.
8. J.P. Thornley. Static analysis and diversity in the software development process — experiences with the use of SPARK. In K. Hardy and J. Briggs, editors, *Reliable software technologies — Ada-Europe '97,* number 1251 in Lecture Notes in Computer Science, pages 266–277. Springer-Verlag, 1997.

Scenario-Based System Assessment

Silke Kuball

Safety Systems Research Centre, Department of Computer Science, University of
Bristol, Merchant Venturers Building, Woodland Road, Bristol BS8 1UB, UK,
silke@cs.bris.ac.uk

Abstract. In this paper we introduce a new approach to the assessment
of risk and reliability of safety-critical software systems: scenario-based
system assessment. This approach uses the notion of input-space scenarios, which are created by a link between system structure and input
space structure. Scenario-based system assessment combines two differing already existing approaches to software reliability and risk assessment: input space partitioning and code partitioning and it draws on
the strengths of both models while at the same time helping to overcome
some of their restrictions.

1 Introduction

The assessment of system dependability for safety–critical software systems used
e.g. in nuclear power plants, aircraft or medical devices is an isssue of key importance. With an increased complexity of these applications, more complex
software systems are required. Dependability claims for the safety–functions in
safety–related systems are high and measures are needed to quantify their dependability effectively. Safety functions are often demand–based, i.e. they are
called upon to act only in the case of critical events. Critical events are rarely
observed in real–life and thus the dependability measure of interest is the probability of the system to fail on demand (*pfd*) at any point in mission time (availability) rather than the probability of the system to fail over a time interval
[0,T] (reliability). Assessment of the *pfd* starts after product development and
debugging has finished and the product is released for use. Most of the currently used assessment methods for safety–critical systems are qualitative and
centred around the use of standards. But the problem is that inspite of the importance of these methods, they do not provide a quantitative measure for the
pfd. A method that can provide such a measure is statistical software testing
(*SST*). It is the only method (apart from formal verification) that can quantify
the system *pfd* and thus monitor the achieved level of dependability against a
given dependability claim. For safety–critical systems, we are particularly interested in the case where SST does not reveal failures or only failures that can be
proven to be tolerable (i.e. that have no effect on safety). A basic requirement
for SST is the generation of independent test cases from the system's *operational
profile* or *operational demand distribution* (ODD). The ODD represents the expected operational use of the system, see also [1], [2]. From the observation of

A. Strohmeier and D. Craeynest (Eds.): Ada-Europe 2001, LNCS 2043, pp. 241–252, 2001.
© Springer-Verlag Berlin Heidelberg 2001

N independent failure–free statistical system test-runs, the system *pfd* is estimated using statistical models. Estimation models for SST were introduced by e.g. [3], [4], [5]. We distinguish classical and Bayesian as well as black–box and white–box SST models. Black–box Bayesian models for SST, [5], [3] benefit from the potential to use prior information on the system's quality. This can lead to higher confidence in system dependability after a fixed number of failure–free statistical system tests. For newly built systems, prior information can however be difficult to obtain. Furthermore the use of a global system prior that is not based on knowledge about the system's structure or complexity yields the same level of dependability after N statistical tests for a simple, small system and for a large system consisting of many interacting components. This has given rise to concern among those in charge for the implementation of safety and has thus been made the focus of recent studies. As a result, structure–based models for statistical software testing have emerged and are currently being further developed [6], [7], [8]. Structure–based approaches to statistical software testing combine knowledge on the system structure/size with prior information on the system components (or units) and system tests. Components could be for example modules, programs, COTS or SOUP components. Prior information on components can stem from unit testing, previous use of COTS components, reported faults etc. The use of qualitative prior information such as the CMM level is potentially interesting, but much more difficult to incorporate and it forms the focus of current studies.

One of the issues that the existing structure–based approaches cannot tackle is the assessment of risk. Risk is another key measure for safety–related systems. In order to assess risk, the probability of the software to fail on a demand has to be weighted with a risk–factor. Risk–factors describe the effect of system failure on specific categories of inputs on the environment. System risk is most commonly estimated using an input-space binning approach. Black–box SST input–space binning models were introduced by [5], [9]. Again, they cannot account for differences in system structure or prior information on system components. Furthermore, the difficulty arises for the practitioner to find a meaningful input-space partition that helps to quantify risk factors for the resulting bins. This is especially difficult for increasingly complex systems. We will combine the approaches introduced in [5], [9] with our structure–based model [8] in order to derive an assessment method for system risk based on system structure, input–space structure, prior information on system components and the results from statistical system testing. We call this approach *scenario–based approach*. It can potentially aid in a more thorough approach to risk–assessment, which accounts for system complexity and prior knowledge on component quality. It can also support the assessment of risk–factors by considering physically meaningful bins in the input–space.

For reliability estimation, the scenario–based approach has the potential advantage that it allows to reuse test data on the components for specific categories of input and to add test data in such categories where the reliability level is not yet sufficiently high rather than generating a set of tests from a global ODD which spreads over all bins identified for that component. The full potential of such a combined approach still needs to be investigated on more examples of safety–critical systems. This paper serves to outline the theoretical background, introduce the model and motivate the necessity of considering such approaches.

After reviewing one state-of the art model for both binning and structure-based approach in section 2, we will introduce the scenario-based approach in section 3 with the help of an example and show how it can be used for both risk and reliability assessment.

2   Input-Space Binning and Structure-Based Approach

The following Bayesian formalism underlies both the binning–model and the structure–based approach.

Bayesian Formalism:

Let $\Theta \in]0, 1[$ be the probability of failure on demand of a software system **S**. Let $\beta[a, b] \propto \Theta^{a-1}(1 - \Theta)^{b-1}$, [10] be a prior probability density function or simply *prior* describing our prior belief about Θ. Let

$$Pr(k \text{ failures in N SST tests}|\Theta) = \binom{N}{k}\Theta^k(1 - \Theta)^{N-k}.$$

Then, after N failure–free SST tests have been performed on **S**, Θ can be estimated as $\Theta = \frac{a}{a+b+N}$.

2.1   Input Space Binning

The following black–box SST model was introduced in [5]. It is based on input–space binning however does not explicitly model system structure or complexity. The input space **I** of software system S is assumed to be partitioned into a number k of subsets I_j, $j = 1, \ldots, k$, which are called *bins*. The set of k bins forms a true partition of **I**, that means they are mutually disjoint and cover all of **I**. Within each bin, there exists a probability distribution $OID_j(x)$ describing the occurrence of inputs x within I_j. Over the set of bins, there exists a set of bin probabilities p_j, $j = 1, \ldots, k$. When statistical system testing is performed, N independent tests are generated from **I** according to the underlying probability distributions $(p_j, OID_j(x))$. The number of tests falling into each bin (n_j) is observed. Using the Bayesian formalism with a $\beta[a_j, b_j]$–prior for the *pfd* of **S** in bin $I_j, j = 1, \ldots, k$, an estimate for the overall system *pfd* is given by

$$\Theta^S = \sum_{j=1}^{k} p_j \cdot \frac{a_j}{a_j + b_j + n_j}.$$

In the absence of any specific prior information, uniform priors $\beta[1,1]$ are often used. This results in $\Theta^S = \sum_{j=1}^{k} p_j \cdot \frac{1}{n_j+2}$.

Θ^S increases with growing number of input–space bins. However it provides information on the probability of failure within particular bins. To make full use of this concept, it is would be helpful to look inside the system to understand which functions execute the inputs in I_j and how complex those functions are. This would help to build more informative priors for the *pfd* of **S** in I_j. Potentially this could lead to a decrease in Θ^S and counter–balance the increase resulting from introducing input–space bins. Component-specific information is used in the structure-based approach, which is introduced next.

2.2   Structure-Based Approach

In the structure-based approach to system reliability estimation [8], it is assumed that a software system S can be split into a set of k major components, either generic or bespoke components. Examples are Commercial–Off–The–Shelf components (COTS) or Software of Unknown Pedigree (SOUP) or simply project-developed modules exercising the various major tasks of the system. We assume that the boundaries of each component can be clearly defined. In this paper we assume that interfaces form part of the components themselves. No loops between components are assumed at this stage. A simple example system **S** is considered consisting of two sequentially executed components C_1 and C_2, where C_1 is executed first and all failure within **S** is assumed to be detected, see also [8]. The overall system *pfd* now measured over the entire input space is

$$\Theta^S = 1 - (1 - \Theta_1)(1 - \Theta_2). \tag{1}$$

Hereby, Θ_1 is the probability of C_1 to fail on an arbitrary system input x and Θ_2 is the probability of C_2 to fail given system input x and data correctly propagated from C_1 to C_2. Thus generally Θ_i, $i = 1,2$ describes the *pfd* of component C_i within the new system **S**. Using the Bayesian formalism with $\beta[a_i, b_i]$–priors for $\Theta_i, i = 1,2$, the following estimator for the overall system *pfd* is obtained after N failure-free statistical system tests have been performed.

$$\Theta^S = 1 - (1 - \frac{a_1}{a_1 + b_1 + N}) \cdot (1 - \frac{a_2}{a_2 + b_2 + N}).$$

In the structure–based approach it is practically more feasible to build informative priors by using information on the components such as data from field-use, unit testing data etc. These data are not necessarily available for the entire system **S**, which is a newly built system, but they will be in many cases available for system components. For example, the parameters a_i, b_i can be retrieved from unit testing as follows: $a_i = 1$, $b_i = m_i + e_i + 1$, where m_i is the number of successful unit tests passed by C_i in some testing environment and e_i is an adjustment term (positive or negative) accounting for the fact that the unit has now been transferred to a different operating environment, see also [5], [8], [11].

Similarly as in the binning model (section 2.1), an increase in testing can be observed with increasing number of components. In the structure–based model however this effect can be more easily counteracted by the use of prior information. Θ^S decreases with increasing b_i. This is natural. If the components have undergone a large number of successful unit tests, then they are likely to have high quality and if on top of that their behaviour within the system environment is tested N times without revealing failure, then this should improve system dependability when compared to the case where system testing starts on non–assessed units or components ($a_i = b_i = 1$).

One of the the difficulties of the structure-based approach is to decide what the "right" decomposition of the system is. The more components one considers, the more sources of error one acknowledges, the more Θ_i occur in equation (1), leading to a potential increase in Θ^S. To justify a given system decomposition it would be advantageous to show that it is directly linked to a natural decomposition of the system input space. Another difficulty of the structure-based approach is that in order to assess risk, one could only use a global risk factor for the system over the entire input space. However, the risk of system failure depends on the nature of the input it processes and thus the use of global risk factors is not possible.

We will show that if system decomposition is based on the major system tasks, then it is directly linked to a natural input space partition, which reflects on system complexity with the number of input bins. The resulting input bins are called InputScenarios. To each InputScenarios a risk factor can be attached depending on the nature of the inputs processed and on the components processing the inputs.

3   Scenario-Based Approach for System Assessment

In 2.1 and 2.2 we have seen that input-space binning and structure-based models for *pfd* estimation are limited in the sense that they cannot use all the information available on the system. In order to take the above described approaches further, we will now introduce the notion of InputScenarios, which define typical situations in the system's operational life and thus play an important role for system risk and reliability. We consider the following simplified example of a software system such as it could be used in the protection system of a nuclear power plant, see Fig.1. System **S** consists of two sequentially arranged components: MessageControl and DataControl. MessageControl receives an input message from the plant in a specified format and it checks whether the message format is correct. If so, the message is passed on to module DataControl. If not, the system is supposed not to enter module DataControl but to go into halt and request an examination of the problem. If entered, the module DataControl looks at the data contained in the input message (e.g. plant temperature, plant power) and checks whether they are within normal range, within warning range

(Input Message)

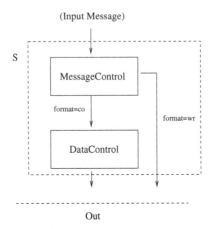

Fig. 1. Example: simplified protection system.

or within trip range. DataControl then diplays either an "all well "message to the system operator or it suggests shutdown of the plant. The input space of the system is the set of all possible input messages. How to partition the input space? Module MessageControl checks the message format for correctness. Thus, in a first step, two different input scenarios can be identified for **S**: a) input has correct message format and b) input has incorrect message format. Module DataControl then checks the data for the range they are in, this leads to three major scenarios: a) data in normal range, b) data in warning range and c) data in trip range. In total, we thus obtain 6 input scenarios, each representing a characteristic situation encountered by the system and requiring a specific action by the system.

Definition 1 (InputScenario). *An InputScenario is a vector*

$$InputScenario_k := (Bin_k, Action_k, Functions(Bin_k, Action_k))$$

The set $Bin_k, k = 1, \ldots, m$ should constitute a partition of the input–space. The notion of an InputScenario expresses that to each input–space bin Bin_k is associated a set of functions[1] ($Functions(Bin_k, Action_k)$) operating on it due to the action the system is supposed to take on that category of input ($Action_k$). InputScenarios pull these elements together. This implies a partition of the input space, which has some meaning for the system since it relates to system components/functions, and for the physical environment of the system since it relates to inputs representing certain fault–scenarios. The entire set of actions $Action_k, k = 1, \ldots, m$ should constitute the system specification.

Examples of InputScenarios for the system in Fig.1:
$InputScenario_1 : Bin_1 = \{$Inputs with distorted message format$\}$. $Action_1$:

---

[1] "Function" is here generally used to cover system components, modules, programs etc.

Halt system. $Functions(Bin_1, Action_1)$: MessageControl. A message with incorrect format and trip data should only be processed by MessageControl, which should bring the system into halt.

$InputScenario_2$: Bin_2 = {Inputs with correct message format and normal data}, $Action_2$: Pass on message, process data and display "all well"-message. $Functions(Bin_2, Action_2)$: MessageControl and DataControl. A message with correct message format and normal data should be passed on from MessageControl and DataControl and then processed by DataControl to display that all is well.

Remark 1 (Scenario-based approach). Assume a software system **S** with input space **I**. If a total of m *InputScenarios* have been established, the overall system *pfd* Θ^S can be calculated by

$$\Theta^S = 1 - \sum_{k=1}^{m} Pr(\text{correct operation of } Functions(Bin_k, Action_k))$$

$$\cdot Pr(Bin_k).$$

We want to apply Remark 1 to the example in Fig.1. Following the approach chosen for the structural model, we will refer to MessageControl as C_1 and to DataControl as C_2. We assume that the data range is in the set $Data = \{T, W, N\}$: Trip, Warning or Normal and will be referred to with the index d. The message format is in the set $Format = \{wr, co\}$: wrong or correct, and it will be referred to with the index f. InputScenarios are thus referred to using the index pair (d, f). We start by writing the overall system *pfd* as

$$\Theta^S =$$

$$1 - \sum_{(d,f) \in \{T,W,N\} \times \{wr,co\}} Pr(\text{correct operation of } C_2 \text{ and } C_1 \text{ on d, f}) Pr((d, f))$$

$$= 1 -$$

$$\sum_{d \in Data} \sum_{f \in Format} Pr(C_2 correct | C_1 correct, d, f) \cdot Pr(C_1 correct | d, f) \cdot Pr(d, f).$$

$$(2)$$

We consider at this stage the total set of 6 bins, each referring to a certain InputScenario, involving certain system functions and contributing to the overall system *pfd* according to a weight $Pr(d, f)$. We will now use the notation

$$Pr(C_2 correct | C_1 correct, d, f) =: 1 - \Theta^{(2)}_{d,f},$$

and

$$Pr(C_1 correct | d, f) =: 1 - \Theta^{(1)}_{d,f}.$$

$\Theta_{d,f}^{(j)}, j = 1, 2$ is the probability of failure on demand for component j in an operating environment defined by the InputScenario (d, f) and - as in the case of C_2 - by the set of (*correctly working*) interacting components. This means that $\Theta_{d,f}^{(j)}$ is the *pfd* of component C_j within system **S** for certain input categories. In the example in Fig.1 above, we can set

$$(a) \quad \Theta_{d,f=wr}^{(2)} = 0, \qquad \text{and} \qquad (b) \quad \Theta_{d,f}^{(1)} = \Theta_f^{(1)}. \tag{3}$$

Equation (3)(a) follows from $Functions(Bin_{d,wr}, Action_{d,wr}) = C_1$. If the message format is wrong and C_1 is operating correctly, C_2 is never executed and thus its *pfd* can be set to 0 for this case. Equation (3)(b) follows from the fact that C_1 is executed before the data ranges are checked, and since C_1 is only concerned with the correctness of the message format its *pfd* is independent of the underlying data ranges. Furthermore, observed message format and data range are assumed to be independent, thus

$$Pr(d, f) = Pr(d) \cdot Pr(f). \tag{4}$$

Using equations (3) and (4), we rearrange (2) to obtain

$$\Theta^S = 1 - \sum_{Format} \left((1 - \Theta_f^{(1)}) Pr(f) \cdot \sum_{Data} (1 - \Theta_{d,f}^{(2)}) Pr(d) \right)$$

$$= 1 - \left[(1 - \Theta_{co}^{(1)}) Pr(f = co) \cdot \left(\sum_{Data} (1 - \Theta_{d,co}^{(2)}) Pr(d) \right) \right. \tag{5}$$

$$\left. + (1 - \Theta_{wr}^{(1)}) Pr(f = wr) \right].$$

If we monitor the number of failure–free SST system tests performed for each InputScenario and assume prior knowledge for example from unit testing of components for different categories of inputs, we can calculate Θ^S as

$$\Theta^S = 1 - \left[(1 - \frac{a_{1,co}}{a_{1,co} + b_{1,co} + n_{co}}) \cdot Pr(f = co) \cdot \left(\sum_{Data} (1 - \frac{a_{2,d}}{a_{2,d} + b_{2,d} + n_{d,co}}) \cdot Pr(d) \right. \right.$$

$$+ (1 - \frac{a_{1,wr}}{a_{1,wr} + b_{1,wr} + n_{wr}}) \cdot Pr(f = wr). \bigg]$$

$$\tag{6}$$

Hereby, $a_{1,co}, b_{1,co}$ describe the prior knowledge about C_1's *pfd* given messages with correct format, $a_{2,d}, b_{2,d}$ describe prior knowledge about the *pfd* of C_2 on different data types. $n_{co} = \sum_d n_{d,co}$ and $n_{co} + n_{wr} = N$. Equation (5) shows that in the example in Fig.1, we can restrict ourselves to the consideration of 4 distinct InputScenarios.

Estimates for $\Theta_{d,f}^{(1)}$ and $\Theta_{d,f}^{(2)}$ are obtained analog to the structure-based approach [8] combining prior knowledge on the components with statistical system test data via a Bayesian formalism. The difference is that now prior knowledge is specifically assessed for each InputScenario. If a component has undergone unit tests, then these will have been performed using some partitioning of the unit's input space as well. For component C_1 for example it would be natural for a tester to test C_1 on messages with flawed format as well as on messages with correct format. The amount of testing performed on C_1 for these cases can be used to establish some prior confidence in system operation under InputScenarios (d, f) where d is any data format. Similarly for component C_2 unit tests will have been performed on sets of Trip-data, Warning-data and Normal-data passed on to C_2 by a presumably correct test driver. This represents use of C_2 under $(N, co), (W, co), (T, co)$ and the amount of testing performed on each category of data would be used to build prior knowledge on $\Theta^{(2)}_{d,co}$.

In equations (5) and (6), we accommodate both the original binning model from section 2.1 and the structure-based approach from section 2.2. If the *pfd* of C_2 was considered to be independent from the message format, we would write (5) as

$$\Theta^S = 1 - (\sum_{Format} (1 - \Theta^{(1)}_f)Pr(f)) \cdot (\sum_{Data} (1 - \Theta^{(2)}_d)Pr(d))$$

$$= 1 - (1 - \Theta_1)(1 - \Theta_2).$$

Hereby Θ_1, Θ_2 are the total failure probabilities of C_1 and C_2 referring to all InputScenarios. This is similar to the structure-based approach.

To compare (5) with the binning model, equation (5) can be re-written as

$$\Theta^S = \sum_{Data} \sum_{Format} (1 - (1 - \Theta^{(1)}_{d,f})(1 - \Theta^{(2)}_{d,f}))Pr(d, f)$$

$$= \sum_{Data} \sum_{Format} Pr(d, f)\Theta^S_{d,f}.$$

Hereby is $\Theta^S_{d,f}$ the probability of the entire system to fail on the bin constituted by Data=d, Format=f. This is similar to the notation of the binning model.

3.1   Risk–Assessment with the Scenario-Based Approach

The advantage of the scenario-based over the binning approach is that in order to assess the system reliability Θ^S, we can make use of prior information available on the component's performance on a subset of inputs. Prior experience is usually lacking for the entire system, since it is a newly built system. Making use of prior information can help to reduce the amount of system tests needed to achieve a given risk or availability requirement, for more detail on this see [8], [7].

The advantage of the scenario-based approach over the structure-based approach is that it supports the assessment of system risk. Risk is generally defined as

$$Risk^S := \sum_{(d,f)} Pr(d, f) \, r_{d,f} \, \Theta^S_{d,f}. \tag{7}$$

Hereby $r_{d,f}$ are risk factors expressing the costs of failure of the entire system on $Bin_{d,f}$. These costs can be expressed for example in million Dollars. This would not make use of any component prior information but instead require prior information $(a_{d,f}, b_{d,f})$ of the system failure behaviour over certain input categories to achieve an estimate

$$Risk^S := \sum_{(d,f)} Pr(d,f)\, r_{d,f}\, \frac{a_{d,f}}{a_{d,f} + b_{d,f} + n_{d,f}}.$$

In the structure-based model without binning, the risk for system S would have to be expressed as

$$Risk' := r_S(1 - (1 - \Theta_1)(1 - \Theta_2))$$

and after N successful system tests, this could be estimated as

$$Risk' = r_S(1 - (1 - \frac{a_1}{a_1 + b_1 + N})(1 - \frac{a_2}{a_2 + b_2 + N}).$$

This would make use of component prior information (a_i, b_i), but a global risk factor r_S would have to be assigned to system failure over the entire input space. However, risk depends to a high degree on the nature of the input processed. It is impossible to specify a risk factor, unless it is based on the question of whether or not the input is in a critical region, i.e. failure can have catastrophic effects and thus involve high costs, or whether the input is uncritical, i.e. failure would be less harmful and involve less costs. Using a scenario-based approach, risk can now more generally be defined as

$$Risk^S = \sum_{InputScenarios} Pr(d,f)\, r_{d,f}(1 - (1 - \Theta_{d,f}^{(1)})(1 - \Theta_{d,f}^{(2)})). \qquad (8)$$

$\Theta_{d,f}$ would be assessed similarly as in (6). Equation (8) incorporates risk factors for system failure on different input–space bins plus prior knowledge on the system components plus system structure.

Risk factors can take on values between $[0, \infty]$ and are associated with the cost of "repair" that would occur if the software failed to perform its task correctly. In the case of protection systems, system failures are usually classified in hazard categories. This could help to assess costs and thus risk-factors. The assessment of risk factors depends on every individual system.

4   Outlook

Scenario–based risk assessment has the potential to be further developed by distinguishing between situations were one, two or more components fail together. For example, using again the example in Fig.1, one could distinguish the situation where both C_1 and C_2 fail together on an input and the situation where just one of them fails. One would then assign different risk factors accordingly.

For example if in the input scenario $Data = T, Format = wr$, C_1 fails to detect that one of the data bytes is not in hexadecimal format and passes on this flawed message to C_2, then if C_2 operates correctly it should not be able to process the incoming data for trip calculations and should issue an error message. No major problem, the cost involved is basically associated with system down-time, we would assign small to medium risk. If C_2 fails as well it could misinterpret the data received and end up signalling that "all is well " when indeed the system has entered trip range. This would lead to catastrophic failure, high cost, high risk. The situation where C_1 or C_2 fail alone or where both fail together should thus be assigned different risk factors.

This would make it necessary to split the term $r_{d,f} \cdot (1 - (1 - \Theta_{d,f}^{(1)})(1 - \Theta_{d,f}^{(2)}))$ into three terms

$$r_{d,f,1}\ P(C_1 fails|f)P(C_2 co|C_1 fails, f, d)+$$

$$r_{d,f,2}\ P(C_1 fails|f)P(C_2 fails|C_1 fails, d, f)+ \qquad (9)$$

$$r_{d,f,3}\ P(C_1 co|f)P(C_2 fails|C_1 co, f, d)$$

and to assign separate risk factors $(r_{d,f,1}), (r_{d,f,2}), (r_{d,f,3})$ to the three failure processes respectively. Even though the definition of risk factors seems to be more meaningful in (9), it will be more difficult to estimate the failure probabilities. It can be shown that in (9)

$$P(C_2 fails|C_1 co, d, f)P(C_1 co|f) = \Theta_{d,f}^{(2)} - \Theta_{d,f}^{(1)}\Theta_{d,f}^{(2)}.$$

This can be calculated from the components' *pfd*'s as before using prior information and system test data over (d, f). However, it is not yet clear how to estimate the remaining failure probabilities in (9) or how to establish upper bounds on them in order to confine the overall system risk and more research is needed here.

5   Conclusion

The approach described in this paper profits from an awareness of input space structure, which is important for meaningful risk assessment, and from the awareness of system structure, which is important to perform efficient reliability and risk assessment by making use of prior information. The link between input space structure and code structure is captured by the notion of input space scenarios. InputScenarios arise from the identification of system actions. They are constituted by bins in the input space to which a set of system functions/components is assigned. A direct influence of system complexity on input-space binning is established.

In scenario-based system assessment, system risk is built up from the effect of failure of a system under a given input condition, the system structure, the failure probabilities of components building the system and the operational frequency with which the scenario occurs. This allows to enter prior knowledge on the component's performance obtained from unit testing, prior operating experience etc. and potentially risk factors associated with failure of a system component on a given input condition. In the example in Fig.1 we can see that the presence of two system modules builds up a maximum of $m = \prod_{i=1}^{2} b_i$, $b_1 = 2, b_2 = 3$, InputScenarios. Adding another component to the system, for example an emergency stop component receiving direct input from a human operator would for example increase the maximum number of input space scenarios from 6 to 12. Investigating this further may shed some light on how increasing system complexity can result in different input space structures and can thus require different testing strategies in order to confine risk. This could help to understand and justify the influence of increasing system complexity on the extent of testing required.

Acknowledgement. The author would like to thank the staff of British Energy and the Nuclear Installations Inspectorate involved in the *New Development of Dynamic Testing (NewDDT)* project.

References

[1] J. Musa, "Operational profiles in software–reliability engineering," *IEEE Software*, pp. 14–32, March 1993.

[2] J. May, G. Hughes, and A. Lunn, "Reliability estimation from appropriate testing of plant protection software," *Software Engineering Journal*, pp. 206–218, 1995.

[3] J. Duran and J. Wiorkowski, "Quantifying software validity by sampling," *IEEE Software Reliability*, vol. R-29, no. 2, pp. 141–144, 1980.

[4] W. Ehrenberger, "Probabilistic techniques for software verification," *paper produced for the IAEA Technical Committee Meeting on Safety Implications of Computerised Process Control in Nuclear Power Plants, Vienna Austria*, vol. November, 1989.

[5] K. Miller, L. Morell, R. E. Noonan, S.K.Park, and D. Nicol, "Estimating the probability of failure when testing reveals no failures," *IEEE Transactions on Software Engineering*, vol. 10, no. 2, pp. 33–43, 1992.

[6] C. Smidts and D. Sova, "An architectural model for software reliability quantification: sources of data," *Reliability Engineering and System Safety*, vol. 64, pp. 279–290, 1999.

[7] J. May, S. Kuball, and G. Hughes, "Test statistics for system design failure," *International Journal of Reliability, Quality and Safety Engineering*, vol. 6, no. 3, pp. 249–264, 1999.

[8] S. Kuball, J. May, and G. Hughes, "Building a system failure rate estimator by identifying component failure rates," *Proceedings from ISSRE'99, IEEE Computer Society Press*, pp. 32–41, 1999.

[9] W. Ehrenberger, "Combining probabilistic and deterministic verification efforts," *Safety of Computers in Safety–Critical Applications*, pp. 299–304, 1992.

[10] D. ed. Zwillinger, *Standard Mathematical Tables and Formulae*. CRS Press, 1996.

[11] S. Kuball, G. Hughes, and J. May, "Review of statistical black–box testing - with particular emphasis on its application to cots," *Deliverable report for the British Energy project NewDDT, PP/40030530*, 2000.

Test Suite Reduction and Fault Detecting Effectiveness: An Empirical Evaluation

Tsong Y. Chen and Man F. Lau*

School of Information Technology
Swinburne University of Technology
Hawthorn, VIC. 3122, AUSTRALIA
{tychen,edmonds}@it.swin.edu.au

Abstract. Test suite reduction is aimed at finding representative sets that can satisfy the same testing objective as their original test suite. As a subset of the original test suite, the representative set may have less fault detection capability. However, researches show that a representative set and its original test suite have similar fault detection capabilities for the case of coverage based criteria. This paper investigates the relationship between the fault detection capabilities of a representative set and its original test suite when the generation of the test suite is based on some fault-based test case selection criteria.

Keywords: Empirical study, software testing, specification based testing, test suite reduction

1   Introduction

Before a program is being tested, test cases must be selected to satisfy a testing objective [11] which can then be considered as a set of *testing requirements* (or, simply *requirements*). For example, if the testing objective is that every statement of the program under test be exercised at least once, each statement can be considered as a requirement.

Test cases are then selected to collectively satisfy the set of requirements. A *test suite* for the set of testing requirements is a set of test cases that can collectively satisfy every requirement. A common approach to generate a test suite is to generate a test case for each requirement [5,9,13,17]. The generated test suite usually contains redundancy in the sense that some test cases can be removed from the test suite without affecting the satisfaction of the set of requirements. It is because a test case may satisfy more than one requirement.

Test suite reduction is aimed at finding subsets for a test suite that can still satisfy the set of all requirements. Such subsets of the test suite are referred to as *representative sets*. Obviously, the representative set as a subset of the test suite might have less fault detection capability although the representative set satisfies the same testing objective as the test suite. However, the results of previous

---

* Corresponding author.

A. Strohmeier and D. Craeynest (Eds.): Ada-Europe 2001, LNCS 2043, pp. 253–265, 2001.

studies [19,20] show that the fault detection effectiveness of the representative sets and their test suites are almost the same in the case of the coverage based criteria. Details will be given in Section 4.

This paper reports an empirical analysis of the relationship between test suite reduction and the fault detection effectiveness when the test suite are minimized according to some fault-based test case selection criteria. Programs whose specifications are in Boolean expressions are selected for the study.

In Section 2, the basic notation and terminology used throughout this paper are introduced. Section 3 briefly describes some fault-based test case selection strategies from Boolean specifications. Section 4 describes related work on the relationship between the size and the fault detection capability of representative sets with respect to their original test suite. Section 5 reports the empirical study and its results. Further possible extension of the work is suggested in Section 6.

2   Notation and Terminology

This section briefly describes the notation and terminology used in this paper.

2.1   Basic Notation

In this paper, the truth values "TRUE" and "FALSE" are denoted by 1 and 0, respectively. The Boolean operators AND, OR and NOT are represented by "$\cdot$", "$+$" and "$^-$", respectively. Usually, "$\cdot$" will be omitted whenever it is clear from the context. The set of all truth values ($\{0,\ 1\}$) and the set of n-dimensional Boolean space are denoted by $\mathbb{B}$ and $\mathbb{B}^n$, respectively.

Given a Boolean expression with n variables, it uniquely defines a Boolean function $f : \mathbb{B}^n \longrightarrow \mathbb{B}$. In this paper, a Boolean function will not be distinguished from a Boolean expression because any testing done on the Boolean specification actually refers to the corresponding functions.

A Boolean formula or expression can be represented in various standard forms including the *disjunctive normal form* and the *conjunctive normal form*. Since there is a dual relationship between the disjunctive normal form and the conjunctive normal form, this paper only considers the disjunctive normal form.

The representation of a Boolean formula in disjunctive normal form is not unique. For example, consider $\bar{a}b\bar{c} + \bar{b}c + abc$ which is in disjunctive normal form. It is equivalent to $\bar{a}b + \bar{b}c + ac$ which is also in disjunctive normal form. However, there exists one special type of disjunctive normal form, namely the *canonical disjunctive normal form*, which guarantees unique representation up to commutativity. A product term is said to be a *minterm* if it consists of every variable or its negation in the formula. An expression is said to be in *canonical disjunctive normal form* if every product term in the expression is a minterm. For example, the above formula when expressed in canonical disjunctive normal form is $\bar{a}\bar{b}c + \bar{a}b\bar{c} + a\bar{b}c + abc$.

A variable in a Boolean expression can be a positive literal or a negative literal. For example, the variable a in $\bar{a}\bar{b}c + \bar{a}b\bar{c} + a\bar{b}c + abc$ is a positive literal whereas $\bar{a}$ is the negation literal. A Boolean expression in disjunctive normal form is said to be *irredundant* [8,12] (or, *irreducible* [18]) if (1) none of its terms may be omitted from the expression; and (2) none of its literals may be omitted from any term in the expression. A disjunctive normal form is *redundant* if it is not irredundant. For example, the formula $\bar{a}b\bar{c} + \bar{b}c + abc$ is redundant because it is equivalent to $\bar{a}b + ac$ which is in irredundant disjunctive normal form. A Boolean expression in disjunctive normal form can be easily transformed into irredundant disjunctive normal form [12]. In general, Boolean expressions in canonical disjunctive normal form may be redundant.

Let $f : \mathbb{B}^n \longrightarrow \mathbb{B}$ be a Boolean function given by the following equation in disjunctive normal form

$$f(t) = p_1(t) + p_2(t) + \cdots + p_m(t) \tag{1}$$

where m is the total number of terms in f and p_i $(i = 1, \ldots, m)$ is the i-th term of f. Whenever there is no ambiguity, $f = p_1 + \cdots + p_m$ will be used instead. A *test case* (or, *test point*) for f is a point in the Boolean space $\mathbb{B}^n$. A point $t \in \mathbb{B}^n$ is said to be a *true point* (*false point*) of f if $f(t)$ evaluates to 1 (0). The sets of all true (false) points of f is denoted by $TP(f)$ ($FP(f)$).

For each term p_i $(i = 1, \ldots, m)$ in f, a point $t \in \mathbb{B}^n$ is said to be a *true point* of p_i in f if $p_i(t)$ evaluates to 1. A point $t \in \mathbb{B}^n$ is said to be a *unique true point* of p_i in f if (1) $p_i(t)$ evaluates to 1 and (2) all other terms evaluate to 0 for t. The sets of all true points and all unique true points of p_i in f are denoted by $TP_i(f)$ and $UTP_i(f)$ $(i = 1, \ldots, m)$, respectively. The set of all unique true points of f is denoted by $UTP(f)$, that is $UTP(f) = \bigcup_i UTP_i(f)$. Those true points which are not unique true points are defined as *overlapping true points*. The set of all overlapping true points of f is denoted by $OTP(f)$. For example, given $f = ab\bar{c} + de$, the unique true points for $p_1 = ab\bar{c}$ are 11000 (that is, $a = b = 1$, $c = d = e = 0$), 11001 and 11010. The set $UTP(f)$ of all unique true points is $\{00011, 00111, 01011, 01111, 10011, 10111, 11000, 11001, 11010, 11111\}$ whereas the set $OTP(f)$ of all overlapping true points is $\{11011\}$.

Suppose that the i-th term, p_i, in f is given by $p_i = x_1^i x_2^i \cdots x_{k_i}^i$ where x_j^i denotes the j-th literal in p_i $(j = 1, \ldots, k_i)$ and k_i is the total number of literals in p_i. For $j = 1, \ldots, k_i$, $p_{i,\bar{j}} = x_1^i \cdots \bar{x}_j^i \cdots x_{k_i}^i$ is used to denote the term obtained from p_i by negating its j-th literal x_j^i. A point $t \in \mathbb{B}^n$ is said to be a *near false point* for the j-th literal x_j^i of the i-th term p_i in f if (1) $p_{i,\bar{j}}$ evaluates to 1 and (2) f evaluates to 0. The set of all near false points for the j-th literal x_j^i of the i-th term p_i in f is denoted by $NFP_{i,\bar{j}}(f)$. Let $NFP_i(f)$ $(= \bigcup_j NFP_{i,\bar{j}}(f))$ denote the set of all near false point for the i-th term p_i in f. The set of all near false points of f is denoted by $NFP(f)$, that is, $NFP(f) = \bigcup_i NFP_i(f)$. Those false points which are not near false points are said to be the *remaining false points*. The set of all remaining false points of f is denoted by $RFP(f)$. For example, for the Boolean function $f = ab\bar{c} + de$, the near false points for $p_{2,\bar{1}}$ $(= \bar{d}e)$ are 00001, 00101, 01001, 01101, 10001, 10101 and 11101. Similarly, $NFP_{2,\bar{2}}(f) = \{00010, 00110, 01010, 01110, 10010, 10110, 11110\}$, $NFP_2(f) =$

$NFP_{2,\bar{1}}(f) \cup NFP_{2,\bar{2}}(f)$ and $NFP(f) = NFP_1(f) \cup NFP_2(f)$. The set $RFP(f)$ of all remaining false points is $\{00000, 00100, 01100, 10100\}$.

Let S be a Boolean specification expressed in the following disjunctive normal form

$$S = p_1 + \cdots + p_m \tag{2}$$

The aim is to derive test cases from S and use them to test whether the implementation denoted by I agrees with the specification S.

If S is expressed in redundant disjunctive normal form, some of the sets of unique true points (that is, $UTP_i(S)$ for some i) or some of the sets of near false points (that is, $NFP_{i,\bar{j}}(S)$ for some i and some j) may be empty. For example, if $S = \bar{a}\bar{b} + \bar{b}c + ac$ ($\equiv \bar{a}\bar{b} + ac$), $UTP_2(S)$ is empty; if $S = ab + \bar{a}bc$ ($\equiv ab + bc$), $NFP_{2,\bar{1}}(S)$ is empty. However, when S is expressed in irredundant disjunctive normal form, it is known that $UTP_i(S)$ and $NFP_{i,\bar{j}}(S)$ are always non-empty.

2.2   Various Types of Faults

In this paper, we only consider Boolean expression without parentheses because it is easy to translate a Boolean expression with parentheses into an equivalent Boolean expression in irredundant disjunctive normal form, that is, without parentheses. This paper only considers Boolean expressions with a single operator or operand fault which may further be classified into the following seven types of faults:-

1. *Expression Negation Fault* (ENF):- The Boolean expression is implemented as its negation. Any point in the Boolean space can be used to detect this type of fault.
2. *Literal Negation Fault* (LNF):- A literal in a particular term in the Boolean expression is replaced by its negation. For example, the Boolean specification $abc + de$ is implemented as $ab\bar{c} + de$. If the literal x_j^i in p_i of S is implemented as its negation, any unique true point in $UTP_i(S)$ or any near false point in $NFP_{i,\bar{j}}(S)$ can reveal this type of fault.
3. *Term Omission Fault* (TOF):- A particular term in the Boolean expression is omitted in its implementation. For example, the Boolean specification $ab + cd + ef$ is implemented as $ab + cd$. If the i-th term p_i of S is omitted in the implementation, any unique true point in $UTP_i(S)$ can reveal this fault.
4. *Operator Reference Fault* (ORF):- A binary Boolean operator '+' in the expression is implemented as '·' or vice versa. For example, the Boolean specification $abe + cd + ef$ is implemented as $abecd + ef$ or $a + be + cd + ef$. For a Boolean specification S with m terms, if the Boolean operator '+' between p_i and p_{i+1} ($1 \leq i < m$) is coded as '·' during the implementation, any unique true point from $UTP_i(S)$ or $UTP_{i+1}(S)$ can detect the fault. On the other hand, if the Boolean operator '·' between x_j^i and x_{j+1}^i ($1 \leq j < k_i$) is coded as '+', any near false point in $NFP_i(S)$ can detect the fault.
5. *Literal Omission Fault* (LOF):- A literal in a particular term of the Boolean expression is omitted in the implementation. For example, $abcd + def$ is

implemented as $abc + def$. If the literal x^i_j in p_i of a Boolean expression S is omitted in p_i, any near false point in $NFP_{i,\bar{j}}(S)$ can detect the fault.

6. *Literal Insertion Fault* (LIF):- A literal not appearing in a particular term of a Boolean specification is inserted into that term. For example, the specification $ab\bar{c} + de$ may be implemented as $ab\bar{c}d + de$ or $ab\bar{c}\bar{d} + de$. It should be noted that inserting a literal does not necessarily cause an error. For example, when the literal b is inserted in the first term of $a + \bar{b}$, the resulting implementation $ab + \bar{b}$ is equivalent to the original specification.

Clearly, if a term in the Boolean expression is a minterm (that is, it contains all variables), it is not necessary to consider a LIF on this particular term. Moreover, it is not necessary to consider inserting those literals whose negation is already in the term because this effectively gives rise to the term omission fault (TOF). For example, after inserting $\bar{a}$, $\bar{b}$, or c in the first term of $ab\bar{c} + de$, the resulting implementation is equivalent to de. This is effectively the same as a TOF.

When a LIF is made on the i-th term, p_i $(i = 1, \ldots, m)$, in S with the literal x_l such that neither x_l nor its negation occurs in p_i (that is, both x_l and $\bar{x}_l$ $\notin \{x^i_1, \ldots, x^i_{k_i}\}$), the implementation denoted by $I_{i,l}$ will be given by

$$I_{i,l} = p_1 + \cdots + p_{i,l} + \cdots + p_m \qquad (3)$$

where $p_{i,l}$ $(= p_i \cdot x_l)$ denotes the expression obtained from p_i by inserting the literal x_l in p_i via a conjunction.

7. *Literal Reference Fault* (LRF):- A literal in a particular term of a Boolean specification is replaced by another literal not appearing in the term during the implementation. For example, the specification $ab\bar{c} + de$ may be implemented as $abd + de$ or $ab\bar{d} + de$. Similar to the case of LIF, the replacement of a literal by another literal may not cause an error. For example, when the literal b in the first term of $bc + \bar{a}b + a\bar{b} + \bar{c}d$ is replaced by the literal a, the implementation $ac + \bar{a}b + a\bar{b} + \bar{c}d$ is equivalent to the original specification. Similar to the LIF, an LRF should only be considered for terms which are not minterms. Moreover, it is not necessary to consider the literal x^i_j being replaced by (1) its negation; (2) any other literal occurring in the term p_i; and (3) the negation of any other literal occurring in the term p_i because these are effectively the same as ENF, LOF and TOF, respectively.

For LRF, when the literal x^i_j of p_i in S is replaced by the literal x_l whose normal form or its negated form does not appear in p_i (that is, both x_l and $\bar{x}_l \notin \{x^i_1, \ldots, x^i_{k_i}\}$), the implementation denoted by $I_{i,\hat{j},l}$ will be given by

$$I_{i,\hat{j},l} = p_1 + \cdots + p_{i,\hat{j},l} + \cdots + p_m \qquad (4)$$

where $p_{i,\hat{j},l}$ $(= x^i_1 \cdots x^i_{j-1} \cdot x^i_{j+1} \cdots x^i_{k_i} \cdot x_l)$ denotes the expression obtained by replacing x^i_j with x_l.

3   Fault-Based Test Case Selection Strategies

Fault-based test case selection strategies are aimed at finding test cases that can guarantee to detect a particular type of fault. For Boolean specification with n variables, 2^{2^n} distinct Boolean functions can be formed because each Boolean function is uniquely determined by a truth table with 2^n rows and the function value can either be TRUE or FALSE. Hence, 2^n test cases can be used to distinguish all the Boolean functions. However, exhaustive testing is practically infeasible when the number of variables, n, is large. Chilenski and Miller [3] have studied the Boolean expressions in an avionics system, EIFS, and they found that it is not uncommon for the Boolean expressions to have 15 or more variables, making it difficult to conduct exhaustive testing.

It is then interesting to investigate strategies to select test cases that can guarantee the detection of a particular type of fault. For fault-based approach to Boolean specifications, test cases are selected from the Boolean space to check whether the implementation is correct. Clearly, a test case can reveal a fault if the Boolean specification S and the corresponding implementation I evaluate to different truth values on the test case.

Various method of generating test cases for Boolean expression have been proposed. Foster [6,7] proposes an algorithm to generate test cases for logical expressions. Foster's approach is expression-driven rather than fault-based.

Tai and Su [16] propose two test cases generation algorithms to detect the Boolean operator errors. However, they restrict themselves to the testing of *singular Boolean expression*. A Boolean expression is said to be *singular* if each of its operands is a simple Boolean variable that cannot occur more than once. For example, $a + bc$ is a singular Boolean expression whereas $ab + ac + bc$ is not. Tai [14,15] extends the work to deal with general expression, and to detect the relational operator faults and a type of fault involving arithmetic expressions. Although Tai's approach is fault-based, those Boolean operand faults mentioned in Section 2.2 are not considered.

Weyuker *et al.* [18] propose a family of meaningful impact strategies for automatically generating test cases from Boolean specifications. The meaningful impact strategies require the selection of test cases such that each literal occurrence in the Boolean expression demonstrates a *meaningful impact* on the outcome of the Boolean expression whenever possible. A literal occurrence in a Boolean expression is said to have a *meaningful impact* on the Boolean expression for a given test case if, assuming that the value of every other literals being the same, the Boolean expression evaluates to a different truth value when the literal is assigned to a different truth value. For the expression $S = ab + bc$, the test case 101 demonstrates a meaningful impact on S because when b is changed from 0 to 1 while keeping the value of a and c constant, S evaluates to 1 instead of 0. On the other hand, the test case 000 cannot demonstrate a meaningful impact on S with respect to the literal b.

The family of strategies proposed by Weyuker *et al.* is described below:

BASIC: It requires the selection of (1) one test case from $UTP_i(S)$ for every i; and (2) one test case from $NFP_{i,\bar{j}}(S)$ for every i, j.

MANY-A: It requires that (1) $\lceil \log_2(|UTP_i(S)|) \rceil$ elements are (arbitrarily) selected from $UTP_i(S)$ for every i; and (2) $\lceil \log_2(|NFP_{i,\bar{j}}(S)|) \rceil$ elements are (arbitrarily) selected from $NFP_{i,j}(S)$ for every i, j. If any set mentioned above contains only one element, the element is selected from the set.

MANY-B: It requires that (1) $\lceil \log_2(|UTP_i(S)|) \rceil$ elements are (arbitrarily) selected from $UTP_i(S)$ for every i; (2) $\lceil \log_2(|NFP_{i,\bar{j}}(S)|) \rceil$ elements are (arbitrarily) selected from $NFP_{i,j}(S)$ for every i, j; (3) $\lceil \log_2(|OTP(S)|) \rceil$ elements are (arbitrarily) selected from $OTP(S)$; and (4) $\lceil \log_2(|RFP(S)|) \rceil$ elements are (arbitrarily) selected from $RFP(S)$. If any set mentioned above contains only one element, the element is selected from the set.

MAX-A: It requires that (1) all elements in $UTP_i(S)$ are selected for every i; and (2) all elements in $NFP_{i,\bar{j}}(S)$ are selected for every i, j.

MAX-B: It requires that (1) all elements in $UTP_i(S)$ are selected for every i; (2) all elements in $NFP_{i,\bar{j}}(S)$ are selected for every i, j; (3) $\lceil \log_2(|OTP(S)|) \rceil$ elements are (arbitrarily) selected from $OTP(S)$; and (4) $\lceil \log_2(|RFP(S)|) \rceil$ elements are (arbitrarily) selected from $RFP(S)$. If $OTP(S)$ or $RFP(S)$ contains only one element, the element is selected from the set.

Chen *et al.* [2] propose the MUMCUT test case selection strategy for generating test cases from Boolean specifications. The test cases generated by the MUMCUT strategy can guarantee the detection of all seven types of faults mentioned in Section 2.2 provided that the Boolean expression is in irredundant disjunctive normal form and at most 1 fault is made during the implementation of the Boolean specification. Under the same assumption, the **MAX-A** and the **MAX-B** strategies can also guarantee the detection of all seven types of faults. However, the empirical study in [2] shows that the MUMCUT strategy uses on the average 74% and 67% of the test cases required by the **MAX-A** and the **MAX-B** strategies, respectively.

In fact, the MUMCUT strategy is the integration of the MUTP strategy, the MNFP strategy and the CUTPNFP strategy. The *multiple unique true point* (MUTP) strategy requires the selection of unique true points from every $UTP_i(S)$ such that all possible truth values (0 and 1) of every missing variable of the term p_i will be covered. For example, if $S = ab + cd$, the set $\{1101, 1110, 0111, 1011\}$ satisfies the MUTP strategy. The *multiple near false point* (MNFP) strategy requires the selection of near false points from $NFP_{i,\bar{j}}(S)$ such that all possible truth values of every missing variable of the term p_i will be covered. For example, for the Boolean specification $S = ab + cd$, the set $\{0101, 0110, 1001, 1010\}$ satisfies the MNFP strategy. The *corresponding unique true point and near false point pair* (CUTPNFP) strategy requires the selection of one unique true point from $UTP_i(S)$ and one near false point from $NFP_{i,\bar{j}}(S)$ (for every i, j pair) such that the two points only differ in the value of the j-th literal of the i-th term p_i in S. For example, for the Boolean specification $S = ab + cd$, the set $\{1100, 0100, 1000, 0011, 0001, 0010\}$ satisfies the CUTPNFP strategy.

4   Related Work

Wong *et al.* [19] perform experiments to study the correlation between test set minimization and fault detection capability. The subject programs are 10 Unix

1. $\overline{(ab)}(d\bar{e}\bar{f} + \bar{d}e\bar{f} + \bar{d}\bar{e}\bar{f})(ac(d+e)h + a(d+e)\bar{h} + b(e+f))$
2. $(a((c+d+e)g + af + c(f+g+h+i)) + (a+b)(c+d+e)i)\ \overline{(ab)}\ \overline{(cd)}\ \overline{(ce)}\ \overline{(de)}\ \overline{(fg)}$
   $\overline{(fh)}\ \overline{(fi)}\ \overline{(gh)}\ \overline{(hi)}$
3. $(a(\bar{d}+\bar{e}+de(\overline{\bar{f}gh\bar{i}} + \bar{g}hi)\ \overline{(\bar{f}glk + \bar{g}\bar{i}k)}) + (\overline{\bar{f}gh\bar{i}} + \bar{g}hi)\ \overline{(\bar{f}glk + \bar{g}\bar{i}k)}\ (b+c\bar{m}+f))(\overline{ab\bar{c}}+$
   $\bar{a}b\bar{c} + \bar{a}\bar{b}c)$
4. $a(\bar{b} + \bar{c})d + e$
5. $a(\bar{b} + \bar{c} + bc(\overline{\bar{f}gh\bar{i}} + \bar{g}hi)\ \overline{(\bar{f}glk + \bar{g}\bar{i}k)}) + f$
6. $(\bar{a}b + a\bar{b})\overline{(cd)}(\bar{f}\bar{g}\bar{h} + \bar{f}g\bar{h} + \bar{f}\bar{g}h)\overline{(jk)}((ac + bd)e(f + (i(gj + hk))))$
7. $(\bar{a}b + a\bar{b})\overline{(cd)}\ \overline{(gh)}\ \overline{(jk)}((ac + bd)e(\bar{i} + \bar{g}k + \bar{j}(\bar{h} + \bar{k})))$
8. $(\bar{a}b + a\bar{b})\overline{(cd)}\ \overline{(gh)}((ac + bd)e(fg + \bar{f}h))$
9. $\overline{(cd)}(\bar{e}f\bar{g}\bar{a}(bc + \bar{b}d))$
10. $a\bar{b}\bar{c}d\bar{e}f(g + \bar{g}(h + i))\overline{(jk + \bar{j}l + m)}$
11. $a\bar{b}\bar{c}(\overline{(\bar{f}(g + \bar{g}(h + i)))} + f(g + \bar{g}(h + i))\bar{d}\bar{e})\overline{(jk + \bar{j}l\bar{m})}$
12. $a\bar{b}\bar{c}(f(g + \bar{g}(h + i))(\bar{e}\bar{n} + d) + \bar{n}(jk + \bar{j}l\bar{m}))$
13. $a + b + c + \bar{c}\bar{d}ef\bar{g}\bar{h} + i(j + k)\bar{l}$
14. $ac(d + e)h + a(d + e)\bar{h} + b(e + f)$
15. $a((c + d + e)g + af + c(f + g + h + i)) + (a + b)(c + d + e)i$
16. $a(\bar{d} + \bar{e} + de(\overline{\bar{f}gh\bar{i}} + \bar{g}hi)\ \overline{(\bar{f}glk + \bar{g}\bar{i}k)}) + (\overline{\bar{f}gh\bar{i}} + \bar{g}hi)\ \overline{(\bar{f}glk + \bar{g}\bar{i}k)}\ (b + c\bar{m} + f)$
17. $(ac + bd)e(f + (i(gj + hk)))$
18. $(ac + bd)e(\bar{i} + \bar{g}k + \bar{j}(\bar{h} + \bar{k}))$
19. $(ac + bd)e(fg + \bar{f}h)$
20. $\bar{e}f\bar{g}\bar{a}(bc + \bar{b}d)$

Fig. 1. Boolean specification

utilities with line of codes ranging from 90 to 842. The generation of test sets is based on block coverage criterion. Each faulty version is generated by manually injecting one fault into the subject programs. Since some blocks may be infeasible, the generated test sets may not satisfy 100% block coverage. Nonetheless, these test sets are minimized with respect to the block coverage criterion, the decision coverage criterion and the all-uses coverage criterion, respectively. The study shows that the *fault detection effectiveness* of the reduced test sets are similar to their original test suites for the block coverage criterion, the decision coverage criterion and the all-uses criterion. The fault detection effectiveness of a reduced test set A is defined as the ratio of the number of faults detected by the reduced test set A to the number of faults detected by the original test set.

Wong *et al.* [20] perform a similar case study on the relationship between size reduction and fault detection effectiveness reduction. In this study, an application software developed for the European Space Agency is used and the test cases are generated based on an operational profile of the application. The faults were obtained from the error-log maintained during the testing and integration phases of the application. Each faulty version is created by manually injecting one fault into the subject program. Since there are no attempts in identifying the infeasible blocks, the generated test set may not achieve 100% block coverage. The results show that the reduced test sets has nearly the same fault detection capability as that of the original test suite.

Table 1. Percentage of Non-equivalent Mutants killed by the original test suite

Spec. Id.	ENF	LNF	TOF	ORF	LOF	LIF	LRF
1	100.0	95.2	100.0	100.0	94.1	98.1	96.1
6	100.0	96.0	100.0	100.0	85.7	100.0	95.1
7	100.0	100.0	100.0	100.0	88.9	100.0	98.4
8	100.0	100.0	100.0	100.0	86.7	100.0	97.6
10	100.0	100.0	100.0	100.0	100.0	99.0	100.0
11	100.0	95.0	100.0	100.0	100.0	100.0	100.0
12	100.0	100.0	100.0	100.0	100.0	99.4	100.0
14	100.0	100.0	100.0	100.0	100.0	97.1	100.0
others	100.0	100.0	100.0	100.0	100.0	100.0	100.0
average	100.0	99.6	100.0	100.0	97.8	99.7	99.4

In summary, the fault detection capabilities of representative sets and their original test suite are similar if the test suite is minimized according to the block coverage criterion, the decision coverage criterion and the all-uses coverage criterion, respectively.

5   An Empirical Analysis on the Fault Detecting Ability of the MUMCUT Strategy

This section reports an empirical study which compares the fault detection capabilities of representative sets and their original test suite satisfying the MUMCUT strategy. As a reminder, when the Boolean specifications are in irredundant disjunctive normal form, the representative set and the original test suite can reveal all seven types of faults.

In this empirical study, the set of Boolean specifications studied by [18] is used (see Figure 1). These Boolean specifications are originated from the specification of TCAS II, an aircraft collision avoidance system, in [10]. Each of the Boolean specifications is first translated into an irredundant disjunctive normal form because the MUMCUT strategy requires the Boolean expression to be in irredundant disjunctive normal form.

Mutation analysis [4] is a common technique used to analyze the fault detection capability of the test sets. It involves the construction of a set of *mutants* for the tested program. A program is a *mutant* of the original program if it differs from the original program by some syntactic changes. The syntactic change is made by a *mutation operator* which is a rule specifying the changes.

The generation of mutants in this study is based on the original Boolean expressions. For each expression in Figure 1, all possible mutants of the seven types of faults in Section 2.2 are generated. The total number of mutants which are not equivalent to the original expression ranges from 1 to 1225.

A test suite is formed by repeated random generation of test cases until the MUMCUT strategy is satisfied. Once the test suite is generated, the heuristic *GRE* for test suite reduction in [1] is then applied to find their corresponding

Table 2. Size of Test Sets that satisfy the MUMCUT strategy

Spec. Id.	Test Suite	Representative sets by GRE (%)
1	46	40 (87.0%)
2	116	116 (100.0%)
3	971	402 (41.4%)
4	21	14 (66.7%)
5	176	50 (28.4%)
6	118	104 (88.1%)
7	166	140 (84.3%)
8	36	36 (100.0%)
9	16	16 (100.0%)
10	164	150 (91.5%)
11	747	223 (29.9%)
12	666	208 (31.2%)
13	1687	52 (3.1%)
14	79	43 (54.4%)
15	186	79 (42.5%)
16	1507	220 (14.6%)
17	259	118 (45.6%)
18	228	123 (53.9%)
19	96	62 (64.6%)
20	24	24 (100.0%)
average		61.4%

representative sets with respect to the MUMCUT strategy. The representative sets are then tested against the mutants which are not equivalent to the original specification. The numbers of non-equivalent mutants killed by the original test suite and their corresponding representative sets are then recorded.

The performance on the fault detection effectiveness of the representative set is judged by the number of mutants killed by the corresponding test sets with respect to the original test suite. The total number of test cases in the original test suite ranges from 16 to 1687.

The following observations are made.

1. Table 1 shows the percentages of mutants killed by the original test suite for various types of faults. The mutation scores range from 97.8% to 100.0% with an average of 99.5%. It shows that, on most occasions, the test suites that satisfy the MUMCUT strategy are very good at detecting the seven types of faults even if the Boolean specification is not in irredundant disjunctive normal form.

2. Table 2 shows the average size of the original test suites and the average percentage of the size of the corresponding representative sets found by the heuristic GRE. The percentages ranges from 3.1% to 100.0% with an average of 61.4%. Hence, the average size reduction is about 40%.

Table 3. Various types of mutants killed

Types of mutants	Spec. Id.	Test Suite	GRE (%)
ENF	all	1	100.0%
LNF	11	20	19 (95.0%)
	others	5–46	100.0%
	average		99.8%
TOF	11	14	13 (92.9%)
	others	3–26	100.0%
	average		99.6%
ORF	all	4–45	100.0%
LOF	11	17	16 (94.1%)
	others	5–41	100.0%
	average		99.7%
LIF	11	721	682 (94.6%)
	15	337	335 (99.4%)
	others	52–1225	100.0%
	average		99.7%
LRF	11	463	444 (95.9%)
	15	284	283 (99.6%)
	others	45–1027	100.0%
	average		99.8%

3. Moreover, from Table 2, there is a general trend that the percentage of representative set delivered by *GRE* decreases as the size of the original test suite increases. This can also been seen from Figure 2.

4. Table 2 shows no reduction in size for specifications 2, 8, 9 and 20. Detailed examinations of these specifications reveal that they are very close to the canonical disjunctive normal form. The number of variables in each term and that in the specification differ by at most 1. Under these circumstances, the numbers of test cases in each $UTP_i(S)$ and $NFP_{i,\bar{j}}(S)$ is at most 2. As a result, all unique true points and near false points are selected.

5. The reduction in the fault detection effectiveness for various types of faults can be seen from Table 3. On average, the values range from 99.6% to 100.0%. This indicates that with regard to the fault detection capability, the representative set is as effective as the original test suite. The average reduction is at most 0.4% which is insignificant.

6   Summary and Future Work

One of the important issues for test suite reduction is whether the representative set has a similar fault detection effectiveness as compared with the original test suite. For the control-flow based coverage criteria, previous researches [19,20] show that there is little or no reduction in the fault detection effectiveness of a representative set.

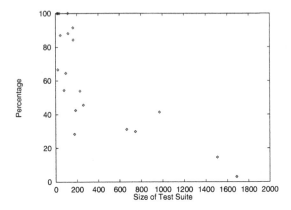

Fig. 2. A plot of the percentages of representative sets by *GRE* against the size of the original test suite

This paper compares the fault detection effectivenesses between a representative set and its original test suite with respect to the MUMCUT strategy which is a fault-based test case selection strategy. The empirical result shows that the fault detection capability of the original test suites that satisfy the MUMCUT strategy are quite high. Moreover, on average, there is a size reduction of about 40% whereas the reduction in the fault detection effectiveness is only about 0.4%. In summary, it is cost-effective to perform test suite reduction because the fault detection capability of the representative sets and their original test suites are nearly the same.

Obviously, the empirical study reported in this paper only confines to a small subset of Boolean specifications and also to the MUMCUT test case selection strategy. Further possible extension of the work may be on the study of the fault detection effectiveness of a representative set for other fault-based test case selection strategies. Moreover, similar investigations for other formal specification frameworks are worth to conduct.

References

1. T.Y. Chen and M.F. Lau, A new heuristic for test suite reduction, *Information and Software Technology*, 40(5–6):347–354, 1998.
2. T.Y. Chen, M.F. Lau, and Y.T. Yu, MUMCUT: A fault-based strategy for testing Boolean specifications, In *Proceedings of APSEC'99*, pp. 606–613, 1999.
3. J.J. Chilenski and S.P. Miller, Applicability of modified condition/decision coverage to software testing, *Software Engineering Journal*, 9(5):193–200, 1994.
4. R.A. DeMillo, R.J. Lipton, and F.G. Sayward, Hints on test data selection: Help for the practicing programmer, *Computer*, 11(4):34–41, 1978.
5. R.A. DeMillo and A.J. Offutt, Constraint-based automatic test data generation, *IEEE Trans. on Software Engineering*, 17(9):900–910, 1991.

6. K.A. Foster, Error sensitive test cases analysis (estca), *IEEE Trans. on Software Engineering*, 6(2):258–264, 1980.
7. K.A. Foster, Sensitive test data for logic expressions, *ACM SIGSOFT Software Engineering Notes*, 9(2):120–125, 1984.
8. D.D. Givone, *Introduction to Switching Circuit Theory*, McGraw-Hill, 1970.
9. B. Korel, Automated software test data generation, *IEEE Trans. on Software Engineering*, 16(8):870–879, 1990.
10. N.G. Leveson, M.P.E. Heimdahl, H. Hildreth, and J.D. Reese, Requirements specification for process-control systems, *IEEE Trans. on Software Engineering*, 20(9):684–707, 1994.
11. G.J. Myers, *The Art of Software Testing*, John Wiley, Second edition, 1979.
12. W.V. Quine, The problem of simplifying truth functions, *American Mathematical Monthly*, 59:521–531, 1952.
13. C.V. Ramamoorthy, S.-B.F. Ho, and W.T. Chen, On the automated generation of program test data, *IEEE Trans. on Software Engineering*, 2(4):293–300, 1976.
14. K.C. Tai, Condition-based software testing strategies, In *Proceedings of COMPSAC 90*, pp. 564–569, Washington, DC, 1990.
15. K.C. Tai, Theory of fault-based predicate testing for computer programs, *IEEE Trans. on Software Engineering*, 22(8):552–563, 1996.
16. K.C. Tai and H.K. Su, Test generation for boolean expressions, In *Proceedings of COMPSAC 87*, pp. 278–284, Washington, DC, 1987.
17. W.T. Tsai, D. Volovik, and T.F. Keefe, Automated test case generation for programs specified by relational algebra queries, *IEEE Trans. on Software Engineering*, 16(3):316–324, 1990.
18. E.J. Weyuker, T. Goradia, and A. Singh, Automatically generating test data from a boolean specification, *IEEE Trans. on Software Engineering*, 20(5):353–363, 1994.
19. W.E. Wong, J.R. Horgan, S. London, and A.P. Mathur, Effect of test set minimization on fault detection effectiveness, *Software–Practice and Experience*, 28(4):347–369, 1998.
20. W.E. Wong, J.R. Horgan, A.P. Mathur, and A. Pasquini, Test set size minimization and fault detection effectiveness: A case study in a space application, *The Journal of Systems and Software*, 48:79–89, 1999.

JEWL: A GUI Library for Educational Use

John English

Faculty of IT, University of Brighton, Brighton BN2 4GJ, UK
je@brighton.ac.uk

Abstract. JEWL (John English's Window Library) is a set of Ada packages for developing GUI-based programs. It has been designed to be usable by complete beginners in an introductory programming course. It does not require a knowledge of any 'advanced' Ada concepts before it can be used, and it allows novices to develop GUI-based applications with a minimum of effort. This paper describes the features of JEWL, its design and the philosophy which underlies the design. JEWL is freeware, and can be downloaded from http://www.it.brighton.ac.uk/staff/je/jewl/.

1 Introduction

Ada is a popular language for introductory programming courses in many university Computer Science departments [4]. It is a highly orthogonal language with a clear, regular syntax, and its strong typing model allows the compiler to trap a range of errors that would be deferred to run time in other languages. It includes support for a range of programming styles, including object-oriented programming and concurrent programming. High quality compilers and documentation including the Language Reference Manual [5] and the Lovelace tutorial [9] are freely available. However, students are often less enthusiastic than faculty about learning Ada as a first language. They perceive it as an old-fashioned language with limited employment potential, and often express a preference for Java, which they see as a modern language with good employment prospects.

From an educator's point of view, a programming language is simply a vehicle to teach introductory (and largely language-independent) programming concepts. Ada is a good choice as it provides a clear, consistent syntax with none of the irritating pitfalls for the unwary that can bog down students learning other languages. The freely available GNAT compiler also provides superb error reporting.

However, Ada is seriously deficient in terms of standard library support by comparison with the Java API [3]. The most important omissions compared to Java are the absence of standard data collections, graphical user interface (GUI) and networking facilities. From a student's point of view, the lack of GUI facilities is a serious problem. Students today are accustomed to working in a graphical environment rather than a traditional text-based environment. It is difficult to inspire

A. Strohmeier and D. Craeynest (Eds.): Ada-Europe 2001, LNCS 2043, pp. 266-277, 2001.

enthusiasm when students are forced to produce text-based programs using packages like Ada.Text_IO.

The major problem with teaching beginners to develop GUI-based software in Ada is the learning curve involved. Existing GUI packages are usually bewildering to novices with the range of facilities they provide, and they achieve flexibility at the price of complexity. As a result, hand-coding a GUI-based application can be extremely difficult. Flexibility is important when developing production software, and experienced developers are capable of dealing with the level of complexity that results. The same is not true in an educational context, where ease of use is of paramount importance. Sacrificing some flexibility in this context is an acceptable trade-off, as the programs which novices will be expected to develop will be relatively simple.

Languages like Visual Basic use a GUI builder to avoid the need for hand-coding, but the code that a GUI builder generates is often difficult to understand (and easy to avoid having to understand). This is not an important issue in a production environment where the primary goal is maximising productivity, but in education it can cloud the student's understanding of what is really going on. It is also easy for students to get sidetracked into perfecting the appearance of the user interface at the expense of perfecting the desired functionality.

JEWL (John English's Window Library) is a set of Ada packages aimed at novices which enables reasonably sophisticated GUI applications to be built with a minimum of effort. It is freely available, and can be downloaded from http://www.it.brighton.ac.uk/staff/je/jewl/. The intention of JEWL is to provide a development kit for GUI-based programming in Ada which is sufficiently simple that it can be used from the 'Hello world' stage onwards. For this reason the emphasis is on ease of use rather than completeness.

JEWL is relatively inflexible by comparison with systems intended for developing production code and only provides access to a limited subset of the underlying facilities, but it is still sufficient for a wide range of novice programs. It is designed so that a program using a graphical interface can be developed by hand-coding, and so that the resulting program will be similar in structure to an equivalent program with a traditional text-based interface. Indeed, it is usually possible to transform text-based applications into graphical ones without fundamental changes to the program structure.

2   The JEWL Library

There are three primary packages included in JEWL:
- **JEWL.IO**: a package with similar functionality to Ada.Text_IO which provides input/output facilities for strings and characters, integers, floats, Booleans and generic enumeration, integral and floating-point types, as well as useful facilities such as message boxes to display error messages. Input is based on GUI dialogs which echo the input received to the standard output, so that a standard text-based program can easily be transformed into a partially GUI-based program.

- **JEWL.Windows**: a GUI package providing a selection of common GUI building blocks (frames, dialog windows, buttons, menus, editboxes, checkboxes, and so on). This is a generic package.
- **JEWL.Simple_Windows**: an instantiation of JEWL.Windows for type Character, which is provided so that the facilities of JEWL.Windows can be used without having to create a generic instantiation explicitly.

JEWL.IO is intended to be used as a more-or-less direct replacement for Ada.Text_IO (although not all the facilities of Ada.Text_IO are supported, and there are some extra features in JEWL.IO). JEWL.IO uses GUI dialogs for input which are built using the facilities of JEWL.Simple_Windows.

JEWL.Windows is a generic package which is instantiated using a discrete type listing the various commands that GUI controls will be required to generate. JEWL.Simple_Windows is a predefined instantiation of JEWL.Windows which generates values of type Character for the command codes. JEWL.IO, JEWL.Windows and JEWL.Simple_Windows can all be used together in a single program if required.

A program based around JEWL.Windows or JEWL.Simple_Windows uses an explicit event loop to get the next command from the user interface and respond to it. This makes programs appear synchronous and procedural, unlike most GUI systems where event handlers are invoked from an invisible implicit event loop. This makes it simple to replace a JEWL graphical user interface with a text-based menu-driven interface, or vice versa.

The current implementation only supports Microsoft Windows, but the package specifications have been designed to be platform-independent. Support for other platforms is envisaged, including a version based on the Java AWT for use with compilers such as JGNAT, a version of GNAT which targets the Java Virtual Machine.

2.1 JEWL.IO

JEWL.IO is a package which is a more-or-less direct replacement for the standard package Ada.Text_IO and the related Ada.Integer_Text_IO and Ada.Float_Text_IO packages, which means that traditional text-based programs can be converted to GUI-based programs with a minimum of effort. It is similar in intent to Woltz and Koffman's simpleIO package for Java novices [10]. JEWL.IO provides conventional text-based output and file I/O operations, but for input it uses GUI dialogs. These dialogs also echo all prompts and user input to the standard output. This means that the input part of any program can be made to use GUI dialogs, while output will still be written to the text-based standard output. The fact that all input is echoed to the standard output means that the output log will exactly mirror an equivalent program whose input is completely text-based.

JEWL.IO provides similar facilities to Ada.Text_IO together with some extra features:

- Input and output of standard types: String, Character, Integer, Float and Boolean;
- Additional operations, e.g. versions of Put_Line for all types rather than just for strings;
- Input and output of user-defined types and subtypes via generic subpackages: enumeration types, integral types and floating point types;
- Type conversions from the above types to strings, and concatenation operations between strings and other types;
- Standard dialog boxes for user alerts: error messages, information messages and queries;
- File operations: opening and creating files using standard dialogs to identify the files to be opened or created.

An example input dialog is shown below (fig 1):

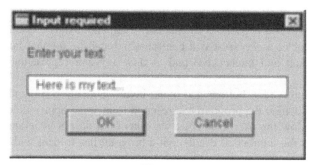

Fig. 1.

This dialog can be generated by the following procedure call:

```
Get (Item    => String_Var,
     Length  => String_Len,
     Prompt  => "Enter your text:",
     Default => "Here is my text...");
```

The Prompt parameter is displayed in the dialog, and the Default parameter is the initial value displayed in the edit field of the dialog. When the OK button is pressed, the value of the edit field and its length will be stored in the Item and Length parameters. The prompt and the input value will also be echoed to the standard output to provide a program log. Both the Prompt and the Default parameter can be omitted, in which case a standard prompt and a blank edit field will be displayed.

All dialogs except the user alerts have a Cancel button which allows input to be aborted. Pressing the Cancel button (or the close button in the dialog's title bar) will close the dialog and raise an Input_Cancelled exception.

Similar dialogs are provided for integral and floating-point types (and subtypes thereof). These dialogs can only be closed if valid input is supplied (or if the Cancel button is pressed); they will display an error alert if the input is not valid when the OK button is pressed. Dialogs for enumeration types use a drop-down list giving the possible choices instead of an edit field. There are also special dialogs for Boolean values; one version provides Yes, No and Cancel buttons, while another uses a checkbox with OK and Cancel buttons.

2.2 JEWL.Windows

JEWL.Windows is the central package in the JEWL library. This is a generic package which needs to be instantiated with a type representing the set of command codes returned by the controls within the GUI. To avoid the need to explicitly define a type and instantiate the package, the package JEWL.Simple_Windows is a predefined instantiation of JEWL.Windows for type Character (that is, the command code that a control returns will be a character).

JEWL provides a number of standard GUI controls including menus, buttons, text labels, checkboxes, radio buttons, edit boxes, list boxes and combo boxes. It also provides a set of container windows to which controls can be attached; for example, a *frame* is a container window which appears as a standard top-level window with a title bar. Controls can be regarded as visual representations of variables in a program. For example, an *editbox* appears as an editable string, and is thus a visual representation of a string variable; a *checkbox* is a control which can be toggled between two visible states (checked and unchecked) and is thus a visual representation of a Boolean variable.

Some controls (e.g. buttons and menu items) generate command codes when they are activated which the program can respond to in some appropriate way; others (e.g. editboxes) allow the user to interact with them but do not generate command codes. This reduces the number of events that a program has to deal with at the expense of some flexibility. A program can wait for a command from a button or menu item and then respond to the command by reading or altering the values of other controls. A simple example is shown below:

```
with JEWL.Simple_Windows;
use  JEWL.Simple_Windows;
procedure My_Program is
  My_Frame : Frame_Type   :=
             Frame (200, 150, "Main Window", 'Q');
  Load_Button : Button_Type :=
             Button(My_Frame, (55,20), 80, 25, "Load", 'L');
  Save_Button : Button_Type :=
             Button(My_Frame, (55,60), 80, 25, "Save", 'S');
begin
  loop
    case Next_Command is
      when 'Q' =>
        exit;
      when 'L' =>
        Show_Message ("Load button pressed!");
      when 'S' =>
        Show_Message ("Save button pressed!");
      when others =>
        null;
    end case;
  end loop;
end My_Program;
```

This program will display a window as shown below (Figure 2).

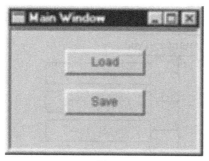

Fig. 2.

The window consists of a frame containing two buttons. When the Load button is pressed, the command code 'L' is generated; when Save is pressed, 'S' is generated; and when the window is closed, the command code 'Q' is generated. The program begins by declaring these three components.

The body of the program consists of an explicit event loop which uses the function Next_Command to wait for a command code to be generated by one of the three components. It then executes the appropriate choice in the *case* statement in response to the command (exit from the loop if the main window is closed, or display a message if either of the buttons are pressed). Show_Message is a procedure which displays a message box; Figure 3 below shows the effect of pressing the Save button.

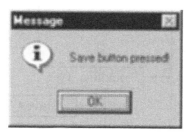

Fig. 3.

2.3 Control Types

JEWL is not intended as a complete binding to the Windows (or any other) API; it is a deliberately simple system intended to allow novices to build GUI-based applications in Ada with minimal effort. It hides much of the complexity involved in building GUI applications, and its use involves no 'advanced' language concepts. Internally, it uses tasks, protected records, tagged types, and many other features which the user does not need to know about. From a user's point of view, the approach is essentially procedural, thus avoiding the potential complexities involved in other approaches to event handling, e.g. using callbacks (scope issues for access to subprogram types), object-oriented approaches (overriding primitives without accidentally defining new

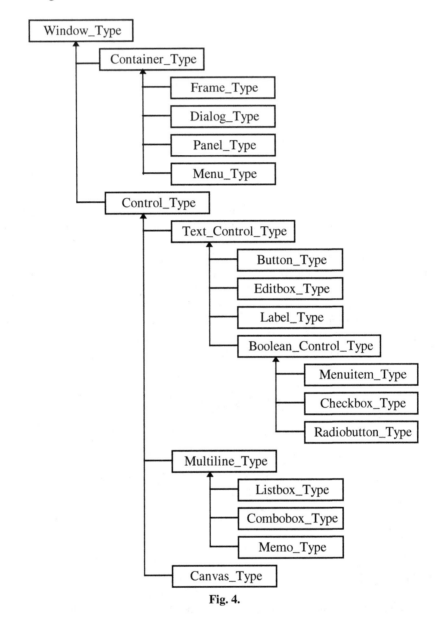

Fig. 4.

methods that are never called) or generic controls (requiring instantiation of individual controls). It provides only a limited set of controls, but these are sufficient for the majority of simple applications.

The available window types are arranged in an inheritance hierarchy as shown in Figure 4. The main types of windows are *containers* and *controls*. Containers are windows which can contain other windows. The container types available are *frames*, *dialogs*, *panels* and *menus*. Frames and dialogs are top-level windows with a title bar; the former are intended for use as main windows in an application, the latter for modal dialog boxes. All other window types must be attached to some other container window. A *panel* is an internal container window intended for grouping controls inside another window; a *menu* is a container for menu items, and can only be attached to a frame.

Controls are primarily divided into *text controls* and *multiline controls*. A further type of control, the *canvas*, is described below. Text controls contain a text string; *Boolean controls* also encapsulate a Boolean state, and can be visibly checked or unchecked. Text controls can be thought of as visual representations of text strings, while Boolean controls also provide a visual representation of a Boolean value. They each have additional properties: buttons generate a command when pressed, editboxes contain editable text, labels contain static text. Menu items generate a command code when they are selected, checkboxes can be toggled between the checked and unchecked states, and radiobuttons act as a group where only one radiobutton in a group can be checked at any time.

A multiline control contains multiple lines of text, and can be regarded as a visual representation of an array of strings. A listbox is a scrollable list of strings from which a single string can be selected; a combobox is a drop-down list combined with an edit box, allowing selection from the list or direct entry of a value; and a memo is a basic text editor which can hold multiple lines of text.

Each type of control provides a set of operations to get and set the values it encapsulates; for example, there are procedures to get and set the text of a menu item as well as its Boolean state. In some cases (e.g. editboxes) the value can be altered directly by the user; in other cases (e.g. labels) the value can only be altered from within the program. Only a few controls are used to generate command codes for processing by the program's event loop:

- Buttons generate a command code when they are pressed;
- Menu items generate a command code when they are selected from a menu;
- Frames and dialogs generate a command code when they are closed;
- Canvases can generate a command code when the mouse button is pressed, and also when a key is pressed.

2.4 Canvases

Canvases are general-purpose drawing surfaces which provide a range of operations for drawing text, lines, rectangles, ellipses, and other shapes. Different fonts, line colours and thicknesses and fill colours can be specified. Each item drawn on a canvas is recorded internally, so that the programmer does not need to worry about explicitly recording the contents of a canvas or redrawing it when the window is refreshed. While this makes the programmer's life simpler, it is sometimes necessary to remove previously-drawn shapes. For example, a program which displays an analogue clock will need to be able to update the position of the hands on the clockface.

To accommodate requirements like this, canvases are able to erase their contents. However, redrawing the complete clock every second would be unacceptable. For this reason, extra operations are provided to save the state of the canvas and to restore that state later, effectively 'forgetting' all additions to the drawing after the state was saved. This can be used to implement an analogue clock as shown by the following code fragment:

```
Draw_Clock_Face (Canvas);
Save (Canvas);
Draw_Hands (Canvas);
loop
  delay 1.0;
  Restore (Canvas);
  Draw_Hands (Canvas);
end loop;
```

First, the clock face is drawn on the canvas as a permanent background, and the state of the canvas is saved. The hands are then drawn on top of the clock face. To update the clockface inside the loop, the saved state is restored (i.e. the clockface as it was before the hands were drawn) and the hands are then redrawn on top of the clock face in their new position.

Canvases can be used interactively by specifying a command code which will be generated whenever the mouse button is pressed within the boundaries of the canvas; another command code can be specified which will be generated when a key is pressed. Additional operations are provided to test whether the button is still down, to test whether the mouse has moved, and to get the current mouse position or key code. Together with the save and restore facilities described above, the mouse operations can be used to write a simple 'rubber-banding' program which tracks the mouse while the button is down:

```
with JEWL.Simple_Windows;  use JEWL.Simple_Windows;
procedure Rubber Band is
  F : Frame_Type  := Frame (200, 150, "Rubber Band", 'Q');
  C : Canvas_Type := Canvas (F, (0,0), 0, 0, 'X');
begin
  loop
    case Next_Command is
      when 'X' =>
        Save (C);
        while Mouse_Down (C) loop
          if Mouse_Moved (C) then
            Restore (C);
            Draw_Line (C, Start_Point(C), End_Point(C));
          end if;
        end loop;
      when others =>
        exit;
    end case;
  end loop;
end Rubber_Band;
```

The state of the canvas is saved when the mouse button is pressed, and each mouse movement will restore this state before drawing a line between the original mouse position and its current position. There will thus appear to be a single line which follows the mouse as it is moved.

3   Implementation Issues

To ensure portability, none of the JEWL package specifications have any dependency on features of the underlying implementation. The window types described above are private tagged types derived ultimately from the private type Window_Type. For example:

```
type Control_Type is abstract new Window_Type
                                  with null record;
type Canvas_Type  is new Control_Type with null record;
```

The definition of Window_Type is deliberately uninformative:

```
type Window_Type is abstract tagged
   record
      Internals : JEWL.Controlled_Type;
   end record;
```

JEWL.Controlled_Type is a type derived from Ada.Finalization.Controlled which is defined in the parent package, and which contains nothing but a pointer to a private tagged type Reference_Counted_Type. The use of a controlled type requires a library-level declaration, so the type is defined in the parent package to avoid forcing users to instantiate JEWL.Windows at library level.

Reference_Counted_Type contains a reference count which is incremented by JEWL.Controlled_Type when a window object is copied and decremented when it is destroyed. When the last reference to a window object is destroyed, the object representing the window's internals is also destroyed. A set of types which incorporate the necessary implementation details for different types of window are then defined in a private package by derivation from Reference_Counted_Type, so that these details are not visible in any way to the user. Each constructor function which creates a particular type of window returns an appropriately constructed window object whose Internals field points to one of these derived types, using the package body's ability to refer to private child packages of the parent package.

Canvases use a list of objects derived from Canvas_Object_Type to record the state of the drawing. Canvas_Object_Type provides a primitive Draw operation which each derived type (Line_Type, Rectangle_Type, Ellipse_Type, and so on) overrides to provide the appropriate behaviour for that type of object. Whenever the canvas needs to be withdrawn, Draw is called for each object in turn. Save is implemented by saving a pointer to the last object in the list, and Restore simply deletes any objects beyond this point in the list. Saving a pointer into the list is safe since the list always grows until either Erase or Restore is called; Erase deletes any saved pointer when it deletes the list of objects.

To ensure responsiveness, a separate event loop task is used to deal with events from the underlying implementation (e.g. Windows messages). This task is started when the first window is created and terminates when the last window is destroyed, and uses a protected record to communicate with the main task. The event loop task puts commands (e.g. when a button is pressed) in the protected record; the

Next_Command function, which the main program calls to get the next command, blocks on an entry in this protected record until a command becomes available.

Task termination is always an issue in designs like this; in JEWL it is dealt with by keeping a count of existing top-level windows, and using a terminate alternative in the event loop which is only open when there are no top-level windows. The event loop will therefore prevent the main program from ending while the program still has any active top-level windows, and will continue dealing with any user interaction with them.

4   Comparison with Other Systems

A number of other GUI packages are available for Ada, but as noted earlier, they are intended for production use rather than educational use. Their goals are therefore somewhat different to JEWL, and they provide greater flexibility at the expense of a steeper learning curve. Examples include GtkAda [1], CLAW [2], Windex [6] and TASH [8]. Each of these systems use an implicit event loop. Hiding the event loop so that event-handling primitives appear to be called 'by magic' can obscure the program behaviour; beginners are often unsure when, why or how event handlers are invoked. Problems can occur when event handlers which share data are not called in the 'expected' sequence, and beginners tend to find these situations difficult to unravel. In the author's experience, an explicit event loop can often help to clarify the essentially procedural, synchronous nature of event handling in GUI-based programs.

CLAW and Windex both use inheritance as a mechanism for implementing event handlers, with derived types overriding event handling primitives. The use of derived types means that users must be familiar with concepts of inheritance, overriding of primitives and the use of packages. These topics are not normally covered until fairly late in an Ada course, and indeed they may not be covered at all in an introductory course.

GtkAda and TASH both use callbacks for event handling, registering them with access-to-subprogram values. Accessibility levels are another potential pitfall for beginners here. The use of access-to-subprogram values means that callback procedures must be declared at the correct lexical level, and since the Unchecked_Access attribute cannot be used with subprograms, there is no way to avoid this problem. Accessibility issues also intrude in other ways. In CLAW, the visible use of controlled types means that derived types must be defined in a library level package. GtkAda also requires library-level generic instantiations for reasons of memory management, with memory being reclaimed when a generic package goes out of scope.

The other major problem for beginners is the sheer size of the learning curve. GtkAda is a large and complex system which is somewhat daunting for the beginner; TASH relies on the user registering callback functions using Tk command strings, so that a knowledge of Tcl/Tk [7] is needed in order to use TASH. All of these problems render systems such as the ones described unsuitable for use by beginners, although they are undoubtedly powerful and flexible systems for experienced users.

5   Conclusions

Unlike other GUI libraries for Ada, JEWL was deliberately designed to be simple to use by novices. This restricts its usefulness for complex systems, but it is nevertheless suitable for a fairly wide range of GUI applications. It has also been designed with portability in mind, although at present it is only available on the Windows platform. It deliberately uses no 'advanced' features of Ada; the user simply calls constructor functions to create graphical interface objects and processes events using an explicit event loop similar to that which would be used in equivalent text-based applications. It thus enables complete beginners to generate reasonably modern-looking applications entirely in Ada.

References

1. Briot, E., Brobecker, J. and Charlet, A.: GtkAda User's Guide.
    http://gtkada.eu.org/docs/gtkada_ug.html (2000)
2. Brukardt, R. and Moran, T.: CLAW, a High-Level, Portable, Ada 95 Binding for Microsoft Windows. Proc. TRI-Ada '97, ACM Press (1997) 91–104
3. Chan, P. and Lee, R.: The Java Developer's Almanac. Addison Wesley (2000)
4. Feldman, M.B.: Ada as a Foundation Programming Language.
    http://www.seas.gwu.edu/~mfeldman/ada-foundation.html (2000)
5. Intermetrics, Inc.: Ada 95 Reference Manual. ANSI/ISO/IEC:8652-1995, Intermetrics (1995)
6. Leake, S.: Comparing Windex and other Ada GUI/Win32 Bindings.
    http://users.erols.com/leakstan/Stephe/Ada/compare.html (2000)
7. Welch, B.: Practical Programming in Tcl/Tk. Prentice Hall (1997)
8. Westley, T.J.: TASH: A Free Platform-Independent Graphical User Interface Development Toolkit for Ada. Proc. TRI-Ada '96, ACM Press (1996) 165–178
9. Wheeler, D.A.: The Lovelace Tutorial. Springer-Verlag (1997)
10. Woltz, U, and Koffman, E.: SimpleIO: A Java Package for Novice Interactive and Graphics Programming. Proc. ITiCSE '99, ACM Press (1999) 139–142

Object-Oriented Stable Storage Based on Mirroring

Xavier Caron, Jörg Kienzle, and Alfred Strohmeier

Swiss Federal Institute of Technology in Lausanne
Department of Computer Science
1015 Lausanne EPFL, Switzerland
{xavier.caron, joerg.kienzle, alfred.strohmeier}@epfl.ch

Abstract. Stable storage can be seen as an ideal storage medium that, given a set of failure assumptions, protects user data from corruption or loss. The integrity of the stored data must be guaranteed even in the presence of crash failures. In this paper, we show how to realize stable storage using a technique called mirroring. The main idea is to write the data to two locations instead of one, in a sequential order. If one write operation fails, the technique ensures that the other copy is in a consistent state. It may be the state that was valid before the write operation, or it may already be the new one. Of course, there must be some mechanism to determine which one is correct. The purpose of the paper is therefore to describe the mirroring algorithm, and to present a state automaton covering all possible situations that can occur in the case of crash failures. Finally, an implementation in Ada 95 is presented.

Keywords. Memory Management, Mirroring, Shadowing, Stable Storage, Fault Tolerance, Ada 95.

1 Introduction

The concept of *Stable Storage* has its origins in the realm of transactions and databases. A stable storage unit can be seen as an ideal storage medium that, given a set of failure assumptions, protects user data from corruption or loss. Such a storage unit offers two operations to the user, *Write* and *Read*, which can be used to store and retrieve user data to and from stable storage.

The name of 'stable storage' has been first introduced in [1]. The paper describes how conventional disk storage, that shows imperfections such as bad write operations or decay, can be transformed into an ideal disk with no failures using a technique called mirroring. In this paper, we present this technique and show how to convert any nonvolatile storage into stable storage.

Stable storage guarantees atomicity of the write operation, e.g. either all data is written to the storage unit, or none at all, even in the case of a crash. So a write operation appears as indivisible. As a result, a read operation will always return consistent data. However, the user of a stable storage unit has to design the application in such a way that, after recovering from a crash failure, it can deal with the system either in the old or in the new state without knowing which one holds.

A. Strohmeier and D. Craeynest (Eds.): Ada-Europe 2001, LNCS 2043, pp. 278-289, 2001.
© Springer-Verlag Berlin Heidelberg 2001

The remainder of this paper is organized as follows: the next section describes mirrored storage and the related algorithms. Section 3 shows how to integrate mirrored storage into a storage hierarchy, how it can be implemented in Ada 95, and how to use it. A conclusion and references complete the paper.

2   The Mirroring Algorithm

In specialized literature, the *"mirroring"* technique, sometimes called *"shadowing"*, often refers to duplication of data. For example, the *Ralston Encyclopedia of Computer Science* [2] says:

> *Another recent trend is to duplicate data to enhance reliability. This technique, called mirroring or shadowing, allows systems to continue operation in spite of media, controller, or channel failure. Sophisticated systems also take advantage of the extra I/O path to enhance throughput. On-line reconstruction ("re-mirroring") of a new second copy when one of the original two is lost is also common.*

The main idea is to write data in two locations instead of one, in a sequential order. If one write operation fails, we assume that the other copy is in a consistent state. It may be the state that was valid before the write operation, or it may already be the new one. Of course, there must be a mechanism to determine which one of the two copies contains the valid data. For this purpose, a third storage unit called the *log* is used. It allows us to distinguish between the three possible situations depending on the moment of the crash:

- The crash happens before or after the write operation, i.e. the log does not indicate any problem,
- The crash happens while writing the first copy, or
- The crash happens while writing the second copy.

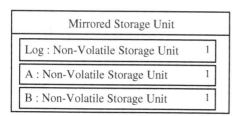

Fig. 1. Components of a Stable Storage Unit based on Mirroring (UML notation)

The three components used for the algorithm are shown in fig. 1. The data copies are called *A* and *B*.

Mirroring can be used for instance in a transactional system in order to keep uncorrupted a log table mapped on sequential files, as explained in [3].

2.1   Preliminary Assumptions
Before describing the mirroring algorithm, we have to specify our failure assumptions i.e. under which conditions we can guarantee the stability of the storage unit.

If any of the storage units used for storing the log and the data copies does not meet one or more of the following assumptions, then the resulting mirrored storage unit can not be considered stable.

Non-volatile Storage. The storage units used for holding the log and the two data copies must be non-volatile, i.e. they must retain their contents even in the case of a crash failure.

Failure Isolation. Our main assumption is that a crash while executing a write operation on a storage unit can only corrupt the contents of that particular storage unit, and no other data stored on the same device or another device.

Non-destructive Reads. Reading from storage will not corrupt the data, even in the presence of crash failures.

Unbuffered Writes. Our algorithm is composed of *sequential* write operations to the log and data copies. It is essential for the correct working of the mirroring algorithm that when a new write operation begins, the previous one has been completed successfully. This assumption may not be met if the storage device uses buffering or caching that writes physically to the device only when the buffer is full. However, such devices often offer a *flush* operation that forces the buffer to be written out to the device. This operation must therefore be called after every write.

Error-free Reading and Writing. We assume that the storage units holding the two data copies and the log provides error-free read and write operations. For the interested reader, more information on how to construct a higher-level abstraction to handle read and write errors can be found in [1].

2.2   Write and Read Operations

Mirrored Write Operation. The algorithm of the mirrored write operation is summarized in fig. 2. The initial value of the log is *OK*.

1. Set Log to A (i.e. *writing to A*)

2. Write the data to A

3. Set Log to B (i.e. *writing to B*)

4. Write the data to B

5. Set Log to *OK*

Fig. 2. Mirrored Write Operation

We can illustrate this algorithm with a state automaton (fig. 3). Each state is composed of three values: the value in the log and the two data copies. The log can take the values OK (in short O), A and B. The data copies can be in the states P or N, where P, respectively N, means that the copy is still in the *previous*, respectively already in the *new* state. The initial state is therefore O | P | P, the final state O | N | N. Each arrow between two states means writing to a storage.

Mirrored Read Operation. The mirrored read operation is just a normal read of any of the two copies, since they are identical after a successful write operation.

2.3   Handling Crashes

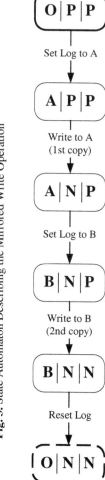

Fig. 3. State Automaton Describing the Mirrored Write Operation

The sequence of the state automaton (fig. 3) can be interrupted at any time by a crash failure. According to our preliminary assumptions, the storage unit that is open in write mode at that moment may get corrupted. Upon restart, before executing any I/O operation, we must check the consistency of the mirrored storage. We *never* check the contents of the data copies itself, only the log. If the log is not set to OK, we have to perform a cleanup operation.

Cleanup Operation. According to our preliminary assumptions only one storage unit can be corrupted by a crash at any given time. The table in fig. 4 summarizes the required cleanup operations based on the information found in the log.

Second Level Crash Failures. We have to pay special attention to new crash failures happening during cleanup, since we always must keep at least one valid data copy. Since we only *read* the valid copy, our failure assumptions guarantee that it will not get corrupted. When a crash occurs there are two possible cases:

- If the new crash happens while repairing a suspected data copy, then the log is unchanged.
- If the new crash happens while resetting the log to OK, then we have successfully repaired the suspected data copy but we cannot know it because the log is corrupted.

In both cases we perform a complete cleanup operation when restarting.

State of Log	Suspected Problem	Cleanup
OK	None.	None.
A (i.e. *writing to A*)	A was not successfully written and might be corrupted.	Copy B to A. Set Log to OK.
B (i.e. *writing to B*)	B was not successfully written and might be corrupted.	Copy A to B. Set Log to OK.
X (i.e. *corrupted*)	Neither A nor B is corrupted, but they might contain different data.	Copy A to B (or B on A). Set Log to OK.

Fig. 4. Cleanup Operation Summary

2.4   State Automaton Describing the Cleanup Algorithm

To verify that our algorithm safely covers all cases, we can represent the complete mirroring algorithm (write and cleanup operation) by a state automaton shown in fig. 5. In addition to being in a normal state, a storage unit can also be corrupted, which is represented by the symbol X. The question mark stands for different possible cases, depending on the damage created by the crash.

We can distinguish four vertical columns in the automaton, each one representing a different kind of system state:

1. *Normal states*: the left vertical column of states represents the normal sequence of write operations in the absence of crash failures.
2. *Crash states*: the states of the second column can only be reached after at least one crash failure. After every new crash, we must restart in one of these states. One or two storage units might be corrupted depending on the number of previous crash failures, but at least one of the data copies is not corrupted.
3. *Re-mirroring states*: the third vertical column is reached when the "re-mirroring" operation, i.e. the copy of one storage unit to the other, is successfully completed.
4. *Final states:* the last column consists of the two possible final states after a successful cleanup operation: either O | P | P or O | N | N, the latter being the normal consistent final state without any crash failure.

The Rubicon Property. There is clearly a separation, shown by a dashed line, between the upper and the lower part of the automaton. When a crash happens in the upper part, the final state after recovery will be the one before calling the mirrored write operation, i.e. O | P | P. Otherwise (writing the first copy to A has been completed successfully), the mirrored write operation will succeed, i.e. the final state will be O | N | N, even if still other crash failures occur.

Unreadable Log and Uncertainty. After a crash, when the log can not be read, i.e. the system is in one of the states X | P | ? or X | N | ?, there is uncertainty about its actual state. However recovery can be performed because the actions to be taken in both states are exactly the same, i.e. copy A to B and set the log to OK.

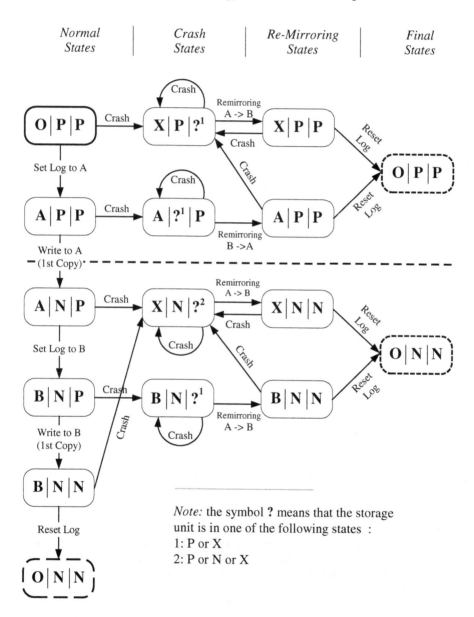

Fig. 5. State Automaton for the Mirroring Algorithm

2.5   Time Needed for the Mirrored Write Operation

Using the automaton of fig. 5 and assigning probabilities to basic operations, we can estimate the time needed to complete a mirrored write.

Time without Crash Failures. We suppose that the two storage units A and B are attached to similar devices. According to our algorithm, the execution time of a mirrored write operation without any crash failure, i.e. the best time, is equal to:

$$t_{normal} = 3t_l + 2t_d \tag{1}$$

where t_l is the time needed to set the log, and t_d the time needed to write the data to A or B.

Time with Crash Failures. To recover from a single crash, it takes the time $t_{restart}$ to restart the application plus the time for one re-mirroring operation, i.e. t_d, plus the time for one log reset, i.e. t_l. However this is only an upper limit, because a crash might occur before the re-mirroring operation is completed. Therefore, if n denotes the total number of crash failures, the time spent in the state automaton is bound by:

$$t_{crash} < t_{normal} + n(\, t_{restart} + t_l + t_d) \tag{2}$$

Conclusion. If we consider that the time needed to set the log is negligible in comparison with the time needed to write a data copy, we can simplify the equation 1 to:

$$t_{normal} \approx 2t_d \tag{3}$$

It means that mirrored storage needs twice the time of conventional storage. With the high speed of actual storage devices, this should be acceptable in most cases.

2.6   Transition Probabilities

Transition Matrix. Let's denote by p_l the probability that there is a crash while setting the log, and p_d the probability that there is a crash while writing a data copy. We can then assign probabilities to the transitions of the state automaton of fig. 5. The transition matrix is shown in Fig. 6. Rows and columns represent the states of the automaton. The value in a cell is the probability to go from the state represented by the row to the one associated with the column. Note that it is a Markov transition matrix since the sum of the probabilities on a line is always 1, except for the final states.

Probabilities for Final States. As said previously, there are two kinds of final states: either O | P | P, which is the starting state, or O | N | N. We saw that if the automaton succeeds in passing through the dashed line (fig. 5), the final state is O | N | N, and otherwise it is O | P | P. Based on this observation, we can compute the probabilities of the final states.

States	O/P/P	A/P/P	X/P/?	A/?/P	X/P/P	A/P/P	O/P/P	A/N/P	B/N/P	X/N/?	B/N/?	X/N/N	B/N/N	O/N/N	B/N/N	O/N/N
O|P|P	0	$1-p_l$	p_l	0	0	0	0	0	0	0	0	0	0	0	0	0
A|P|P	0	0	0	p_d	0	0	0	$1-p_d$	0	0	0	0	0	0	0	0
X|P|?	0	0	p_d	0	$1-p_d$	0	0	0	0	0	0	0	0	0	0	0
A|?|P	0	0	0	p_d	0	$1-p_d$	0	0	0	0	0	0	0	0	0	0
A|P|P	0	0	p_l	0	0	0	$1-p_l$	0	0	0	0	0	0	0	0	0
O|P|P	0	0	0	0	0	0	0	0	0	0	0	0	0	0	0	0
A|N|P	0	0	0	0	0	0	0	0	$1-p_l$	p_l	0	0	0	0	0	0
B|N|P	0	0	0	0	0	0	0	0	0	0	p_d	0	0	0	$1-p_d$	0
X|N|?	0	0	0	0	0	0	0	0	0	p_d	0	$1-p_d$	0	0	0	0
B|N|?	0	0	0	0	0	0	0	0	0	0	p_d	0	$1-p_d$	0	0	0
X|N|N	0	0	0	0	0	0	0	0	0	p_l	0	0	0	$1-p_l$	0	0
B|N|N	0	0	0	0	0	0	0	0	0	p_l	0	0	$1-p_l$	0	0	0
O|N|N	0	0	0	0	0	0	0	0	0	0	0	0	0	0	0	0
B|N|N	0	0	0	0	0	0	0	0	0	p_l	0	0	0	0	0	$1-p_l$
O|N|N	0	0	0	0	0	0	0	0	0	0	0	0	0	0	0	0

Fig. 6. Transition Matrix for the Mirroring State Automaton

1. To finish in the state O I N I N, the dashed line must be crossed. The unique possibility is to go directly from O I P I P to A I P I P (with a probability $1-p_l$) and then directly from A I P I P to A I N I P (with a probability $1-p_d$):

$$P_{O/N/N} = (1-p_l) \cdot (1-p_d) \tag{4}$$

2. Because the mirroring algorithm guarantees to finish in one of the two kinds of final states, the probability to finish back in the state O I P I P is the complement to 1 of the previous probability:

$$P_{O/P/P} = 1 - P_{O/N/N}$$
$$\Leftrightarrow P_{O/P/P} = 1 - (1-p_l) \cdot (1-p_d)$$
$$\Leftrightarrow P_{O/P/P} = 1 - (1 - p_l - p_d + p_l \cdot p_d)$$
$$\Leftrightarrow P_{O/P/P} = p_l + p_d - p_l \cdot p_d \tag{5}$$

3   Implementation in Ada 95

We want to be able to write the state of any object to our storage. Ada *streams* can be used for that purpose [4]. A stream is a sequence of elements comprising values of possibly different types. The standard package Ada.streams defines the interface for streams in Ada 95. It declares an abstract type `Root_Stream_Type`, from which all other stream types must derive.

In Ada 95, the predefined attributes `'Write` and `'Output` are used to write values to a stream by converting them into a flat sequence of stream elements. Reconstructing the values from a stream is performed with the predefined attributes `'Read` and `'Input`. These two attributes make dispatching calls to the `Read` and `Write` operations of the `Root_Stream_Type`. With `'Write` and `'Read`, neither array bounds nor tags of tagged types are written to or read from the stream. `'Output` and `'Input` must be used for that purpose.

[5], [6] construct a framework for providing persistence for Ada objects based on streams. It classifies storage devices in a class hierarchy according to essential properties, like volatility, stability, etc. The abstract root class Storage (fig. 7) defines the common interface for all storage classes, including Read and Write operations. The storage hierarchy is then split into *volatile* and *non-volatile* storage. Data stored in non-volatile storage remain intact even when the program terminates. Among the different types of non-volatile storage, there is then the distinction between *stable* and *non-stable* storage. The mirrored storage finally is a subclass of the stable storage class.

For storing the log and the data copies, we need non-volatile storage units, but the mirroring algorithm is independent of the kind of non-volatile storage actually used.

Using the *Strategy design pattern* [7], we can implement a mirrored storage class, whose instances are supplied with parameters at creation time. These parameters specify the kinds of non-volatile storage the application programmer chooses, depending on the needs of the application. To help him make this choice, a concrete non-volatile storage class must document any applicable constraints and provide information about the performance of its instances. E.g. the log is frequently accessed, but holds only a small piece of information, to the contrary of the data copies.

The structure of the collaboration is shown in fig. 7. The class is an aggregation of three non-volatile storage objects (Log, A and B). The specific kinds of these three objects are chosen when creating an object of the mirrored storage class. It is therefore possible to *reuse* concrete implementations of the non-volatile storage class to create a variety of mirrored storage devices.

Storage Parameters. Because we want to provide persistent storage, there must be some means to uniquely identify storage objects. Storage identification is usually device dependent. Files for instance have file names associated with them, but other storage devices may use different identification means. In order to provide correct identification for each storage type, a parallel hierarchy of storage parameter classes has been introduced. A concrete parameter class contains the necessary identification data for a particular storage device. Each parameter class must also provide operations to convert the parameter to and from a string. This string will be used as a common, device-independent means for identifying storage objects.

3.1   Implementation Details

The mirroring class is defined as follows:

```
type Mirrored_Storage_Type is new Stable_Storage_Type with private;
type Mirrored_Storage_Ref is access all Mirrored_Storage_Type'Class;
... -- Usual operations declarations for non-volatile storage
... -- Read, Write, Get_Current_Size, Open, Close, Delete
```

```
private
   type Mirrored_Members_Type is new Limited_Controlled
      with record
         Log : Non_Volatile_Storage_Ref;
         B : Non_Volatile_Storage_Ref;
         A : Non_Volatile_Storage_Ref;
      end record;

   procedure Finalize (Members : in out Mirrored_Members_Type);

   type Mirrored_Storage_Type is new Stable_Storage_Type
      with record
         Members : Mirrored_Members_Type;
      end record;
```

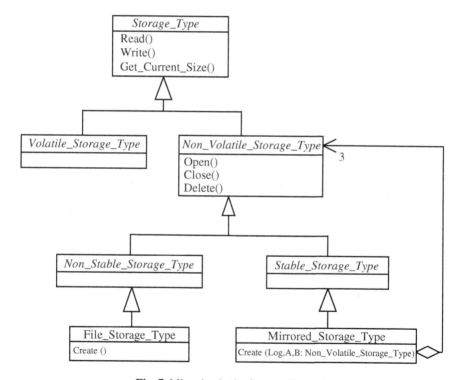

Fig. 7. Mirroring in the Storage Hierarchy

First of all, note how we declare the three components `Log`, `A` and `B` as references to the non-volatile storage class-wide type `Non_Volatile_Storage_Ref`. It means that the implementation does not rely on any specific type of non-volatile storage.

Deriving the members of the mirrored storage from a controlled type allows one to deallocate the three non-volatile storage components in the `Finalize` procedure. In this way, we ensure that the three storage components are released when the mirrored storage is deleted.

3.2   Example of Use

The example shows how to save integers to a mirrored storage unit.

```
with Mirrored_Storage_Params; use Mirrored_Storage_Params;
with Mirrored_Storages; use Mirrored_Storages;
with Streams; use Streams;

procedure Save_Integer is
   My_Params : Mirrored_Storage_Params_Type;
   My_Storage : Mirrored_Storage_Ref;
   My_Stream : Stream_Ref;

begin
   My_Params := String_To_Storage_Params ("AdaEurope");
   My_Storage :=
      Mirrored_Storage_Ref (Create_Storage (My_Params));
   My_Stream := new Stream_Type (My_Storage);
   Integer'Write (My_Stream, 6577);
   Close (My_Storage.all);
end Save_Integer;
```

The package Streams contains the type Stream_Type. A new instance of a stream is associated with a storage object at creation time, as shown in the code. The attribute `'write` makes a dispatching call to the write operation of the associated storage object.

4   Conclusion

We proposed a technique called *mirroring* to convert non-volatile storage into *stable storage*. A stable storage unit can be seen as an ideal storage medium that, given a set of failure assumptions, protects user data from corruption or loss in the presence of crash failures. The technique uses two data storage units instead of one, completed by a log that indicates if data was corrupted during the crash needing cleanup.

The algorithm can be represented by a *state automaton* showing that all cases of even multiple crash failures can be handled. Based on the state automaton we established upper limits for the time behavior. We also showed how to assign probabilities to the transitions and estimate the probability of reaching the final state.

The mirrored storage can easily be integrated in a storage hierarchy, transforming any non-volatile, non-stable storage (e.g. a local file) into stable storage. This design was successfully implemented in Ada 95, but the technique does not rely on any specific feature of the programming language.

References

1. Lampson, B.W., Sturgis, H.E.: "Crash Recovery in a Distributed Data Storage System". *Technical report, XEROX Research*, Palo Alto (June 1979). Much of the material appeared in *Distributed Systems-Architecture and Implementation*, ed. Lampson, Paul, and Siegert, *Lecture Notes in Computer Science*, Vol. 105. Springer Verlag (1981), pp. 246-265 and 357-370.
2. Ralston, A., Reilly, E.D.: *Encyclopedia of Computer Science Third Edition*. Van Nostrand Reinhold, New York (1993).
3. Gray, J., Reuter A.: *Transaction Processing: Concepts and Techniques*. Morgan Kaufmann, San Francisco, California (1993).
4. ISO: International Standard ISO/IEC 8652:1995(E): *Ada Reference Manual, Lecture Notes in Computer Science*, Vol. 1246. Springer Verlag (1997); ISO 1995.
5. Kienzle, J., Romanovsky, A.: "On Persistent and Reliable Streaming in Ada". In *Reliable Software Technologies - Ada-Europe'2000, Potsdam, Germany, Lecture Notes in Computer Science*, Vol. 1845. Springer Verlag (2000), pp. 82-95.
6. Kienzle, J., Jiménez-Peris, R., Romanovsky, A., Patiño-Martinez, M.: "Transaction Support for Ada". *International Conference on Reliable Software Technologies - Ada-Europe'2001, Leuven, Belgium, May 14 - 18, 2001*, to be published in Lecture Notes in Computer Science, Springer Verlag (2001).
7. Gamma, E., Helm, R., Johnson, R., Vlissides, J.: *Design Patterns*. Addison Wesley, Reading, MA(1995).
8. Kienzle, J., Strohmeier, A.: "Shared Recoverable Objects". In *Reliable Software Technologies - Ada-Europe'99, Santander, Spain, Lecture Notes in Computer Science*, Vol. 1622. Springer Verlag (1999), pp. 387-411.
9. Wolf, T., Strohmeier, A.: "Fault Tolerance by Transparent Replication for Distributed Ada 95". In *Reliable Software Technologies - Ada-Europe'99, Santander, Spain, Lecture Notes in Computer Science*, Vol. 1622. Springer Verlag (1999), pp. 412-424.

Transaction Support for Ada

Jörg Kienzle[1], Ricardo Jiménez-Peris[2], Alexander Romanovsky[3], M. Patiño Martinez[2]

[1] Software Engineering Laboratory
Swiss Federal Institute of Technology Lausanne
CH - 1015 Lausanne EPFL
Switzerland
Joerg.Kienzle@epfl.ch

[2] Facultad de Informática
Universidad Politécnica de Madrid
E - 28660 Boadilla del Monte, Madrid
Spain
{rjimenez,mpatino}@fi.upm.es

[3] Department of Computing Science
University of Newcastle
NE1 7RU, Newcastle upon Tyne
United Kingdom
Alexander.Romanovsky@newcastle.ac.uk

Abstract. This paper describes the transaction support framework OPTIMA and its implementation for Ada 95. First, a transaction model that fits concurrent programming languages is presented. Then the design of the framework is given. Applications from many different domains can benefit from using transactions; it is therefore important to provide means to customize the framework depending on the application requirements. This flexibility is achieved by using design patterns. Class hierarchies with classes implementing standard transactional behavior are provided, but a programmer is free to extend the hierarchies by implementing application-specific functionalities. An interface for Ada programmers is presented and its use demonstrated via a simple example.

Keywords. Transactions, Open Multithreaded Transactions, OPTIMA Framework, Design Patterns, Fault-Tolerance, Ada 95.

1 Introduction

Ada [1] has a strong reputation for its error-prevention qualities, such as strong typing, modularity, and separate compilation; it has been extensively used for the development of mission-critical and safety-critical software. It is not surprising that there has also been various research in the fault-tolerant area, such as providing replication for Ada 95 partitions [2].

Ada also provides support for lightweight and heavyweight concurrency (tasks and partitions). But among these active entities, concurrency control and synchronization are reduced to single method, procedure or entry calls (protected objects, rendezvous). These mechanisms are adequate to build small-scale applications where tasks and their synchronization are designed together. However, these mechanisms do no scale well (e.g. several method calls can not be executed as one atomic operation). Complex systems often need more elaborate features that can span multiple operations.

Transactions [3] are such a feature. A transaction groups an arbitrary number of simple actions together, making the whole appear indivisible with respect to other concurrent transactions. Using transactions, data updates that involve multiple objects can be executed without worrying about concurrency. Transactions have the so-called

A. Strohmeier and D. Craeynest (Eds.): Ada-Europe 2001, LNCS 2043, pp. 290–304, 2001.
© Springer-Verlag Berlin Heidelberg 2001

ACID properties: *Atomicity, Consistency, Isolation* and *Durability*. If something unexpected happens during the execution of a transaction that prevents the operation to continue, the transaction is aborted, which will undo all state changes made on behalf of the transaction. The ability of transactions to hide the effects of concurrency and at the same time act as firewalls for failures makes them appropriate building blocks for structuring reliable distributed systems in general.

This paper presents a framework called OPTIMA (OPen Transaction Integration for Multithreaded Applications) that provides transaction support for Ada 95. The next section introduces a new transaction model that fits our needs; section 3 outlines how an Ada programmer should interface with our transaction service; section 4 presents the design of the framework that provides support for open multithreaded transactions; section 5 presents an example program and the last section draws some conclusions and presents future work.

2   Open Multithreaded Transactions

When introducing transactions into a concurrent programming language such as the Ada language, it is important to support concurrency inside a transaction in a natural way. In Ada, a task can terminate or fork another task at any time. This section presents a new transaction model named *Open Multithreaded Transactions*. For a complete description of the model see [4]. It allows tasks to join an ongoing transaction at any time. Tasks can also be forked and terminated inside a transaction. There are only two rules that restrict task behavior:

- It is not allowed for a task that has been created outside a transaction to terminate inside the transaction.

- A task created inside a transaction must also terminate inside this transaction.

Exceptions [5], a standard Ada feature, are also integrated into the model. Transactions are atomic units of system structuring that move the system from a consistent state to some other consistent state if the transaction commits. Otherwise the state remains unchanged. The exception mechanism is typically used to signal foreseen and unforeseen errors that prevent an invoked operation from completing successfully. Exceptions are events that must be handled in order to guarantee correct results. If such a situation is not handled, the application data might be left in an inconsistent state. Aborting the transaction and thus restoring the application state to the state it had had before the beginning of the transaction will guarantee correct behavior. For this reason we have decided that unhandled exceptions crossing the transaction boundary result in aborting the open multithreaded transaction [6, 7].

The following rules describe open multithreaded transactions in detail. Tasks working on behalf of a transaction are referred to as participants. External tasks that create or join a transaction are called *joined participants*; tasks created inside a transaction by a participant are called a *spawned participants*. The data that can be modified from inside a transaction is stored in so called *transactional objects*. The transaction support guarantees the ACID properties for this data. Participants of a transaction collaborate by accessing the same transactional objects.

Starting Open Multithreaded Transactions

- Any task can start a transaction. This task will be the first joined participant of the transaction. A newly created transaction is *open*.
- Transactions can be nested. A participant of an open multithreaded transaction can start a new (nested) transaction. Sibling transactions can execute concurrently.

Joining Open Multithreaded Transactions

- A task can join a transaction as long as it is still open, thus becoming a joined participant. To do this it has to learn (at run-time) or to know (statically) the transaction context or the identity of this transaction.
- A task can join a top-level transaction if and only if it does not participate in any other transaction. To join a nested transaction, a task must first join all parent transactions. A task can only participate in one sibling transaction at a time.
- A task spawned by a participant automatically becomes a spawned participant of the transaction in which the spawning task participates. A spawned participant can join a nested transaction, in which case it becomes a joined participant of the nested transaction.
- Any participant of an open multithreaded transaction can decide to *close* the transaction at any time. Once the transaction is closed, no new joined participants are accepted anymore. If no participant closes the transaction explicitly, it closes once all participants have finished.

Concurrency Control in Open Multithreaded Transactions

- Participant accesses to transactional objects inside a transaction are isolated with respect to other transactions. The only visible information that might be available to the outside world is the transaction identity to be used by tasks willing to join it.
- Accesses of child transactions are isolated with respect to their parent transaction.
- Classic consistency techniques are used to guarantee consistent access to the transactional objects by participants of the same transaction.

Ending Open Multithreaded Transactions

- All transaction participants vote on the outcome of the transaction. After that they do not execute any application activity inside this transaction anymore. Possible votes are *commit* or *abort*.
- The transaction commits if and only if all participants vote commit. In that case, the changes made to transactional objects on behalf of the transaction are made visible to the outside world. If any of the participants votes abort, the transaction aborts. In that case, all changes made to transactional objects on behalf of the transaction are undone.
- Once a spawned participant has given its vote, it terminates immediately.
- Joined participants are not allowed to leave the transaction (they are blocked) until the outcome of the transaction has been determined. This means that all joined participants of a committing transaction exit synchronously. Only then, the changes made to transactional objects are made visible to the outside world. If the transac-

tion is aborted, the joined participants may exit asynchronously, once changes made to the transactional objects have been undone.

- If a task participating in a transaction disappears without voting on the outcome of the transaction (a deserter task), the transaction is aborted.

Exceptions and Open Multithreaded Transactions

- Each participant has a set of internal exceptions that it can handle inside the transaction and a set of external exceptions which it can signal to the outside, when needed. An additional external exception `Transaction_Abort` is always included in the set of external exceptions.

Internal Exceptions

- Inside a transaction each participant has a set of handlers, one for each internal exception that can occur during its execution.
- The termination model is adhered to: after an internal exception is raised in a participant, the corresponding handler is called to handle it and to complete the participant's activity within the transaction. The handler can signal an external exception if it is not able to deal with the situation.
- If a participant "forgets" to handle an internal exception, the external exception `Transaction_Abort` is signalled.

External Exceptions

- External exceptions are signalled explicitly. Each participant can signal any of its external exceptions.
- Each joined participant of a transaction has a containing exception context.
- When an external exception is signalled by a joined participant, it is propagated to its containing context. If several joined participants signal an external exception, each of them propagates its own exception to its own context.
- If any participant of a transaction signals an external exception, the transaction is aborted, and the exception `Transaction_Abort` is signalled to all joined participants that vote commit.
- Because spawned participants don not outlive the transaction, they cannot signal any external exception except `Transaction_Abort`, which results in aborting the transaction.

3   Ada Interface

The support for open multithreaded transactions in Ada has been implemented in form of a library, without introducing any language changes. This approach has many advantages. It allows us to stay within the standard Ada language, hence making our approach useful for any settings and platforms which have standard Ada compilers and run-times. On the other hand, it requires the application programmer to adhere to certain programming guidelines in order to guarantee correct handling of transactions.

Our transaction support must be called at the beginning (procedure `Begin_Transaction` or `Join_Transaction`) and end of every transaction (procedure `Commit_Transaction` or `Abort_Transaction`). When a transaction is started, the calling task is linked to the transaction using the package `Ada.Task_Attributes`, which offers the possibility to declare data structures for which there is a copy for each task in the system. From that moment on, the transaction support can always determine on behalf of which transaction a task is executing its operations.

```
begin
    Begin_Transaction;
    -- perform work
    Commit_Transaction;
exception
    when ...
        -- handle internal
        -- exceptions
        Commit_Transaction;
    when others =>
        Abort_Transaction;
        raise;
end;
```

Fig. 1: Procedural Interface

In order to correctly handle exceptions, a programmer must associate a transaction with an Ada block statement. Using the procedural interface described above, the code of a transaction must look like the code presented in figure 1. Internal exceptions can be handled in the exception section, and if the handling is successful, the transaction can still commit. Any unhandled exception crossing the block boundary will cause the transaction to abort.

To avoid forgetting to vote on the outcome of a transaction and at the same time force the programmer to declare a new block for each transaction, an interface based on controlled types can be used as shown in figure 2.

What is important here is that the Ada block construct is at the same time the transaction and the exception context. Declaring the transaction object calls the `Initialize` procedure of the transaction type, which on its part calls the transaction support and starts a new transaction. The task can now work on behalf of the transaction. In order to commit the transaction, the `Commit_Transaction` procedure must be called before exiting the block. If a programmer forgets to commit the transaction, or if an unhandled exception crosses the block boundary, the transaction object is finalized. From

```
declare
    T : Transaction;
begin
    -- perform work
    Commit_Transaction;
exception
    when ...
    -- handle internal
    -- exceptions
    Commit_Transaction;
end;
```

Fig. 2: Interface based on Controlled Types

within the `Finalize` procedure, `Abort_Transaction` is called.

The state of an application using the transaction support will be stored in a set of data objects. Our transaction service must also be called before and after every operation invocation on such a data object. This can be automated by writing a wrapper object (a *proxy*) offering the same interface as the data object, thus transforming it into a *transactional object*. The implementations of the operations in the transactional object will call the transaction support, and only then invoke the real operations on the data object.

If writing a proxy object for each data object, and adhering to the programming conventions mentioned earlier is too much of a burden for an application programmer, she/he can opt to use Transactional Drago [8], which is an extension to Ada that introduces transactions into the language itself. One of the advantages of having linguistic support is that many programming errors can be detected at compilation time (e.g. correct nesting of transactions). Concurrency control is automatically set in Transactional Drago. Therefore, transactions are programmed just as any other piece of code. The only thing the programmer needs to do is to enclose the transaction code within a transactional block statement.

4   The OPTIMA Framework

A framework providing support for open multithreaded transactions must allow tasks working on behalf of transactions to access transactional objects in a consistent manner, guaranteeing the transactional ACID properties.

The design of the framework is a further development of our previous work described in [9]. It makes heavy use of design patterns in order to maximize modularity and flexibility. Using object-oriented programming techniques it can be easily customized and tailored to specific application needs. The design of the framework can be broken into three important components, namely *transaction support*, *concurrency control* and *recovery support*.

4.1   Transaction Support

The transaction support is responsible of keeping track of the lifetime of an open multithreaded transaction. For each transaction, it creates a transaction object that holds the transaction context containing the following data:

- The status of the transaction (open, closed, aborted, committed),
- The current number of participants, their identity and their status (joined participant, or spawned participant),
- A list of subtransactions, and a reference to the parent transaction, if there is one,
- A list of all transactional objects that have been accessed from within the open multithreaded transaction.

When a participant votes on the outcome of an open multithreaded transaction, the transaction support is notified. If a joined participant votes *commit*, and there are still other participants working on behalf of the transaction, the calling task is suspended. Only in case of an abort, or if all participants have voted commit, the transaction support passes the decision on to the recovery support.

4.2   Concurrency Control

The main objective of the concurrency control support is to handle the cooperative and competitive concurrency in open multithreaded transactions. Dealing with *competitive concurrency* comes down to guaranteeing the *isolation* property for each transaction. Transactions running concurrently are not allowed to interfere with each other; participants of a transaction access transactional objects as if they were the only tasks executing in the system. Handling *cooperative concurrency* means ensuring data *consistency* despite concurrent accesses to transactional objects by participants of the same transaction.

These problems can be solved by synchronizing the accesses to transactional objects made by tasks participating in some transaction. Providing consistency among participants of the same transaction requires that operations that update the state of the transactional object execute with mutual exclusion. Competitive concurrency control among concurrent transactions can be *pessimistic (conservative)* or *optimistic (aggressive)*, both having advantages and disadvantages. In any case, the serializability of all transactions must be guaranteed.

The principle underlying pessimistic concurrency control schemes is that, before attempting to perform an operation on any transactional object, a transaction has to get permission to do so. If a transaction invokes an operation that causes a conflict, the transaction is blocked or aborted. Read/write locks are common examples of pessimistic concurrency control.

In optimistic concurrency control schemes [10], transactions are allowed to perform conflicting operations on objects without being blocked, but when they attempt to commit, the transactions are validated to ensure that they preserve serializability. If a transaction is successfully validated, it means that it has not executed operations that conflict with the operations of other concurrent transactions. It can then commit safely.

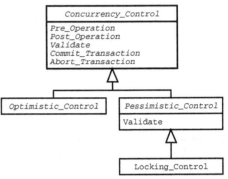

Fig. 3: Concurrency Control

The common interface for concurrency control is shown in the abstract class `Concurrency_Control` in figure 3. The `Pre_` and `Post_Operation` operations must be called before (resp. after) executing any operation on a transactional object.

A call to `Pre_Operation` comprises two phases. First, competitive concurrency must be handled. In optimistic concurrency control schemes based on timestamps for instance, `Pre_Operation` must remember the invocation time of the operation. In a pessimistic scheme based on locking, the calling task must acquire the lock in order to proceed with the operation. If the lock is not compatible with all other locks granted for this transactional object, the calling task is suspended.

The second phase deals with cooperative concurrency. In both concurrency control schemes, `Pre_Operation` will acquire the mutual exclusion lock to access the transactional object. This is needed to guarantee consistent access to the data among participants inside an open multithreaded transaction. `Post_Operation` releases the mutual exclusion lock again, but does not discard the competitive concurrency control information (i.e. discarding the timestamps, or releasing the transaction locks). In general, information about the competitive concurrency control must be kept at least until the outcome of the transaction is known.

When the transaction support is ready to commit a transaction, the `Validate` operation is called for each accessed transactional object. In optimistic concurrency control schemes, `Validate` verifies that there the serializability property has not been violated. If this has happened, the transaction will abort. For pessimistic concurrency control schemes, `Validate` always succeeds.

Optimistic and pessimistic concurrency control schemes must be able to decide if there are conflicts between operations that would compromise the serializability of transactions. They must also know if an operation modifies the state of the transactional object.

This is what the operation information hierarchy shown in figure 4 is there for. For each operation of a transactional object, an operation information object must be written providing the operations Is_Update and Is_Compatible. Is_Update is needed for dealing with cooperative concurrency. It returns true if the operation modifies the state of the transactional object. This determines if mutual exclusion is needed among participants of the same transaction.

Is_Compatible is necessary for dealing with competitive concurrency. It must determine whether an operation conflicts with the other operations available for this transactional object with respect to transaction serializability.

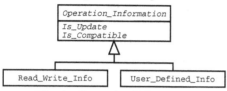

Fig. 4: Operation Information

Without knowledge of the semantics of operations, one can easily see that update operations conflict with each other, and also with read operations. Read operations however do not conflict with other read operations, since they do not modify the state of the transactional object. The operation information hierarchy contains a Read_Write_Info class that provides this behavior. Inter-transaction concurrency can be increased if one knows more about the semantics of the operation itself. For instance two invocations of an insert operation that inserts an element into a set do not conflict with each other. They *commute*. An application programmer can provide his own operation information class if she/he wants to use commutativity-based concurrency control [11].

Once the outcome of a transaction has been determined by the transaction support, the concurrency control is notified by means of the operations Commit_Transaction or Abort_Transaction. When a transaction aborts, the collected information can be discarded (timestamps, locks). When a transaction commits, the information must be passed to the parent transaction (the parent transaction "inherits" the modifications made on behalf of a nested transaction). Only when a top-level transaction commits, the information can be discarded safely.

4.3 Recovery Support

The recovery support provides open multithreaded transactions with *atomicity* and *durability* properties in spite of system failures. To achieve durability the state of transactional objects is stored on a non-volatile storage device. Atomicity means that either all modifications made on behalf of an open multithreaded transaction are reflected in the state of the accessed transactional objects, or else none is.

The recovery support must therefore keep track of all the modifications that the participants have made to transactional objects on behalf of a transaction. In order to recover from a crash failure, this information, also called a transaction *trace*, must be stored on some kind of storage, called a *log*, that will not be affected by the system failure. That way, once the system restarts, the recovery support can consult the log and perform the cleanup actions necessary to restore the system to a consistent state. The information that must be written to the log depends on the chosen recovery strategy, and the necessary cleanup actions depend on the strategy, the status of the transaction and whether the modifications made to the transactional objects have already been propagated from the cache to the non-volatile storage unit or not.

The essential components of the recovery support are the *Persistence_Support*, the *Cache_Manager*, the *Recovery_Manager* and the *Log_Manager*. The following sub-sections present these components in more detail.

4.3.1 Persistence Support

The persistence support provides three basic functionalities:

- It provides a device independent interface that is used by the cache manager to store the state of transactional objects on some non-volatile storage.
- It provides stable storage (not affected by crash failures) to the log manager.
- It provides a means for identifying transactional objects stored on some storage device which is independent of the actual device used.

The implementation is based on the persistence support presented in [12].

4.3.2 The Cache Manager

The state of transactional objects is kept in main memory in order to improve the performance of the overall system, since accessing memory is in general significantly faster than accessing non-volatile storage. However, in systems that are composed of lots of transactional objects, it is often not possible to keep the state of all objects in memory at a given time, and therefore it is sometimes necessary to replace objects that are already in the cache.

In a conventional cache, any object can be chosen. The situation for a cache used in a transaction system is more complicated [13]. Firstly, we distinguish between *Steal* and *No-Steal* policy. In the *Steal* policy, objects modified by a transaction may be propagated to the storage at any time, whereas in the *No-Steal* policy, modified objects are kept in the cache at least until the commitment of the modifying transaction. We also make a distinction on what happens during transaction commit. In the *Force* policy, all objects that a transaction has modified are propagated to their associated storage unit during the commit processing, whereas in the *No-Force* policy no propagation is initiated upon transaction commit.

In practice, caches are very effective because of the *principle of locality*, which is an empirical observation that, most of the time, the information in use is either the same information that was recently in use (temporal locality), or is information "nearby" the information recently used (spacial locality). The behavior of caches can be tailored in order to get a better hit ratio, i.e. by adjusting the size of the cache, or by choosing appropriate fetch and replacement algorithms. It is therefore important for our framework to allow a user to define his own cache policy.

Again this flexibility is achieved by providing an abstract root class Cache_Manager, with abstract methods such as Apply_Replacement_Policy. An application programmer can choose the appropriate cache policy depending

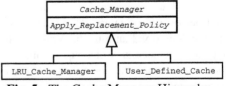

Fig. 5: The Cache Manager Hierarchy

on the application requirements. She/he can also extend the cache manager hierarchy, providing his own implementation as shown in figure 5.

Although introducing a cache is completely transparent for the users of the transaction support, it significantly complicates the reasoning about the consistency of the state of the system. When using a cache, the current state of a transactional object is determined by the state of the object in the cache, or if it is not present in the cache, by the state of the object on the storage. When a transaction aborts, the state changes made on behalf of the transaction are undone in the cache. It might be that these changes have already been propagated to the storage. However, we do not have to undo them, since they will be undone the next time we update the state of the object on the storage. When a transaction commits, we must ensure that at some time in the future, the changes of the transaction will be propagated to the associated storage unit.

Using a cache has a significant impact on the actions that must be taken when recovering from a crash failure. On a system crash, the content of the cache is lost, and therefore, in general, the state of the objects on the storage can be inconsistent for the following reasons:

- The storage does not contain updates of committed transactions.
- The storage contains updates of uncommitted transactions.

When recovering from a system crash, these situations must be remedied. The former problem can be solved by *redoing* the changes made by the corresponding transactions, the latter by *undoing* the changes made by the corresponding transactions. Depending on the cache policy, undo, redo or both are necessary [14].

Undo/Redo

The *Undo/Redo* recovery protocol requires both undo and redo actions and allows great flexibility in the management of the cache by permitting *Steal* and *No-Force* object replacement policies. It maximizes efficiency during normal operation at the expense of less efficient recovery processing.

Undo/No-Redo

The *Undo/No-Redo* recovery protocol requires undo but never redo actions by ensuring that all the updates of committed transactions are reflected in the storage. It therefore relies on *Steal* and *Force* object replacement policies. The commitment of a transaction is delayed until all its updates are recorded on non-volatile storage.

No-Undo/Redo

The *No-Undo/Redo* recovery protocol, also known as *logging with deferred updates*, never requires undo actions, but relies on redo actions. Updates of active transactions are not propagated to the storage, but recorded in the system log, either in the form of an after-image of the state or as a list of invoked operations, also called an *intention list*.

4.3.3 The Log Manager

The system log is a sequential storage area located on stable storage. It is important that the log is stored on stable storage, since it must always remain readable even in the presence of failures in order to guarantee the correct functioning of the transaction system. The purpose of the log is to store the information necessary to reconstruct a consistent state of the system in case a transaction aborts or a system crash occurs. The required information can be split into 3 categories:

- Undo Information
- Redo Information
- Transaction Status Information

This information is organized in a hierarchy as shown in figure 6.

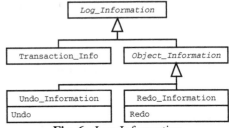

Fig. 6: Log Information

There are two situations in which the log must be updated:

- A transaction is committed or aborted.
- An operation that modifies the state of a transactional object is invoked.

Undo and redo information can be stored in the log in two ways. In the first technique, called *physical logging* [3], copies of the state of a transactional object are stored in the log. These copies are called *before-images* or *after-images*, depending on if the snapshot of the state of the object has been taken before or after invoking the operation. Unfortunately, physical logging only works if read/write concurrency control is used. If semantic-based concurrency control such as commutative locking schemes are used, undo and redo information must be saved using *logical logging*. In this technique, the operation invocations and their parameters are written to the log. In order to support undo, every operation op of a transactional object must provide an *inverse operation* op^{-1}, i.e. an operation that undoes the effects of calling op.

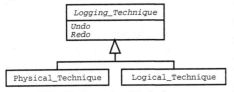

Fig. 7: Logging Techniques

These two logging techniques are captured in the class hierarchy presented in figure 7.

After a system crash, the entire log needs to be scanned in order to perform all the required redo and undo actions. What algorithm must be used to recover from a crash, depends on the chosen recovery strategy and is detailed in [13]. The same paper also shows how to prevent the log from growing too long by using a technique called *checkpointing*.

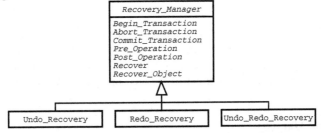

Fig. 8: The Recovery Manager Hierarchy

4.3.4 The Recovery Manager

The *Recovery_Manager* implements the recovery strategy, and therefore controls the *Cache_Manager* and the *Log_Manager*. Again, a class hierarchy of recovery managers is provided to the application programmer. She/he can select the most appropriate recovery strategy for his application by instantiating one of the concrete recovery managers shown in figure 8.

5   Auction System

This section describes how open multithreaded transactions can be used to structure an electronic auction system. The general idea of such a system is the following: First, a user must register with the system by providing a username and password, and deposit some money, most of the time in form of a credit card number. From then on, the user can login and consult the current auctions. He can decide to bid for items he wants to acquire, or sell items by starting new auctions.

Such an auction system is an example of a dynamic system with cooperative and competitive concurrency. The concurrency originates from the multiple connected users, that each may participate in or initiate multiple auctions simultaneously. Inside an auction, the users cooperate by bidding for the item on sale. On the outside, the auctions compete for external resources such as the user accounts. The system is dynamic, since a user must be able to join an ongoing auction at any time. An additional non-functional requirement of such a system is that it must be fault-tolerant, e.g. money transfer from one account to the other should not be executed partially, even in the presence of crash failures.

All these requirements can be met if an individual auction is encapsulated inside an open multithreaded transaction. The seller starts the auction, the individual bidders join it if they want to place a bid.

Implementation in Ada

Figure 9 shows how the main program must initialize the transaction support. The package `Object_Based_Transaction_Interface` defines the object-based interface to the transaction support as mentioned in section 3. The other context clauses define the transactional objects that are used in this example, namely auctions and accounts.

Before starting a transaction, the programmer must call the `System_Init` procedure. This procedure can take additional parameters that allow the application programmer to customize the transaction support according to his needs. In particular, a recovery manager, a cache manager, and a

```
with Object_Based_Transaction_Interface;
use Object_Based_Transaction_Interface;

with Transactional_Auctions;
use Transactional_Auctions;

with Transactional_Accounts;
use Transactional_Accounts;

with File_Storage_Params;
use File_Storage_Params;

procedure Main is
   -- Task and other declarations
begin
   System_Init;
   -- Run auctions
   System_Shutdown;
exception
   when others =>
      System_Shutdown;
end;
```

Fig. 9: System Initialization

storage unit to be used to store the log can be specified. The default implementation chooses a LRU cache manager, a Redo/NoUndo recovery manager, and a mirrored file for storing the log.

The package `Transactional_Auct-ions` defines the auction objects, with the operations `Create_Auction`, `Restore_ Auction`, `Get_Current_Bid`, `Accept_Bid`, `Finished` and `Bid_Accepted`. The package `Transactional_Accounts` defines the account objects, with the usual operations `Deposit`, `Withdraw` and `Get_Balance`. Figure 10 shows how the seller tasks and bidder tasks make use of these objects when performing an auction.

The seller task begins its work by declaring a reference to a transactional auction, and then asks the user to input the duration of the auction. Next, a new open multi-threaded transaction named "Auction" is started by declaring a `Transaction` object; the scope of the transaction is linked to the scope of this object. Inside the transaction, a new auction object is created by calling the `Create_Auction` operation. The `Storage_Params_To_String` function of the `File_Storage_Params` package is called in order to tell the system to store the state of the auction object in the file "Auction.file". Then, the seller task suspends itself for the duration previously specified by the user.

```
task body Seller_Task is                task body Bidder_Task is
   Auction : Transactional_Auction_Ref;     Auction_Transaction : Transaction
   Auction_Time : Duration := Ask_User;        (new String' ("Auction"));
   Auction_Transaction : Transaction         Auction : Transactional_Auction_Ref
      (new String' ("Auction"));                := Get_Auction;
   Current_Bid : Natural;                    Current_Bid : Natural;
begin                                        My_Bid : Natural;
   Auction := Create_Auction (String_To_  begin
      Storage_Params ("Auction.file"),        while not Finished (Auction.all) loop
      -- + initialization parameters,            Current_Bid :=
      -- e.g. description, minimum bid...          Get_Current_Bid (Auction.all);
   delay Auction_Time;                          My_Bid := Ask_User (Current_Bid);
   Current_Bid :=                               Bid (Auction.all, My_Bid);
      Get_Current_Bid (Auction.all);         end loop;
   if Current_Bid >= Minimum_Bid then        if Bid_Accepted (Auction.all) then
      Accept_Bid (Auction.all);                 declare
      declare                                      My_Account : Transactional_
         My_Account : Transactional_                  Account_Ref := Restore_Account
            Account_Ref := Restore_                    (Storage_Params_To_String
            Account (String_To_Storage_                ("Bidder_Acc.file"));
            Params ("Seller_Acc.file"));        begin
      begin                                         Withdraw
         Deposit                                        (My_Account.all, My_Bid);
            (My_Account.all, Current_Bid);      end;
      end;                                     end if;
   end if;                                     Commit_Transaction
   Commit_Transaction                            (Auction_Transaction);
      (Auction_Transaction);               end Bidder_Task;
end Seller_Task;
```

Fig. 10: Seller and Bidder Tasks

The bidder tasks join the ongoing transaction by also declaring a transaction object. This time, the object is initialized with a call to `Join_Transaction`. The bidder task then obtains the current bid from the auction object, and asks the user for his new bid. Next, the `Bid` operation of the auction object is invoked. Other bidder tasks will see the new bid, for they are all participants of the same transaction, and, in turn, are allowed to place new bids. When the time-out expires, the seller task accepts the current bid, deposits the money on his account and commits the transaction. The bidders leave the loop and the bidder that won the auction withdraws the money from its account. The open multithreaded transaction ends once the last bidder calls `Commit_Transaction`.

If any unforeseen exception is raised inside the transaction, the transaction is aborted and the predefined external exception `Transaction_Abort` is raised in all other participants. The abort results in undoing the deposit and withdrawal, and in deleting the created auction object. This also holds in case of a crash failure.

6   Conclusions and Future Work

This paper has presented the design of the OPTIMA framework supporting *Open Multithreaded Transactions*, a transaction model that does not restrict the concurrency features found in Ada, but still keeps the tasks participating in a transaction under control, enforcing the ACID properties. The framework makes heavy use of design patterns in order to maximize modularity and flexibility. Using object-oriented programming techniques it can be easily customized and tailored to specific application needs. A more detailed description of the OPTIMA framework can be found in [15].

Interfaces for the Ada programmer have been laid out. The framework has been implemented in form of a library based on standard Ada only. This makes our approach useful for any settings and platforms which have standard Ada compilers.

The paper also describes parts of an implementation of an auction system based on open multithreaded transactions. This case study has shown the benefits of using open multithreaded transactions for system structuring and fault-tolerance in concurrent systems.

The open multithreaded transaction model does support distribution, but the current framework only addresses single nodes. In the future, we intend to add distribution to our framework. This has an impact on the transaction support component, which must be extended to provide distributed transaction control (i.e. two phase commit protocol), and on the cache manager, which must provide distributed access to transactional objects. Another promising direction of the research is to try and integrate the transaction support with the CORBA Object Transaction Service [16]. Using our transaction support an application programmer can easily implement a transactional CORBA resource. Our intentions are to provide a bridge that will intercept calls to the `prepare`, `rollback` and `commit` methods of CORBA resources and forward them to our transaction support.

7   Acknowledgements

Jörg Kienzle has been partially supported by the Swiss National Science Foundation project FN 2000-057187.99/1. Alexander Romanovsky has been partially supported by the EC IST RTD Project on Dependable Systems of Systems (DSoS). Ricardo Jimenez-Peris and Marta Patino-Martinez have been partially supported by the Spanish Research Council (CICYT) grant #TIC98-1032-C03-01 and by the Madrid Research Council (CAM) grant #CAM-07T/0012/1998.

References

[1] ISO: *International Standard ISO/IEC 8652:1995(E): Ada Reference Manual*, Lecture Notes in Computer Science **1246**, Springer Verlag, 1997; ISO, 1995.

[2] Wolf, T.; Strohmeier, A.: "Fault Tolerance by Transparent Replication for Distributed Ada 95". In Harbour, M. G.; de la Puente, J. A. (Eds.), *Ada-Europe'99*, pp. 411 – 424, Lecture Notes in Computer Science **1622**, 1999.

[3] Gray, J.; Reuter, A.: *Transaction Processing: Concepts and Techniques*. Morgan Kaufmann Publishers, San Mateo, California, 1993.

[4] Kienzle, J.; Romanovsky, A.: "Combining Tasking and Transactions, Part II: Open Multithreaded Transactions". *10th International Real-Time Ada Workshop, Castillo de Magalia, Spain*, to be published in Ada Letters, ACM Press, 2001.

[5] Goodenough, J. B.: "Exception Handling: Issues and a Proposed Notation". *Communications of the ACM 18(12)*, pp. 683 – 696, December 1975.

[6] Kienzle, J.: "Exception Handling in Open Multithreaded Transactions". In *ECOOP Workshop on Exception Handling in Object-Oriented Systems, Cannes, France*, June 2000.

[7] Patiño-Martinez, M.; Jiménez-Peris, R.; Arevalo, S.: "Exception Handling in Transactional Object Groups". In *Advances in Exception Handling Techniques*, Lecture Notes in Computer Science **2022**, Springer Verlag, 2001.

[8] Patiño-Martinez, M.; Jiménez-Peris, R.; Arevalo, S.: "Integrating Groups and Transactions: A Fault-Tolerant Extension of Ada". *Reliable Software Technologies - Ada-Europe'98*, pp. 78 – 89, Lecture Notes in Computer Science **1411**, 1998.

[9] Jiménez-Peris, R.; Patiño-Martinez, M.; Arevalo, S.: "TransLib: An Ada 95 Object-Oriented Framework for Building Transactional Applications". *Computer Systems: Science & Engineering Journal 15(1)*, 2000.

[10] Kung, H. T.; Robinson, J. T.: "On Optimistic Methods for Concurrency Control". *ACM Transactions on Database Systems 6(2)*, pp. 213 – 226, June 1981.

[11] García-Molina, H.: "Using Semantic Knowledge for Transaction Processing in a Distributed Database". *ACM Transactions on Database Systems 8(2)*, pp. 186 – 213, June 1983.

[12] Kienzle, J.; Romanovsky, A.: "On Persistent and Reliable Streaming in Ada". In Keller, H. B.; Plöderer, E. (Eds.), *Reliable Software Technologies - Ada-Europe'2000*, pp. 82 – 95, Lecture Notes in Computer Science **1845**, 2000.

[13] Haerder, T.; Reuter, A.: "Principles of Transaction Oriented Database Recovery". *ACM Computing Surveys 15(4)*, pp. 287 – 317, December 1983.

[14] Bernstein, P. A.; Goodman, N.: "Concurrency Control in Distributed Database Systems". *ACM Computing Surveys 13(2)*, pp. 185 – 221, June 1981.

[15] Kienzle, J.: *Open Multithreaded Transactions: A Transaction Model for Concurrent Object-Oriented Programming*. Ph.D. Thesis, Swiss Federal Institute of Technology Lausanne, Switzerland, April 2001, to be published.

[16] Object Management Group, Inc.: *Object Transaction Service*, May 2000.

MaRTE OS: An Ada Kernel for Real-Time Embedded Applications

Mario Aldea Rivas and Michael González Harbour

Departamento de Electrónica y Computadores
Universidad de Cantabria,
39005- Santander, SPAIN
{aldeam, mgh}@unican.es

Abstract: MaRTE OS (Minimal Real-Time Operating System for Embedded Applications) is a real-time kernel for embedded applications that follows the Minimal Real-Time POSIX.13 subset, providing both the C and Ada language POSIX interfaces. It allows cross-development of Ada and C real-time applications. Mixed Ada-C applications can also be developed, with a globally consistent scheduling of Ada tasks and C threads. Details on the architecture and implementation of the kernel are described, together with some performance metrics.

Keywords: Real-Time Systems, Kernel, Operating System, Embedded Systems, Ada 95, POSIX.

1 Introduction[1]

MaRTE OS (Minimal Real-Time Operating System for Embedded Applications) is a real-time kernel for embedded applications that follows the Minimal Real-Time POSIX.13 subset, providing both the C- and Ada-language POSIX interfaces. Although POSIX [3] is a fairly large interface, standard subsets of POSIX have been defined in the IEEE 1003.13 standard [6]. The smallest of these subsets requires only a reduced set of the system services, which can be implemented as a small and very efficient kernel that can be used to effectively implement embedded systems with real-time requirements.

Most existing POSIX real-time operating systems are commercial systems that do not provide their source code. Open-source implementations exist, like RTEMS [12], but because they were not built following the POSIX model from the beginning they offer POSIX just as an external interface layer. Another popular open-source implementation is RT-Linux [14]. Although this implementation currently offers a partial Minimal Real-Time POSIX.13 interface, it is not suitable for embedded systems, because it requires support for a full Linux operating system.

For these reasons, our research group decided to design and implement a real-time kernel for embedded applications that could be used on different platforms, including

---

1. This work has been funded by the *Comisión Interministerial de Ciencia y Tecnología* of the Spanish Government under grants TIC99-1043-C03-03 and 1FD 1997-1799 (TAP)

A. Strohmeier and D. Craeynest (Eds.): Ada-Europe 2001, LNCS 2043, pp. 305–316, 2001.

microcontrollers, and that would follow the Minimal Real-Time POSIX.13 subset. This kernel, called MaRTE OS, is usable both as a vehicle for the development of real-time applications such as robot controllers, and as a research tool on which we can prototype new OS interfaces, such as user-defined real-time scheduling, interrupt control, etc. In addition, it serves as a proof that a POSIX operating system can be implemented in Ada, while providing a C-language interface that allows multithreaded C applications to run on top of it.

This paper presents an overview of the architecture and internal details of MaRTE OS. In Section 2 we describe the objectives and basic requirements of our kernel. Section 3 describes its general architecture, and Section 4 describes some of the most relevant aspects of the implementation of its different components. Section 5 describes some performance metrics. Finally, Section 6 describes the current status of the project and gives our conclusions and future work.

2   Objectives and Basic Requirements

The main objective is to develop a real-time kernel for embedded systems, that conforms to the POSIX minimal real-time system profile specified in POSIX.13. In addition to the services defined in this profile, we have implemented some services from the POSIX.1d [4] and POSIX.1j [5] newly approved standards, which we think are very important for the kind of real-time applications at which MaRTE OS is targeted. Among these services are execution-time clocks and timers, and the absolute high resolution sleep.

The applications that we plan for this kernel are industrial embedded systems, such as data acquisition systems and robot controllers. We also plan on using the kernel as a research tool for investigating in operating systems and scheduling mechanisms. Based upon these objectives, the main requirements that we have formulated for our kernel are:

- Targeted for applications that are mostly static, with the number of threads and system resources well known at compile time. This allows these resources (i.e., threads, mutexes, thread stacks, number of priority levels, timers, etc.) to be preallocated at system configuration time, thus saving a lot of time when the application requests creation of one of these objects.

- All services with bounded response times, for hard real-time performance.

- Non protected. For efficiency purposes, no protection boundaries will be established between the application and the kernel. This means that a misbehaved application may corrupt kernel data, but this should be no problem in thoroughly tested static systems, like the targeted applications.

- Multiplatform. The kernel shall be implemented for multiple target platforms, using cross-development tools.

- Multilanguage: The kernel shall support Ada and C as well as mixed Ada/C applications. In the future, addition of a Java virtual machine will be explored, to allow also real-time Java applications [8].

3   Kernel Architecture

MaRTE OS allows software cross-development of both Ada and C applications using the GNU compilers gnat and gcc. Most of its code is written in Ada with some C and assembler parts. Multithreaded C applications can make use of the Ada kernel through a C-language interface that has been created on top it.

The kernel has a low-level abstract interface for accessing the hardware. This interface encapsulates operations for interrupt management, clock and timer management, and thread context switches. Its objective is to facilitate migration from one platform to another. Only the implementation of this hardware abstraction layer needs to be modified. For our initial platform (a PC) some of the functions of this hardware abstract interface come from a publicly available toolset called *OSKit* [1], which is intended to ease the low-level aspects of the development of an operating system. They are written in assembly and C language. We also use the facilities of *OSKit* for booting the application from a diskette or from the net.

The kernel is directly usable as the basis for the gnat run-time system, and thus applications may be programmed in Ada using its language-specific tasks. The gnat compiler is free software and provides the sources, including its run-time system called GNARL [2]; this is extremely important for us because we need to modify part of that run time system to adapt it to our kernel.

The gnat distribution that we have adapted is the version developed for Linux, and compiled to use the Florida State University (FSU) threads, which are a library implementation of the POSIX threads. Adapting the run-time system has implied modifying part of the GNARL lower level layer, called GNU Low-Level (GNULL). In particular, we have modified packages System.Os_Primitives, System.OS_Interface, and System.Task_Primitives.Operations, which define the interface between GNARL and the POSIX interface provided by the FSU threads and the Linux operating system, now replaced by the MaRTE kernel.

The modifications made are very minor, and mainly consist of type conversions between the internal types used by gnat (some of which are private), and their equivalent types in MaRTE. When a new version of the compiler is available, if we wish to migrate MaRTE to the new version, a careful check needs to be made to make sure that the modifications are correctly applied, and that the changes introduced in the new version are not incompatible with them. But because the modifications are very minor, if the changes in the compiler itself are not significant this migration process takes just a few hours, as we have experienced when migrating from gnat 3.12 to gnat 3.13.

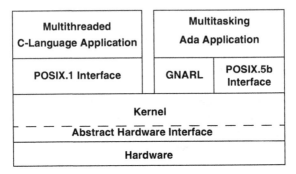

Fig. 1. Layers for applications in C and Ada

The kernel interface has been developed mainly according to the POSIX C-language interface, instead of the POSIX.5b specification [7], even though it is written in Ada. There were two reasons behind this decision. One was that GNULL is layered on top of the POSIX C interfaces. The other reason is that, because we had to provide both the Ada and C-language interfaces, we were not able to use exceptions inside the kernel, because C programs running on top of it would not know how to handle them. Therefore, the kernel interface uses only function return values to notify errors. The POSIX-Ada interfaces are implemented using an additional layer, that maps those interfaces to MaRTE , and raises the appropriate exceptions to the Ada applications. Fig. 1 shows the layered architecture for applications using our kernel and written in the Ada and C languages.

MaRTE OS works in a cross development environment. The host computer is a Linux PC with the gnat and gcc compilers, and the gdb debugger. The target platform is any 386 PC or higher, with a floppy disk (or equivalent) for booting the application, but not requiring a hard disk. An ethernet link is recommended for speeding the uploading of the application, and a serial line is required if remote debugging is desired. Fig. 2 shows the architecture of the cross-development platform. The *bootp* and *nfs* protocols are used to remotely boot an application stored in the host, through the ethernet link. The final application can be downloaded directly from the floppy (or

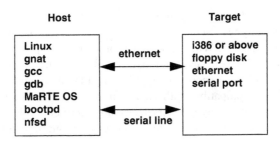

Fig. 2. Cross-Development Platform

a functionally equivalent device, such as a flash memory), without requiring the net, nor the serial line.

4   Implementation

Currently MaRTE OS implements the following POSIX functionalities. They cover the POSIX.13 minimal profile, plus some extensions from POSIX.1j and POSIX.1d:

- *POSIX Thread Management*: thread creation, finalization, attributes, etc. All threads and thread stacks are preallocated, so thread creation is extremely fast. The number of threads and the sizes of the stacks are configurable.

- *Priority Scheduling*. The two preemptive priority scheduling policies required by POSIX are implemented: FIFO within priorities, and round robin within priorities.

- *Mutexes*. For mutually exclusive synchronization among threads. Both priority inheritance and immediate priority ceilings are implemented for avoiding unbounded priority inversions.

- *Condition Variables*. For condition wait synchronization.

- *Signals*. They are the basic event notification mechanism. In particular, this mechanism is used by the timers to notify about timer expirations.

- *Clocks*. The POSIX real-time clock is implemented, for measuring time.

- *Timers*. They are software objects that measure time intervals or detect when a clock reaches a given time.

- *Execution-Time Clocks and Timers*. They enable CPU-time accounting and budgeting. This is an extremely interesting feature for detecting and limiting CPU-time overruns in real-time applications, that would make the results of real-time schedulability analysis invalid.

- *Console I/O*. For I/O using the PC console. Other I/O drivers will be provided in the future.

- *Time Services*: Thread suspension with absolute and relative high-resolution delays. Absolute delays are not yet part of POSIX.13, but were included because they are extremely useful; otherwise, a heavier-weight timer needs to be used.

- *Dynamic Memory Management*. Although not part of the POSIX interfaces, this functionality is required by the programming languages.

These POSIX functionalities support the whole gnat run time library, so the current MaRTE OS implementation allows running complex C and Ada applications with the restriction that they do not use a file system. This limitation is imposed by the Minimal Real-Time POSIX.13 subset.

4.1. Implementation Details

Implementation details on some of the most relevant services are given next.

- *Mutexes.* Each thread contains in its thread control block the list of mutexes that it owns, in order to keep track of priorities or priority ceilings that need to be inherited. In turn, each mutex has a queue with the threads that are waiting on that mutex. Despite what would seem natural, the mutex queues are not implemented as priority queues, although they behave as such as required by the POSIX specification. Under the immediate priority ceiling protocol, usually no thread will be queued in the mutex queue as a consequence of normal mutual exclusion. By not providing a priority queue, we avoid having to reorder it whenever priorities change. We have optimized the priority protection mechanism for mutexes by implementing a "deferred priority change". In this mechanism, when a thread becomes the owner of a mutex and thus inherits its ceiling priority, the priority is not immediately raised, but a flag is set to indicate that the priority change is pending. In most of the cases, the critical section during which the thread holds the lock is very short, and thus the priority is returned back to its normal level very soon, with no other thread being scheduled in between. In that case, the deferred priority change flag is reset and nothing else needs to be done. If indeed a scheduling point occurs after setting the flag, then the scheduler would check the flag and make the required priority change. The effect of this optimization is that in most cases we save two full priority changes (with their associated queue reordering), and consequently the average-case response time for the priority protection protocol is extremely low, similar to that of the priority inheritance protocol.

- *Condition Variables.* Each condition variable needs a queue of waiting threads. If the number of threads simultaneously waiting is under four, a simple linked list is the best implementation for the queue. However, for a larger number of threads, a priority queue is faster. The implementation chosen has a priority queue built with a linked list for each priority level, and a priority bit map to rapidly determine the highest non-empty priority level. To make the implementation of the "Signal" and "Broadcast" operations for condition variables faster, we check the priorities of the set of activated threads; within this set, and if the mutex is not locked, the thread with the highest priority is made the owner of the mutex, and put into the ready queue, while the other threads, if any, are inserted in the mutex wait queue. If the mutex was already locked, all threads are put in the mutex wait queue.

- *Signals.* Suspension inside a signal handler has been restricted to make signals more efficient. If a signal handler was allowed to suspend itself, and the interrupted thread was already suspended at some other OS service, the thread would be suspended twice, in different places. This makes the implementation very complex. Since we can use a user-defined thread to handle signals, such complexity for signal handlers is not really justified. With the proposed restriction, we can use a single special-purpose thread to execute all signal handlers, and the implementation becomes very simple and efficient. This restriction is being proposed for the next revision of POSIX.13.

- *Dynamic Memory Management.* The current implementation is very simple, and is optimized for real-time threads that make the allocations at initialization time, and then do not release the allocated memory. For each allocation (i.e., `malloc`), a consecutive block of memory is reserved. The `free` operation has no effect. Another possibility would be to use the Buddy algorithm for memory allocation and deallocation [9], which has a bounded response time.

In addition to these application-visible services, there are other internal services in the kernel:

- *Time services.* The system timer chosen is of the "alarm clock" kind, in which the timer is programmed at every scheduling point to expire at the next nearest scheduling point. This implementation reduces the overhead of the traditional "ticker" or periodic timer, and reduces the jitter in determining the scheduling points, provided that the underlying timer has sufficient resolution. Details on the low-level implementation of the clocks are given in Subsection 4.2.

- *Ready Queue.* This is one of the most fundamental objects in the kernel, because its performance is crucial to the overall performance of the system. For this reason, the queuing and dequeuing operations must be extremely fast, and with bounded execution time. We have tested different implementations of priority queues for numbers of threads between 20 and 50, which we estimate typical for the kind of embedded applications that we target. We have focused on systems in which the number of threads per each priority level is very low, because with normal Rate Monotonic or Deadline Monotonic scheduling each thread usually has a distinct priority. As a result of these tests, we have chosen an array of ordered singly linked lists, one for each priority level, together with a map of bits that indicates whether there is an active thread at any given priority. This map of bits can be tested in a very short time (typically one instruction) to determine the highest active priority level.

- *Timed Events Queue.* This is another structure that is crucial to the performance of the overall system. We cannot use the same priority queue implementation as for the ready queue, because this queue is ordered by time values, and the time may have very many different values. For this queue we have chosen the heapform heap structure, which provided the best worst-case results for a number of timed events roughly similar to the number of threads, between 20 and 50.

- *Execution-Time Events Queue.* Each thread has a queue of pending execution-time events which can represent the expiration of execution-time timers, or the expiration of their round robin quantum in case the thread is scheduled using the round robin policy. This queue is implemented as a singly-linked list, ordered by execution time, because the number of elements in it is usually very small. When a thread is made a running thread, the implementation calculates the absolute time at which the execution-time event found at the head of the queue should expire.

The hardware timer is then programmed to generate an interrupt at the smallest of that time and the time associated with the head of the Timed Events Queue. When the thread is blocked or preempted, the consumed execution time is added to its registered execution time.

4.2. Low-Level Timing Services

The implementation of clocks and timing services in MaRTE OS depends on the underlying processor architecture. If the processor is an 80386 or 80486, the Programmable Interval Timer (PIT) is used [13], both for the clocks (i.e., for measuring absolute or system time) and timing services (i.e., those requiring the generation of a timed event, at the requested time). The PIT is a standard device in the PC architecture that has three 16-bit counters driven through a hardware clock signal of 838.1 ns period. The main problem with the PIT is that its registers are accessed through the old I/O bus in the PC architecture, which makes accessing any of these registers a very slow operation, typically taking several microseconds.

The strategy used for programming the PIT is the same used in RT-Linux [11]. Counter 0 is used both to generate the timer interrupts required by the timing services, and to implement the clocks used in the OS to measure time. For this purpose, if an interrupt is required to occur within the next 50 ms, the counter is programmed with that interval; otherwise, if there are no urgent timer interrupts required, Counter 0 is programmed to generate an interrupt after 50 ms. After each interrupt occurs, the programmed interval is added to the total time count, and the counter is reprogrammed. The time required to reprogram the counter is measured using Counter 2 (which is commonly used in PCs to produce sounds of different tones through the speaker). This time is also added to the total time count. In this way, we make sure that the delays caused by reprogramming the counters do not cause a cumulative error in the measurement of time for the system clock.

With this strategy, an invocation of the get-time operation to obtain the current time consists of adding the total system time to the current value of Counter 0. The total system time variable is initialized at boot time with the value read from the PC's Real-Time Clock (RTC). The resolution of the clock implemented with this strategy is the same as for the underlying counters (838.1 ns).

If a Pentium processor is available, the measurement of absolute time can be implemented using the time-stamp counter (TSC). This counter (as implemented in the Pentium and P6 family processors) is a 64-bit counter that is set to zero following the hardware reset of the processor. Following reset, the counter is incremented every processor clock cycle, even when the processor is halted by the HLT instruction or the external STPCLK# pin [10]. Reading the value of this counter requires only a single machine instruction and, because this counter is internal to the processor and the I/O bus is not used, the operation is very fast (89 ns in a Pentium III at 550 MHz).

The system time is obtained by adding the initial boot time of MaRTE OS (read from the Real-Time Clock) to the number of cycles counted by the TSC at the present time minus the number of cycles already counted at boot time, and multiplied by the corresponding conversion factor. The clock resolution with this strategy is 1.8 ns in a Pentium III at 550 MHz.

In this implementation, timer interrupts are still generated with the PIT's Counter 0. In this case there is no need to use Counter 2 to measure reprogramming times, because the current time is measured with the TSC. Because Counter 0 cannot be programmed to measure intervals greater than 50 ms, if the next timed event is more that 50 ms away from the current time, one or more intermediate activations are programmed. With this strategy, we still have to pay the price of using the PC I/O bus to access the PIT counter.

For P6 processors (Pentium II or higher) the overhead can be greatly diminished by using the timer included in the Advanced Programmable Interrupt Controller (Local APIC). The local APIC is included in all P6 family processors. Although its main function is the dispatching of interrupts, it also contains a 32-bit programmable timer for use by the local processor whose time base is derived from the processor's bus clock. It can be configured to interrupt the local processor with an arbitrary vector. The frequency of the processor's bus clock in the Pentium III-500 MHz that we have used for testing is 100 MHz, and thus the timers in this machine have a resolution of 10 ns.

The local APIC is disabled after the hardware reset of the processor. Enabling the APIC requires two steps: first, a bit needs to be set in the model-specific register of the APIC [10], which enables access to the APIC registers; then, the APIC must be enabled explicitly by writing the appropriate value in its Spurious-Interrupt Vector Register.

Access to the local APIC registers is achieved by reading from and writing to specific memory addresses. With the APIC enabled, accesses to those memory addresses are mapped onto the APIC registers. Read and write access times for those registers are very short. For example writing to the Initial Count Register of the APIC Timer takes 62 ns in our Pentium III at 550MHz.

Table 1 shows some performance metrics comparing the three implementations of the time services. It can be seen that the overheads of using the local APIC are at least an order of magnitude less than when using the PIT.

Table 1. Comparison of the overheads of the time services implementations (ns)

Operation	PIT	TSC+PIT	TSC+APIC
Get time	3100	105	105
Program timer	12900	3000	324

5   Performance Metrics

Table 2 shows performance metrics for some of the most important services, measured on a Pentium III at 550 MHz.

Table 2. Performance metrics

Service	Time (μs)
Context switch, after `yield` operation, low priority thread	0.748
Context switch, after `yield` operation, high priority thread	0.734
Read the clock	0.089
Send signal followed by context switch and await signal	0.927
Send signal followed by context switch and await signal, with deferred priority change	1.316
Mutex lock followed by unlock (with deferred priority change)	0.399
Signal a condition variable on which a high priority thread is waiting, followed by context switch and end of condition wait call	1.262
Minimum Ada rendezvous, including two context switches	6.8
Two ada rendezvous, passing an integer from a producer task through a buffer task to a consumer task	15.1
Relative `delay` operation, until lower priority task starts running, including one context switch	5.0
Absolute `delay until` operation, until lower priority task starts running, including one context switch	5.0
Wake up from a relative `delay` operation, including one context switch	8.7
Wake up from an absolute `delay until` operation, including one context switch	8.8
Delay resolution (difference between requested delay and actual delay)	11.0
Minimum period thread (C program using `nanosleep`)	7.9 (126 KHz)
Minimum period task (Ada program using `delay`)	11.5 (87 KHz)

The number of lines of our implementation is around 10300, which gives an idea that the POSIX minimal real-time profile is really suited for embedded systems.

6   Conclusions and Further Work

With the kernel described in this paper we are able to develop real-time embedded applications running on a bare PC. These applications can be written in Ada, C, or both languages. More important, we can use this kernel as a vehicle for research in new scheduling mechanisms for real-time, and also as a teaching platform for real-time operating systems and programming.

The implementation of the kernel is now complete for a bare Pentium-PC platform. The next steps in the development of this kernel will be to add services for managing application-defined scheduling policies, application-defined interrupt management, network communications (ethernet and CAN bus), and additional I/O drivers. In addition, we need to port the implementation to other platforms, such as microcontrollers, and Power PC boards.

MaRTE OS is available under the GNU General Public License, and can be found at: `http://ctrpc17.ctr.unican.es/marte.html`

References

[1]   Ford, B., G. Back, G. Benson, J. Lepreau, A. Lin, and O. Shivers. (1997). The Flux OSKit: a Substrate for OS and Language Research. *Proceedings of the 16th ACM Symposium on Operating Systems Principles*, Saint Malo, France (http://www.cs.utah.edu/flux/oskit)

[2]   Giering, E.W. and T.P. Baker (1994). The GNU Ada Runtime Library (GNARL): Design and Implementation. *Wadas'94 Proceedings*.

[3]   ISO/IEC 9945-1 (1996). *ISO/IEC Standard 9945-1:1996. Information Technology - Portable Operating System Interface (POSIX)- Part 1: System Application Program Interface (API) [C Language]*. Institute of Electrical and electronic Engineers.

[4]   POSIX.1d (1999). *IEEE Std. 1003.d-1999. Information Technology -Portable Operating System Interface (POSIX)- Part 1: System Application Program Interface (API) Amendment: Additional Realtime Extensions [C Language]*. The Institute of Electrical and Electronics Engineers.

[5]   POSIX.1j (2000). *IEEE Std. 1003.j-2000. Information Technology -Portable Operating System Interface (POSIX)- Part 1: System Application Program Interface (API) Amendment: Advanced Realtime Extensions [C Language]*. The Institute of Electrical and Electronics Engineers.

[6]   POSIX.13 (1998). *IEEE Std. 1003.13-1998. Information Technology -Standardized Application Environment Profile- POSIX Realtime Application Support (AEP)*. The Institute of Electrical and Electronics Engineers.

[7]   POSIX.5b (1996). *IEEE Std 1003.5b-1996, Information Technology—POSIX Ada Language Interfaces—Part 1: Binding for System Application Program Interface (API)— Amendment 1: Realtime Extensions*. The Institute of Electrical and Engineering Electronics.

[8]   RTSJ (1999). The Real-Time for Java Experts Group, "Real-Time Specification for Java", Version 0.8.2, November 1999 (http://www.rtj.org).

[9]   Rusling, D.A. (1999). *The Linux Kernel*, Version 0.8-3 (http://www.linuxhq.com/guides/TLK/tlk.html).

[10]   Intel. Intel Architecture Software Developer's Manual. Vol. 3. System Programming. (ftp://download.intel.nl/design/pentiumii/manuals/24319202.pdf)

[11] Real-Time Linux operating system web page (http://luz.cs.nmt.edu/~rtlinux)

[12] "Real-Time Executive for Multiprocessor Systems: Reference Manual". U.S. Army Missile Command, redstone Arsenal, Alabama, USA, January 1996.

[13] Triebel W.A., "The 80386DX Microprocessor", Prentice Hall, 1992.

[14] Yodaiken V., "An RT-Linux Manifesto". Proceedings of the 5th Linux Expo, Raleigh, North Carolina, USA, May 1999.

Implementing Ada.Real_Time.Clock and Absolute Delays in Real-Time Kernels*

Juan Zamorano[1], José F. Ruiz[2], and Juan Antonio de la Puente[2]

[1] Departamento de Arquitectura y Tecnología de Sistemas Informáticos
Universidad Politécnica de Madrid, E-28660 Madrid, Spain
[2] Departamento de Ingeniería de Sistemas Telemáticos
Universidad Politécnica de Madrid, E-28040 Madrid, Spain
jzamora@fi.upm.es jfruiz@dit.upm.es jpuente@dit.upm.es

Abstract. A real-time kernel providing multitasking and timing services is a fundamental component of any real-time system. Timing services, which are crucial to the correct execution of this kind of applications, are usually provided by a real-time clock and timer manager, which is part of the kernel and implements the required functionality on top of the one or more hardware timers. Kernel timing services must be implemented carefully in order to avoid race problems and inconsistencies which may be caused by the fact that many common hardware timer chips are not intended at a direct implementation of software timing services. This paper provides advice on the implementation of two of the Ada timing services: Ada.Real_Time.Clock, and absolute delays (delay until). The example implementation of both services in the Open Ravenscar Kernel, which is based on the ideas presented in the paper, is also described.

1 Introduction

Real-time systems are required to react to external signals within specified time intervals [18]. These systems are often built as a set of concurrent periodic and sporadic tasks, implemented on top of a real-time kernel that provides multitasking and timing services, among others. The Ada 95 language [1] supports tasking and real-time at the programming language level, thus providing appropriate high-level abstractions for real-time applications. Tasking and timing constructs are usually implemented by an Ada run-time system, which is built on top of a general-purpose operating system or, as it is customary for real-time systems, a real-time kernel [4].

Ada 95 provides two kinds of timing services. The core language includes the Ada.Calendar package, where a Time type and a time-of-the-day Clock function are defined [1, ch. 9]. The real-time systems annex [1, Annex D] defines the Ada.Real_Time package, with more appropriate definitions of Time and Clock for real-time systems. In the following, we will concentrate on the timing facilities

---

* This work has been funded by ESA/ESTEC contract no. No.13863/99/NL/MV.

A. Strohmeier and D. Craeynest (Eds.): Ada-Europe 2001, LNCS 2043, pp. 317–327, 2001.

defined in Ada.Real_Time, together with the absolute delay statement (delay until), as these are the ones most likely to be used by real-time applications (and the only ones supported in the Ravenscar profile [3]).

Ada 95 timing facilities are usually implemented by some parts of the Ada run-time system, which in turn relies on kernel services. These kernel services are built on top of different kinds of clock and timer hardware devices, which are usually based on a high-frequency oscillator which feeds a frequency divider counting register set. The kernel implementation of timing services has to be both accurate and efficient, providing low granularity time measurements and delays together with a low overhead operation. These properties are often in conflict when using commercial hardware timers, which requires a careful design to be carried out in order to prevent race conditions, inconsistencies, and other problems that may compromise the performance and correctness of real-time applications.

In the rest of the paper we provide advice on the implementation of kernel services for Ada real-time facilities, based on our experience with the Open Ravenscar Kernel [5], an open-source real-time kernel for the GNAT compilation system targeted to the ERC32 (SPARC 7) architecture. Section 2 provides some background on the operation of hardware timers. Section 3 gives some guidelines for implementing Ada.Real_Time. Clock, and section 4 describes the current ORK implementation as an example. Section 5 discusses some important issues related to accurate timer implementation, and sections 6 and 7 provide guidelines and implementation examples for the Ada delay until statement. Finally, some conclusions are drawn in section 8.

2   Hardware Timers

A hardware timer is a device which takes an oscillator signal as an input. In order to operate with a range of clock frequencies, the input signal is usually fed through a component called the *scaler*, which divides its frequency by a configurable integer value. The resulting clock signal is used to decrement a down-count register, which outputs a signal when its value reaches zero (figure 1).

The way of configuring a timer device is by writing into its registers, which have their own addresses in the memory map of the computer. The timer registers can also be read (for instance, to query the current value of the down-count register).

Hardware timers have several programmable operational modes, providing additional flexibility for the implementation of software timer modules. The most common and important modes are:

- Periodic counter mode. In this operational mode, the initial value of the down-count register is automatically reloaded by the hardware when the count reaches zero, and then the down-count starts again.
- Interval counter mode. In this mode, the initial value is not reloaded when the down-count ends. Hence, the timer operation finishes and the down-count register remains with a zero value.

The level of the output signal changes every time the down-count reaches zero. The output pin is usually connected to a computer line, and the role of the timer device in the computer depends on the line to which the output is connected and the operational mode selected.

The most common configurations of hardware timers in a computer system are:

- Watchdog timer. The output pin is connected to the reset line of the computer, and the device is programmed as an interval counter. As a result, the computer is reset whenever the down-count reaches zero.
- Periodic timer. The output pin is connected to an interrupt request line, and the device is programmed as a periodic counter. As a result, an interrupt request is periodically generated every time the down-count reaches zero.
- Single-shot timer. The output pin is connected to an interrupt request line, and the device is programmed as an interval counter. As a result, an interrupt request is generated when the down-count reaches zero.
- Sound generator. The output pin is connected to a loudspeaker or a similar device, and the device is programmed as a periodic counter. By properly adjusting the scaler and down-count preset values, the output signal changes at an audible frequency, thus producing a sound.

Although watchdog timers are common in real-time systems, only periodic and single-shot timers are relevant from the point of view of this paper.

3   Implementing Ada.Real_Time.Clock

Annex D of the Ada Language Reference Manual [1] requires a maximum resolution of 1 ms and a minimum range of 50 years for Ada.Real_Time.Time. Therefore, at least 41 bits are needed to implement this data type.

An easy way to implement Ada.Real_Time.Clock would be to use a hardware periodic timer with a period equal to the required resolution. Unfortunately, the down-count registers of most hardware timers are at most 32 bits wide (8 and 16 bits are the most common sizes), which means that in most cases Ada.Real_Time.Clock cannot be implemented directly in hardware. However, it is possible to use a hardware periodic timer to store only the least significant part of the clock value, while the most significant part of the same value is stored in main memory, and incremented by the timer interrupt handler. Since the timer down-count is automatically restarted by the hardware, the clock resolution is given by the scaled oscillator frequency. The interrupt period can be much longer (actually up to the down-count register capacity) without loss of precision.

This method makes it possible to implement Ada.Real_Time.Clock with the required resolution and range. However, there is a consistency problem (race condition), as reading the clock is not an atomic operation. Incorrect clock values may be obtained if an interrupt occurs between the reading of the hardware and software components of the time. The order of magnitude of the error is about one interrupt period, which should be considered unacceptable. It must be noticed that masking the timer interrupt does not solve the problem, because the down-count register is automatically reloaded by the hardware when it reaches zero, even if interrupts are disabled.

It is also possible to use a single-shot hardware timer. In this case, the down-count register is reloaded by the interrupt handler, and the consistency problem can be solved by masking the timer interrupt in order to make the reading of both components of the clock an atomic operation. However, this method introduces another problem related to the precision of the clock, as the time spent by the processor to recognize an interrupt varies depending on the behavior of the software. For example, interrupts may be delayed after a kernel procedure has raised the processor priority, or the handler may execute a variable sequence of instructions before the timer is restarted. This variation in time introduces an additional drift in the value of the clock, which is different from the usual manufacturing drift which deviates the clock in a linear way. The drift induced by the variation in interrupt handling changes the clock in a different amount of time at every interrupt. Therefore, it is difficult to compensate, and even the kind of clock synchronization algorithms that can be used in other situations to get an accurate time keeping (see, e.g. [11]) are harder to implement. It should be noticed that, although the additional drift could be overcome by taking into account the average time to restart the timer after an interrupt request, this would result in a acceptable loss of monotonicity for the clock.

4   Implementation of Ada.Real_Time.Clock in ORK

The Open Ravenscar Real-Time Kernel (ORK) [5,6] is a tasking kernel for the Ada language which provides full conformance with the Ravenscar profile [3] on ERC32-based computers. ERC32 is a radiation-hardened implementation of the SPARC V7 architecture, which has been adopted by the European Space Agency (ESA) as the current standard processor for spacecraft on-board computer systems [8].

The ERC32 hardware provides two timers (apart from a special *Watchdog timer*): the *Real-Time Clock* (RTC) and the *General Purpose Timer* (GPT). Both timers can be programmed to operate in either single-shot or periodic mode [19]. The timers are driven by the internal system clock, and they include a two-stage counter which operates as described in section 2 (figure 1).

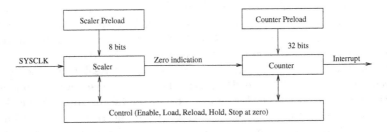

Fig. 1. Structure of the ERC32 timers.

The kernel uses one of the hardware timers, namely the Real-Time Clock, to implement Ada.Real_Time.Clock. The maximum time value that can be kept in the RTC is:

$$MaxTime = \frac{(RTCC + 1)(RTCS + 1)}{SYSCLK} = \frac{2^{32} \times 2^{8}}{10^{7}} \approx 109\_951s$$

where $RTCC$ is the maximum value of the RTC counter register (32 bits wide), $RTCS$ is the maximum value of the RTC scaler (8 bits wide), and $SYSCLK$ is the system clock frequency (10 MHz). Not only this value is much shorter than required time range (50 years), but the clock resolution provided by a hardware-only implementation (25.6 μs) is too coarse for many applications. Therefore, the clock cannot be implemented only with the available hardware, and a mixed hardware-software mechanism, as discussed above in section 3, is necessary.

ORK uses the first of the methods in section 3. The RTC device is configured by the kernel so that it generates periodic interrupts. The interrupt handler updates the most significant part of the clock (MSP_Clock), which is kept in memory, while the least significant part of the clock is held in the RTCC register. In order to obtain the highest possible resolution, ORK sets the RTCS preload value to zero. As a result, the resolution of Ada.Real_Time.Clock is the same as the $SYSCLK$ period, that is 100 ns. The periodic interrupt period (which is given by the RTCC preload value) can be up to 429 s $(= 2^{32}/10^{7})$. These values are valid for the usual ERC32 system clock frequency of 10 MHz.

In order to prevent the race condition which was mentioned in section 3, the Clock function reads the hardware clock twice. This arrangement is valid because the long interrupt period of the RTC prevents the occurrence of two interrupts during two consecutive clock readings. This solves the race condition problem, at the price of a slight performance penalty in Ada.Real_Time.Clock function calls. The code of this function is shown in figure 2.

5 Using Hardware Timers to Provide High Resolution Timing

It is very common to implement software timers based on the same periodic interrupt timer that is used for the real-time clock (see, e.g. [14,12]). In order to improve the resolution of the software timers, the timer chip can be programmed to interrupt at a higher frequency than strictly required for keeping the clock.

The problem with this approach is that the overhead due to interrupt handling may raise to unacceptable levels for high frequency values. Actually, interrupts need to be programmed only when there is some timing event that has to be signaled. The key point is that, even when a microsecond resolution is required, there is no need to have timing events every microsecond. What is needed is a mechanism by which timer interrupts are allowed to occur at any microsecond, but not necessarily every microsecond.

Single-shot timers provide just the right kind of support for this behavior, where interrupts are generated on demand, and not periodically. However, this kind of devices are not appropriate for implementing a monotonic, precise clock

```
MSP Clock : Time := 0;
pragma Atomic (MSP Clock);
-- pragma Atomic (MSP Clock) is needed because MSP Clock
-- is updated by Clock Handler.
                                                                        5
function Clock return Time is
   Before, After : constant Time :=
     MSP Clock + Time (Kernel.Peripherals.Read Clock);
begin
   if After > Before then                                              10
      -- an interrupt may have occurred while Before was being built
      return After;
   else
      -- an interrupt has occurred while After was being built
      return Before;                                                   15
   end if;
end Clock;
```

Fig. 2. ORK implementation of Ada.Real_Time.Clock.

(see section 3). Therefore, the best arrangement is to use two hardware timers: a periodic interrupt timer for the high resolution clock, and a single-shot timer for software timers. The single-shot timer is reprogrammed on demand every time an alarm is set so that it interrupts when the alarm expires. This arrangement provides high resolution software timers with a low overhead. Many real-time kernels, such as RT-Linux [2], KURT [9], Linux/RK [15], JTK [16], and ORK [5, 6] follow this approach.

6   Implementing Absolute Delays

The implementation of absolute delays (delay until in Ada) is based on software timers. Timing events are kept in a delay queue ordered by expiration time. A single-shot timer is programmed to interrupt at the expiration time of the first pending delay. When the interrupt occurs, the first event is removed form the queue and the timer is programmed for the next delay, and so on.

The best way to store delay expiration times is to use absolute time values. Otherwise, the timer interrupt routine would have to perform additional operations in order to maintain the relative times of the events in the queue, which would increase the interrupt handling overhead and, even worse, the worst case execution time of the kernel timing services. However, single-shot timers are programmed with relative times. This means that the timer interrupt routine has to read the clock and subtract its value from the absolute time of the next event, in order to compute the right preset value for the timer down-count register.

It must be noticed that periodic timer interrupts must be enabled during the execution of the single-shot timer interrupt routine. Otherwise, the interrupt routine might get an erroneous clock value if a periodic timer interrupt were pending. Such a situation would result in an error of almost one periodic timer interrupt period in the single-shot timer interval. The easiest way to prevent this kind of problems is to configure the timer with the lowest interrupt priority as the single-shot timer, and the other one as the periodic timer. Some timer chips, however, cannot be configured in this way, which may lead to very complex code in the timer interrupt routines. Luckily enough, the ERC32 timers have different priorities each, thus making this approach feasible for ORK.

The last point to be considered is the way to deal with delays which are longer than the maximum time interval which can be programmed in the hardware timer. If only a single-shot timer is used, the timer has to be restarted several times in order to get such a long delay. Another possibility is to use both a single-shot and a periodic timer, in such a way that the single-shot timer is only used when the next event expires before the next periodic timer interrupt.

The first approach has only a small overhead, but raises the issue of how to model the additional interrupts for response time analysis. On the other hand, the second approach may not work properly if the next event occurs before the next periodic timer interrupt, but close to it. If the code which calculates the relative time for the next alarm and programs the interval timer takes too long to execute, the single-shot timer can actually be set to interrupt just a little bit after the next periodic timer interrupt. This possibility has to be taken into account when coding the interrupt routines, as it may give raise to race conditions resulting in alarms being lost or scheduled twice, depending on the actual implementation. However, there is a trivial solution, which is to record the pending alarm status in a boolean flag. It must be noticed that this flag is also needed by the low-level delay until procedure, because a current timer expiration may have to be canceled by a new, but closer, delay request.

7   Implementation of Absolute Delays in ORK

Following the discussion of the previous section, the ORK implementation of absolute delays is based on two timers: a periodic interrupt timer and a single-shot timer. The first timer is the RTC, which is also used to support Ada.Real_Time.Clock (see section 3, and the second one is the ERC32 GPT, which is used to set alarms on demand. This timer is only used when the next alarm is closer than the next periodic interrupt. A boolean flag called Pending_Alarm is used to indicate that the single-shot timer is set.

As explained before, the RTC timer must have a higher interrupt priority than the GPT. ORK allows the nesting of interrupts in the usual way: high priority interrupt requests can preempt the execution of interrupt handlers with a lower priority, but lower priority interrupts are masked during the execution of an interrupt handler. Therefore, the periodic (RTC) interrupt handler can preempt the execution of the single-shot (GPT) interrupt handler. On the other hand, single-shot timer interrupts are not recognized during the execution of the periodic interrupter handler.

The kernel achieves mutual exclusion on its internal data structures (e.g. ready and delay queues) by means of a monolithic monitor [13,7], which is implemented by disabling interrupts, so that interrupt recognition is postponed while a kernel function is being executed [17,16].

```
Pending Alarm : Boolean := False;
pragma Atomic (Pending Alarm);

procedure Clock Handler is
   Next Alarm : Time;                                              5
begin
   KP.Clear Clock Interrupt;
   KT.Protection.Enter Kernel;
   MSP Clock := MSP Clock + KPA.Clock Interrupt Period;
   if not Pending Alarm then                                       10
      Next Alarm := KT.Queues.Get Next Alarm Time;
      -- if the head of the alarm queue is scheduled before the next
      -- clock interrupt
      if Next Alarm < MSP Clock + KPA.Clock Interrupt Period then
         -- set alarm                                              15
         KP.Set Alarm (To Safe Timer Interval (Next Alarm -
                  MSP Clock - Time (KP.Read Clock)));
         Pending Alarm := True;
      end if;
   end if;                                                         20
   KT.Protection.Leave Kernel;
end Clock Handler;
```

Fig. 3. ORK RTC interrupt handler.

The code of the RTC interrupt handler is shown in figure 3. The procedures Kernel. Threads.Protection.Enter_Kernel and Kernel.Threads.Protection.Leave_Kernel change the running priority in order to disable and restore interrupts for mutual exclusion, as above described. The handler increments the most significant part of the monotonic clock (MSP_Clock) with the clock interrupt period. The interrupt handler also checks whether the alarm timer is set, which is recorded in Pending_Alarm, so that the current alarm, if there is one, is not lost by setting a new one. More in detail, if the alarm timer is set then nothing is done, as an alarm timer interrupt is coming soon. Otherwise, it checks the alarm queue and sets the alarm timer if the next alarm is closer than the next clock interrupt. The function KT.Queues.Get_Next_Alarm_Time returns Time'Last when the alarm queue is empty. The timer is programmed by the procedure KP.Set_Alarm, which takes the relative delay to the alarm as a parameter. The clock value can be explicitly evaluated from its components (MSP_Clock + Time (KP.Read_Clock)) because the clock interrupts are disabled during the execution of the clock handler. The function To_Safe_Timer_Interval is used to avoid possible negative values of the next alarm caused by delays in the code execution.

The code of the alarm timer handler is shown in figure 4. The handler wakes up all the tasks whose expiration times have already been reached. It then checks the alarm queue and sets the alarm timer if needed. The clock is read again after waking up the tasks in order to avoid an excessive jitter. It must be noticed that the alarm interrupt priority must be restored (thus leaving the kernel monitor) in order to prevent an incorrect time value to be read because of a pending clock interrupt request. The kernel is requested to execute the dispatching routine so as to enable a newly awaken task to preempt the previously running task if it has a higher priority.

```
procedure Alarm Handler is
 Now, Next Alarm : Time;
begin
 -- Pending Alarm must be true
 KP.Clear Alarm Interrupt;                                         5
 Now := Clock;
 KT.Protection.Enter Kernel;
 while KT.Queues.Get Next Alarm Time <= Now loop
   -- extract the tasks that were waiting on the alarm
   -- queue and insert them into the ready queue.               10
   KT.Queues.Insert At Tail (KT.Queues.Extract First Alarm);
 end loop;
 Next Alarm := KT.Queues.Get Next Alarm Time;
 -- the dispatcher is now called.
 KT.Protection.Dispatch;                                         15
 KT.Protection.Leave Kernel;
 -- if the head of alarm queue is closer than the next clock interrupt
 if Next Alarm < MSP Clock + KPA.Clock Interrupt Period then
   -- set alarm but read clock again to avoid an excessive jitter
   KP.Set Alarm (To Safe Timer Interval (Next Alarm - Clock));  20
 else
   Pending Alarm := False;
 end if;
end Alarm Handler;

                                                                 25
```

Fig. 4. ORK GPT interrupt handler.

It could be argued that the head of the alarm queue might change after waking up all the tasks with expired alarms, but it can be easily shown that such a situation cannot happen under the Ravenscar profile, for which ORK has been designed. Only sporadic tasks which are waken up by higher priority interrupts can preempt the alarm handler, and such tasks cannot execute a delay until statement due to the single invocation restriction. Since the execution of a delay until statement is the only way to put tasks in the alarm queue under the Ravenscar profile restrictions, it can be concluded that the alarm queue cannot change.

8 Conclusions

Hardware timers provide the low-level functionality required to support time features of real-time kernels. A number of different approaches for implementing the Ada real-time clock and absolute delays on top of this kind of hardware devices have been introduced in the paper, and some problems related to the accuracy and efficiency of the implementation have been discussed. As an example, representative parts of the Open Ravenscar Kernel implementation for ERC32 computers have been described in detail. Unfortunately, these solutions are not of general nature because of the diversity of timer device arrangements in computers.

As we have shown, a hardware real-time clock provides the simplest and more efficient implementation of a clock. Unfortunately, this solution cannot be used with most current hardware timers, which have only 32 bits or less. Timers with counting registers up to 64 bits wide, such as the ones that can be found in Pentium processors [10], provide the required accuracy with an extended time range, and therefore are more suitable for real-time applications. An advantage of hardware-only clocks is that there are no race conditions or inconsistencies as the timer registers are read or written in an atomic fashion.

An efficient and effective implementation of shared timers needs some help from the software, though. It is not reasonable to force the hardware to maintain a list of pending timers. Therefore, this function has to be provided by the software, with a hardware support based on an efficient and a high resolution mechanism for programming timer interrupts. This mechanism can be based on a single-shot interrupt timer with a 64 bit counter.

Acknowledgments. The Open Ravenscar Real-Time Kernel was developed by a team of the Department of Telematics Engineering, Technical University of Madrid (DIT/UPM), lead by Juan Antonio de la Puente. The other members of the team were Juan Zamorano, José F. Ruiz, Ramón Fernández, and Rodrigo García. Alejandro Alonso and Ángel Álvarez acted as document and code reviewers, and contributed to the technical discussions with many fruitful comments and suggestions. The same team developed the adapted run-time packages that enable GNAT to work with ORK.

The ORK software was validated by Jesús Borruel and Juan Carlos Morcuende, from Construcciones Aeronáuticas (CASA), Space Division. We also relied very much on Andy Wellings and Alan Burns, of York University, for reviewing and discussions about the Ravenscar profile and its implementation.

ORK was developed under contract with ESA, the European Space Agency. Jorge Amador, Tullio Vardanega and Jean-Loup Terraillon provided many positive criticism and contributed the user's view during the development. The project was carried out from September, 1999 to early June, 2000, with some extensions being made in the first half of 2001.

References

1. *Ada 95 Reference Manual: Language and Standard Libraries. International Standard ANSI/ISO/IEC-8652:1995*, 1995. Available from Springer-Verlag, LNCS no. 1246.
2. Michael Barabanov. A Linux-based real-time operating system. Master's thesis, New Mexico Institute of Mining and Technology, June 1997. Available at http://www.rtlinux. org/ baraban/thesis.
3. Alan Burns. The Ravenscar profile. *Ada Letters*, XIX(4):49-52, 1999.

4. Alan Burns and Andy J. Wellings. *Real-Time Systems and Programming Languages*. Addison-Wesley, 2 edition, 1996.
5. Juan A. de la Puente, José F. Ruiz, and Juan Zamorano. An open Ravenscar real-time kernel for GNAT. In Hubert B. Keller and Erhard Ploedereder, editors, *Reliable Software Technologies — Ada-Europe 2000*, number 1845 in LNCS, pages 5-15. Springer-Verlag, 2000.
6. Juan A. de la Puente, José F. Ruiz, Juan Zamorano, Rodrigo García, and Ramón Fernández-Marina. ORK: An open source real-time kernel for on-board software systems. In *DASIA 2000 - Data Systems in Aerospace*, Montreal, Canada, May 2000.
7. Juan A. de la Puente, Juan Zamorano, José F. Ruiz, Ramón Fernández, and Rodrigo García. The design and implementation of the Open Ravenscar Kernel. *Ada Letters*, XXI(1), March 2001. 10th International Real-Time Ada Workshop, Las Navas del Marqués, Ávila, Spain. 8.
8. ESA. *32 Bit Microprocessor and Computer System Development*, 1992. Report 9848/92/NL/FM.
9. Robert Hill, Balaji Srinivasan, Shyam Pather, and Douglas Niehaus. Temporal resolution and real-time extensions to Linux. Technical Report ITTC-FY98-TR-11510-03, Information and Telecommunication Technology Center, Department of Electrical Engineering and Computer Sciences, University of Kansas, June 1998.
10. Intel Corp. *Survey of Pentium Processor Performance Monitoring Capabilities and Tools*, 1996. Available at http://developer.intel.com/software/idap/resources/technical_collateral%/mmx/.
11. Hermann Kopetz. Clock synchronization in distributed real-time systems. *IEEE Tr. on Software Engineering*, 36(8), 1987.
12. Lynx Real-Time Systems, Inc. *LynxOS Appplication Writer's Guide*, 1993.
13. A.K. Mok. The design of real-time programming systems based on process models. In *IEEE Real-Time Systems Symposium*. IEEE Computer Society Press, 1984.
14. OAR. *RTEMS SPARC Applications Supplement*, 1997.
15. Shuichi Oikawa and Ragunathan Rajkumar. Linux/RK: A portable resource kernel in Linux. IEEE Real-Time Systems Symposium Work-in-progress Session, December 1998.
16. José F. Ruiz and Jesús M. González-Barahona. Implementing a new low-level tasking support for the GNAT runtime system. In Michael González-Harbour and Juan A. de la Puente, editors, *Reliable Software Technologies — Ada-Europe'99*, number 1622 in LNCS, pages 298-307. Springer-Verlag, 1999.
17. J.S. Snyder, D.B. Whalley, and T.P. Baker. Fast context switches: Compiler and architectural support for preemptive scheduling. *Microprocessors and Microsystems*, 19(1):35-42, February 1995.
18. J.A. Stankovic. Misconceptions about real-time programming: A serious problem for next-generation systems. *IEEE Computer*, 21(10):10-19, 1988.
19. Temic/Matra Marconi Space. *SPARC RT Memory Controller (MEC) User's Manual*, April 1997.

Defining New Non-preemptive Dispatching and Locking Policies for Ada

Alan Burns

Real-Time Systems Research Group
Department of Computer Science
University of York, UK

Abstract. In many high-integrity applications, non-preemptive execution is preferred. This paper motivates and defines such a dispatching policy for Ada. It also describes an associated locking policy for protected objects. To deliver non-preemptive execution a new processing resource is introduced – the execution token. In addition to defining these new policies the paper also reviews how non-preemptive tasking systems can be analysed for their schedulability.

1 Introduction

The Real-Time Annex of the ARM (Ada Reference Manual) requires that a preemptive dispatching policy is always provided by an implementation. It also allows implementa- tion-defined policies to be supplied. For many system builders, particularly in the safety-critical area, the policy of choice is *non-preemption*.

The standard way of implementing many high-integrity applications is with a cyclic executive. Here a sequence of procedures is called within a defined time interval. Each procedure runs to completion, there is no concept of preemption. Data is passed from one procedure to another via shared variables, no synchronisation constraints are needed, as the procedures never run concurrently.

Recent advances in Ada technology (the production of the Ravenscar[2,4] Profile) has shown how a simple subset of the language's tasking features can give effective support to high-integrity real-time systems. Whilst many system builders are prepared to move to use tasking (as defined by Ravenscar) some are reluctant to embrace the preemptive dispatching policy. They prefer the reduced non-determinism of non-preemptive dispatching. Non-preemption also increases the effectiveness of testing [5].

At the last three IRTAWs (International Real-Time Ada Workshops) consideration has been given to a non-preemptive version of Ravenscar and non-preemptive execution in general. This paper aims to provide a definition of a new `Task_ Dispatching_ Policy` and a new `Locking_Policy` (for the entire language - not just Ravenscar). It builds on an earlier workshop paper [1] and reflects the discussion that have occurred during this workshop series.

It should be noted that non-preemption is not synonymous with non-interruptible. With non-preemption a task may lose its processor while an interrupt is being handled (including the timer interrupt). But control will pass back

A. Strohmeier and D. Craeynest (Eds.): Ada-Europe 2001, LNCS 2043, pp. 328–336, 2001.

to the original task when the handler has completed - and this will occur even if a higher priority task has been released by the action of the handler.

The organisation of the paper is as follows. The next section gives an overview of the approach. Section 3 gives the Ada definitions, and section 4 reviews the appropriate scheduling theory. Conclusions are provided in section 5.

2 Basic Approach

In defining this new policy an attempt has been made to keep as close as possible to the pre-defined `Fifo_Within_Priority` policy. The ARM (D.2.1.9) allows an implementation to define "additional resources as execution resources". For non-preemptive dispatching we introduce a new type of resource: the *execution token*. In an implementation there will be a token per processor. Hence on a single processor system there will be just one execution token. A task must acquire a token before it can execute; it retains the token until it blocks or completes.

Priorities are still used to control dispatching. A task is selected for execution when there is a free execution token and the task is at the head of a non-empty ready queue (ARM, D.2.1.6). The existing task dispatching points still apply but the execution token is not released at these points (unless the task with the token is blocked).

One of the advantages of non-preemption is that, on a single processor, shared data does not require any form of lock to furnish mutual exclusion - provided the task does not block within the critical section. Ada defines the code within a protected object (PO) to be free of potential suspension. Hence POs remain the means of defining critical sections of code. However, no lock or priority ceiling protocol is needed around the action of the PO; the non-preemptive dispatching policy will ensure serialised access to the PO. Note that POs that act as interrupt handlers must be dealt with differently as interrupts can still occur asynchronously.

The major disadvantage with non-preemption is that it will usually (though not always) leads to reduced schedulability. For example, consider a low priority (long deadline) task with a long execution time. Once it starts executing, no high priority (short deadline) task will be able to even start its execution until the low priority task has finished. This is an example of excessive priority inversion. To reduce its impact the low priority task needs to periodically offer to be preempted. Within Ada the obvious way to do this is to execute 'delay 0.0' (or delay until 'yesterday'). This scheme is known as a *deferred preemption* or *co-operative scheduling*. In section 4 a way of testing the schedulability of task sets undertaking co-operative scheduling is described.

3 Definition of New Policies

The style of the ARM is used to introduce the new features.

3.1 Syntax

```
pragma Task_Dispatching_Policy (
    Non_Preemptive_Fifo_Within_Priorities);
pragma Locking_Policy (Non_Preemptive_Locking);
```

3.2   Post-compilation Rules

If the Non_Preemptive_Locking policy is specified for a partition then Non_ Pre-Emptive_Fifo_Within_Priorities shall also be specified for that partition.

3.3   Dynamic Semantics - for Synchronous Behaviour

Each processor has one execution token resource. A ready task must acquire the execution token before it can become the running task. When the Non_Pre-Emptive_Fi- Fo_Within_Priorities policy is in effect the modification to the ready queues are identical to the existing preemptive policy Fifo_Within_Priorities.

The running task releases the execution token whenever it becomes blocked (or completed). It also releases the execution token whenever it executes a delay statement (whether this results in blocking or not).

A new running task is selected and is assigned the execution token whenever the previously running task on that processor becomes blocked or otherwise releases the execution token. The rule for selecting the new running task follows the policy of Fifo_Within_ Priorities. On a multiprocessor system there may be further restrictions on where tasks may execute (as covered in ARM D.2.1.11).

The locking policy, Non_Preemptive_Locking is defined as follows:

- if the protected object contains either an Interrupt_Priority pragma, an Interrupt_Handler or Attach_Handler then the rules defined for locking policy Ceiling_Locking apply;
- if none of the above pragmas are present then, on a single processor, no run-time code need be generated to protect the object, in particular the priority of the calling task need not be changed;
- pragma Priority must not be present in any protected object.

NOTE:

1. The running task may release the execution token, by executing, 'delay 0.0'[1] but be reassigned it immediately if it is at the head of highest priority ready queue.
2. Implementation Permission 9.5.3 (22) still applies[2].
3. It remains a bounded error to call a potentially blocking operation from within a PO.
4. A task executing an accept statement on which there is an outstanding call, proceeds without releasing the execution token (either before or after the execution of the accept statement). Select statements are treated similarly.
5. A task calling an entry of a task releases the execution token even if the entry is open.
6. It remains implementation defined, on a multiprocessor, whether a task waiting for access to a protected agent keeps the processor busy (i.e. retains the execution token), see ARM (D.2.1.3).

---

[1] or delaying for a negative time interval, or delay until some time in the past
[2] This allows the code of a protected entry to be executed on the stack of another task (the one that has caused the blocked task to become runnable again).

3.4   Dynamic Semantics - for Asynchronous Behaviour

All of the above discussion has concern synchronous actions where the required behaviour of the non-preemptive policy is uncontroversial and relatively straight-forward to define. There are however other, asynchronous, situations where the choice of semantics is not as clear-cut:

- a task is being aborted.
- a task executing within a 'then abort' sequence.
- a task having its priority changed (using dynamic priorities)
- a task being 'held' using Asynchronous Task Control.

In this paper it is proposed that the first two should lead to 'immediate' preemption, whilst the later two should not. The rationale for these choices will now be given. Note that if the non-preemptive policy is being used with the Ravenscar Profile none of these issues would apply (as the language features are outside the profile).

If a programmer uses abort or select-then-abort then a conscious decision has been made to use a particular style of programming. This style accepts that code segments may be abandoned. The ARM, by defining abort-deferred regions, allows controlled abandonment to be programmed; but the intention is clear - control is asynchronously removed from the code segment. It is perfectly in keeping with the use of non-preemptive dispatching to view the completion of an aborted construct as an action that should take place as soon as possible - the construct is being abandoned not preempted.

In contrast, dynamic priority changes and the use of Asynchronous Task Control effect the 'progress' of a task but not its execution sequence. Hence it is reasonable for these constructs to have an 'immediate' impact on a task's base priority but for the execution token (if it is currently in use by the affected task) to be retained. This will reduce the effectiveness of these constructs but this is to be expected with a non-preemptive dispatching policy.

Having defined the semantics in these asynchronous situations it must be noted that on a single processor system the number of occasions during which they could occur is quite small. If there is only one execution token and task T has it, then no other task can possible execute abort T (for example). Actions from within interrupt handles (programmed as protected procedures) being one remaining means of asynchrony. The other is the use of a select-then-abort construct where the triggering action is either a delay statement or a protected entry call that is executed as a result of either an interrupt or the action of the task itself (e.g. a call to the triggering object from within the 'then abort' code). In these situations the 'then abort' code is completed but the task continues its execution at the point after the triggering call. From these considerations the definition of the non-preemptive dispatching policy is completed as follows.

- If a task holding an execution token is aborted it releases the execution token when it completes.
- If a task holding an execution token executes a select-then-abort construct, and the trigger occurs, then the aborted construct is completed following the rules of the ARM (D.6) but the token is retained.

- If a task holding an execution token is subject to a priority change (Set_Priority) or asynchronous control (Hold) then it retains the execution token.

The above definitions have centered on the notion of a processor and non-preemptive execution on that processor. In Ada terms, however, this is not the full story. Dispatching policies are set on a per-partition basis and it is possible for an implementation to put more than one partition on a processor. The ARM is silent about multi-partition scheduling, and there is clearly more than one way to schedule such a system:

- use 'priority' across all partitions on the same processor;
- assign overriding priorities to each partition;
- use priority dispatching within a partition and time-slicing between partitions.

The notion of 'non-preemption' is different in each case. But as Ada only allows the dispatching policy within a partition to be defined, no further refinement of the language model can be given. Hence it would be possible to have an execution token per processor or per partition.

4   Scheduling Analysis

In this section we show how response time analysis (RTA), which is usually applied to preemptive systems, can be applied to non-preemptive dispatching. There is insufficient space here to fully introduce schedulability analysis; this can be found in textbooks [6].

First some nomenclature - see Table 4 for the definition of the standard terms for priority based dispatching. The analysis process takes the following steps:

- assign priorities (P) to tasks;
- calculate the worst-case response times (R) for each task;
- check worst-case response times are all within the required deadlines $(R \le D)$.

Table 1. Standard notation

Notation	Description
B	Worst-case blocking time for the task
C	Worst-case computation time (WCET) of the task
D	Deadline of the task
P	Priority assigned to the task
R	Worst-case response time of the task
T	Minimum time between task releases (task period)

For a straightforward set of task attributes (e.g. all tasks having deadline less than period) an optimal priority ordering is obtained by undertaking Deadline Monotonic Priority Assignment which simply assigns high priorities to the tasks with the shortest deadlines: $(D_i < D_j \Rightarrow P_i > P_j)$.

The worst-case response times (R) is obtained from the following formulation[7]:

$$R_i = C_i + B_i + \sum_{j \in hp(i)} \left\lceil \frac{R_i}{T_j} \right\rceil C_j \qquad (1)$$

where $hp(i)$ is the set of higher-priority tasks (than i).

With preemptive scheduling the blocking factor (B) is the maximum time task i can be prevented from executing by the action of the priority ceiling protocol.

Although the formulation of the interference equation is exact, the actual amounts of interference is unknown as R_i is unknown (it is the value being calculated). Equation (1) has R_i on both sides, but is difficult to solve due to the ceiling functions. It is actually an example of a fixed-point equation. In general, there will be many values of R_i that form solutions to equation (1). The smallest such (positive) value of R_i represents the worst-case response time for the task. The simplest way of solving equation (1) is to form a recurrence relationship [3]:

$$w_i^{n+1} = C_i + B_i + \sum_{j \in hp(i)} \left\lceil \frac{w_i^n}{T_j} \right\rceil C_j \qquad (2)$$

The set of values $\{w_i^0, w_i^1, w_i^2, ..., w_i^n, ...\}$ is, clearly, monotonically non-decreasing. When $w_i^n = w_i^{n+1}$, the solution to the equation has been found. If $w_i^0 < R_i$ then w_i^n is the smallest solution and hence is the value required. If the equation does not have a solution then the w values will continue to rise (this will occur for a low priority task if the full set has a utilization greater than 100%). Once they get bigger than the task's period, D, it can be assumed that the task will not meet its deadline.

For non-preemptive scheduling the same formulation can be used (and the same solution strategy). The only term that changes is the blocking factor. With pure non-preemption, the maximum time a task can be prevented from making progress (other then by the action of higher priority tasks) is equal to the maximum computation time of any lower priority task:

$$B_i = \max_{k \in lp(i)} C_k \qquad (3)$$

where $lp(i)$ is the set of lower-priority tasks (than i).

If deferred preemption (cooperative scheduling) is used then the blocking factor is reduced to the longest non-preemptive section of code in all lower priority tasks.

To illustrate the application of this analysis consider the task set given in Table 4. In this table the response times are produced by equation (1) (i.e.

preemptive scheduling) assuming a blocking factor for 1 for tasks a, b and c (the lowest priority task never suffers blocking).

Table 2. Example task set - Preemptive Scheduling

Task	Period T	Deadline D	Computation Time, C	Priority P	Response Time, R
a	20	6	2	4	3
b	15	8	2	3	5
c	10	10	3	2	8
d	20	20	4	1	14

If pure non-preemption is used then the values in Table 4 apply. Note now that task c is unschedulable because of the large blocking induced by task d. However if task d has a preemption point inserted half way through then it will only induce a maximum blocking factor of 2 and the system becomes schedulable (see Table 4).

Table 3. Example task set - Non-Preemptive Scheduling

Task	Period T	Deadline D	Computation Time, C	Priority P	Response Time, R
a	20	6	2	4	6
b	15	8	2	3	8
c	10	10	3	2	F
d	20	20	4	1	14

Table 4. Example task set - Cooperative Scheduling

Task	Period T	Deadline D	Computation Time, C	Priority P	Response Time, R
a	20	6	2	4	4
b	15	8	2	3	6
c	10	10	3	2	9
d	20	20	4	1	14

Actually there is a further improvement that can be undertaken for non-preemptive scheduling. Consider the lowest priority task, d (with its preemption point after 2 ticks). Once it starts its final two ticks it cannot be preempted (even if a high priority task is released). Its worst-case response time for 2 ticks is 9. Its last 2 ticks are non-preemptive and hence its overall worst-case response time is 11. This value is better than the preemptive case and explains why non-preemption is sometime preferred even from a scheduling point of view.

The formulation for this latter case is as follows. Let F be the length of the final non-preemptive section of code. Equation (4) is solved for $(C_i - F_i)$:

$$R_i^* = C_i - F_i + B_i + \sum_{j \in hp(i)} \left\lceil \frac{R_i^*}{T_j} \right\rceil C_j \tag{4}$$

and then the final time interval is added back on:

$$R_i = R_i^* + F_i \tag{5}$$

5   Conclusion

A definition of non-preemptive scheduling has been given. This could be used with the full Ada tasking facilities or with a restricted subset such as Ravenscar. Non-preemptive execution can deduce schedulability if a low priority task has a long execution time. However, this can be countered by restricting the maximum length of any non-preemptive section of code. Thereby providing a simple means of increasing schedulability – the judicious introduction of delay statements.

The most restricted subset of language features comes from using non-preemption, the Ravenscar subset and by also disallowing application interrupts. Although this is a very static approach, it has a number of advantages over the conventional use of a cyclic executive.

Although any implementation is free to introduce new dispatching policies, the motivation for this paper is to define a standard scheme that could be incorporated in a future definition of the language.

References

1. A. Burns. Non-preemptive dispatching and locking policies. In M.G. Harbour, editor, *Proceedings of the 10th International Real-Time Ada Workshop*. ACM Ada Letters, 2001.
2. L. Asplund, B. Johnson, and K. Lundqvist. Session summary: The Ravenscar profile and implementation issues. In A. Burns, editor, *Proceedings of the 9th International Real-Time Ada Workshop*, volume XIX(2), pages 12–14. ACM Ada Letters, June 1999.
3. N. C. Audsley, A. Burns, M. Richardson, K. Tindell, and A. J. Wellings. Applying new scheduling theory to static priority pre-emptive scheduling. *Software Engineering Journal*, 8(5):284–292, 1993.
4. T. Baker and T. Vardanega. Session summary: Tasking profiles. In A.J. Wellings, editor, *Proceedings of the 8th International Real-Time Ada Workshop*, pages 5–7. ACM Ada Letters, 1997.
5. A. Burns and A.J. Welling. Restricted tasking models. In A.J. Wellings, editor, *Proceedings of the 8th International Real-Time Ada Workshop*, pages 27–32. ACM Ada Letters, 1997.

6. A. Burns and A. J. Wellings. *Real-Time Systems and Programming Languages.* Addison Wesley Longman, 3rd edition, 2001.

7. M. Joseph and P. Pandya. Finding response times in a real-time system. *BCS Computer Journal*, 29(5):390–395, 1986.

Modelling Communication Interfaces with ComiX

Frank Oppenheimer[1], Dongming Zhang[1], and Wolfgang Nebel[2]

[1] Carl v. Ossietzky University of Oldenburg, 26111 Oldenburg, Germany
[2] OFFIS, Escherweg 2, 26121 Oldenburg, Germany

Abstract. For the communication of hardware and software via memory mapped I/O e.g. in an embedded system, it is necessary to specify the communication registers in every detail. Since this work usually needs to be done for hardware and software independently, this work is time consuming, difficult, and error prone. This paper presents an approach to model hw/sw interfaces in an XML-based[8] interface description language called ComiX. We believe that an abstract and target language independent modelling technique based on ComiX can improve designers productivity and the systems reliability through reuse and automatically generated target code. Furthermore this paper describes a tool architecture to generate software device drivers and hardware I/O components automatically from a ComiX specification.

1 Introduction

Many embedded systems contain software components which react on sensor data by controlling actuators. Since sensors and actuators are located in hardware, the data from the sensors as well as the controlling values for the actuators need to be exchanged between hardware and software through device registers[1] as depicted in Fig.1. The task to model such hw/sw interfaces is in general time consuming, difficult, and error prone. The representation of data in the device registers must be exactly the same for both communicating partners. Thus the layout and representation of the data type must be determined unambiguously by the designer.

Very few research has been done in this area. Hovater presents in [4] an ASIS[6] based tool to generate documentation for existing Ada83 representation clauses. The approach presented in his paper analyses the code rather than generate it from an abstract specification. In contrast, our approach starts with an abstract interface specification and generates the target code or the documentation for the specification automatically. Standards like [10] or [9] also provide detailed formal methods to specify data types but with these methods the designer cannot specify the particular layout of device registers. While XDR and ASN.1 are able to specify communication using various protocols the method

---

[1] Control registers accessed through memory-mapped I/O

A. Strohmeier and D. Craeynest (Eds.): Ada-Europe 2001, LNCS 2043, pp. 337–348, 2001.

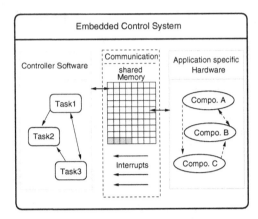

Fig. 1. HW/SW interface in an embedded system

presented here focuses a particular communication architecture based on memory mapped I/O and interrupts.

In Ada95 [1] representation clauses allow to specify the layout and location of data items in the memory. This specification must be very detailed to guarantee a deterministic layout. If the representation clauses leave any property undefined the compiler will generate a potentially undesired layout for the data item leading to severe communication problems. Automatically generated code can guarantee that all attributes are set to an appropriate value even if the designer does not specify them explicitly which can improve the safety of the interface.

The right side of Fig.2 shows a snapshot of the memory-mapped I/O area with a rather simple device register at the octal memory address 8#104# representing an integer with the range from 0 to 10000.

The left side of the figure illustrates the use of Ada95 representation clauses to determine the desired layout. The representation of types and data structures can be indicated by attributes like bitorder, size, alignment and address (lines 2,8,9,18). Lines 10-13 in our example determine the layout within a record. A bigger example will be presented in Sect.5.

In this paper we will introduce an interface description language (IDL) called COMIX (Communication Interfaces in XML) for the specification of hw/sw interfaces. From a COMIX description device drivers for the software and I/O components for the hardware can be generated automatically.

Since COMIX is not restricted to a particular target language it can be employed in various design flows (Sect.3). COMIX is the intermediate format between the code generator (Sect.4) providing the back-end for different output formats and the front-end. Possible front-ends can be as simple as an XML text editor or as elaborated as an interactive graphical tool producing COMIX.

We have chosen a XML based approach for COMIX for several reasons. XML seems to become an accepted standard for data description languages. It is less

```
type Speed_T is range 0..10000;
for Speed_T'bitorder use Low_Order_First;
type Speed_DR_T is
  record
     Speed : Speed_T;
  end record;

for Speed_DR_T'Alignment use 2;
for Speed_DR_T'Size use 14;
for Speed_DR_T use
  record
     Speed at 0 range 2..15;
  end record;
pragma Pack(Speed_DR_T);

Speed_DR : Speed_DR_T;
pragma Atomic(Speed_DR);
for Speed_DR'Address use To_Address(8#104#);
```

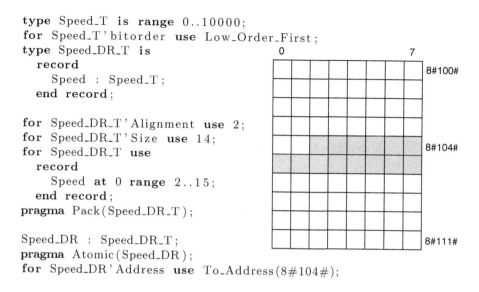

Fig. 2. Ada95 description of a device register

complex than similar languages like SGML and many tools for XML processing are available as open source. XML parsers generators like jaxp [7] make it easy to define, validate, and parse XML based languages. Since XML is a mark-up language like HTML, many web browsers and other tools are able to process XML. Thus generating documentation for interfaces specified in CoMiX can be done easily.

The remaining paper is organised as follows: in Sect.2 we introduce the CoMiX language in terms of syntax and semantics. Sect.4 describes the code generation concept. Section 3 presents perspectives for the application of CoMiX and how it could become part of an embedded system design flow. Section 5 gives an example of a small hw/sw interface modelled in CoMiX including the Ada95 code generated from the CoMiX specification. The paper ends with a conclusion and an outlook on further developments.

2   ComiX

In this section we will begin with a list of required features for an interface definition language like CoMiX. Then the structure of the language in its current state is presented. In the last paragraph we explain the approach for the code generation.

2.1   Requirements for ComiX

The main requirement CoMiX has to fulfil is to provide a universal intermediate format to describe hw/sw interfaces. Thus it was necessary to find an abstract format that neither depends on a particular input tool at the front end nor on a particular target language at the back-end.

An IDL like COMIX must enable the designer to specify the exact layout of the intended communication interface. This is especially necessary if the interface is already predefined by e.g. an off-the-shelf component [2]. On the other extreme if no off-the-shelf components are involved it should also be possible to neglect details in the description which can be determined by an intelligent code generator. In this case the consistency of the interface can be guaranteed because the code generator chooses the same alternatives for both sides of the communication.

As embedded systems become larger and more complex the interfaces modelling technique should be able to separate the description into several interface modules possibly organised in a hierarchy. The designer might want to reuse some interface components defined in previous designs. Thus the IDL should provide a simple to use library mechanism.

Flexibility is a big issue. With ongoing research it might be necessary to extend COMIX to cope with new requirements. For this aspect it is not enough to make changes to the language itself extend-able if every modification means to write a new code generator. Thus Sect.4 introduces a modular, template based concept for the code generation.

2.2   The Language Itself

Like all XML-based languages COMIX is specified by a document type definition (DTD)[3]. A reduced DTD for COMIX can be found in App.A.

A COMIX interface description consists of four major levels depicted in Fig.3. The first level describes the overall architecture of the interface, i.e. the size and organisation of the I/O memory area, the bit-order etc.. The environment level allows to include library components such as type definitions or predefined register-sets. This level enables the reuse of former work and the decomposition of complex designs. The third level defines the types and the related layout information (size, representation of enumeration literals,..) which can be used in the register-set definitions which form the fourth level of a COMIX document.

Well formed ComiX Descriptions. Only well formed COMIX descriptions can be used to generate working interfaces implementations. Syntactical correctness can be guaranteed by the XML parser which validates the document against its DTD. But well formed COMIX descriptions must fulfil many other requirements. We can not name all requirements here but the following list is to illustrate what is meant:

---

[2] Imagine an off the shelf hardware device providing a device register in a particular layout. In such situation the designer needs to describe the interface rather than design a new one.

[3] A DTD is like a grammar for a XML-document. It defines the allowed tags and attributes for the language.

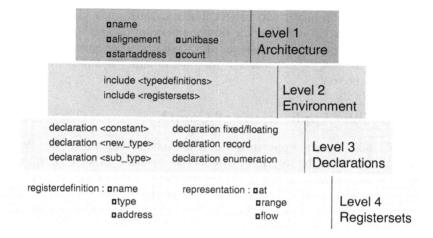

Fig. 3. Structure of a COMIX description

- The addresses for all registers must be in the allowed range given at architecture level.
- Registers may not overlap i.e. share the same memory space or violate the alignment.
- The size given for a type must be big enough to represent all values. For example the device register in the introductory example needs at least 15 bit.

One might argue that a compiler for the target language could check these requirements. Although this is true for Ada, compilers for other languages might not be able to do this. Even worse is that the error messages produced by the compiler are related to the target code but not to the COMIX document. Thus the designer needs to understand the target code and the way it was generated. Since this is obviously not intended we decided to check the well-formedness before the code generation automatically.

Default Patterns. We believe that in many embedded system design it is not necessary to specify the communication interface down to every single detail as long as both communication partners use the same representation for the data items. Thus we keep many components in the COMIX DTD optional. If the designers leave these aspects of the interface unspecified the code generation scheme can determine a reasonable value for it. This of course only makes sense when the designer does not need to meet the requirements of a predefined interface component. Only if the generator is able to define both communication sides it can be guaranteed that the interfaces works well.

For example one may want to put some registers into a particular memory mapped I/O area but the concrete addresses are arbitrary. The exact representation may not be important as well. The generator must only guarantee that both communication units use the same representation and the same addresses.

With this approach we hope to allow a much easier specification of device registers. The designer can now concentrate on the important properties and leave the rest to the tool.

3   Possible Applications of ComiX

COMIX offers various opportunities for its integration into design-flows. The simplest way would be to use a text-editor to create a COMIX interface specification. The designer can now generate the target code in e.g. Ada95 or VHDL and use the generated interface component in the further design-flow. Changes in the interface can be applied easily by changing the COMIX document and generation of the new interface.

This is exactly the way we are using COMIX in the OOCOSIM [3,5] design flow shown in Fig.4. In the OOCOSIM design flow we start from an extended HRT-HOOD specification which consists of software objects like in classical HRT-HOOD [2], hardware objects, and interface objects. From the interface objects we can easily generate a COMIX specification. The co-simulation environment in OOCOSIM allows to evaluate the entire specification. By synthesis and compilation for the hardware and software components we finally reach the implementation of a prototype embedded system.

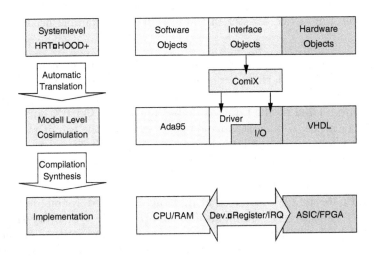

Fig. 4. ComiX in the OOCOSIM design flow

Other applications of COMIX could be to use it for the documentation of existing interfaces. One could use an ASIS based tool like presented in [4] and generate COMIX. Based on this COMIX specification it is easy to generate the documentation or to do re-engineering of the interface.

4   Code Generation with TempliX

COMIX was designed to describe interfaces independently of their later implementation. Nevertheless it is viable for a modelling method to fill the gap between specification and implementation or documentation.

We decided not to implement a fixed code generator for each target format but to use a template based approach. Thus we developed a meta language called TempliX (Templates in XML) and an abstract code generator applying the templates on COMIX documents. The abstract code generator can be seen as an abstract machine executing a TempliX program on a COMIX document (Fig.5). With TempliX we can define code generation schemes for different sections of the COMIX DTD. The code generation for a target language is defined by a set of templates.

We use different template sets for each target language or documentation format without changing the abstract code generator.

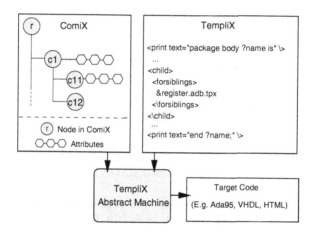

Fig. 5. Code generation with TempliX

TempliX is a simple XML-based language with commands and control structures for processing COMIX parse trees. These commands allow to traverse the COMIX documents, search for nodes, examine attributes or simply print the output.

5   Example

To demonstrate the COMIX method we will introduce a small example of a device driver for a temperature controlled heat sink. The software could periodically monitor the temperature of the heat sink and increase or decrease the fan speed appropriately. Since for this paper the hw/sw communication is the most important part, we will neglect the software tasks of the application and concentrate on the interface modelling. For the hw/sw-interface (Fig.6) we will use three device registers namely :

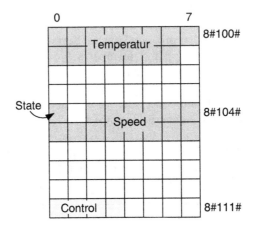

Fig. 6. HW/SW interface for a heat-sink

- Temperature : A fixedpoint register at address octal 100 with a range between -20.0 and +120.0 with an accuracy of 0.01.
- State_And_Speed : A register indicating the fan speed in a range of 0 to 10000 and the state of the power switch (ON/OFF). The register address is octal 104.
- Control : A register that represents four command states for the fan (TURN_ON, TURN_OFF, INCREASE, DECREASE in 'one-hot encoding'). This register has no predefined address thus the generator can determine it freely within the given address range.

The architecture level in the following COMIX specification allows an address range between octal 100 and 111 with alignment on the word borders. To keep the example simple we don't use the environment level here. The declaration level defines the types for the three registers mentioned above and the register set completes the specification with the definition of known addresses.

```
<?xml version="1.0"?> <!DOCTYPE ComiX SYSTEM "ComiX.dtd">
<ComiX name="FanControl">
<architecture name="FanControlArch" unitbase="8"
   alignment="word" count="10" startaddress="8#100#"/>
<declaration>
<enumeration name="State_T" size="1">
  <item name="OFF" use="2#0#"/>
  <item name="ON" use="2#1#"/>
</enumeration>
```

```
<enumeration name="Control_T"  size="4">
  <item name="TURN_OFF"  use="2#0001#"/>
  <item name="TURN_ON"   use="2#0010#"/>
  <item name="INCREASE"  use="2#0100#"/>
  <item name="DECREASE"  use="2#1000#"/>
</enumeration>
<fixed name="Temperatur_T" delta="0.01"
  range="-20..+120"  size="15"  small="1.0/128.0"/>
<newtype name="Speed_T" range="0..10000"/>
<record name="Temperatur_DR_T">
  <component name="Temperature"
    type="Temperature_T"  init="0.0">
    <representation at="0"  range="0..14"/>
  </component>
</record>
<record name="State_Speed_DR_T">
  <component name="State" type="State_T">
    <representation at="0"  range="0..0"/>
  </component>
  <component name="Speed"  type="Speed_T">
    <representation at="0"  range="2..15"/>
  </component>
<record name="Control_DR_T">
  <component name="Control"  type="Control_T">
    <representation at="0"  range="0..3"/>
  </component>
</record>
</declaration>
<registerset name="FanController">
  <register address="8#100#"
        type="Temperatur_DR_T"
        name="Temperatur_IF">
  </register>
  <register address="8#104#"
        type="State_Speed_DR_T"
        name="State_Speed_IF">
  </register>
  <register
        type="Control_DR_T"
        name="Control_IF">
  </register>
</registerset>
</CoMiX>
```

Example 1.1. CoMiX specification for the heat-sink interface

The generated code (in our example in Ada95) must provide an easy to use interface to the device registers. We decided to generate a package for the register set and a protected object for each device register which provides get and set routines to access the information stored in the register and its components. The following listing shows partially the output of our prototype code-generator.

```
package FanController is
  type Control_T is (SWITCH_ON, SWITCH_OFF, INCREASE, DECREASE);
  for Control_T use (SWITCH_ON=> 2#0001#, SWITCH_OFF=> 2#0010#,
```

```
                               INCREASE => 2#0100#,  DECREASE => 2#1000#);
   type State_T is (OFF, ON);
   for State_T use (OFF => 2#0#, ON => 2#1#);

   type Temperature_T is delta 0.01 range −20.0 .. 120.0;
   for Temperature_T'Size use 15;
   for Temperature_T'Small use 1.0/128.0;


   type Speed_T is new Integer range 0 .. 10000;

   protected Control_IF is
     procedure Set(value : Control_T);
   end Control ;

   protected State_Speed_IF is
     function Get_Speed return Speed_T;
     function Get_State return State_T;
   end State_And_Speed ;

   protected Temperature_IF is
     function Get return Temperature_T;
   end Temperature;
end FanControl;

package body FanControl is
  type Control_DR_T is
     record
        Control_Register : Control_T := SWITCH_OFF;
     end record;

   −− Representation clauses for Record Control_DR
   for Control_DR_T use
     record
        Control_Register at 0 range 0..3;
     end record;
   for Control_DR_T'Size use 4;
   for Control_DR_T'Bit_Order use System.Low_Order_First;
   Control_DR : Control_DR_T;
   pragma ATOMIC(Control_DR);
   for Control_DR'Address use To_Address(8#111#);

   −− Operations for Register Control_DR
   protected body Control_IF is
     procedure Set(value : Control_T) is
     begin
        Control_DR.Control_Register := value;
     end Set;
     ...
end FanControl;
```

Example 1.2. Device driver for the heat-sink interface

6   Conclusions

In this paper we presented a new approach for the modelling of hw/sw interfaces. We introduced the interface description language COMIX and a code generation mechanism to generate different target code from a COMIX specification. To illustrate the practical implications we have shown how our approach can be integrated into design-flows for embedded systems. Furthermore we have given a design example to describe the way designers could use COMIX.

In the future we are going to extend the set of supported target languages. While interface code generation for Ada95 is quite easy this might be more difficult for other languages such as C/C++ as this involves direct operating system calls and is thus not portable.

For the front end we are working on more comfortable user interfaces such as graphical specification methods. Since the current version of COMIX does not support the specification of interrupts for asynchronous communication, we will add this to COMIX in the very near future.

A   COMIX Syntax

```
<!ENTITY % UNITBASE    "8|16|32|64">
<!ENTITY % ALIGNMENT   "byte|word|longword|double|int64">
<!ENTITY % FLOW        "2sw|2hw|sh|hs">
<!ENTITY % PRAGMA      "volatile|atomic">

<!ELEMENT ComiX              ( architecture+, environment?,
                               declaration, registerset*)>
<!ATTLIST ComiX              name NMTOKEN #REQUIRED>

<!ELEMENT architecture       EMPTY>
<!ATTLIST architecture       name ID #REQUIRED
                             startaddress CDATA #REQUIRED
                             unitbase (%UNITBASE;) #REQUIRED
                             alignment (%ALIGNMENT;) #REQUIRED
                             bitorder #REQUIRED
                             count CDATA #IMPLIED>

<!ELEMENT environment        (include*, alias*)>
<!ELEMENT include            EMPTY>
<!ATTLIST include            name CDATA #REQUIRED>
<!ELEMENT alias              EMPTY>
<!ATTLIST alias              name ID #REQUIRED
                             value CDATA #REQUIRED>
<!ELEMENT declaration        (fixed|enumeration|record)+>

<!ELEMENT fixed              EMPTY>
<!ATTLIST fixed              name ID #REQUIRED
                             delta CDATA #REQUIRED
                             range CDATA #IMPLIED
                             size CDATA #IMPLIED
                             small CDATA #IMPLIED>
```

```
<!ELEMENT enumeration    (item)+>
<!ATTLIST enumeration    name ID #REQUIRED
                         size CDATA #IMPLIED>
<!ELEMENT item           EMPTY>
<!ATTLIST item           name ID #REQUIRED
                         use CDATA #IMPLIED>
<!ELEMENT record         (component)+>
<!ATTLIST record         name ID #REQUIRED
                         size CDATA #IMPLIED>
<!ELEMENT component      (representation)?>
<!ATTLIST component      name ID #REQUIRED
                         type IDREF #REQUIRED
                         init CDATA #IMPLIED>
<!ELEMENT representation EMPTY>
<!ATTLIST representation at CDATA #REQUIRED
                         range CDATA #REQUIRED>


<!ELEMENT registerset    (register)+>
<!ATTLIST registerset    name ID #REQUIRED>
<!ELEMENT register       (configuration*)>
<!ATTLIST register       name ID #REQUIRED
                         type IDREF #REQUIRED
                         size CDATA #IMPLIED
                         pragma (%PRAGMA;)#IMPLIED
                         address CDATA #IMPLIED>


<!ELEMENT configuration  EMPTY>
<!ATTLIST configuration  name IDREF #REQUIRED
                         at CDATA #REQUIRED
                         flow (%FLOW;)#REQUIRED
                         range CDATA #REQUIRED>
```

References

1. J. Barnes: *Programming in Ada95*. Addison-Wesley, 1995.
2. A. Burns, A. Wellings: *HRT-HOOD: A Structured Design Method for Hard Real-Time Ada Systems*. Elsevier, 1995.
3. G. Gorla, E. Moser, W. Nebel and E. Villar: *System Benchmarking on a Common Benchmark : Protal Crane cosimulation in Ada95/VHDL*. IEEE Design & Test of Computers. IEEE Computer Society, 2000.
4. S. Hovater, W. Marksteiner, A. Butturini: *Generation of Interface Design Description Using ASIS*. Proceedings of Reliable Software Technologies Ada-Europe 2000. pp.138-148. LNCS 1845, Springer-Verlag, 2000.
5. W. Nebel, F. Oppenheimer, G. Schumacher, L. Kabous, M. Radetzki and W. Putzke-Röming: *Object-Oriented Specification and Design of Embedded Hard Real-Time Systems*. Proceedings of the ICDA2000.
6. *Ada Semantic Interface Specification (ASIS)*; Int. Std. ISO/IEC 15291. 1999(E)
7. *Java Technology and XML*. http://java.sun.com/xml/
8. *Extensible Markup Language (XML) 1.0*. http://www.w3.org/TR/REC-xml
9. Oliver Dubuisson *ASN.1 - Communication between heterogeneous systems*. Morgan Kaufmann Publishers, 2000.
10. *XDR : External Data Representation standard*. RFC 1014, http://jandfield.com/rfcs/rfc1014.html, SUN Microsystems, Inc. 1987.

Safe Web Forms and XML Processing with Ada

Mário Amado Alves*

Faculdade de Ciências e Tecnologia da Universidade Nova de Lisboa
2815-114 Caparica, Portugal
maa@di.fct.unl.pt

Abstract. We present a method for the development of complex web services. The method was tested with a service case featuring user authentication, multiple forms, recorded data, and automated page creation. The method emphasises safety at two stages: development and execution. It comprises selected and created "open source" software components, notably Ada packages CGI by David Wheeler and XML_Parser by the author. The method is presented with examples from the real development case, and with incursions into the detail of selected aspects.

Keywords: web services development, Ada, CGI, XML, HTML

1 Introduction and General Issues

HTTP, CGI are the GOTOs of the 1990s. [2]

We present a method for the development of complex web services. The method was tested with a service case featuring:

- user authentication
- multiple forms
- recorded data
- automated page creation

The method emphasises safety at two stages: development and execution (meaning runtime execution of the service). The method comprises selected and created "open source" software tools and components: package CGI by David Wheeler (modified version included in [1]), package XML_Parser by the author [1], and *GNAT* by *GNU, NYU* and *ACT* (cf. adapower.com).

Here we use the words *method* and *safety* in a wide sense, viz. with *method* ranging from architecture to coding, and *safety* including effectiveness and efficiency both in development (cost safety) and execution.

In this paper the method is presented with examples from the real development case, and with incursions into the detail of selected aspects.

The method is continually evolving, due to both external technological change and internal planned increments. Some of these planned increments are also exposed in this paper, as a means of obtaining feedback from the reliable software development community.

---

* My research is supported by *PRAXIS XXI* and the *Fundação para a Ciência e a Tecnologia* (vd. Acknowledgements).

A. Strohmeier and D. Craeynest (Eds.): Ada-Europe 2001, LNCS 2043, pp. 349–358, 2001.

2   The Case

The most recent application of the method was in the implementation of an official inquiry to schools via Internet. This was in Portugal, in the year 2000. The purpose of the inquiry was to evaluate a recent reform in school administration.

The inquirer, and my client, was $CEESCOLA$[1], a state-funded research centre in education—henceforth simply the *Centre*.

The inquirees were 350 secondary schools and school-groups randomly chosen out of a nation-wide universe of 1472 such entities.

The service was required to be accessible only by the selected schools, so these were previously given, via surface mail, private access elements (identifier and password). A time window for answering the inquiry was fixed, and the system was required to make the answers available to the Centre as soon as they were submited.

The inquiry itself took the form of a number of long and complex questionnaires: each questionnaire had hundreds of questions, and the answer to certain questions determines the existence of other questions or their domain of possible answers.

Note that this case is very similar to electronic commerce services in complexity and safety issues.

3   The Method

The top level features of the method are:

- HTML
- CGI
- separation of HTML code (documents) and service logic (program)
- HTML extended internally
- documents prepared through XML transformations
- both the service logic and the transformations written in Ada
- session state maintained in the served pages
- a single meta-HTML unit
- a single service procedure

The separation of HTML code and service logic is a crucial design premise. Our rationale for this converges for the most part with that described in [2]. In order to attain separation, the stored pages are written in a slightly extended HTML, call it *meta-HTML*, which is transformed by the service, upon each request, into the served pages in standard HTML.

Also, *minimalized* HTML was preferred as a basis for meta-HTML, because minimalized HTML is more readable by humans than its non-minimalized counterpart or XHTML—and the ultimate reviewers of the meta-document are human.

---

[1] *Centro de Estudos da Escola* = Centre for School Studies, Faculty of Psychology and Education Sciences of the University of Lisbon.

Now, HTML, minimalized HTML, XHTML, and the designed meta-HTML are all subsumed by a slightly relaxed XML, notably one not requiring pairing end tags. This may seem nonsensical to XML formalist eyes and sound of heresy to XML purist ears, but in practice such a "dirty" version of XML is very convenient. With a *robust* XML processor one can easily control that one dirty aspect of not requiring pairing end tags. Package XML_Parser has such a robustness feature. The gains include:

- a single processing component for all dirty XML instances (HTML, minimalized HTML, meta-HTML, XHTML)
- increased readability of the input units
- an easy path to proper XML representations (not taken, but the current trend from HTML towards XML in the Web was a concern)

So, in this paper we take the liberty of calling simply *XML* to all that— and hence the pervasive use of the term and the inclusion of XML tools in the method.

XML processing happens at two stages: data preparation and service execution.

Data preparation. The questionnaires are created by client staff using WYSIWYG editors like Microsoft FrontPage and Word. Then these items are transformed into the final, static meta-HTML items. The major part of this transformation is automated, by means of Ada procedures utilizing package XML_Parser. The transformation consists of:
- rectify the messy HTML emited by Microsoft tools
- rectify and insert control elements and attributes
- structure the items into identified groups

Because the necessary ad hoc transformation programs are small (c. 1k lines), and the compiler is fast and easily installable on any site, Ada can also be used here, instead of the usual unsafe scripting languages.

Service execution. The pages are not served directly: they have a number of markers that must be replaced by the definitive values. This is done at runtime by the main service procedure, again utilizing XML_Parser. The rest of this section focuses on this.

Input values from one form are relayed onto the next as hidden input elements. This provides for:

- data communication between session points, or forms—this implements sessions
- general tests on input values to be run on any session point—this increases safety

All input values are relayed, so careful naming of input elements is required (in order to avoid collision). The localization of all forms in a single meta-unit promotes this.

The method evidently relies on the usual external pieces of web technology: an HTTP/CGI server and web browsers. The service was deployed with the Apache server running on a Linux system. Some problems were felt here, notably an access security hole: the service internal database files, in order to be accessible by the main procedure, had to be configured in such a way that they were also accessible by all local Linux system users! This problem is perhaps corrigible with the proper Apache settings; but this server's documentation is hardly comprehensible.

3.1   The Service Procedure

The service procedure is a non-reactive program, i.e. it terminates, as usual CGI procedures are. It is designed as the sequence of blocks sketched in Figure 1.

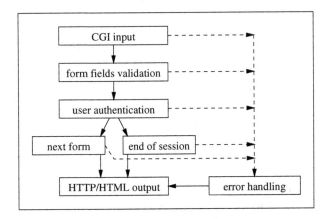

Fig. 1. Service procedure blocks

The computation is data-driven by form input values, meta-HTML markers, and system database files (users, passwords, etc.) The form input values and the files are totally case-dependent, so we focus on the meta-HTML markers, and dedicate the next section to them.

The exception handling is crucial. All errors are captured in a report page served to the user with a wealth of useful information, including instructions for error recovery, illustrated in Figure 2.[2] This happens even during development and testing, facilitating these tasks greatly.

---

[2] Original text on the left column; applicable aligned translation on the right. This parallel text scheme is used throughout the paper, because the original data have formal identifiers in Portuguese (sometimes in English, e.g. when they emanate from the compiler), and we wanted to ensure referential consistency between all data items shown in this paper and at its presentations (e.g. at the Ada-Europe 2001 conference, which featured code views).

Erro	Error
	There are errors in the filling out of the questionnaire, or in the submition acceptance system. The errors are described below. Go back (using the browser "back" button), correct the errors (if applicable), and resubmit. Upon persistent system error please contact us. Thank you.
Há erros de preenchimento do questionário, ou do sistema de recolha de respostas, abaixo indicados. Retroceda (com o botão de retrocesso do navegador), corrija os erros de preenchimento (se os houver), e ressubmeta. Perante erros de sistema persistentes é favor contactar-nos. Obrigado.	
ACEITAR_QUESTIONARIO.SITUACAO-_INDEFINIDA	*Accept questionnaire.undefined situation*
aceitar_questionario.adb:246	*Accept questionnaire*
Exception name: ACEITAR-_QUESTIONARIO.SITUACAO_INDEFINIDA	*... accept questionnaire.undefined situation*
Message: aceitar_questionario.adb:246	*... accept questionnaire*
Id_Respondente:A=ceescola	*Replier_Id:...*
_Continuar=Continuar	*Continue*
_Escolher_Kestionario=A. Questionário de descrição do processo	*Choose questionnaire=A. Process description questionnaire*
_Situacao_Requerida=	*Required situation=*
_Continuar=Continuar	*Continue*
_Seguinte:e=kestionario.htm	*Next:...*

Fig. 2. Example error page

4 Meta-HTML

This section describes the meta-HTML used in the example case. Other HTML extensions are possible. In fact this possibility is a major plus of the method: it provides applicability to a wide range of possible web services, through case-by-case adaptation of the meta-documentary language. It can even go beyond XML eventually, but that is another story.

4.1 Input Field Types

The names of the form/input fields are extended with a type suffix of the form :t, where t is a single letter as described in Table 1.

The upper case versions of t (I, A, E) additionally require a non-null value. The set is easily extended with more basic types, e.g. float and date. Type e (from the Portuguese word *especial* = special) requires a case-by-case treatment in the main procedure. The relevant section in the procedure is structured as

Table 1. Type suffixes

t	Description
i	integer
a	alphanumeric
e	subject to special verification

a **case** construct: any e type value falling back to the **others** case raises a `System_Error` (or something similar). This together with the proper test data set increases safety in the development stage.

4.2   Conditional Inclusion

Meta-element `if` provides conditional selection of parts of the meta-document to be included in the served page. The selected part is the enclosed content of this element. This is similar to the C preprocessor directive `#if`. The condition is expressed in the element attributes

$$\texttt{Name}_1 = |\,\texttt{Value}_{1_1}\,|\, \ldots \,|\,\texttt{Value}_{1_{m_1}}\,|$$
$$\vdots$$
$$\texttt{Name}_n = |\,\texttt{Value}_{n_1}\,|\, \ldots \,|\,\texttt{Value}_{n_{m_n}}\,|$$

which contain references to form/input element names and values. The set of attributes is a conjunction of disjunctions. The (positive) boolean value of the set determines inclusion of the element's content. Figure 3 shows an excerpt[3] of the example meta-document with heavy use of conditional inclusion, and Figure 4 shows the corresponding HTML result for a particular session.

Note the pervasive use of E suffixes in the meta-text: this was very helpful in assuring completness of treatment of all cases—and therefore the correctness of the service.

4.3   Session Control

A special hidden input element named `_Seguinte:e` (portuguese for *next*) specifies the next meta-HTML unit to be processed. This is non-trivial at the start of the session, when moving from an authentication form to the main set.

Also, the absence of this element may be used to signal to the main procedure that the session is in its final step, usually submission of the combined data of all forms.

A small number (circa 5) of other special elements were found necessary to control very specific aspects of the service. It was technically easy to implement them in the same vein, notably with the CGI and XML processing resources already available.

---

[3] The excerpt was slightly abridged in order to fit in the figure.

`<h2>`Situação da Escola/Agrupamento em 30 Abril 2000`</h2>`	*Status of the School/Group on the 30th April 2000*
`<if orgao:E="|CEI|CPN|not|">` Estava em regime de transição. `<p>`Órgão responsável pela gestão da Escola/Agrupamento: `</if>`	*body:... Was in transition regime.* `<p>` *Body in charge of the School/Group*
`<if orgao:E="|CEI|">` Comissão Executiva Instaladora. `</if>`	*body:... Executive instalation commitee.*
`<if orgao:E="|CPN|">` Comissão provisória nomeada pela DRE. `</if>`	*body:... Temporary comission appointed by the DRE.*
`<if orgao:E="|not|">` Órgão de gestão anterior à publicação do 115-A/98. `</if>`	*body:... Older body than reglement 115-A/98.*
`<if orgao:E="|CEI|CPN|not|">` `<p>`Fase do processo de instalação em que se encontrava: `</if>`	*body:... Instalation process phase the school was at:*
`<if orgao:E="|CEI|CPN|not|" fase="|notAC|">` ainda não tinha Assembleia Constituinte. `</if>`	*body:... phase=... No Constituting Assembly yet.*
`<if orgao:E="|CEI|CPN|not|" fase="|notRI|">` já tinha Assembleia Constituinte, mas não Regulamento Interno. `</if>`	*body:... phase=... Having Constituting Assembly, but no Internal Regulations.*
`<if orgao:E="|CEI|CPN|not|" fase="|notAE|">` já tinha Regulamento Interno, mas não Assembleia de Escola. `</if>`	*body:... phase=... Having Internal Regulations, but no School Assembly.*
`<if orgao:E="|CEI|CPN|not|" fase="|AE|">` já tinha Assembleia de Escola. `</if>`	*body:... phase=... Having School Assembly.*
`<p>`(Se estes dados estão incorrectos volte atrás e corrija.)	*If these data are not right go back and correct them.*

Fig. 3. Conditional inclusion example: meta-text

`<h2>`Situação da Escola/Agrupamento em 30 Abril 2000`</h2>`	*Status of the School/Group on the 30th April 2000*
Estava em regime de transição.	*Was in transition regime.*
`<p>`Órgão responsável pela gestão da Escola/Agrupamento: Comissão Executiva Instaladora.`</p>`	*Body in charge of the School/Group: Installation Executive Commitee.*
`<p>`Fase do processo de instalação em que se encontrava: ainda não tinha Assembleia Constituinte.`</p>`	*Instalation process phase the school was at: No Constituting Assembly yet.*
`<p>`(Se estes dados estão incorrectos volte atrás e corrija.)`</p>`	*If these data are not right go back and correct them.*

Fig. 4. Conditional inclusion example: after processing with `orgao:E=CEI` and `fase=notAC`

5   The Tools and Components

To see the next transactional "transfer" happen, ignore the XML (and SOAP) hype and *watch for actual* XML implementations. (Mike Radow, in [1])

A modified version of package CGI by David Wheeler served well as the CGI component. The modifications, done by myself, included:

- Elimination of auxiliary overloading which caused ambiguity problems to the GNAT compiler. I suspect GNAT's complaints were legitimate, language-wise; perhaps Wheeler used another, non-validated, compiler; or the problem was not detected until my use of the package.
- Redesign of the output format of procedure Put_Variables.

The modified version is now in [1]. Further modifications are planned and described there.

Package XML_Parser by myself, also in [1], was used to transform the HTML emited by the non-technical staff into extended HTML and then into the served HTML pages. Although XML_Parser served well as the (extended) HTML component of the current project case, it has severe limitations with respect to XML proper, noticeable in its documentation; it has also some design drawbacks, viz. the finite state device is entangled with the rest of the code.

To overcome this limitations, I have already developed a new XML processing package, XML_Automaton. This package properly encapsulates the finite state device. A new XML parser package, XML_Parser_2, will use XML_Automaton as its engine, in order to produce a more localized interpretation of the XML input. XML_Parser_2 is designed after XML_Parser with respect to the (internal) treatment of XML element containment, and I am trying to make the expression of this containment generic, probably with an array of packages drawing on XML-_Parser_2, each dedicated to a certain expression: an Ada linked list, Prolog facts, a DOM (Document Object Model, w3.org) structure, etc.

A rather specific but interesting point is the character-by-character vs. chunking way of processing XML input. XML elements may span over more than one text line. In chunk-based parsers, the chunk is normally the line. These parsers, especially if also based on character string pattern matching libraries, have a real problem here. XML_Automaton does not.

XML_Parser_2 design includes an unbounded array of stacks. Currently I am choosing between two basis for the implementation of this structure: GNAT.Table or Unbounded_Array. I am inclined to the latter because it is compiler-independent.

6   Evaluation and Some Remarks

The software metrics available for the example case are:

$$\begin{aligned}
\text{Cost} &= 0.5 \text{ programmer/month} \\
\text{Lines of code (Ada)} &= 1.0 \text{ k lines} \\
\text{Meta-document size} &= 1.5 \text{ k lines}
\end{aligned}$$

Note the cost. We are missing precise comparison data with other experiments, but our experience and intuition tells us that it is a very good number—given the degree of correctness attained in the final service; notably, no fatal defaults were found. I have worked also recently with a team developing a service similar to the example in intrinsic complexity but with much less form data, implemented with inter-calling PERL (www.perl.com/pub) scripts (essentially a *Great Ball of Mud*)—it required much more work and delivered much less correctness. The service is still plagued with detected bugs that no one rectifies anymore.

Why not use PHP3 (www.php.net)? Our reasons include:

– our method offers more control over the design and processing of the meta-language
– PHP3 documentation is incomprehensible

Why not use Mawl [2]?

– it is not extensible
– it seems to be very hard to achieve a working installation

I am particularly fond of the inevitable conclusion that Ada is a good choice for programming in the small. So, there is a real small software engineering after all, and it is not confined to the unadjusted Personal Software Process we read about [3]—but never practice.

Acknowledgements. I wish to thank my research advisor at *CENTRIA*[4], Doctor Gabriel Pereira Lopes. His correct envisionment of research in informatics as a rich network of diversified competences and interests has made possible the

---

[4] Centre for Artificial Intelligence, Universidade Nova de Lisboa.

degree of reusability seen here, notably of the XML tools which were firstly developed for our research projects in information retrieval and natural language processing.[5] I am also indebted to Professor João Barroso of *CEESCOLA* for providing such an interesting case of Internet usage as the one described here. Thanks to my colleagues Nuno Marques, Pablo Otero and Alexandre Agustini for useful remarks on an early version of the paper—and to the Ada-Europe 2001 anonymous reviewers, and especially to the final reviewer Dr. Michael Feldman, for their invaluable assistence in shaping it up. Thanks to my family, for letting our home be also a software house. And to Our Lord, for everything.

References

1. *Ad^{a}lib*: the software process and programming library [web site] / by Mário Amado Alves. — (http://lexis.di.fct.unl.pt/ADaLIB)
2. Mawl : A Domain-Specific Language for Form-Based Services / David L. Atkins ; Thomas Ball ; Glenn Bruns ; Kenneth Cox. — pp. 334-346 — //In: IEEE Transactions on Software Engineering, vol. 25, no. 3, May/June 1999
3. Results of applying the personal software process / P. Ferguson ; W. S. Humphrey ; S. Khajenoori ; S. Macke ; A. Matvya. — pp. 24-32 — //In: IEEE Computer, 30(5), 1997. — (description in [4])
4. Software Engineering : An Engineering Approach / James F. Peters ; Witold Pedrycz. — John Wiley & Sons, Inc. : New York, 2000. — xviii, 702 p.

---

[5] Projects *Corpora de Português Medieval*, *PGR*, *IGM*, and, in great part, my postgraduation scholarship *PRAXIS XXI/BM/20800/99*, granted by the *Fundação para a Ciência e a Tecnologia* of Portugal.

Mapping UML to Ada

Bill Taylor[1] and Einar W. Karlsen[2]

[1]Rational Software, 2 Portersbridge Mews, Romsey, SO51 8DJ, United Kingdom
btaylor@rational.com
[2]Rational Software, Keltring 15, 82041 Oberhaching, Germany
ekarlsen@rational.com

Abstract. The Unified Modeling Language (UML) is now the most common language for capturing the design of an object oriented system. Ada has all the features expected of an object oriented programming language. This paper describes how most of the features of UML readily map to Ada and many of the Ada features can be mapped to from UML. It also shows how an Ada package specification could be automatically generated from a UML model.

1   Introduction

This paper describes how a design captured in UML [BRJ99a, BRJ99b] can be mapped to Ada – that is Ada 95 [TD95]. UML is now the most common notation for capturing an object-oriented design. Ada, on the other hand, is a standardized programming language frequently used for developing safety critical applications.

Unlike most of the popular object oriented programming languages (including C++ and Java), Ada does not treat the class construct as a compilation unit. This accords a great deal of flexibility when mapping a UML class to Ada. The most useful mapping therefore is to map an Ada tagged type declared in the visible part of an Ada package. In addition, there are a number of useful Ada features that could not be mapped from UML directly, such as: subtypes, scalar types, array types, private types, limited types, record types, task types, protected types, discriminants, child packages, subunits, parameter modes, access parameters, representation clauses, generic parameters, and class-wide parameters.

In this paper we shall describe a mapping from UML to Ada that maps UML to a large subset of Ada. The mapping, currently implemented in Rational Rose/Ada [Rati98], is achieved by associating *code generation properties* with individual UML elements. In this way, a UML class can be mapped to any one of a number of Ada types. Similar, a UML operation may be mapped to an Ada procedure declaration, entry declaration or renaming declaration – as requested by the designer.

A major issue with the current mapping is that it has been designed with *tool support* and *automation* in mind. Many auxiliary operations, such as attribute access operations and memory allocation routines (create, copy, free), can therefore be generated automatically upon need. Moreover, it is feasible for package specifications to be automatically generated from a UML model. For full flexibility, the mapping utilises *preserve code sections* – annotated sections of the Ada program where

A. Strohmeier and D. Craeynest (Eds.): Ada-Europe 2001, LNCS 2043, pp. 359-370, 2001.

declarations and code fragments can be entered that has no counterpart in the model, in order to avoid cluttering up the design model with implementation details.

The remainder of this paper is structured as follows. The default mapping is described first. Then follow individual sections that show how UML components, classes, attributes, parameterized classes, inheritance links and finally association links are mapped to a large subset of Ada using code generation properties. The last section presents the conclusion and areas of future work.

2   Default Mapping of UML to Ada

The default mapping of UML features is as follows:
1. A UML class maps to a tagged type.
2. A UML package maps to a directory or folder.
3. A UML attribute maps to a record component.
4. A UML operation maps to a subprogram.
5. A UML association maps to a record component.
6. A UML class dependency maps to a "with clause".
7. A UML parameterized class maps to a generic package.
8. A UML specialisation relationship maps to a derived tagged type.

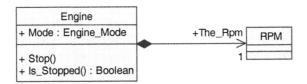

Fig. 1. UML Model of class Engine

By default, the class Engine in Figure 1 maps to the following Ada code:

```
with Rpm;
package Engine is

    type Object is tagged private;

    function Get_Mode (This : in Object) return Engine_Mode;

    procedure Set_Mode (This : in out Object;
                        Mode : in Engine_Mode);

    procedure Stop (This : in out Object);
    function Is_Stopped (This : in Object) return Boolean;

    function Get_The_Rpm (This :in Object) return Rpm.Object;
    procedure Set_The_Rpm (This : in out Object;
                           The_Rpm : in Rpm.Object);
```

```
private
   type Object is tagged
         record
               Mode : Engine_Mode;
               The_Rpm : Rpm.Object;
         end record;
end Engine;
```

A UML *class* is mapped to a type declared in an Ada package. By default, the class is mapped to a tagged type consisting of a private type declaration in the visible part followed by a full type declaration in the private part of the package to promote information hiding. Because the type name is unlikely to be used outside its defining package without also naming the package, the package is named after the class and "Object" is used as the type name.

The *operations* of the UML class such as Stop and IsStopped map naturally to primitive subprograms of the tagged type. Because in UML, the instance of the class on which the operation is to operate is implicit, this needs to be explicitly added to the Ada subprogram. The name "This" has been chosen for the parameter – the type would be "Object". UML allows the visibility of an operation to be specified as one of "Public", "Protected" or "Private". A public operation would be declared in the visible part of the package and a private operation in the private part. "Protected" has no obvious equivalent in Ada so would be treated as private. In Ada, a visibility of "Implementation" could be supported in which the operation only appeared in the package body.

The *attributes* of the UML class map naturally to record components of the tagged type. UML allows the visibility of an attribute to be specified as one of "Public", "Protected" or "Private". Because Ada can only support all record components being defined in the visible part of a package or all being defined in the private part, then either the type is fully defined in the visible part of the package or the type is fully defined in the private part of the package and assessor functions (Set and/or Get) provided to give access to the attributes designated "public". The latter will be the default mapping. The alternative of introducing an intermediate type to reflect a mixture of visibilities has not be adopted, because it is considered that allowing public access to attributes is not good software engineering practice.

If a class has an *association relationship* (including *aggregation* and *composition*), such as the relationship between the class Engine and the class RPM, this can be represented in a similar way to attributes, i.e. as record components. Special considerations would be multiplicity – whether there are at most one or more than one instance of the associated class for each instance of the class, navigability and containment.

In addition to the record components, *accessor operations* are provided for getting (Get_Mode, Get_The_Rpm) and setting (Set_Mode, Set_The_Rpm) the value of the associated attributes and roles. These subprograms are in turn given an implicit class parameter named This for representing the target of the operation. To avoid a runtime penalty compared to record selection, pragma Inline's could be provided. The major advantage of this code generation scheme is that *information hiding* is preserved.

Notice that it would be feasible using UML to represent the type Engine_Mode in terms of a UML class (see Figure 2). A UML dependency link is here used to specify the fact that class `Engine_Mode` is used by class `Engine`. When mapping this class diagram to Ada two questions must be answered: how to map the two classes to declarations of a single Ada package, and how to map the class `Engine_Mode` into an enumeration type. We shall deal with these issues in the next two sections.

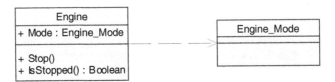

Fig. 2. Dependency links

3   Components

The mapping of UML components to Ada compilation units can be controlled using UML stereotypes. Using stereotypes, a UML component can be set up to map to an Ada package specification, package body, main program, subprogram specification, or subprogram body – as required. Ada additionally provides two important concepts for managing large and complicated systems: child packages and sub-units.

In general, dependency links between UML components are mapped to Ada *with clauses*. If the default mapping of a class to an Ada package of the same name is acceptable, a component diagram is superfluous. In cases where a more refined mapping of classes to components is necessary, component diagrams may be created and the relevant classes associated with the components as shown in Figure 3.

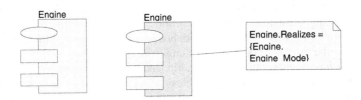

Fig. 3. Component diagram for Engine

Two `Engine` components are defined – one for the package specification and another for the package body. The two classes, `Engine` and `Engine_Mode`, must then be assigned to the component `Engine`[1], to indicate that a single Ada package realizes the class `Engine` as well as the class `Engine_Mode`. This is an alternative to adding the declaration for `Engine_Mode` in a preserve code section.

---

[1] Throughout his paper we will illustrate properties associated with a UML element using a UML note. Notice however that in reality these properties are not provided at the level of the UML diagram, rather they are associated with the UML elements in terms of meta-data.

A more explicit control of the mapping of classes to components is for example necessary in case of circular dependencies between two or more classes, in which case the classes need to be implemented by one and the same component. At the same time, private type declarations are conveniently used to introduce the names of all the involved types before the full type declarations appear.

4   Classes

A UML class can be mapped to an Ada construct in the following way:

☐ A regular UML class maps to an Ada type (by default a *tagged type*).
☐ A UML utility class maps to an Ada package that defines the attributes and operations of the class.
☐ A parameterized UML class maps to an Ada *generic package* or in special cases, to an *unconstrained type*.

In this section we shall focus on mapping classes to Ada types, and then deal with utility classes and parameterized classes later. In mapping a UML class to an Ada type, several properties become relevant:

☐ The TypeImplementation property controls whether a class is mapped to a tagged type (Tagged), a *record* type (Record), a *task* type (Task) or a *protected* type (Protected).
☐ The Type_Definition property is a general-purpose property for providing the type definition of an Ada type (i.e. a *subtype, derived, enumeration, numeric, array, access, private* and *incomplete* type).
☐ The IsLimited property is set to True in order to map a class to a *limited* type.
☐ The IsSubtype property is set to True in order to map a class to a *subtype*.

For example, to change the implementation of class Engine from a tagged to a limited record type, TypeImplementation for class Engine is simply set to Record and IsLimited to True. It is also possible to map the class Engine_Mode to an enumeration type (see Figure 4). For this purpose, the Type_Definition property is used, as well as two properties that are used to control the visibility of the corresponding declaration (TypeVisibility) and the name of the class (TypeName).

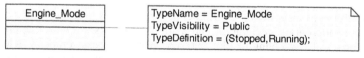

Fig. 4. Mapping of class Engine_Mode to a visible enumeration type

5 Attributes

By default a UML attribute is mapped to a *record component* of a tagged type. However, UML attributes can be mapped to other Ada declarations as follows:

- A static UML attribute maps to an Ada *object* declaration.
- A static attribute of "type" constant maps to an Ada *constant* declaration.
- A static attribute of "type" exception maps to an Ada *exception* declaration.
- An attribute where the property RecordFieldImplementation is set to Discriminant rather than Component maps to a *discriminant* declaration.
- An attribute where the property IsAliased is set to True maps to an *aliased* Ada record component.

```
                Engine_Aux
+ max_rpm : constant = 15000
+ engine_failure : exception
- no_of_engines : Natural = 0
```

Fig. 5. UML Attributes

Notice that all attributes of a UML class utility are treated as static declarations. This has the implication that the class Engine_Aux in Figure 5 maps to the following package:

```
package Engine_Aux is
   Max_Rpm : constant := 15000;
   Engine_Failure : exception;
private
   No_Of_Engines : Natural := 0;
end Engine_Aux;
```

Regarding visibility, a "Public" UML attribute will be mapped to a declaration in the visible part of the package, a "Private" or "Protected" UML attribute to the private part of the package, and a "Implementation" attribute to the body of the Ada package. Similar visibility rules apply to UML operations.

6 Operations

A straightforward mapping of UML operations to Ada is to represent the operation in terms of a subprogram declaration and a subprogram body. Other mappings may be enforced as well by changing the SubprogramImplementation property whose default value is Body. The property is also used to generate *abstract* operations (Abstract), *renaming* declarations (Renaming), *separate* units (Separate), as well as *imported* operations (Spec).

For renaming declarations the property is used in conjunction with the Renaming property, which specifies the name of the renamed operation. For imported subprograms, a Representation property is furthermore used to specify the representation, i.e. in terms of a suitable pragma Import. Special mappings may in turn be provided for task and protected types: for a class that maps to a task (or protected) type, the class operation can naturally be mapped to an entry declaration of the type.

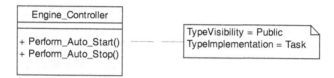

Fig. 6. Task type with associated entry declarations

For example, the UML class in Figure 6 maps to the following Ada code:

```
package Engine_Controller is
    task type Object is
        entry Perform_Auto_Start;
        entry Perform_Auto_Stop;
    end Object;
    procedure Perform_Auto_Start (This : in out Object);
    procedure Perform_Auto_Stop (This : in out Object);
end Engine_Controller;
```

The procedures `Perform_Auto_Start` and `Perform_Auto_Stop` are here defined in the package body and call the corresponding task entries.

A major advantage of using a tool based mapping from UML to Ada is that the tool, combined with suitable properties, can be set up to generate a number of useful utility subprograms such as:

☐ Accessor operations providing access to the attributes of the class.
☐ Standard operations such as a constructor (`Initialize`), copy constructor (`Adjust`) and destructor (`Finalize`) for controlled as well as uncontrolled types.
☐ Relational operations such as equality and inequality.

7 Parameterized Classes

A parameterized UML class maps to an Ada *generic declaration* or an *unconstrained type declaration*, depending on whether the value of the Parameterized property is set to Unconstrained or Generic (default). Conversely, a UML class instance maps to an Ada *generic instantiation* or a constrained Ada type, provided that a dependency/use link exists between the generic (target) and the instance (source). The generic formal and actual parameters are simply treated as strings and need in principle no further consideration.

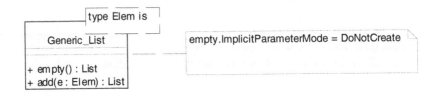

Fig. 7. Parameterized class

According to these simple rules, the class diagram in Figure 7 will map to the following Ada declarations:

```
generic
    type Elem is private;
package Generic_List is
    type Object is tagged private;

    function Empty return Object;
    function Add (This : in Object; E : Elem) return Object;
end Generic_List;
```

Notice that the operation property ImplicitParameterMode has been set to DoNotCreate in order to ensure that the operation empty does not get an implicit "This" parameter of type `Generic_List.Object`.

8   Inheritance Links

Inheritance (or specialization) is one of the key concepts of OO languages and allows one subclass to inherit, extend and overwrite the properties of one or more superclasses. The UML inheritance relationship may map to Ada in several ways. We shall demonstrate the mapping in terms of a specialization of the `Engine` class called `Aero_Engine` with an additional Boolean attribute named `Is_Turbo` (see Figure 8).

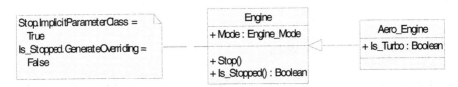

Fig. 8. Inheritance Link

A natural presentation of (public) inheritance would be to represent both the superclass and subclass in terms of Ada tagged types where the additional attributes of the subclass are defined in terms of a record extension. A mapping of the class `Aero_Engine` using this mapping scheme will look like:

```
with Engine;
package Aero_Engine is
    type Object is new Engine.Object with private;

    function Get_Is_Turbo (This : in Object) return Boolean;
    procedure Set_Is_Turbo (This : in out Object;
                                Is_Turbo : in Boolean);
    procedure Stop (This : in out Object);
private
    type Object is new Engine.Object with
        record
            Is_Turbo : Boolean;
        end record;
end Aero_Engine;
```

Similar to class `Engine`, the class `Aero_Engine` maps to a package specification with a private type declaration in the visible part named `Object` that extends `Engine.Object`. Visibility of the base type is achieved by a *with* clause. The full type declaration follows in the private part and contains a record extension that defines the attribute `Is_Turbo`. Associated accessor operations for the attribute(s) of the subclass are furthermore generated in the visible part.

Inherited operation of the superclass can be overwritten with local declarations of the subclass, provided that the property GenerateOverriding is set to True (default). For these operations, such as `Stop`, default definitions can be provided in the package body:

```
procedure Stop (This : in out Object) is
begin
    --##begin Aero_Engine.Stop.statements preserve=no
    Engine.Stop (This => Engine.Object (This));
    --##end    Aero_Engine.Stop.statements
end Stop;
```

Additional properties can then in turn be used to specify the type of the implicit "This" parameter. This way, it becomes possible to turn the `Stop` operation into class wide operations by setting the property ImplicitParameterClassWide to True. Furthermore, it is possible using properties to specify whether an operation should be overwritten or not for any of the subclasses. This has been turned off for `Is_Stopped`.

Safety critical applications may prohibit the use of tagged types since they allow dynamic binding/dispatching. For such applications, the superclass can be represented as a record type with a variant part defining the additional attributes for all the subclasses in the inheritance hierarchy. The subclasses are in turn mapped to derived type declarations with a constraint that defines the actual value of the discriminant. This requires that both classes have TypeImplementation set to Record and that the visibility of `Aero_Engine` is set to Public (see Figure 9).

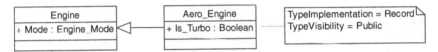

Fig. 9. Mapping Inheritance Hierarchy to a Single Record Type

In this case the Engine class maps to the following Ada code:

```
package Engine is
    type Engine_Kinds is (A_Engine, A_Aero_Engine);
    type Object (Kind : Engine_Kinds := A_Engine) is private;
    ...
private
    type Object (Kind : Engine_Kinds := A_Engine) is
        record
            Mode : Engine_Mode;
            case Kind is
                when A_Aero_Engine => Is_Turbo : Boolean;
                when others => null;
            end case;
        end record;
end Engine;
```

The enumeration type Engine_Kinds serves as a discriminator for all objects in the inheritance hierarchy, i.e. for objects of class Engine and Aero_Engine. The Engine.Object type uses this discriminant named Kind to define the variant part for each subclass. The subclass is then itself represented by a derived type declaration that constraints the value of the discriminant:

```
with Engine;
package Aero_Engine is
    type Object is new Engine.Object (Engine.A_Aero_Engine);
    ...
end Aero_Engine;
```

The two examples given show a limited set of the possibilities that exist in mapping UML inheritance to Ada. The second alternative avoids the use of tagged types. However, additional schemes have been provided for representing multiple inheritance (via mix-ins) and private inheritance in Ada.

9   Association Links

UML provide association relationships between two or more classes. For such relationships, the mapping to Ada is highly dependent on the properties of the individual roles of the association link, i.e. the *multiplicity* of the roles, whether the roles are *navigable* or not and whether the roles have by-value or by-reference *containment*. One simple example of a UML association relationship and its associated mapping to Ada has already been given in Figure 1 in terms of a unidirectional composition relationship with multiplicity one-to-one. Such a relationship maps quite naturally to a record component and is in fact very similar to an attribute declaration with an associated dependency link giving visibility to the contained class.

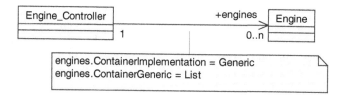

Fig. 10. Uni-directional Association Link

The mapping of more complicated association relationships is considered next in Figure 10. The association link is only navigable in one direction, namely from class `Engine_Controller` to class `Engine`. However, the given multiplicity of the link implies that an `Engine_Controller` may have zero or more associated `Engine`'s and that containment of the link is by reference rather than by value. This implies in turn that the references to objects of class `Engine` must be provided in terms of Ada access types. For this purpose, it makes sense to automatically map the class `Engine` to a tagged type declaration followed by an associated access type declaration (by default the type name `Handle` is used)

```
type Object is tagged private;
type Handle is access Object'Class;
```

Notice that a tool would be able to provide these associated handle types. The next question however is to provide an Ada mapping of the container needed to hold the handles. A default mapping would be to use an Ada array type, but in principle any container type may do the trick such as for example a list. Such a mapping can be achieved by setting the properties as shown in Figure 10. The following Ada code is then produced for class `Engine_Controller`:

```
with Engine;
with List_Generic;
package Engine_Controller is
    type Object is tagged private;

    package Engine_Handle_List is
       new List_Generic (Engine.Handle);

    function Get_Engines (This : in Object)
        return Engine_Handle_List.List;
    procedure Set_Engines (This : in out Object;
                            Engines : in Engine_Handle_List.List);
private
    type Object is tagged
        record
            Engines : Engine_Handle_List.List;
        end record;
end Engine_Controller;
```

An instantiation of the generic list container is provided first (including the with clause giving visibility to the generic). The referenced engines are then in turn provided as a record component of the instantiated list type. To provide access to this attribute, appropriate accessor operations are provided.

When an association link is navigable in both directions, both classes are preferable mapped to one and the same component. In this case, access types are usually provided for both types, unless of course, one of the roles has by-value containment.

10 Conclusion and Future Work

This paper has shown how UML maps to Ada and that most features of Ada can be mapped to from UML. It has also been demonstrated how such a mapping could be automated.

The current mapping scheme, based on attaching code generation properties to each UML element, can cover a large number of the declarative subset of Ada. This paper only touches upon some of the many possibilities. Moreover, the paper does not provide a complete mapping of all of UML to Ada. For example, the mapping of interface classes and realization relationships to Ada is left for future work.

References

[BRJ99a] G. Booch, J. Rumbaugh, I. Jacobsen: *The Unified Modeling Language User Guide*, Addison Wesley, 1999.

[BRJ99b] G. Booch, J. Rumbaugh, I. Jacobsen: *The Unified Modeling Language Reference Manual*, Addison Wesley, 1999.

[Rati98]   Rational Software: *Rational Rose Forward and Reverse Engineering with Ada95*, Cupertino, 1998.

[TD95]   S. Tucker Taft, R. A. Duff (editors): *Ada95 Reference Manual, Language and Standard Libraries*, International Standards ISO/IEC 8652:1995(E), LNCS 1241, Springer Verlag, 1995.

Ship System 2000, a Stable Architecture under Continuous Evolution

Björn Källberg[1] and Rei Stråhle[2]

[1]SaabTech Systems AB
SE-175 88 Järfälla
Sweden
bjkae@systems.saab.se

[2]SaabTech Systems AB
S:t Olofsgatan 9 A
SE-753 21 Uppsala
Sweden
rest@systems.saab.se

Abstract. Ship System2000 was conceived in the middle of the 1980s. It was started as a development project for a general Command and Control and Weapon Control Systems for naval ships (C2 and WCS), intended for reuse. Its first use was for three different ship types. Following these orders, later deliveries with similar functionality were made. From the beginning the company chose to use the Ada language for future systems in this area and selected Rational for the first compiler, editor and programming environment. A strategic decision was made to include all the Ada components developed in a family of reusable components. The number of components has grown and variants for different platforms and compilers have been included. In the early days the word was *Reuse*, and later the terms *Dual Life Cycle* and *Product Line Management* have been introduced for the same concept. Since then, the 1st generation has been successfully reused for ships from many other navies and air forces. However, the architecture has evolved in two major steps, and several minor steps. Thus, it is still a modern architecture, but with a heritage.

1   System Design

The system is a distributed system, where typically 20 nodes are connected using a double Local Area Network (LAN), for redundancy reasons. Each node is a single or multi-CPU node. In principle there is one node for each sensor, weapon and operator.

From the start, we tried to use as much commercially available equipment and software as possible. The first generation used M68K series computers, and the Ethernet LAN was based on the ISO standard (i.e. not IP). At that time, (the end of 1980s,) the coming dominance of IP was not easy to foresee. The operating system was OS9, which is mostly used for industrial automation purposes. The networking system was mostly custom made by us.

A. Strohmeier and D. Craeynest (Eds.): Ada-Europe 2001, LNCS 2043, pp. 371-379, 2001.

The latest version is based on Windows NT on the Intel architecture, using IP on top of FDDI (a 100 MHz fibre network, with standardised redundancy and excellent fallover characteristics, especially compared to Ethernet).

Software-wise, the system consists of some hundred different software components, CSCs. Each component typically consists of many Ada packages, with ten to a hundred thousand lines of code. All of the application components are written in Ada, but a number of the lower level components are written in C.

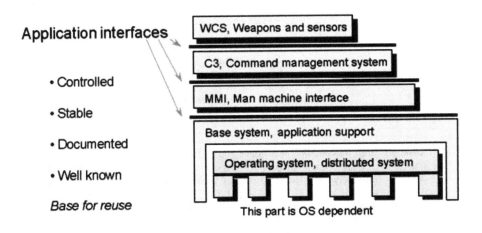

Fig. 1. Layered structure

The components are organised in a layered structure, which hides the operating system and other implementation issues from the application programmer. The reuse degree between different systems is very high, typically 80-90%. In the base system and application support, the reuse is 100%, but in the higher, more application-oriented layers the reuse is lower. As an example, if a system has a new type of radar that has not been used previously, a completely new component is written for that sensor.

The unit of distribution is an Ada program. Each program consists of many CSCs, linked together. The programs send messages to each other over the LAN.

The fundamental design decision of the components is that all interfaces are software interfaces, defined by Ada packages. Thus, the actual format of a message transmitted over the LAN is completely hidden within one component. It is never the case that a message is transmitted by one component and received by another component. Instead, those components essentially consist of two parts, a client package that is linked together with other components, and a server side, which receives the data transmitted by the client package. See fig 2 below.

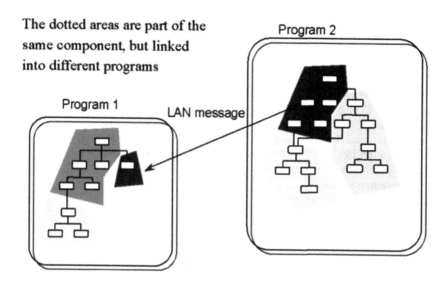

The dotted areas are part of the same component, but linked into different programs

Program 2

Program 1

LAN message

Fig. 2. Ada program structure

2   Application Interface Standard

A number of guideline documents for writing applications was developed very early in the development of the base system. This set of instructions defines the fundamental rules for a component. A component must follow these rules to be integrated and work within the architectural rules of the system.

The fundamental areas covered are the following:
- **System Start and Redundancy.** The system will automatically reconfigure in case of problems. This requires special uniform start up and shut down procedures.
- **Error Handling Principles.** Naturally, error handling is performed uniformly over the system.
- **Overload Behaviour.** Programs shall be designed to minimize effects of overload and always cause a graceful degradation.
- **Parameterisation.** Rules the process of parameterisation of software in the system.
- **Inter-Program Communication.** Principles for communication between programs.
- **Man-Machine Interface (MMI).** All communication with the operator is done using a special subsystem that isolates the program from the actual I/O.
- **Task Priorities.** How to set priorities. Essentially we use the Rate Monotonic Scheduling algorithm.
- **Input and Output.** Input and output to devices that are not MMI devices.
- **Time.** How time is implemented. This chapter was specially included to handle monotonic time in Ada83.
- **Operating Modes, System and Local.** Used to handle different modes, i.e. simulation and live.

3   Education / Training

Very early on it was clear that education in the principles of writing code for the base system was needed. Also training in selecting from the existing components and their proper use was defined.

Since 1991 there have been 15 formal training workshops, including about 12 – 15 students each. Typical length of such a workshop is some 7 – 10 days with a mixture of both lectures and programming. Some basic concepts like the inter-program communication and the error handling principles are included, as well as areas closer to the application like coordinate conversions and track distribution.

The following topics are normally covered:

- Base system overview
- Inter program communication
- Error handling principles
- Program start and stop
- Base types and coordinate conversions
- Track distribution
- System parameters
- Man-machine interface

4   Ada95 Transition

When the Ada95 standard was released, some worries arose in the company that the existing code, written in ANSI Ada83 / ISO Ada87 over 10 years by a great number of different programmers, needed to be modified to a large extent in order to conform to the new standard. A first conversion was made with a relatively small system, some 700k lines of code.

The results of this first conversion were very promising:

- Of the 6 new keywords, only one was used in 1 place.
- The transition to 8-bit character set required changes in 3 places, where an "array of character" was used.
- New type Wide_Character made concatenation of string literals ambiguous in 10 places.
- Generic parameters can in Ada95 not be instantiated with unlimited types, unless a specific syntax is used. This required changes in 4 places.
- Changed attributes for Float, 10 changes.

In the following cases deviations from the company programming standards were detected and the code was in some sense unsafe or erroneous which was detected by the Ada95-compiler.

- In Ada95 the parameters for the pragma are checked and are in some sense valid. This was found to be erroneous in 6 places.
- The fact that Numeric_Error and Constraint_Error are the same in Ada95 required changes in 3 places.
- In Ada95 it can be determined by the package specification if a package body is required or not, it is never optional. That required changes in 20 places.

Hence a total of 60 changes were required. Since the code in the study encompassed 735 846 lines of Ada source code (comments not included), it can be estimated that the backward compatibility is 99,99%. In Ada95 there is a standardised pragma Interface, which differed between the compilers earlier used in the company. If this had been utilised, changes would have been required at about 100 more places.

It is now an accepted fact that we use Ada95 compilers to develop our systems with a minimum of local design rules and rely heavily on the Ada95 Quality and Style.

5   Unexpected Experiences

In this chapter some difficulties (actually both expected and unexpected) are highlighted.

5.1   Documentation

During development we followed a typical military development model, which requires thorough documentation for each component and subsystem.
We had hoped to be able to reuse almost all of the documentation between the different projects. However, this was not possible to the extent we had hoped. The reason was security problems. The requirement specifications for each system is of course classified, although they mostly contain similar requirements. The problem is shown by the following example:

Assume customer A has the requirement that 800 tracks shall be presented every second, but customer B requires 1500 tracks per second. The requirement for the reusable component must then be that it shall handle 1500 tracks per second. This is written in the SRS, Software requirement specification for the component. However, this SRS can not be shown to customer A, because he then can deduce the secret requirement of customer B. Thus, different SRS had to be produced for the same component.

Similar problems occurred for other documents, but at least some could be reused.

5.2   Dead Code

The customer does not necessarily see reuse of code as an advantage. The following disadvantages can be seen. Reuse almost always means, that a general component is used, which does not exactly match the specific customer need. As customers have specific requirements, it means that a component that shall handle requirements from multiple customers must be the union of all requirements. Thus, the component will contain code that does not correspond to the requirement for that specific customer. This code can occur in many forms, with different forms of disadvantages:

- Extra functionality which can be used. This makes the system larger, more difficult to learn for the operators. Of course, in some cases this may also be an advantage, the customer gets useful extra functionality for free.

- Executing code with functionality that can not be used due to absence of accompanying MMI. Uses system resources.
- Code that is loaded, but will not be executed - uses memory.
- Code that is not loaded, but is part of the total system anyway - uses disk space.

As the code is larger than strictly necessary, maintenance, if done by the customer, will be more difficult.

Against this we have the advantages of reuse:

5.3   Complexity

An important part of the system design process is to divide the components in such a way that the union of the requirements is not too much different from the requirements from the individual customer. If this is not successful, the complexity of the system will grow beyond control.

Assume we have three different systems, each consisting of 4 CSCs. The requirements for each CSC, and the complexity for the CSC, had it been made specifically for that project, varies according to the table below. Assume further, that the complexity of the system is the product of the complexity of the individual components.

In the simple system below, the complexity of the reusable system is than 25 times as complex as the most complex delivered system. Obviously this is not a good component design.

Table 1. Complexity for individual projects, compared to system complexity

	Project A	Project B	Project C	Reusable system
CSC 1	1	7	8	8
CSC 2	4	10	2	10
CSC 3	5	1	9	9
CSC 4	10	1	2	10
Total complexity	200	70	288	7200

Thus, a component must not be too general. If the requirements are very diversified, it is better to make a new, simple component for that specific case.

We have used both ways, both general components, where the functional adaptation was made by setting parameters controlling the behaviour of the component, and having different components. Early in the development program, we could probably have benefited by separating more components.

Our reuse effort has been successful. One of the reasons probably is that the application domain is clearly defined, and limited. For larger, more general domains, the complexity problems will be more difficult, or even impossible, to handle.

6   Portability

The system has been ported to many different environments, operating systems, and Ada compilers. The latest is the port to Windows NT.

The transfer of code to a new compiler is always difficult. We use a rather complicated structure of nested generics. Thus, no compiler has ever compiled our code the first time, it has always required some bug fixes to the compiler.

Porting to a new operating system is relatively straightforward, due to the layered structure of the system.

7   Porting to Windows NT

Porting to a new windowing system was a more exciting challenge. In the older system, we used a proprietary windowing system, with a limited number of windows. The challenge was to port this to Windows NT, and getting the look and feel of a modern windowing system. This was possible due to the MMI structure of our system. The application programs never directly access the MMI, but read and write all MMI data to a real time database. There are then different MMI programs, that also reads and writes from the same database. In this way, the applications are completely decoupled from the actual layout and implementation of the MMI, see fig 3 below.

In the first generation, all general MMI programs were proprietary, written in Ada. In the NT version, about 50% of the Ada programs are kept, in modified version. These modified Ada programs now send messages to Visual C++ programs, which handle the direct operation with the operator. In this way, most of the application logic is still kept in Ada, but we can utilise the power of the GUI tools that come with Visual C++. All application programs are unmodified.

8   Evolution

Looking back at more than 15 years of development in this product line, a number of important evolutionary steps can be recognised. The first major step was a conversion to Unix, IBM AIX, and a different application domain, an intercept control system for the Swedish Air force. It also includes a large simulator for the same system.

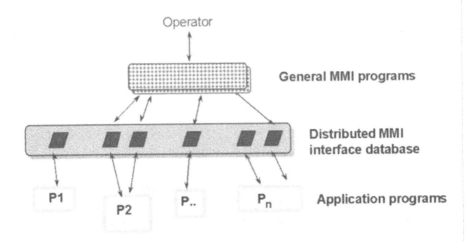

Fig. 3. MMI architecture

The second major step is a sibling to the first, and involves a conversion to Windows NT. Some of the architectural aspects that have made this continuous evolution possible are:

- Layered structure
- Fine grained structure, not monolithic
- Openness to other architectures, both hardware and software
- Location independency
- Asynchronous messages
- Parameterised components
- MMI definition language
- COTS Operating system
- Ada

The different steps have not only involved a change of operating system, but also other major changes such as:

- Use of commercially available windowing system (X-windows and Windows NT) instead of proprietary systems
- Change of network protocol
- Replacement of custom made bit slice boards with general purpose computers
- Porting between different Ada compilers
- Coexistence of different languages (Ada for the applications, C and C++ for lower level functions and window handling)

The majority of the application components are unaffected by these changes. The components have however been maintained and upgraded over the years, by many different programmers. We attribute this to a large degree to the use of Ada.

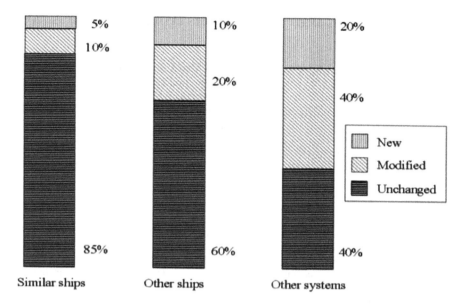

Fig. 4. Degree of reuse

9   Conclusions

Some of the experiences we have drawn from the continuous development are that reuse is not easy to accomplish. This architecture has been able to evolve with different requirements, different platforms and different people over a time period of more than 15 years. We attribute a large degree of the success to the fact that we chose to use the Ada language from the very beginning.

There is however a great need to use different ways to control the increase in complexity that can be introduced by too general components, and perhaps the most important factor is that reuse should be applied to a limited application domain.

Documentation can not be underestimated. It must be complete and relevant in order to bridge the information gap between the developer and the user of a component. And often many years have passed from the time of development until the reuse.

Remember that reuse is not necessarily seen as an advantage by the customers, but can still be very successful, if applied with a large degree of skill through the analysis, design and coding phases.

Reference

Bass, Len; Clements, Paul; Kazman, Rick: "Software Architecture in Practice", Addison & Wesley, 1998.

Migrating Large Applications from Ada83 to Ada95

Philippe Waroquiers, Stef Van Vlierberghe,
Dirk Craeynest, Andrew Hately, and Erik Duvinage

Eurocontrol/CFMU, Development Division
Rue de la Fusée, 96,
B-1130 Brussels, Belgium
{philippe.waroquiers, stef.van-vlierberghe, dirk.craeynest,
andrew.hately, erik.duvinage}@eurocontrol.be

Abstract. The CFMU has developed mission critical applications for Europe-wide flight plan processing and air traffic management activities using Ada83. This paper presents the techniques and tools used for the migration from an Ada83 to an Ada95 compiler and run-time. It puts a particular emphasis on both the software management aspects and the technical aspects e.g. language aspects, run-time evolution, how to cater for incompatibilities between Ada83 and Ada95, elaboration order, etc...

1 Introduction

EUROCONTROL, the European Organization for the Safety of Air Navigation, was tasked in the late 80's by its control body - the ministers of transport of its member states - to establish a Central Flow Management Unit. The CFMU is responsible for the following activities:

- Flight plan processing: receiving flight plans filed by the Aircraft Operators; flight plan validation and correction - manual or automatic. The corrected flight plans are redistributed to the Aircraft Operators and the overflown Airspace Control Centers.
- Air Traffic Flow Management: when the planned traffic load exceeds the capacity of Air Traffic Control (ATC), the CFMU is responsible for balancing the number of flights and available ATC capacity, the objective being optimum use of European airspace and prevention of air traffic congestion.

To support flight plan processing and short term - two days ahead - tactical air traffic flow management, the CFMU has developed the IFPS (Integrated Flight plan Processing System) and the TACT (tactical) system. Both systems were developed with common tools and techniques: HP servers and workstations, Ada83, Motif, Oracle, ... A large proportion of the code is common between the TACT and the IFPS system (see [1] for a more detailed description of some aspects of the architecture and development of the TACT system).

The TACT and IFPS systems became operational in 1995. Since then, major functional evolutions have been applied to both systems to cope with the expansion of air traffic. The traffic has grown by 27% between 1996 and 2000 (see [2]). The number of messages to be handled by the TACT system increased by almost 50%

A. Strohmeier and D. Craeynest (Eds.): Ada-Europe 2001, LNCS 2043, pp. 380-391, 2001.

over the same period (see figure 1). Currently, the system handles ± 25000 flights per day, with peak days up to 28000.

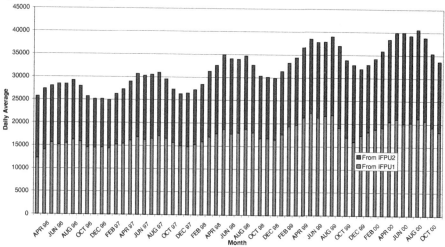

Fig. 1. Daily average of number of messages received by TACT system, per month

The systems have also been upgraded technically to follow up the evolution of the system software; operating system, database and to cope with the increasing demand both in volume and in terms of functionality, all of which necessitated increasing the power of the computers.

The software is large: in total, more than 1.4 million lines of Ada83 source code and 150 thousand lines of C, ksh, TCL/Tk, awk, PL/SQL, ... The software is structured in more than 60 software sub-systems and contains more than 2100 Ada packages.

The systems are also complex and integrate a lot of different techniques and technologies to provide the needed functions:

– Shared memories, semaphore, ...
– Network access: synchronous and asynchronous IO, TCP/IP, SNA, ...
– Low level access, e.g. for tracing (signal tracing, signal mask, stack trace, memory use, ...)
– Alsys Ada83 compiler
– Oracle database with SQL language access
– Usage of a POSIX Ada binding
– X and Motif
– ...

The short and medium term technical evolutions (2001/2002) are the introduction of version 11 of the HP-UX operating system and the use of CORBA for interfacing with other components.

On the functional side, major evolutions are also under way, in particular for the TACT system which will receive and process radar position data for flights over Europe. These radar positions will enable better prediction of the time, altitude and geographical positions of airborne flights leading to better-optimized management of airspace capacity. Receiving radar data will imply that the peak number of messages handled by the TACT system will increase from 10 per second to about 200 per second.

These heavy technical and functional evolutions are the main factors that have lead to the project of Ada95 compiler evaluations. The expected benefits of migrating to an Ada95 compiler were:

- The Ada83 compilers (e.g. Alsys) have become mature over the years. With the standardization of the new version of the Ada language [3], a lot of effort has been invested in new compilers. No major evolution or improvement of the Ada83 compiler was to be expected, which means that the use of newly available features such as the thread support by the HP-UX 11 operating system would not be possible while staying with Alsys Ada83.
- Use of CORBA with an Ada83 compiler is possible (see [4] for the description of an Ada83 targeted CORBA IDL compiler) but does not follow the standard CORBA Ada Mapping ([5]) thereby making the selection of a CORBA ORB product more difficult and making the code less portable.
- The Ada95 features like child units, protected objects, controlled types, tagged types, are also believed to bring better ways to develop and maintain our systems.
- Improvement of compilation speed.
- Easier integration of other technologies (e.g. C++).

2   Selection of an Ada95 Compiler

There are some major planning constraints that are imposed by others systems that depend on CFMU systems: air traffic control systems, aircraft operators fleet management systems, and national air traffic management systems. Delivery of new versions must be planned well in advance to give the external users time to adapt their operational procedures and systems. Meeting these planned installation dates - each year around March/April before the summer season - is crucial to the CFMU.

When planning a major change, having a contingency solution in case unexpected technical difficulties are encountered reduces risk. Hence it was decided to select and use an Ada95 compiler for the release to be installed in March 2001, but to keep the complete TACT and IFPS software compatible with Ada83. The evaluation of different Ada95 compilers was done between December 1999 and March 2000. After initial selection, the evaluated compilers were GNAT and ObjectAda. The main criteria used to evaluate the compilers are

- quality/performance of the generated code,
- quality of the associated tools (debugger, profiler, coverage, editor, ...),
- integration (multi-language, available products, ...), and
- quality of support provided by the compiler supplier.

From the beginning, a full-scale evaluation was deemed necessary to minimize the uncertainty. A complete port of TACT and IFPS to GNAT and ObjectAda was made between December 1999 and February 2000 by 4 people working ± 50% of their time on this activity. Our automated battery of regression tests was used to evaluate the functional quality of the code generated by the compiler. Some limited performance measurements were done with different scenarios.

Due to the very limited incompatibilities between Ada83 and Ada95, the necessary adaptations of the software - for example needed by the switch to a thread-based Ada tasking runtime - were done together with the development and finalization of the March 2000 release of the CFMU software. At the end of the compiler evaluation, the baseline code could be compiled by both the Alsys Ada83 compiler and by both of the Ada95 compilers.

After evaluation, the GNAT compiler was selected. The main positive points of GNAT are the quality of the support provided by the compiler supplier, the compilation speed, in particular on a multi-CPU computer, the very well appreciated simplicity of use, the robust make facility, the integration with other tools and the availability of products for GNAT. The main negative points were the poor quality of some aspects closely related to the operating system and the processor, poor quality of the gdb debugger, no support for zero cost exception handling, relative lack of performance of the generated code, no support for task switches in gdb, bugs in the profiling support, ...

EUROCONTROL has signed a contract with ACT-Europe in order to improve various aspects of the GNAT compiler (e.g. additional tracing features for exceptions) and to enhance most of the points mentioned above.

3   Ada83/Ada95 Differences and Incompatibilities Encountered

One of the main design factors of Ada95 was to keep a very high level of compatibility with the Ada83 version of the language (see [6] e.g. I.2, I.4 and [7]). This section explains the incompatibilities that were encountered and how they were solved. In most cases, an incompatibility between Ada83 and Ada95 can be removed by trivial adaptation of the code. In some cases, such a compatible modification is not possible, e.g. the generic formal indefinite types.

In case no compatible code can be written, two techniques have been used to still have one common source file to be handled by both the Ada83 and the Ada95 compiler: using a preprocessor, and automatic editing of the file using emacs scripts (see [8] and [9] for a description of the GNU emacs editor).

Preprocessing techniques are widely used in programming despite their drawbacks. A common problem is that the preprocessor directives make Ada source code syntactically invalid, as is the case for the preprocessor delivered with GNAT.

To preprocess our code, we use "ccf" (see [10]), a tool that provides preprocessing features by "commenting/uncommenting" the lines. Using this particular preprocessor in contrast to most others, for example gnatprep, m4, the C preprocessor or the Oracle embedded SQL preprocessor, has as advantage that the source files are still valid Ada and can thus still be handled properly by all the tools that expect "valid" Ada (code analyzers, syntax-aware editors, ...).

3.1   Indefinite Generic Parameter

In our code six generic packages are instantiated with indefinite actual parameter type. As explained in [6] Appendix X.4, this incompatibility is likely to occur. To remedy this incompatibility - which was detected at compile time- required a trivial change; add (<>) after the generic formal type name. However, this change is not compatible with our Ada83 compiler. So all the generic packages that were instantiated with unconstrained types were changed to obtain a preprocessable source as in

```
--## if language = Ada95 then
--##!type T (<>) is private;
--## else
type T is private;
--## end if
```

The ccf preprocessor can switch the sources between Ada83 and Ada95 version by commenting/uncommenting the relevant lines. Currently, the default source layout is Ada83. A preprocessing step is thus needed to compile our sources with GNAT. We plan to drop this preprocessing step when we no longer need compatibility with the Ada83 compiler.

3.2   Character Type Having 256 Values Instead of 128

This incompatibility, also characterized as likely to happen in [6] was present in one test program. The program looped over all characters in Ada 83. To continue to give the expected result, the loop was changed to explicitly loop on the first 128 character values. Note that this is the only incompatibility that was not detected at compile time.

3.3   String and Wide_String

The addition of Wide_Character and Wide_String is classified as an unlikely source of incompatibility in [6]. This unlikely incompatibility was present at multiple places (> 20) in our software due to the use of the POSIX function To_Posix_String with a string literal argument. The incompatibility, detected at compile time, was trivially avoided by qualifying the string literal with String'.

3.4   Generic Elementary Functions

The software is using some services of generic elementary functions (sin, cos, ...) present in the Alsys provided package Generic_Elementary_Functions, which was not in the Ada83 standard. As these functions are now part of the Ada95 standard, we use library level renaming of generics, provided in Ada95, to resolve this issue. Preprocessing is used to avoid compiling this with the Alsys 83 compiler:

```
--## if language = Ada95
--##!with Ada.Numerics.Generic_Elementary_Functions;
--##!generic package Generic_Elementary_Functions
--##!renames Ada.Numerics.Generic_Elementary_Functions;
--## end if
```

3.5   Numeric Attributes

An obsolete numeric attribute was used in a test program that was checking boundary values. This incompatibility, detected at compile time, was solved by replacing 'Small by 'Model_Small.

3.6   Illegal Non-required Package Bodies

A few empty package bodies had to be removed. For a few packages, a pragma Elaborate_Body was added. These illegal "non-required" package bodies were detected at compile time.

3.7   Use of New Ada95 Keywords

There were a few uses of the new reserved keyword "protected". These incompatibilities, also detected at compile time, were trivially solved by changing the name of the variable or parameter.

4   Adaptation of Non-portable Code

The TACT and IFPS code has proven to be quite portable; indicated by the limited time and effort needed to port it from one compiler to another. However, some non-portable features had to be used, for example Alsys specific pragmas, or compiler/run-time/operating system specific features. The following sections list the different points at which non-portable code had to be changed or alternative code developed, either due to the migration to Ada95 or to use the new Ada tasking run-time based on operating system threads.

4.1   Alsys Specific Mutex

For performance reasons Alsys specific low level mutexes had been used to implement critical sections, instead of implementing this via a monitor task. The direct use of these non-portable mutexes was centralized inside one package body (safe_mutex.adb). It was thus very easy to implement an alternate body for Ada95.

The performance of two different versions was compared: pure Ada95, based on protected objects, and access to the low-level pthread mutex via GNAT specific packages. Implementing a mutex on top of a protected object is an abstraction inversion: we are using a high level structure to implement a low-level concept. The direct access to the low-level resource was more efficient by a factor of 6 and was, similarly to Alsys code, centralized into the safe_mutex package body.

4.2   Access to Command Arguments

Access to the command arguments was done via an Alsys specific package. An alternate implementation of this package was implemented on top of the new standard Ada.Command_Line package.

4.3   "System.Offset"

In some packages, some low-level pointer arithmetic was done (e.g. to pack some bytes into a piece of shared memory). Some Alsys specific features - Offset type and related functions – were used. These incompatibilities were solved by doing 'renames' using the preprocessor, renaming either the Alsys type and functions, or the new Ada95 standard features provided in System.Storage_Elements.

4.4   Heap and Memory Use Information

When suspecting a memory leak or when measuring the memory use of some algorithm, the state of the heap has to be reported. The state of the Alsys heap was reported using Alsys specific calls. The package body reporting the heap status was modified, with preprocessing, so as to have either code that reported the state of the Alsys heap or the state of the GNAT heap, which is based on the operating system memory allocation malloc library.

4.5   Pragmas

The graphical interface of the TACT and IFPS system is based on Motif. Motif widgets make intensive use of callbacks; a callback has to be defined for each action such as a button push, a list selection, etc. In Ada83, there was no portable way to define these callbacks. Hence there were a large number of uses - more than 500 - of non-portable Alsys specific or obsolete Ada83 pragmas (Call_In, External_Name, Interface, Interface_Name). Due to the number of these non-portable pragmas we did not want to use the preprocessor to solve this incompatibility. Instead, a GNU emacs lisp script [9] was written that automatically converts the old style pragmas into a set of pragmas accepted by GNAT.

Note that this automatic conversion is not switching to a pure Ada95 solution but rather to an intermediate solution (accepted by GNAT) that is halfway between the Alsys specific version and the pure Ada95 version:

Ada Calls C (e.g. Access to Motif, System Calls):

Alsys Ada83 specific:

```
function A_System_Call (Foo: Bar);
pragma Interface (C, A_System_Call);
pragma Interface_Name (A_System_Call, "system_call");
```

Ada95:

```
pragma Import (C, A_System_Call, "system_call");
```

C Calls Ada

Alsys Ada83 specific:

```
procedure Doit (Some_Thing: Some_Type);
pragma Call_In (C, Doit);
pragma External_Name (Doit, "externaldoit");
```

Ada95:

```
pragma Export (C, Doit, "externaldoit");
```

C Calls Pointer to Ada (Motif Callbacks)

Alsys Ada83

```
procedure Button_Clicked (Button: Motif.Button.T);
pragma Call_In (C, Button_Clicked);
  -- Button_Clicked callable from C
pragma External_Name
  (Button_Clicked, "screenx_buttony_click");
  -- via linkname screenx_buttony_click

procedure Button_Clicked_Entry
  (Button: Motif.Button.T);
pragma Call_In (C, Button_Clicked_Entry);
pragma Interface_Name
  (Button_Clicked_Entry, "screenx_buttony_click");

Motif.Button.Create
  (When_Click => Button_Clicked_Entry'Address);
```

Pure Ada95: elegant, type safe, no name collision e.g. in generics

```
procedure Button_Clicked (Button: Motif.Button.T);
pragma Convention (C, Button_Clicked);

Motif.Button.Create
  (When_Click => Button_Clicked'Access);
```

"Alsys-ified" Ada95 Accepted by GNAT:

```
pragma Export + pragma Import + 'Address
```

4.6   Differences Due to Tasking Run-Time Behavior

We did not encounter incompatibilities or run-time differences for "pure" use of tasking, e.g. when using monitor tasks protecting access to an object. However, some code providing access to TCP/IP uses non-trivial Unix features such as asynchronous signal based IO to avoid having the complete process being blocked when one task calls a blocking Unix system-call during TCP/IP input-output.

The first idea was to make the minimum of changes to this complex code to get it work with the new runtime. This was not too difficult but afterwards we decided to simplify the code using the thread-based Ada tasking run-time: with GNAT, Ada tasks are mapped on operating system HP-UX threads. From HP-UX 10 onwards (DCE threads) or HP-UX 11 (real kernel pthreads), a blocking system call does not block the complete process.

The package implementing the non-blocking TCP/IP layer was then simplified for the Ada95 version as each task could directly do its "own" IO system calls instead of going though a central IO task intercepting the SIGIO signal and waking up the task(s) for which IO was possible. This new IO schema based on the improved Ada tasking based on OS threads is also more efficient than the signal based IO.

4.7   Elaboration Order

During the development of the TACT and IFPS system, little attention was paid to elaboration problems, mainly because the Alsys compiler is quite good at finding a working elaboration order.

The GNAT compiler has multiple ways to handle elaboration order. The default GNAT behavior is to find a working static order. This means that at compile time, the compiler determines an elaboration order that is guaranteed to work always.

When such an order cannot be found, the GNAT binder reports this fact. Multiple options are then available to obtain an elaboration order:

- Change the code to allow a static elaboration order to be found. There are many advantages to this solution. See section 9 of the GNAT user manual [11] for a detailed explanation of elaboration handling in GNAT and the advantages of this static solution.
- Ask the compiler to try to find a "good" order. In this case, the compiler inserts elaboration checks to make sure at run-time that the order is valid.
- Tell the compiler that the programmer has taken care of elaboration order problems. This is a dangerous option to use because, in case of human error, some packages might not have been elaborated yet when used. Note that this is the standard C++ and Java approach (see the Java and C++ language specifications [12] [13]).

We had a few executables where no static elaboration order was found by the GNAT compiler. We first tried to have GNAT finding a "good" elaboration. This did not work very well for us, either because the Alsys compiler is better at finding a working order or because our code was "naturally" developed over the years to fit well with the Alsys way of choosing an elaboration order.

We then decided to change the code in order to obtain a static elaboration order. This was quite easy to do in all cases except one. What is interesting to note is that the code changes needed to obtain a static elaboration resulted in better-structured code. When the GNAT compiler could not find a static elaboration order, in most cases this indicated that the package structure was not very good and that artificial dependencies had been introduced by this inadequate structure.

The case for which we were not able to obtain a static elaboration order was tasking code that had not been developed at Eurocontrol. We took over the support of this code due to contractual changes with the product supplier. With limited knowledge of this code and its complex structure we were unable to change it to elaborate statically. For this particular case the solution chosen was to tell the compiler that there was no elaboration problem.

4.8 By-Reference Types

We had code that needed by-reference types for memory management. If an access type value is passed mode **in out** to a procedure that deallocates it, then, if control returns to the caller via exception propagation, we do not want the caller to still have access to the dangling reference. The Alsys compiler chose a by-reference mechanism when an access value was encapsulated in a record type, while GNAT uses by-value parameter passing for such types. Luckily these access values were already encapsulated in limited private types, so we could easily use the Ada95 non-private limited type construct to force the appropriate mechanism on the full type declaration.

```
generic
  type Access_Type is private;
  -- unprotected reference type to be encapsulated
package Mem_Mgmt_G is
  type T is limited private;
  -- "managed" reference type to be re-exported
private
  type T is limited record -- becomes by-reference
    Component: Access_Type;
  end record;
end Mem_Mgmt_G;
```

5   Software Management Aspects

As explained in the introduction, one of the main factors for the CFMU at Eurocontrol is to minimize the risk related to the technology change. This is why the compatibility with Ada83 must be maintained until the code compiled with the new Ada95 compiler has enjoyed a long period of operational validation.

Also we do not want to have two separate sets of sources, one each for Ada83 and Ada95. Hence our compilation and build procedures have been modified to support the compilation by multiple compilers. Currently the source control system contains the version of the sources that can be compiled directly by the Ada83 compiler.

As long as Ada83 compatibility is kept, all developers have the option of using either the Ada83 or the GNAT compiler to compile, link and test. If the developer chooses to use the Ada83 compiler, he compiles the source files directly. To use the GNAT compiler, the developer uses a script that wraps up the compiler so that the following actions are executed automatically:

- Copy the source file into a sub-directory.
- Launch the preprocessor in order to switch from the Ada83 to the Ada95 version.
- If the source file contains pragmas then it is automatically edited by emacs to convert the pragmas to the Ada95 version.
- The GNAT compiler is then launched on the modified source file.
- In case of compilation error, the developer edits the Ada83 version.

While not completely comfortable, the above scheme worked quite well, particularly as the editing scripts and preprocessor do not modify the code much. The editing scripts have been constructed so that the line numbers stay the same. Hence compilation errors referring to preprocessed automatically edited code refer to the correct line in the Ada83 version even if the code to change was the "commented" Ada95 code.

6   Future Developments

As explained before, in a first phase, the strategy was to keep compatible code between Ada83 and Ada95. The final validation of the new compiler was deemed OK after a period of 3 months of operational evaluation (between November 2000 and January 2001). After this period the software to be put into operation in March 2001 should be stable. From then on development of the next version for March 2002 can be done without the constraints of keeping the compatibility with Ada83.

Once Ada83 compatibility is no longer needed, the source files in our source management system will be converted to the Ada95 form, so that preprocessing and automatic editing is not needed anymore when compiling with GNAT. From that point onwards, the source lines specific for Alsys or Ada83 becomes useless and can also be removed.

We also intend to increase the use of Ada95 features in the coming months. One of the first Ada95 specific features we expect to use is child units. Previously our code made a lot of use of Ada83's subunits (separate bodies). Child units provide better code structure. Also, the GNAT compilation model has not been optimized for the compilation of subunits: modifying one subunit means you have to recompile the parent unit and all the other "sibling" subunits. We hope to obtain better-structured code and faster compilation by limited restructuring to replace some subunits with child units.

We have also decided that using controlled objects can ease the development and maintenance of the system in cases where dynamic memory is heavily used, or had previously been necessary but not used due to the difficulty of avoiding memory leaks and dangling pointers.

7   Conclusion

On these large real life applications, the compatibility between Ada83 and Ada95 is very good. Where not compatible, the differences were almost always trivial to solve and were all - except one - detected during compilation. Porting from Ada83 to Ada95 was in fact a non-event that was done in parallel with normal system evolution. The progress in compiler technology visible in the Ada95 compilers - both GNAT and ObjectAda - has already brought in benefits even during the port. For example both compilers give warning messages for some dubious constructs. In some cases these warnings have revealed genuine problems in our code, or code that could be optimized.

Despite some aspects of the technology that have still to be improved, in particular the gdb debugger, the GNAT compiler and tool suite brings some major improvement and comfort in many aspects, for example compilation speed and better diagnostics. We also expect that for future developments, the increased use of Ada95 concepts will make the evolution of our systems easier and our software even more portable.

References

[1]   Waroquiers, P.: Ada Tasking and Dynamic Memory: To Use or Not To Use, That's a Question!. In Alfred Strohmeier (Ed.): Reliable Software Technologies – Ada-Europe'96. Springer-Verlag, Lecture Notes in Computer Science vol. 1088, ISBN 3-540-61317-X (1996) pp. 460-470

[2]   ATFM Operations Summer 2000 Report, Eurocontrol/CFMU (2000)

[3]   Taft, T.S., Duff, R.A., (Eds.): Ada 95 Reference Manual: Language and Standard Libraries, International Standard ISO/IEC 8652:1995(E). Springer-Verlag, Lecture Notes in Computer Science vol. 1246, ISBN 3-540-63144-5 (1997)

[4]   Ada 83 CORBA IDL Compiler. http://www.eurocontrol.fr/projects/arh-spv_ext/comp/ (1996)

[5]   Object Management Group: Ada Language Mapping Specification. Edition June 1999, http://www.omg.org/technology/documents/formal/ada_language_mapping.htm (1999)

[6]   Barnes, J., (Ed.): Ada 95 Rationale: The Language, The Standard Libraries. Springer-Verlag, Lecture Notes in Computer Science vol. 1247, ISBN 3-540-63143-7 (1997)

[7]   Bill Taylor: Ada Compatibility Guide, Version 6.0, http://www.adaic.com/AdaIC/docs/compat-guide (1995)

[8]   Richard M. Stallman: GNU Emacs Manual. Thirteenth Edition (1997)

[9]   Bill Lewis, Dans LaLiberte and the GNU Manual Group: The GNU Emacs Lisp Reference Manual. Edition 2.5 (1998)

[10] CCF: a Conditional Compilation Facility. http://users.swing.be/imw/ccf/ (2000)

[11] Ada Core Technologies: GNAT User's Guide. Document revision level 1.317 (2000)

[12] Java Language Specification. The part where something like elaboration is mentioned (Static Initializers):
      http://www.javasoft.com/docs/books/jls/html/8.doc.html#39245 (1996)

[13] C++ Language Standard: ISO/IEC 14882:1998. http://www.ncits.org/cplusplus.htm (1998)

An Application Case for Ravenscar Technology: Porting OBOSS to GNAT/ORK

Tullio Vardanega[1], Rodrigo García[2], and Juan Antonio de la Puente[2]

[1] Directorate of Technical and Operational Support
European Space Research and Technology Centre, 2200 AG Noordwijk, Netherlands
[2] Departamento de Ingeniería de Sistemas Telemáticos
Universidad Politécnica de Madrid, E-28040 Madrid, Spain
tullio.vardanega@esa.int {rodrigo,jpuente}@dit.upm.es

Abstract. As Ada compilation systems with specific support for the Ravenscar Profile become available, users have the opportunity to assess the expressive power of the profile and the effectiveness of the relevant technology. User feedback in both respects may significantly contribute to furthering the maturity of the profile and the confidence of the user community. This paper provides some such feedback discussing the lessons learned on the port of a space application to GNAT/ORK, an open-source implementation of the profile.

1 Introduction

The Ravenscar Profile [1] captures a subset of the tasking model of the Ada 95 programming language [2], which is especially suited for the implementation of concurrent real-time systems with high integrity requirements. High integrity applications prohibit the use of language features that are deemed to complicate static analysis. Ada tasking is traditionally seen as one of those 'dangerous' features. The profile promotes a set of tasking features that enable direct expression of the inherent concurrency of real-time system and that are directly amenable to static analysis.

The Ravenscar Profile seeks predictability of execution at application level along with resource-efficient and time-bounded behaviour at runtime level. These characteristics make implementations of the profile especially attractive to applications that operate under stringent resource constraints (like most spacecraft systems) and to those that need to seek certification before deployment (like aircraft systems).

The GNAT/ORK compilation system [3] is the product of a technology research contract that the European Space Agency (ESA) recently awarded to the Technical University of Madrid. As the name suggests, GNAT/ORK stems from the integration of two distinct components: the open-source Ada 95 GNAT compiler, currently supported by Ada Core Technologies (ACT) [4], which constitutes the target-independent component of the product; and the Open Ravenscar Real-Time Kernel (ORK), an open-source, small-size, reliable and efficient

A. Strohmeier and D. Craeynest (Eds.): Ada-Europe 2001, LNCS 2043, pp. 392–404, 2001.

kernel that implements the tasking model defined by the Ravenscar Profile and is distributed under GPL license. The open-source nature of the product reflects the interest that ESA places into the open-source movement in so far as it facilitates the long-term maintenance typical of long-lived space projects and it promotes and enforces standards [5]. The latter aspect in particular was especially important to the promotion of the Ravenscar concept within the space community.

GNAT/ORK is currently available on Linux platforms as a cross compilation system targeting the ERC32, a radiation tolerant version of the SPARC v7 computer architecture [6]. To date, GNAT/ORK has been validated using TSIM [7], an ERC32 instruction set simulator originally developed for use in ESA-funded projects. On account of the task-intensive nature of Ravenscar applications, the GNAT/ORK product package includes task-aware debug support via specific adaptations to the well-know GDB and DDD free-software utilities.

Systematic reuse is one the development paradigms that may be able to raise the productivity of the software process and the dependability of the software product. Aware of this potential, ESA has over the last few years funded studies aimed at promoting systematic software reuse within the industrial practice of space business. One of those studies has resulted in the development of OBOSS [8], a collection of reusable software components designed for the implementation of spacecraft data handling systems. Earlier work (cf. e.g.: [9]) describes the structure of the OBOSS library.

Although the needs of reuse are somewhat orthogonal to the motivations for the Ravenscar Profile, the combined exploitation of the two notions arguably offers important advantages. The reduction in the demand of user code (i.e. the code that the user has to add to the reusable asset) is one of the parameters with the most direct impact on the economic value of reuse. As Reference [10] observes, several Ravenscar-related factors arguably contribute to this reduction. In particular, a reuse library that fully determines the control architecture of the system whilst only presenting standard requirements on the runtime interface of the application saves the user a considerable amount of coding effort. Similarly, a control architecture that complies with the Ravenscar Profile makes the execution model of the system easy to understand, low in support requirements and easy to port across standard Ada platforms.

In fact, several distinct aspects of the OBOSS implementation provided an attractive 'window of opportunity' for us to effectively transition it to Ravenscar technology:

1. The original design of OBOSS used Ada tasking in the form promoted by HRT-HOOD [11] as the means to express the inherent concurrency of systems in the target application domain.
2. The HRT-HOOD model of concurrency embodied distinct elements of what has later become the Ravenscar Profile.
3. The Ada 83 compiler technology on which OBOSS was first ported to ERC32 targets incorporated tasking constructs with equivalent semantics to those of the Ravenscar Profile.

A full port of OBOSS to genuine Ravenscar technology is attractive for at least two reasons:

a. The port helps the Ada community determine whether the restrictions of the profile leave room for a language subset expressive enough to meet the demands of real-world systems.

b. The wealth of language constructs used by the OBOSS library and the very dimension of it, make the port a truly comprehensive benchmark for any given Ravenscar technology.

Reference [10] covers the former aspect arguing that the profile has proven able to implement real-world systems in the class and range of OBOSS. The port of OBOSS to GNAT/ORK discussed in this paper specifically addresses the latter aspect while attempting to draw lessons with the widest possible applicability.

2   Syntactic and Semantic Ada Coding Issues

One of the key aspects of the port was to ensure that the transition from pre-Ravenscar technology to a genuine implementation of the profile would preserve the intended tasking semantics of the application without violating any of the enforced restrictions.

In fact, the whole of the OBOSS concurrency model proved to be a perfect semantic match to the GNAT/ORK implementation of the profile. A few syntactic adaptations were of course needed but none of those had any semantic impact.

OBOSS used passive tasks with at most one entry to play the role of protected objects. Passive tasks were marked by an implementation-specific pragma Passive, which caused the compiler to refrain from assigning the task its own thread of control and its own task control block. Those tasks were turned into Ravenscar protected objects without difficulty.

Contrary to the prescription of the profile, OBOSS active tasks did have one entry, notionally denominated Go, which the main unit would employ to determine the order of release after elaboration. Quite like Ravenscar tasks, however, OBOSS active tasks were designed to infinitely revolve around a single activation event, which would be either a time event or a hardware interrupt or else a software synchronisation. The one-time nature of the Go entry invocation by the main unit made it logically and physically distinct from the activation event controlling the main loop. Hence, all it took us to accomplish the transformation was to replace the Go accept outside the main loop by a delay until statement with a suitable activation time.

OBOSS is geared toward reuse. As such, it makes extensive use of generic units, which were the prime support provided by Ada 83 to the cause. One difficult aspect with the language definition of generics is that formal generic parameters are not treated as static expressions even if the corresponding actual values are defined as such. Let us suppose we use a generic unit to implement an abstract data type like a queue. Also suppose that we want to express the size attribute of the queue as a formal generic parameter. Unfortunately, this option is incompatible with the use of a modular type based in the generic parameter size to index the elements of the queue. As a result, the declaration of type Queue_Index in the following code fragment is illegal:

```
generic
   Queue_Size : in Natural;
   . . .
package Queue is
   . . .
end Queue;
package body Queue is
   type Queue_Index is mod Queue_Size; – non-static value in bound - illegal.
   . . .
end Queue;
```

Had the construct been legal, we would have been able to profit from the primitive cyclic arithmetic associated to the definition of the modular type. Instead, the declaration of the modular type wants a static expression for the bound, which formal generic parameters cannot provide.

There are of course several work-arounds for this problem, none of which, however is fully satisfactory. One solution, which preserves the configurability of individual queue sizes but drops the modular type, uses the generic parameter and explicit bound checking to build the range attribute of an unconstrained array defined in a general configuration package. This is certainly doable, except that it forces the user into the undesirable practice of re-coding an existing language feature. Another solution is to define the whole modular type as the formal generic parameter in the place of the queue size only. This is also doable, but also not commendable as it contravenes a basic principle of information hiding. A third solution is to renounce expressing the queue size as a generic formal parameter while retaining the convenience of the modular type with the bound expressed as a global, static value. In this way, however, any instantiation of the queue ought to have the same size.

3   Technology Issues

3.1   Ravenscar-Specific Issues

The Ravenscar Profile is relatively new to both the user and the implementor community. It is therefore important that demanding applications be targeted to the profile to expose undesirable limitations and shortcomings in the general nature and in the specific implementation of Ravenscar technology.

As part of the ORK implementation and the port of OBOSS we experienced a number of limitations in the GNAT implementation and enforcement of some Ravenscar restrictions.

The following restrictions appeared to be ignored altogether:

1. The Max_Tasks => N restriction, which expresses a user assertion on a static property of the program, is not checked at compilation time. An application can thus exceed the maximum number of tasks set by the restriction without incurring a violation error.
2. The No_Protected_Type_Allocators restriction, which contributes to making the use of protected objects static throughout the program, is not checked at compilation time. An application can thus erroneously declare and use protected types without incurring a violation error.

Those restrictions are integral part of the Ravenscar Profile and their violation may break the integrity of the program. Accordingly, the expected behaviour of Ravenscar technology on violation of any such restriction should definitely be to raise compilation error.

Early versions of the profile contemplated including restriction Static_Storage_Size to ensure that the stack requirements of all tasks in the program be statically known. GNAT Ravenscar does in fact enforce the restriction while ObjectAda Real-Time RAVEN [13] (RAVEN for short), the only other Ravenscar technology presently available, makes it optional (and disabled by default). Burns in [1] does *not* include the restriction in the 'official' manifesto of the profile.

Unfortunately, the restriction has a nasty interaction with OBOSS. Reference [10] discusses how OBOSS uses generic units embedding Ravenscar tasks as 'generic task templates'. As part of the OBOSS design approach, the desired stack size is designed to be a specific task attribute determined at generic instantiation with a pragma Storage_Size clause. In keeping with the Ravenscar principle, all OBOSS tasks are library level, embedded in library level instantiations. Yet, when attempting to use a formal generic parameter to set the size of a library level task stack in the presence of pragma Restrictions (Static_Storage_Size), both GNAT Ravenscar and RAVEN fail on account of the parameter not being static. As a consequence, *library level* instantiations of the following unit appear to be illegal with GNAT in Ravenscar mode as well as with RAVEN with pragma Storage_Size enabled:

```
generic
    Task_Stack_Size : in Natural;
package Cyclic_Task is
    task Cyclic_Task is – library level task for library level instantiation
        pragma Storage_Size (Task_Stack_Size);
        – violation of restriction Static_Storage_Size: expression must be static.
    end Cyclic_Task;
end Cyclic_Task;
```

Arguably, this code should be legal for it does comply with the restriction as long as the generic actual parameter is a static expression and the generic instantiation is library level. The brute-force solution to this problem would be to selectively disable the restriction, which we could do with RAVEN but not with

GNAT Ravenscar, which bundles the restriction in the single pragma Ravenscar that selects the Ravenscar runtime. Hence, we were compelled to assign the stack size of all generic task templates a single, global, static value; which is not quite an acceptable solution.

Ravenscar applications should not use dynamic memory. The IRTAW group gathered at Las Navas del Marqués, Ávila (Spain) to discuss the profile concluded that restriction No_Implicit_Heap_Allocation should be added to the profile to prohibit *implicit* use of dynamic memory by the runtime and that the profile should remain silent on the use of allocators and storage pools at application level [12].

RAVEN   takes   a   stronger   stance   by   enforcing   restriction No_Standard_Storage_Pools to compel the application to explicitly provide user-specific (Ravenscar compliant) management of memory. Because restriction No_Standard_Storage_Pools has no interaction with pragma Storage_Size, the above code fragment compiles without problems under RAVEN.

Had restriction No_Implicit_Heap_Allocation been supported by GNAT Ravenscar (or even by RAVEN) we would have been able to catch instances of code that may require use of implicit heap allocations, for example to treat the return of objects of unconstrained type.

OBOSS does include an instance of code that may cause the compiler to make implicit use of heap:

```
type Internal_TC_Representation
    (Result : Interpretation_Result := Failed;
    Subservice : TC_Subservice := TC_Subservice'First) is
    record
        case Result is
            when Failed => Status : Verification_Types.Verification_Status;
            when Passed => Src_Data : Internal_TC_Source_Data (Subservice);
                - which is a variant record with an unconstrained array component
        end case;
    end record;
...
    return Internal_TC_Representation'
        (Result => Passed,
        Subservice => The_Source_Data.Subservice,
        Src_Data => The_Source_Data);
end;
```

Not surprisingly, GNAT did in fact use heap for the implementation of the return statement, which we detected by setting a breakpoint in __gnat_malloc, the function that GNAT uses to reserve dynamic memory. This detection technique however is not fit to exhaustively catch all occurrences of allocation violation, which in fact requires full object code analysis. Of course, the most direct and efficient way to achieve this objective is definitely to have compiler support for the No_Implicit_Heap_Allocation restriction.

The different approach taken by GNAT Ravenscar to the use of dynamic memory with respect to RAVEN had another interesting effect on the port of OBOSS. The OBOSS library includes a unit with the following code:

```
generic
   type Key is (<>);
   ...
package Cell_Pool is
   ...
end Cell_Pool;
package body Cell_Pool is
   ...
   subtype Cell is ...;
   type Cell_Ref is access Cell;
   type Cell_Collection is array (Key) of Cell_Ref;
   Source_Data_Store : Cell_Collection;
begin - Cell_Pool
   for Index in Key loop
      Source_Data_Store (Index) := new Cell;
   end loop;
end Cell_Pool;
```

Arguably, code of this kind does not violate restriction Static_Storage_Size, because it only allocates from the heap once in elaboration code. Instantiation of package Cell_Pool however contravenes restriction No_Standard_Storage_Pools. Neither of the two restrictions is part of the 'official' Ravenscar profile. Yet, the code compiles without errors under GNAT Ravenscar while it obviously incurs violation of the No_Standard_Storage_Pools restriction under RAVEN.

A genuine bug in the GNAT Ravenscar technology, fully acknowledged by the implementor, causes program termination when the main unit attempts to terminate, thereby hindering the portability of Ravenscar-compliant code.

Ravenscar applications use explicit library level tasks to carry out the whole range of non-terminating activities required of the system. The main unit, which is not an explicit task at program level, translates to the environment task (and the master of all other tasks in the system) upon compilation. When outlining the Ravenscar Profile, Reference [1] allows the assumption that none of the program tasks will terminate, but it does not distinguish between explicit library level tasks and implicit environment task. By the rules of master termination, however, the main unit implicitly becomes non-terminating as any (all for Ravenscar) of its dependent tasks are non-terminating. This notion suggests that the main unit should not be treated as an explicit task and, thus, that it should not be expected or even required to be non-terminating.

When Ravenscar restrictions are enforced it is crucial that this be done in a manner that captures the prescription of the profile exactly and that does not cause unwanted secondary effects. Any glitches in this area may dramatically reduce the value of the Ravenscar technology. The ORK implementation experienced problems of this kind with GNAT, which would have been genuine show-stoppers for the port of OBOSS, had the open nature of GNAT not allowed the ORK development team to fix them in their build. In particular, we found that restriction Boolean_Entry_Barriers is not correctly implemented, for it causes some spurious errors when compiling valid Ravenscar programs. Furthermore, we observed that the restricted GNAT runtime selected on the use of the implementation-specific pragma Ravenscar does not support interrupt protected handlers. This limitation is especially disturbing in that interrupt protected handlers constitute an integral component of the language subset captured by the profile and are obviously essential to typical Ravenscar applications.

Three important lessons may be learned from this sort of incidents:

a. Users and implementors of Ravenscar technology need an agreed conformance test suite respectively to ascertain correct and exhaustive implementation of the profile and to claim full conformance to it.

b. By the same token, technology providers should clearly specify what additional restrictions they support and what side effects (if any) those may have on the application.

c. An implementation-specific pragma Ravenscar that does not meet condition a. is neither desirable nor proper, for it does not warrant program portability (which should be wholly obvious for Ravenscar applications) and it does not bear a formally sanctioned relationship with the whole collection of individual restrictions of the profile.

3.2   General Issues

Generic units provide the foundation upon which the OBOSS architecture achieves its intensively reusable character. The Ravenscar Profile is silent about generic units, for they are genuinely orthogonal to the issue of concurrency. Yet, systems in the application domains addressed by the profile obviously need to pay a great deal of attention to the intended use of generics and to the way the compiler technology treats them. Reference [14] provides guidance on the use of generic units in the face of high integrity requirements.

In fact, the way GNAT treats generic units caused distinct problems to the OBOSS port. Section 2.6 'Source Dependencies' of Reference [15] documents the very special way in which GNAT handles generic units. Quoting verbatim: *If a file being compiled instantiates a library level generic unit, the object file depends on both the spec and body files for this generic unit.*

This notion ties with the fact that GNAT subjects the success of a generic instantiation to the successful elaboration of all the units which the generic unit (specification *and* body) depends upon. The net consequence of this notion for the OBOSS port is that the following code fragment, which compiles successfully with other Ada technology, yields an elaboration circularity problem and fails:

```
generic
   ...
   with procedure Operation (...);
package Sporadic_Task is – library level generic unit.
```

```
    . . .
    procedure Start ( . . . ); – to activate sporadic task.
end Sporadic_Task;

with Event_Reporting;
package body Sporadic_Task is – unit body depends on Event_Reporting.

    . . .
    task body Sporadic_Task is

      . . .
    exception
      when others => Event_Reporting.Make_Exception_Report ( . . . );
    end Sporadic_Task;
end Sporadic_Task;

package Packet_Router is
    procedure Deposit ( . . . );
end Packet_Router;

with Sporadic_Task;
pragma Elaborate (Sporadic_Task); – to ensure unit elaboration before instantiation.
package body Packet_Router is

    . . .
    procedure Distribute_Packet ( . . . ) is . . . ;
    package Packet_Forwarder is new Sporadic_Task ( . . . ,Distribute_Packet);
      – GNAT makes Packet_Router depend on the body of Sporadic_Task.
    procedure Deposit ( . . . ) is begin . . . Packet_Forwarder.Start ( . . . ); end Deposit;
end Packet_Router;

package Event_Reporting is
    procedure Make_Exception_Report ( . . . );
end Event_Reporting;

with Packet_Router;
package body Event_Reporting is – unit body depends on Packet_Router.
    procedure Make_Exception_Report ( . . . ) is
    begin

      . . .
      Packet_Router.Deposit ( . . . );
    end Make_Exception_Report;
end Event_Reporting;
```

In practice, the compilation dependency introduced by GNAT makes legal Ada code incur a circular dependency in the elaboration of the bodies of Packet_Router, Sporadic_Task and Event_Reporting even though the respective specifications have no dependency on one another at all.

Section 9.6 'Elaboration Order Handling in GNAT' of Reference [15] suggests that the problem arises because the *default* behaviour of the binder is to force a pragma Elaborate_All clause in all units with elaboration code that instantiates a generic unit in a with'ed unit (or, equivalently, a pragma Elaborate_Body in the with'ed unit concerned).

The intent of this provision is to warrant avoidance of Program_Error exceptions at elaboration upon calls of subprograms not yet elaborated. The user needs to use a switch (-gnatE) to explicitly override the default behaviour of the binder, whereby GNAT generates dynamic checks for instances of calls of code not yet elaborated.

In essence, if the user wants the compilation system to flag areas of problem with elaboration order, legal (and arguably reasonable) code like ours may not compile. To any rate, we contend that the default behaviour of the binder should definitely comply with the language reference manual, which is not the case at the moment.

We preferred to preserve the issue of elaboration problem warnings and therefore opted not to use the overriding switch. The only way we had to circumvent the problem while preserving code portability was thus to break the circularity rooted in the body of Sporadic_Task by introducing a self-standing artificial unit to interface Event_Reporting to Packet_Router.

The other serious problem that occurred in the regard of generic units was in the exceedingly large size of the code produced by GNAT for units that make instantiations. In relation with figures obtained from the Ada 83 compiler technology with which OBOSS was originally built, we observed the size of key instantiations inflate by a factor of 2 to 3. For an instantiation-intensive system like OBOSS this phenomenon alone was so important to defeat the size reduction attained on the use of the resource-friendly constructs of the Ravenscar Profile.

Ravenscar applications seek predictability of execution (as opposed to mere speed up) in conjunction with efficient use of computation resources. Accordingly, the compilation strategy of Ravenscar technology for language constructs allowed by the profile and by high integrity coding guidance (cf. e.g.: [14]) should be as resource-efficient as possible.

The Ravenscar Profile is silent on whether compliant technology should support exceptions. The role of exceptions in systems with integrity requirements still makes a contentious issue. OBOSS sides with those who consider exceptions as an important component of the system.

The OBOSS design philosophy accepts that certain operations may fail at run time and requires that those should report the failure event in the form of a specific exception. Notable examples of such operations in OBOSS are those that have to take data input from unreliable sources and those that have to cope with user demands in the event of temporary shortage of resources. In order to ensure that the control flow modification resulting from exception events be always statically analysable and would not induce hazards to the system, OBOSS requires that operations that may raise exceptions be encapsulated within blocks equipped with appropriate handlers. In fact these prescriptions are in keeping with the provisions that Reference [16] assumes for the static timing analysis of Ada exception handlers.

GNAT/ORK and RAVEN feature different strategies with regard to exceptions:

- RAVEN prohibits the use of user-defined exceptions altogether and only supports the occurrence of predefined exceptions, the handling of which simply involves direct transfer of control to designated 'last-rites' routines explicitly supplied by the user. This strategy is obviously insufficient to OBOSS, short of revamping it all.
- GNAT/ORK does not pose any major restrictions to the use of exceptions and therefore fully supports the OBOSS needs, yet at some cost in terms of resources. Arguably in fact, exception support includes far more (e.g.: the whole Ada.Exceptions) than what OBOSS and its Ravenscar application equivalents would probably ever need.

Our contention in this respect is that Ravenscar technology needs (optional) resource-efficient exception support, ideally designed as middle ground between those two extremes.

4   Interactions with Object Orientation

As OBOSS is intended for reuse, object orientation is naturally the next frontier of it. Because its origin is rooted in Ada 83, OBOSS only had generic units and variant records as support for primitive inheritance (effectively, instantiation) and static polymorphism. The (abstract) tagged type of Ada 95 extends the potential of the language to true object orientation, including multiple inheritance and dynamic dispatching.

The Ravenscar Profile is silent about the sequential component of the language. Concrete implementations of the profile however may make choices that restrict the sequential features of the language, which specific coding standards perceive (or identify) as detracting from the integrity of the application.

Tagged types are the natural substitute for the range of variant records that the OBOSS implementation used as the encompassing abstraction for data structures that are polymorphic by nature. Tagged types better factor the commonality of recurrent types and provide better support for their (local) extension.

The use of tagged types directly interacts with Ravenscar technology in (at least) two distinct respects: the occurrence of run-time dispatching and the memory cost of type derivation.

Reference [14] considers the use of tagged types without class-wide operations as tractable under all (usual) forms of static analysis. Class-wide operations, however, generally involve run-time dispatching, which the cited reference finds to make flow analysis, symbolic analysis (and, possibly, timing analysis) considerably harder. The impact of run-time dispatching on the predictability of the system is obviously of direct concern to Ravenscar applications. The Ada Language Reference Manual at H.4(19) introduces restriction No_Dispatch to disallow the use of 'Class (hence the use of class-wide operations) but the limitation obviously impairs the expressive power of tagged types. Future work will investigate what use of tagged types in OBOSS is compatible with Ravenscar technology and with the integrity requirements of the application domain.

Derivation of a tagged type causes the automatic overloading of all primitives subprograms of the type. This notion is bound to bear some cost in terms of memory resources. Some instances of variant records in OBOSS proved to be extremely memory-intensive. The fear is that, as those are replaced by suitable derivation of tagged types, the ensuing memory occupation may further inflate and by a significant factor.

5   Conclusions

The Ravenscar Profile proved an excellent framework for the development of hard real-time applications. The concurrent architecture of OBOSS owes the profile its statically analysable yet flexible character and its predictable run-time behaviour. This evidence will hopefully motivate designers of high integrity systems to increase their confidence in the use of (Ravenscar) concurrency.

OBOSS, in turn, proved an optimal benchmark for Ravenscar technology and for the interactions between the direct concerns of the profile and the sequential component of the language under high integrity requirements. This paper highlighted areas where those interactions may give rise to disturbing conflicts.

Based on the experience discussed in this paper we contend that the profile promulgated at IRTAW 2000 [12] is solid and arguably complete but that its interactions with the sequential component of the language need to be further explored and possibly sanctioned in guidance material to the profile.

The profile has evolved and matured since its first appearance in 1997. Understandably, therefore, Ravenscar technology still has to catch up with the latest version and implications of the profile. The existence of two products that aim to support the profile is a definite indicator of the success of this IRTAW product. Yet, implementors of Ravenscar technology and developers of Ravenscar applications need a formal definition of the profile as well as a conformance assessment test suite to base their respective conformance claims and judgements upon.

GNAT/ORK has shown the value of open source software to high integrity applications, particularly by providing a very attractive entry level to Ravenscar technology. RAVEN, which is a more mature product in several respects, takes users further down the road to high integrity levels and certification. The competition between the two products may produce a positive spin for the (public) standardisation of the profile and the growth of its market penetration.

GNAT/ORK still needs considerable work to address the shortcomings and drawbacks highlighted in this paper and other ORK reports, especially in the way of being more resource efficient and suited for certification.

OBOSS has important lessons to draw from the port to GNAT/ORK, the implementation of which may contribute to highlighting the interaction of Ravenscar technology restrictions with design paradigms, coding styles and resource requirements.

References

1. Burns, A.: The Ravenscar Profile. Ada Letters, **XIX**:4. ACM Press (1999) 49–52.
2. Taft, S.T., Duff, R.A.: Ada 95 Reference Manual. Language and Standard Libraries. International Standard ISO/IEC 8652:1995(E). Lecture Notes in Computer Science, **1246**. Springer-Verlag (1997).
3. de la Puente, J.A., Ruiz, J.F, and Zamorano, J.: An Open Ravenscar Real-Time Kernel for GNAT. In: Keller, H.B., and Ploedereder,E.: Reliable Software Technologies — Ada-Europe 2000. Lecture Notes in Computer Science, **1845**. Springer-Verlag (2000), 5–15.
4. Ada Core Technologies Inc.: GNAT web page. http://www.gnat.com
5. Vardanega, T., Terraillon, J.-L. (ed.): Proceedings of the Seminar: The Role of Open-Source Software in the Space Business Technical Issues, Use Guidance, Legal Implications. European Space Agency (2000).
   ftp://ftp.estec.esa.nl/pub/ws/opensource/OpenSourceSeminar.htm
6. European Space Agency (1996): 32-bit Microprocessor and Computer System Development. Deliverable on Contract 9848/92/NL/FM.
   http://www.estec.esa.nl/wsmwww/erc32/erc32.html
7. Gaisler Research. TSIM/ERC32 simulator.
   http://www.gaisler.com →Simulators→TSIM/ERC32
8. TERMA Elektronik (1999): Software System Development for Spacecraft Data Handling Control. Deliverable on ESTEC Contract 12797/98/NL/PA.
   http://spd-web.terma.com/Projects/OBOSS/Home_Page
9. Vardanega, T., Caspersen, G., Storbank Pedersen, J.: A Case Study in the Reuse of On-board Embedded Real-Time Software. In: González Harbour (ed.): Reliable Software Technologies — Ada Europe'99. Lecture Notes in Computer Science, **1622**. Springer-Verlag (1999) 425–436.
10. Vardanega, T., Caspersen, G.: Using the Ravenscar Profile for Space Applications: the OBOSS Case. In: González Harbour (ed.): Proc. of the 10th International Real-Time Ada Workshop. Ada Letters, **XXI**:2. ACM Press (2001) to appear.
11. Burns, A., Wellings, A.: HRT-HOOD: A Structured Design Method for Hard Real-Time Systems. Elsevier Science (1995). ISBN 0-444-82164-3.
12. Wellings, A.: Status and Future of the Ravenscar Profile: Session Summary. In: González Harbour (ed.): Proc. of the 10th International Real-Time Ada Workshop. Ada Letters, **XXI**:2. ACM Press (2001) to appear.
13. Aonix. ObjectAda Real-Time RAVEN.
   http://www.aonix.com/content/products/objectada/raven.html
14. Wichmann, B. (ed.): Programming Languages - Guide for the Use of the Ada Programming Language in High Integrity Systems. Technical Report ISO/IEC **TR 15942**. International Standardisation Organisation (2000).
   http://www.dkuug.dk/jtc1/sc22/wg9/n359.pdf
15. Ada Core Technologies: GNAT User's Guide. Version 3.13a. March 2000.
16. Chapman, R., Burns, A., Wellings, A.: Worst-case timing analysis of exception handling in Ada. In: Collingbourne, L. (ed.): Proc. of the Ada UK Conference. IOS Press (1993) 148–164.

Author Index

Lecture Notes in Computer Science

For information about Vols. 1–1964
please contact your bookseller or Springer-Verlag